Developments in American Politics 2

Developments in American Politics 2

Gillian Peele
Christopher J. Bailey
Bruce Cain
B. Guy Peters
Editors

MACMILLAN

Editorial matter and selection © Gillian Peele, Christopher J. Bailey,
Bruce Cain, B. Guy Peters 1994
Individual chapters (in order) © Pippa Norris, Bruce Cain,
Paul S. Herrnson, Frank L. Davis, John Hart, Roger H. Davidson,
Gillian Peele, Martin Laffin, John Kincaid, Desmond S. King,
Paul Peretz, B. Guy Peters, John Francis, Phil Williams,
Calum Paton, Barbara Burrell, Tim Hames, Christopher J. Bailey 1994

First published as *Developments in American Politics*, 1992
Reprinted 1992, 1993
Second edition 1994

Published by
THE MACMILLAN PRESS LTD
Houndmills, Basingstoke, Hampshire RG21 2XS
and London
Companies and representatives
throughout the world

ISBN 0–333–59652–8 hardcover
ISBN 0–333–59653–6 paperback

A catalogue record for this book is available
from the British Library.

Copy-edited and typeset by Povey–Edmondson
Okehampton and Rochdale, England

Printed and bound in Great Britain by
Biddles Ltd, Guildford and King's Lynn

Contents

Preface   xi
List of Contributors   xiii
List of Tables and Figures   xv
List of Abbreviations   xvi
Map of the United States of America   xviii

1 **Introduction** Gillian Peele, Christopher J. Bailey,
   B. Guy Peters and Bruce Cain   1

PART ONE: DYNAMICS

2 **The 1992 Presidential Election, Voting Behavior and
   Legitimacy** Pippa Norris   18
   The Social and Geographic Basis of the Vote   20
     Changes in the geographic basis of the vote   24
     Changes in the social basis of the vote   26
   Evaluations of the Bush Presidency   30
   Perot and the Challenge to Two-party Politics   36
   Conclusions   41

3 **Racial and Ethnic Politics** Bruce Cain   45
   The Spread of Multiculturalism   49
   Political Diversity and Multiracialism   53
   The Political Consequences of Multiracialism   60

4 **American Political Parties: Growth and Change**
   Paul S. Herrnson   67
   Emergence and Decline   68
   Party Reform and Renewal   71
   Party Organizations and Campaign Activities   75
   Conclusion   82

5 **Interest Groups and Policymaking** Frank L. Davis   85
   Interest Groups' Narrower Focus   86

Variation in Involvement   90
Private Versus Public Interest Groups   91
Representativeness of Interest Groups   92
Bias?   93
How Involved in Health Care are Interest Groups?   94
Subsystems Versus Issue Networks   94
Resources, Tactics, and 'Interested Publics'   97
   Interest group tactics   98
   Lobbying   98
   Advertisements aimed at government officials   98
   Campaign contributions   99
   Appealing to the courts   100
   Publicizing public support   101
   News coverage and mass advertising   101
Tactics in the Health Care Debate   102
A Coordinated Campaign   105
Legitimation of Policy   106
Final Conclusions   107

PART TWO: THE INSTITUTIONAL FRAMEWORK

6 The Presidency in the 1990s *John Hart*   **110**
The Clinton Inheritance   112
The Context of the Clinton Presidency   118
   The election and the mandate   118
   The policy agenda   120
   Leadership style   121
The Clinton Presidency: Problems and Prospects   123
   Managing Congress   125
   Managing the media   127
   Managing public opinion   128
   Institutional support   130
The Post-Watergate Presidency and Presidential
   Leadership   131

7 Congress in Crisis . . . Once Again *Roger H. Davidson* **134**
Sources of Crisis   135
Congress as Representative: Parochialism and
   Professionalism   137
   Constituency outreach   138

The 'Incumbency Party'   139
Congress as Lawmaker: Organizational Fissures   141
   The Committee system   141
   Leadership and management   145
Paths to the Present Crisis   147
Conclusion: The Two Congresses Problem   150

8 The Supreme Court and the Constitution *Gillian Peele* **152**
The Clinton Administration and the Department of
   Justice   156
The Composition of the Supreme Court   160
The Judicial Role   163
The Conservative Legacy   165
Abortion   169
Church and State   169
Conclusion   170

9 Reinventing the Federal Government *Martin Laffin*   **172**
The Challenges of the 1990s   173
The Role of the Federal Government   175
The Structure of the Federal Government   176
Presidential Leadership of the Federal Government   179
Congress and the Bureaucracy   182
Inspectors General   185
The Management of Federal Departments   186
Bureaucrats as 'Political Entrepreneurs'   188
The Role of Political Appointees   189
Appointee–Careerist Relations   191
The 'Quiet Crisis' and Reinvigorating the Bureaucracy   192
The National Performance Review   193
Third Party Government   196
The Prospects for Change   198

10 Governing the American States *John Kincaid*   **200**
Explaining the Paradox   201
Origins of American Federalism   203
Dual, Cooperative, and Coercive Federalism   205
Characteristics of Coercive Federalism   208
   Diminished federal aid to states and localities   208
   Aid to persons over places   209

Conditions of aid to states and localities 210
Federal mandates on states and localities 211
Federal preemption of state and local authority 212
Intergovernmental tax immunities 213
Decline of cooperative programs 213
Federal court orders 214
Conclusion 216

PART THREE: PUBLIC POLICY

11 The Politics of Urban Policy *Desmond S. King* **220**
The Problems of Cities 220
The Politics of the Cities 224
Federal Policy and the Cities 229
Conclusion 233

12 Economic Policy *Paul Peretz* **237**
Introduction 237
The 1980–86 Period 238
The Post-1986 Period 239
Fiscal policy under Bush 241
Monetary policy under Bush 244
Fiscal policy under Clinton 246
Monetary policy under Clinton 249
International trade 250
Policy Outcomes 251

13 Social Policy *B. Guy Peters* **253**
The United States as a Welfare State Laggard 253
The Fundamental Problem: Inequality 257
The politics of poverty 259
The 'New Poverty' 264
Reagan, Bush, and the loosening of the social safety net 267
The Challenges for President Clinton 268
Fiscal Restraints – the Mortmain of Reagan and Bush 269

14 Environmental Policy *John Francis* **271**
The Character of American Environmental Politics 272

The Expanding Range and Persisting Nature of
   Environmental Policies   272
The Institutional Context   275
Political Parties, Interest Groups, and Environmental
   Politics   278
The Western Landscape and the Reccurring Question
   of Federal Land Use   281
Logging   284
Toxic substances   285
Transnational Dimensions   286
Conclusion   288

15 Foreign Policy *Phil Williams*   **289**
Introduction   289
The End of the Cold War   290
New Challenges and Issues   293
The Domestic Context   299
Implications for Policy   307

PART FOUR: CONTEMPORARY ISSUES

**16 Health Policy: The Analytics and Politics of Attempted
Reform** *Calum Paton*   **312**
The Legacy   313
The Reemergence of Regulation   314
The Main Proposal   315
The Political Environment   319
Toward the Clintons' Plan   320
The 'Oregon Plan'   322
Conclusion   323

17 Women in American Politics *Barbara Burrell*   **325**
The Range of Women's Organizations   326
Open Seats   329
General Elections   330
Policy Representation for Women   331

18 The Changing Media *Tim Hames*   **335**
The New American Media   335
The Press Post-mortem on 1988   338

The Candidates' New Media Strategies   340
The Media's Strategy to the Candidates   342
President Clinton's Media Strategy   344
Conclusion   346

PART FIVE: THEORETICAL PERSPECTIVES

19 Visions of American Politics *Christopher J. Bailey*   **350**
    The Study of American Politics   351
        The institutional approach   353
        The behavioral approach   356
        The rational choice approach   358
    Visions of American Politics   361
        Interest Groups   364
        Voting   365
        The presidency   366
        The US Congress   367
        The Supreme Court   369
        Bureaucracy   370
        The policy process   371
    The Study of Politics in the Post-Cold War Era   373

Guide to Further Reading   374
Bibliography   379
Index   407

Preface

This is the second *Developments in American Politics* volume. All the chapters are new and, with the exception of the editors and Desmond King, there is a new group of contributors. We have been fortunate in attracting a truly international team of prominent scholars from the United States, Australia, and Great Britain. The editorial team has been greatly strengthened by the addition of Professor B. Guy Peters who has brought his wide range of contacts and scholarly expertise to bear on this project.

As in the last volume, individual authors were asked both to analyze recent developments in American politics, and to review some of the crucial theories and models available for interpreting them. All authors were asked to concentrate on the contemporary American scene, and especially on the impact of the Clinton administration on the politics and policies of the United States.

Writing about the United States using an international team of authors presents certain stylistic problems. As in the previous volume, the editors have decided that spelling should be Americanized throughout to promote consistency. On the other hand, some specifically American usages have been excised. Where appropriate, the party and state of members of Congress have been included. The references to works cited in the chapters are collected together at the end of the book. There is also a short guide to further reading for each of the chapters (on p. 374).

The editors would like to thank our publisher Steven Kennedy for the help and encouragement he has given to this volume. We would also like to thank our anonymous referees and especially Steve Reilly, who read the entire manuscript of this book and its predecessor.

The editors acknowledge with gratitude the intellectual support given by their colleagues at the University of Oxford, Keele University, the University of California at Berkeley, and the University of Pittsburgh. Chris Bailey would specifically like to thank Dick Engstrom, Peter John, Mike Tappin, Jonathan Knuckey, and Ian Scott for listening, reading, and criticizing.

Others whom the editors and the contributors would like to thank are Mick Moran, Nigel Stanier, Cornell Clayton and Brian Hatch.

The production of this book would have been impossible without the assistance of the highly professional administrative and secretarial staff in our various academic institutions. A particular word of thanks is due to Pauline Shepheard, the College Secretary at Lady Margaret Hall, and to Susan Waters, the Tutors' Secretary. Their calm efficiency and helpfulness have been invaluable in the various stages of the book's life. The editorial team is also grateful to Wiltrandt Grashoff at the University of Pittsburg and to the staff of the Institute of Governmental Studies at Berkeley for all their help and hospitality.

On a personal level, the British editors realize how much they owe to the hospitality of American colleagues and friends. We should particularly like to mention Paul Herrnson, Cathy Helms, Maggie Fish, Laura Doan, Marlene Mussell, Chris Hall, Jackie Wardell, John and Leslie Francis, Colin Campbell, Jim Thurber, and John and Marjorie O'Shaugnessy and Steve and Cindy Saboe.

Finally, we should like to thank our contributors, whose patience and prompt responses to queries have helped to get this book to the finishing line roughly on time.

Gillian Peele
Christopher Bailey
Bruce Cain
B. Guy Peters

List of Contributors

Christopher J. Bailey is Senior Lecturer in American Studies at Keele University.

Barbara Burrell is a researcher at the Wisconsin Survey Research Laboratory at the University of Wisconsin Extension.

Bruce Cain is Professor of Government at the University of California, Berkeley, where he is also Associate Director of the Institute of Government Studies, Berkeley.

Roger H. Davidson is Professor of Government at the University of Maryland, College Park.

Frank L. Davis is Associate Professor of Government at Lehigh University.

John Francis is Professor of Politics at the University of Utah.

Tim Hames is American Studies Research Officer at Nuffield College, Oxford.

John Hart is Reader in Political Science at the Australian National University.

Paul Herrnson is Associate Professor of Government at the University of Maryland, College Park.

John Kincaid is Executive Director of A.C.I.R.

Desmond S. King is Fellow and Tutor in Politics at St John's College, Oxford.

Martin Laffin is Senior Lecturer in Public Policy at the Graduate School of Business, University of Sydney, and was Visiting Fellow in the Graduate Public Policy Program, Georgetown University, Washington D.C., 1992–93.

Pippa Norris is Associate Director and Lecturer, Joan Shorenstein Barone Center on Press, Politics and Public Policy at Harvard University.

Calum Paton is Professor of Health Care Management at Keele University.

Gillian Peele is Fellow and Tutor in Politics at Lady Margaret Hall, Oxford.

Paul Peretz is Associate Professor of Political Science at California State University, Fullerton.

B. Guy Peters is Maurice Falk Professor of American Government at the University of Pittsburgh.

Phil Williams is Professor of Public and International Affairs and Director of the Ridgeway Center, University of Pittsburgh.

List of Tables and Figures

Tables

2.1	Presidential elections 1968–92	21
2.2	Structural change in the size of voting groups	23
2.3	Social basis of the Democratic vote, 1952–92	29
2.4	Changes in the Presidential vote, 1988–92	30
2.5	Approval of President Bush	33
2.6	Economic evaluations and voting choice	34
2.7	Model of voting choice	35
2.8	Timing of voting decision	35
2.9	Change in the vote, 1988–92	40
2.10	Trust and cynicism in government, 1992	42
3.1	Distribution of states by percent minority populations	51
3.2	Distribution of Congressional districts by minority populations	52
3.3	Party identification and ideology	65
5.1	Examples of interest groups involved in health policy	88
5.2	Examples of the campaign expenditures of health-related Political Action Committees for the 1991–2 election cycle	104
13.1	Major welfare state beneficiaries and expenditures, 1990	256
13.2	Poverty and program participation by race	260

Figures

2.1	Electoral college 1992 U.S. election	25
4.1	Party receipts, 1976–92	76
12.1	Unemployment and real per capita disposable income, 1987–93	246

List of Abbreviations

A.A.R.P.	American Association of Retired Persons
A.B.C.	American Broadcasting Corporation
A.C.I.R.	Advisory Commission on Intergovernmental Relations
A.F.D.C.	Aid to Families with Dependent Children
A.F.L.-C.I.O.	American Federation of Labor–Congress of Industrial Organizations
A.H.P.	Accountable Health Partnership
A.M.A.	American Medical Association
A.P.A.	Administrative Procedures Act
Ark.	Arkansas
bn.	Billion
C.B.S.	Columbia Broadcasting System
C.D.B.G.	Community Development Block Grant
C.E.T.A.	Comprehensive Employment and Training Act
D.	Democrat
D.C.	District of Columbia
D.C.C.C.	Democratic Congressional Campaign Committee
D.N.C.	Democratic National Committee
D.S.C.C.	Democratic Senatorial Campaign Committee
D.O.D.	Department of Defense
D.O.J.	Department of Justice
D.R.G.s	Diagnostic Related Groups
E.E.A.	Economic Equity Act
E.I.S.	Environmental Impact Statement
EMILY	Early Money Increases Like Yeast
E.P.A.	Environmental Protection Agency
E.R.A.	Equal Rights Amendment
F.B.I.	Federal Bureau of Investigation
F.D.A.	Food and Drug Administration
F.D.R.	Franklin Delano Roosevelt
F.E.C.A.	Federal Election Campaign Act
F.Y.	Fiscal Year
G.A.O.	General Accounting Office

G.O.P.	Grand Old Party (Republican Party)
G.R.S.	General Revenue Sharing
G.S.	General Schedule
H.I.A.A.	Health Insurance Association of America
H.I.P.C.	Health Insurance Purchasing Cooperative
H.M.O.s	Health Maintenace Organizations
H.U.D.	Housing and Urban Development
I.G.	Inspector General
Ill.	Illinois
I.N.S.	Immigration and Naturalization Service
L.A.	Los Angeles
Miss.	Mississippi
M.T.V.	Multiple Transferable Vote
N.A.F.T.A.	North American Free Trade Agreement
N.A.S.A.	National American Space Agency
N.B.C.	National Broadcasting Corporation
N.C.P.S.	National Commission on the Public Service
N.E.P.A.	National Environmental Policy Act
N.E.S.	National Election Survey
N.I.H.	National Institutes of Health
N.O.W.	National Organization of Women
N.W.P.C.	National Women's Political Caucus
O.E.C.D.	Organization for Economic Cooperation and Development
P.A.C.	Political Action Committee
P.A.S.	Presidential Appointment [with] Senate Confirmation
P.P.I.	Progressive Policy Institute
P.R.	Proportional Representation
R.	Republican
R.N.C.	Republican National Committee
S.E.S.	Senior Executive Service
S.M.S.P.	Single Member Simple Plurality (First Past the Post)
T.C.O.s	Transnational Criminal Organizations
T.Q.M.	Total Quality Management
U.D.A.G.	Urban Development Action Grant

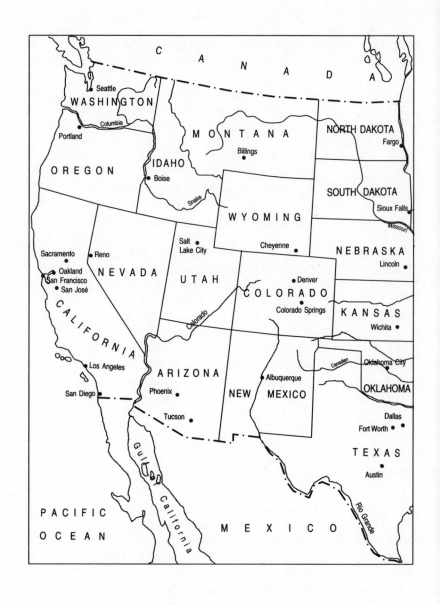

The United States of America: states and main cities

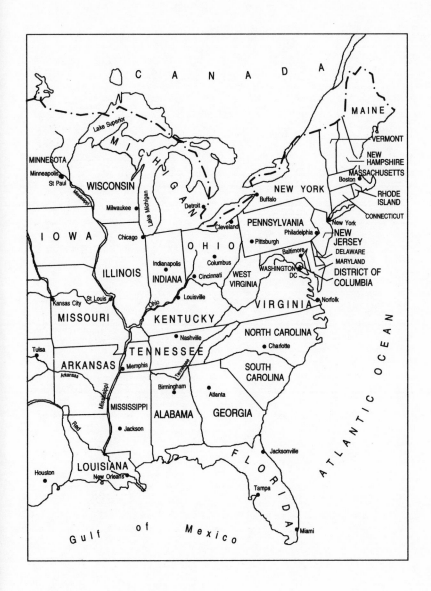

(excluding Alaska and Hawaii)

1

Introduction

The inauguration of William Clinton as the 42nd President of the United States in January 1993 seemed to foreshadow a real transition in American politics. Although all inaugurations tend to use the symbolism of new opportunities, the advent of the Clinton presidency on the surface suggested a particularly radical break with the past and raised the expectation of a fundamental shift in public policy. Clinton's inaugural address was redolent with references to an American "renewal" and to a "spring reborn" that "brings forth the vision and courage to reinvent America".

A New Beginning?

There were several reasons why Clinton's presidency could be presented as a new beginning in American political life. First, the Clinton electoral victory brought a Democrat to the White House after 12 years of Republican dominance – a dominance that was associated with the ideological tides of Reaganism and of the new right. Clinton was only the second Democrat to be elected to the presidency in the period 1968–92, so that for the Democratic Party, and its many supporters throughout the United States, the moment was sweet indeed.

Secondly, Clinton himself symbolized a generational change in the exercise of political power in America. Clinton, at the age of 46, was over 20 years younger than Bush, who was rising 70 in early 1993, and over 30 years younger than Ronald Reagan, who had been nearly 80 when he left the White House in 1989. Clinton's formative experiences had not been of the Second World War, but of the Cold War, the civil rights movement, and the Vietnam War. As Clinton's hero President J. F. Kennedy had used the image of the torch passing to a new generation of Americans, so Clinton

1

challenged a 'new generation of young Americans to a season of service' and spoke of a generation raised in the shadows of the Cold War assuming new responsibilities.

The final aspect of the Clinton presidency (which marked it off from other presidencies) was that by January 1993 the United States was no longer locked in an implacable battle with the communist bloc. The collapse of the Soviet Union and its empire in eastern Europe – symbolized so graphically by the fall of the Berlin Wall in November 1989 – meant that the international situation that faced President Clinton was manifestly different from that which had confronted any of his post-1945 predecessors.

These optimistic features for the new President were, however, paralleled by less favorable ones. Clinton's own mandate was shaky. Although he had reached the White House, Clinton had achieved his victory on the basis of 43 percent of the popular vote and had actually obtained less support than 1988 Democratic contender Michael Dukakis. Clinton probably owed his victory to the independent candidacy of Ross Perot, who ran on a platform that was deeply critical of established political parties and processes. Perot's 19 percent of the popular vote damaged Bush more than Clinton in the election of 1992. However, Clinton's legitimacy was also undermined by the size of the Perot vote, which itself reflected a general national mood of disillusionment and cynicism.

For the Democratic Party as a whole, the victory was equally double-edged. Although the Democrats had done well across the country on the basis of a moderate appeal to mainstream America, the unravelling of the New Deal coalition had not been reversed. The unusual strategy of running a totally southern Democratic ticket in the form of Clinton (from Arkansas) and Gore (from Tennessee) helped the Democrats remain competitive in the south; but Bush still took Virginia, Alabama, Mississippi, Florida, and Texas, as well as both North and South Carolina of the southern states. And while the Democratic Party had run a tight campaign and maintained its unity – in marked contrast to the Republicans – few doubted that the Democrats' unity was precarious and that factional tensions within the party remained.

The most disturbing question of all was whether the strategy for an effective election campaign could be translated into an effective strategy for government. This concern was evident even before the allegations associated with "Whitewater" and Paula Jones surfaced.

The fragmentation of American politics and the difficulty of governing the country have been frequent themes in recent writing about the United States. The Clinton administration entered office with an unhappy legacy of raised expectations about what a Democratic president could do and an agenda of domestic policy problems ignored or neglected by previous administrations.

The Limits to Change

The collapse of communism and the consequent reduction of super-power tension inevitably switched the focus of electoral attention from the international to the domestic arena. Indeed it was the new primacy of the domestic agenda – especially the economy – that had destroyed George Bush's chances of winning a second term and created the conditions that brought Clinton to the White House. Clinton had indeed run on a domestic agenda. Yet for Clinton, as for any American president, domestic politics is an arena which is increasingly inhospitable, requiring negotiation and compromise with a host of other political players and with only limited opportunities for imaginative policy initiatives. Of course, difficulties exist in the making of American foreign policy; but presidents have frequently preferred to concentrate on this aspect of their role because of the relative lack of constraint on their freedom of action and the absence of so many of the tensions that mark the conduct of domestic policy.

One source of tension in American domestic policy is the immense complexity of American society. The divisions of race, of national origin, class, and of religion – as well as newly salient ones such as gender, age, and sexual preference – make the United States a country rich in sub-cultures, pressure groups, and voluntary activity, even if at times those divisions have seemed to threaten the very identity of the United States. The 1990 census underlined the complexity of many of these divisions and confronted America with a very different cultural future. For although immigration has always been a major factor in shaping the politics and consciousness of the United States, the census revealed that the decade of the 1980s had brought in 9 million new immigrants, the highest rate of entry since the first decade of the twentieth century. Just as the early twentieth century immigration transformed the

United States, so this more recent wave has had a major impact on the political system and suggests a more radical impact on American society in the future. For the fastest-growing minority groups in the United States by the 1990s – Hispanic and Asian – were those likely to want to retain their distinct cultural identities rather than merge them in the melting pot of American social integration.

The changing dynamics of American society also produced more tangible policy issues. Differences of race and gender, of national origin and language, also continued to produce savage inequalities and consequently conflict, disillusion, and poverty, despite the formal constitutional promise of equality and more than three decades of public efforts to reduce discrimination and disadvantage.

Clinton tried to speak to these divisions in American society and to revel in its pluralism. He pledged himself to create a government that would be more like America, meaning that it would deliberately include additional representatives of its distinctive social groupings and would include more women. Clinton was, however, also aware of the polarisation caused by many of these cleavages and of the acute controversy caused by such policies as affirmative action. Also, he was inevitably conscious of the extent to which these divisions and inequalities overlapped with other social problems, most notably poverty, inner city decay, declining educational standards, inadequate medical provision, and crime.

The agenda was not so different from that identified by Lyndon Johnson at the start of his ambitious, but ultimately unsuccessful, efforts to harness American wealth to the solution of American social ills in the war on poverty. Yet the contrast between 1965 and 1993 in America's ability to address that agenda was stark, even though by 1993 America could contemplate the reduction of the massive international security burdens that she had borne since 1941.

Why had the United States become daunted by problems that so recently had been accepted with enthusiasm and energy? Although a full exploration of this complex question is well beyond the limits of this introduction three interrelated factors make Bill Clinton's task in the 1990s inexorably more difficult than that which had faced Lyndon Johnson nearly 30 years earlier.

Ideology and leadership style

The first factor that made the climate very different for Clinton than for Johnson or even Carter relates to ideology. By the early 1990s the United States appeared to have reached the end of a cycle that had taken the country through an optimistic belief in the power of government to solve social problems and an equally compelling ideological movement which rejected a positive role for government and believed that there were few spheres in which market solutions were not preferable to collectivist ones. Thus the early 1990s witnessed a certain exhaustion of ideas in the United States, comparable to that which Daniel Bell had detected in relation to the 1950s (Bell, 1965).

On one level, of course, this fitted nicely with the end of the cold war. Much attention was devoted to the implications of the demise of communism and to what one author called the "end of history": the possibility that America was entering an era in which liberal democracy would become the only form of government (Fukuyama, 1989). Technocratic, not ideological, solutions would dominate discussion of international and national policy problems within a liberal capitalist world order.

Clinton himself reflected the transition from ideology to pragmatism. He had won the nomination and the presidency as a politician closely identified with the Democratic Leadership Council of the Democratic Party. The Democratic Leadership Council explicitly rejected the liberalism of the Jesse Jackson Rainbow Coalition and that of Edward Kennedy; and it sought to reposition the Democratic Party around mainstream foreign, economic, and social policies. The think-tank associated with the Clinton campaign – the Progressive Policy Institute (P.P.I.) – had explored policies that had much in common with ideas emerging within conservative and free market circles, especially notions of the new paradigm (which envisaged a new style of public intervention in conjunction with the private sector) and ideas associated with Jack Kemp, William Bennett, and James Pinkerton on the Republican side. There was inevitably more emphasis in the Democratic Party than in the Republican Party on the role of government; but there was also a very real awareness of its limitations and none of the heady optimism associated with the Great Society years.

The emphasis on pragmatism rather than ideology could in many respects be seen as an advantage to a new president, and certainly it, rather than Reaganite conservatism, or more radical liberalism associated with the rainbow coalition or the Committee for Democratic Values, ought to aid rather than impede competent policy analysis. The problem is that competent policy analysis may not be enough in a system where there is a marked tendency for an administration to lose its direction and coherence once elected. If a president has not developed a central set of ideas to inspire his presidency, the drive that is necessary to initiate, pursue, and implement policy will be missing. George Bush's apparent lack of an overall vision of the goals of his presidency was widely blamed for his sudden loss of popularity and his ultimate electoral failure. Reagan, by contrast, although much less involved than Bush in the detail of decision-making and arguably much less fitted for the job of chief executive, never failed to communicate the purpose of *his* presidency and maintained his popularity. In short, while Clinton seemed in little danger of being trapped by the dictates of ideology, his pragmatic approach meant that he might underestimate the need and the potential for change and might lack the philosophical tenets to give his presidency momentum.

Economic constraints

A marked intellectual uncertainty is thus one factor shaping the capacity of the United States and its political leadership to cope with its diverse and difficult domestic problems. Equally marked, and more immediate, is the awareness that the United States now lacks the economic capacity to spend extensive sums of money on social policies. It was of course the case that the simple remedy of 'throwing money' at problems such as poverty and racial inequality was always going to be inadequate. However, efforts to ameliorate America's social problems need funding and even the most carefully crafted policies require some public expenditure by the federal government. Yet the size of American budget deficits in the early 1990s – over 290 billion dollars – has effectively restricted the scope for further governmental initiative.

The restrictions on federal expenditure and the financial problems facing federal government generally were not confined to Washington. Similar problems faced the states and local government, which found themselves starved of federal grants and with a less buoyant fiscal base to meet a range of new policy demands, some of which had been transferred to them from Washington.

Governmental weakness

The third impediment to America's ability to manage its domestic problems relates directly to the structure and quality of government itself. Much attention had been paid to the extent to which (if at all) the split party control of the presidency and Congress – which had marked the years 1969–77 and 1981–93 – had damaged the American policy process, as well as to the causes of divided government (Fiorina, 1992; Mayhew, 1991; Thurber, 1991; Cox and Kernell, 1991), Certainly Clinton in his inaugural address encouraged the expectation that Democratic control of the White House and Congress might end the "era of deadlock and drift."

In a sense, however, the relationship between the executive and the legislature is only the most visible of the constitutional, organizational, and policymaking tensions that constrain the political system. The tendency to fragmentation and conflict marks the policymaking process itself *within* departments and agencies, as much as *between* branches of government. And the multi-layered federal system adds its own complexity, not just to the policy-making process, but also to the implementation of policy. Part of the problem undoubtedly stems from the pluralistic nature of American society, but part of it is also a reflection of institutional design and culture. Although American politics can on occasion sustain radical change, such change usually requires a large and bipartisan consensus behind it. The system has a bias towards continuity, and the normal style of government in the United States involves extensively negotiated policy initiatives and incremental change.

These themes run through the various chapters of the book. The continued erosion of the Democratic Party's social base and the implications of the Perot candidacy for the American political system are explored in Pippa Norris's discussion of American voting behavior and the presidential election of 1992. Pippa Norris underlines the extent to which Clinton's fragile victory made him vulnerable to an erosion of popular support on taking office. In a system where selling the policies to the public has become at least as important as mobilizing Washington elites, an uncertain mandate can soon deprive even a newly elected president of leverage.

The new pattern of minority politics is explored in Bruce Cain's chapter (Chaper 3). Dramatic alterations in the character of the American population are only slowly translated into political changes. Nevertheless, demographic developments have already had a political impact in a number of ways. Thus racial conflict has been transformed from a bipolar black–white issue to a much more variegated and complex equation involving Latinos and Asians. In the absence of affluence, there is greater potential for conflict between minority groups; and anti-discrimination policies designed primarily for blacks may not work well for Latinos and new minorities whose political agenda includes recognition of their distinct linguistic and cultural identity.

The simple existence of ethnic minorities does not by itself mean that they will be able to exercise political influence. The successful mobilization of ethnic minorities at the electoral level is one key to advancing their agenda, but here there are, as Cain notes, factors that may limit their political clout. Electoral rules, in particular, especially the districting system, may work to weaken or strengthen minority power and delay or hasten the successful pursuit of an ethnic group's goals.

Political parties can facilitate the integration of minority groups into the political process, although parties can also be undermined if minority factions dominate and distort the party regular processes, as has often happened recently in the United States. Paul Herrnson's exploration of the state of American parties underlines the extent to which, even with an enhanced role, American political parties are primarily in the business of providing support services to individual candidates, not developing or promoting public policy.

If it is a mistake to look to political parties to impose cohesion on the American public policy process, it is equally vital not to underestimate the role of interest groups in shaping that process. The relative weakness of parties and the relative strength of pressure groups has a number of important policy effects, including the expansion of the number of policy actors and the premium that it places on negotiated rather than imposed policy developments. Frank Davis shows the variety of tactics that groups may use to advance their cause. He illustrates much of his argument by reference to one of the most daunting domestic policy challenges facing President Clinton – health care reform – and delineates the range of different interests involved in the debate. The evolution of policy toward the provision of health care (which is also examined in Calum Paton's chapter) is more likely to be determined by the political dynamics of these interests than by abstract arguments about the merits of competing policies. Interest group activity is ubiquitous and it shapes not merely the attitudes of supporters of those groups, but of the general public as well.

In Part Two of the book, the chapters examine the institutional structure of American government and its capacity to respond to the myriad demands on it. John Hart's discussion of the Clinton presidency sets the position of the chief executive in the 1990s in the context of a constitutional and political system where the exercise of executive power has become ever harder, although expectations about what a president can achieve are always high. Hart argues that Franklin Roosevelt's achievements in his first hundred days set an impossible target for future presidents, especially given the range of new constraints on presidential power which include statutory restrictions from a more assertive Congress, an adversarial media, the decline of party linkages, and the deficit.

Competition between the executive and legislative branches is built into the American constitutional framework. But the way that competition operates in practice has been changed since the Congressional reforms of the 1970s, although, as Roger Davidson shows, the line of development is not a simple one from less to more Congressional power *vis-à-vis* the executive or from centralization to decentralization. Davidson emphasizes the inherent duality of Congress's role – as an institution in which local interests are reflected and as an institution where national public policy is made. The difficulty of reconciling these two roles, especially in the period of cut-back politics that has dominated America since the early 1980s, produced both gridlock in the system and shaped many of the characteristics of Congress today. Although Congress has never been particularly keen on taking unpopular decisions, there is a sense in which the desire to avoid responsibility for tough policy choices has been magnified in recent years. The trend to blame avoidance explains such features as the reluctance of many

Congressmen to attach their names to legislative proposals and their determination to ensure that they as individuals cannot be identified with unpopular policies.

It is not just the executive and legislative branches that can influence the character of public policy in the United States. The unusual degree of power accorded to the courts in America means that not only do they act as a check on legislative or executive action, but also that in some circumstances the courts can effectively initiate new policy mandates. Clinton's two predecessors were keenly aware of the long-term power of the judiciary and sought to shape it to promote conservative values. Gillian Peele's chapter examines Clinton's strategy in relation to the judiciary and the wider legal system. She notes the extent to which the Supreme Court, although dominated by a conservative majority in 1993, has been cautious in its rulings and appears anxious to leave a wide degree of discretion in the hands of democratic bodies at federal, state, and local level. She suggests that the judiciary's efforts to transfer many of the more contentious issues of contemporary American politics to elective bodies is unlikely to prove entirely satisfactory. Many of the issues that trouble the Court touch the democratic process itself (such as questions of fairness in relation to electoral rules) and are hence difficult for those institutions to decide for themselves. Others (such as the abortion issue) involve claims that many see as fundamental rights, and are therefore not suitable for resolution in the ordinary political process.

Martin Laffin's essay on the role of the federal government picks up on the theme of the weakness of the federal governmental system and the highly fragmented nature of the policy process. He stresses, like Hart, the way in which presidents find it difficult to control the administrative system from the top down through a command system. But he emphasizes how far Clinton – through such devices as the Gore Commission – has committed himself to reform of the governmental machine and the administrative process, especially by encouraging a new, more entrepreneurial style of management in government.

Many of the ideas of the Gore Commission have been drawn from the blueprint outlined in *Reinventing Government* and from the wider movement for a new public management (Osborne and Gaebler, 1992). Yet, as Laffin concedes,there has been only a limited amount of experiment in government at the federal level over the past few years. Rather, it has been the states and the system of local government that have provided most of the impetus for experiment with new ideas.

The general resurgence of state politics and the innovations of such groups as the Council of American Governors has not reversed the general post-New Deal trend toward centralization. Indeed, as John Kincaid shows in his examination of American federalism, the two developments constitute a paradox. Kincaid's discussion underlines the expansion of federal powers in state and local affairs and shows how this expansion has in large part occurred as a result of conditions attached to grants in aid. Deficit politics and the anti-government ideology of the Reagan–Bush years frequently left the conditions, but reduced the grants. Additionally, there was a tendency for Congress to pass legislation that created new mandates for the states (such as eliminating discrimination against the disabled), even though Congress had provided no money for these policies. Clinton, as a former governor, might have been expected to bring a new approach to the federal relationship; in fact, federalism did not feature in Clinton's 1992 campaign – an omission that presumably reflects his appreciation of the constraints on future federal action.

The dynamics of the federal system inevitably affect both the making of policy and the delivery of services. Nowhere is this more true than in relation to policy problems confronting American cities. In King's view, any realistic effort to address these problems requires federal action. However, he too emphasizes that even an activist president such as Clinton is unlikely to be able to target the cities in the way they need.

Dealing with the problems of the cities is constrained both by lack of fiscal resources and by the political reality of conflicting constituency interests. As a result, even a sympathetic Democratic cabinet secretary such as Cisneros is likely to shun redistributive programs and urge an emphasis on general problems aimed at securing economic growth for the country as a whole.

The advent of a Democratic administration in Washington inevitably created expectations that there would be a change in economic policy. But, as Paul Peretz argues, in many ways the transition from the Reagan–Bush years to Clinton is unlikely to be that marked as far as economic policy is concerned. Partly that is because in Peretz's view the real break in policy is between the radical Reaganite supply-side policies and those of the more conservative Bush; partly because Clinton adopted a rather conservative economic strategy and gave the key economic posts of Treasury Secretary and Director of O.M.B. to conservative Democrats Lloyd Bentsen and Leon Panetta.

Controversy continues to swirl around the significance of the budget deficit. Even those who deny its long-term significance generally agree that it is seen as a restriction on policy innovation. As has been noted, it appears to preclude any radical revision of the federal relationship with the states and the cities. In terms of substantive policy, it also appears to limit the policy options for dealing with America's complex problems of poverty and social disadvantage. Guy Peters shows in his article the extent to which the United States' range of social welfare programs reflect the country's distinctive values. By comparison with many other western countries, the United States is a welfare "laggard" in the sense that its welfare programs are of limited scope and application. Severe gaps in coverage exist – most notably, of course, in terms of medical coverage. Even those programs that do exist are now facing funding and administrative problems. To some extent, the deficiencies of American public provision have been masked by the existence of private provision, which both fills an important policy need and allows many Americans to neglect the need for social policy reform. Yet, as Peters shows, although much of the social policy of the United States relies heavily on private provision – e.g., in relation to pensions – that private provision is in turn dependent in many ways on the public sector.

Poverty and the programs designed to address it are not unidimensional. Peters distinguishes between programs designed to smooth out periods of poverty that occur within an individual's life cycle as a result of sudden illness or old age. More intractable is the poverty that seems to be transmitted from generation to generation – the cycle that has created an underclass. The United States' inability to sustain coherent policies to cope with this more entrenched form of poverty is partly a result of the extent to which victims of such social disadvantage can be distinguished from "mainstream" America by race, and partly the result of cultural beliefs that continue to emphasize individual mobility. It will be interesting to see how far the stereotypes of the poor will be transformed by the advent of what Peters calls the "new poor."

These are groups whose skills have ceased to be needed by American society as a result of structural change in the economy, technological developments, and a decline in America's international competitiveness. Such people include the workers in industries under threat from growing Asian economies; but they also include middle managers squeezed by a revolution in business organization. This group has greater capacity to exert political clout than the traditional poor. It remains to be seen whether Clinton can respond to the new social agenda, despite the deficit and an unwillingness to commit the administration to policies akin to those of the Great Society. In a sense, the Family Support Act of 1988 provided the United States with a new paradigm in welfare policy to the extent that it combined an emphasis on self-help and willingness to work with welfare. What remains unclear is how far such an approach can really touch the deepest pockets of poverty in the United States or cope with the scale of its problems.

The difficulties of reforming social policy are compounded by the highly fragmented political system of the United States. Not only is there vertical and horizontal institutional fragmentation; but there is also a further fragmentation that results from the proliferation of interest groups which are so much a feature of every policy area in the United States. John Francis shows in his discussion of environmental policy how the vertical relationships of the federal system can affect substantive areas such as environmental policy and how in the Reagan–Bush years the states became seen as more positive protectors of environmental standards than ever before. He also shows how entrenched a feature of the American scene the environmental movement has become and how environmental activists constitute an important component of the Democratic Party in many states, especially in the west. His general argument emphasizes the extent to which in many respects environmental policy has become decentralized partly as a result of political factors, but partly also as a result of a decline in support for authoritative scientific judgment emanating from Washington. In some ways, such decentralization encourages a refreshing opportunity for greater participation; but it also further fragments an already incoherent policy process.

Observers since Tocqueville have commented on the extent to which the American political system with its divisions of powers and its pluralism makes the management of foreign policy difficult.

Phil Williams in his chapter examines the extent to which the end of the Cold War, while it has appeared to create a greater freedom for the United States in foreign policy, has also weakened America's foreign policymaking capacity, removing both its intellectual framework and one of the restraints on its "rampant pluralism." Williams shows how the new problems of the international arena are more complex than before and suggests that foreign policy is now unlikely to be so attractive a field for American presidents. The disappearance of the communist threat has removed a key element in the United States' ability to manage its internal disagreements over foreign policy issues, leaving greater room for issues to be influenced by popular opinion and the media.

Two other consequences of the end of the Cold War highlighted by Williams have extensive implications for the conduct of American government. The removal of the major security threat from the Soviet Union has switched foreign policy from a security focus to an economic focus, especially the conditions of trade. This new emphasis is likely to insert divisions between old allies, not merely in relationships between the United States and Japan, but also in general relationships between North America and Europe. Secondly, the decline of the communist threat reduces the leverage of the United States in its relations with its allies. Ironically, this reduced leverage is occurring at the point at which the US must contemplate more rather than less collaborative ventures. Whether it has the capacity to manage new and more equal alliances remains to be seen.

The overall picture painted by Williams suggests an uncertain future both in terms of the substance of American foreign policy and in terms of the capacity of the system to deliver a coherent policy. If so, there are profound implications for America's allies, particularly given the need to take into account important new issues such as the future relationship between N.A.T.O. and the countries of eastern and central Europe.

Part Four of the book highlights issues of immediate relevance to the policy process or themes that have emerged in the contemporary debate about politics. Here three themes are highlighted. There was little doubt that the future of American medical care should form the basis of one of the chapters. This issue had risen to the top of the political agenda for a variety of reasons, not least the spiralling costs of medical care that has engaged the attention of policymakers in a number of countries. As Calum Paton shows in his chapter, there is an irony in America's efforts to reform its system of medical care because many European health care systems are facing administrative and funding difficulties and much of the language of the debate in Europe has come from the United States. Calum Paton's chapter places the Clinton plan in the context of other efforts at reform, including the Oregon system. Although it is not yet clear whether the Clinton plan will overcome the vested interests ranged against reform, the effort must surely count as one of the most ambitious in recent years.

It was also obvious to the editors that women's issues needed additional treatment in this volume. The 1992 Congressional elections saw the return of an unprecedented number of women legislators, partly no doubt as part of the protest against entrenched Congressional attitudes and behavior. Barbara Burrell places the drive to get more women elected to office throughout the United States in the wider contexts of theories of representation and the feminist movement. It is uncertain how far these newly elected women will be able to make a difference on key issues of concern to women, nor for how long they will retain any distinctive approach to politics. However, it is significant that not merely did women make a significant advance in terms of legislative representation in 1992, but also that Clinton made determined efforts to place women in key positions in his administration.

Tim Hames's chapter on the media draws attention to an institution that has agenda-setting power both in elections and between them. The media has in many ways itself become a key political player in the Washington power game; but its character is also itself an issue, and its capacity to stymie an administration is considerable.

Part Five of the book aims to fulfill a rather different function from the previous four parts. The first four parts of the book survey the changing landscape of American politics. Chris Bailey's chapter surveys the contrasting approaches to the study of American politics and offers a guide to many of the debates between political scientists. As Bailey suggests, there is a strong relationship between the ideological spirit of the age and its preferred methodologies – between, for example, the recent interest in public choice approaches and the mind-set of neo-conservative America. Bailey identifies three dominant approaches to the study of politics –

institutionalism, behavioralism, and rational choice, and he shows how these different approaches have affected the writing and research about different aspects of American government. Although Bailey is necessarily wary of pushing his generalizations too far, he does believe that the present state of the discipline and the likely future development of it are much more diverse than many previous periods, and that a pluralism of intellectual approaches rather than the dominance of any single methodology is likely to prevail.

In terms of the broader theme of the American system's capacity to respond to changing demands, it may be that political scientists have contributed, albeit unconsciously, to its inherent continuity. By reflecting the values of the system rather than seeking to question its assumptions from some more radical viewpoint, they may have reinforced the conservatism already there. Such a view would no doubt be widely contested. What can be said with more certainty is that the tension between the rhetoric of political change and the constraints on reform in the American political system is likely to endure throughout the Clinton presidency.

PART ONE

Dynamics

2

The 1992 Presidential Election: Voting Behavior and Legitimacy

PIPPA NORRIS

On November 2nd, 1992, Bill Clinton, who had seemed irredeemably damaged in the spring primaries, won the first Democratic presidential victory since 1976. In a coast-to-coast triumph, Clinton captured 43 percent of the popular vote, with 370 electoral college votes in 32 states. The result could not be claimed as a Democratic landslide; Clinton's share of the popular vote was similar to that won by Mondale in 1984 and Carter in 1980, and less than Dukakis in 1988. Nevertheless, the Democratic Party reasserted control of both ends of Pennsylvania Avenue, and held almost two-thirds of governorships and state legislative chambers. Despite record-breaking levels of approval after the victorious Gulf War, President Bush lost badly, with only 37.5 percent of the popular vote, the lowest share of any incumbent president for 80 years. Even more unexpectedly, the independent, Ross Perot, won a remarkable 19 percent of the vote, the highest share for any third party candidate since Teddy Roosevelt in 1912. Unlike previous independents such as Strom Thurmond in 1948, or George Wallace in 1968, Perot attracted nation-wide support which cut across most social and ideological divisions.

Beyond the bare results, the election signified certain developments that promise to have significant consequences for interpretations of the future of American politics. The outcome refuted theories of a Republican lock on the White House; produced a serious challenge to the dominance of two-party politics in America; undermined conventional wisdom about campaign strategy, especially the effectiveness of negative personal attacks; saw the highest turnout since 1968, reversing the long-term slide in participation and political interest; brought about a baby-boom generational shift in American leadership; created a more socially diverse Congress; and last, but not least, ended the period of divided party government that many blamed for gridlock in Washington.

Understanding the dynamics of the 1992 campaign that produced these results – vote switches from the primaries and conventions through to election day, the influence of the old and new media, the effects of advertising, the impact of candidate strategy and tactics, the influence of issues like health care and the economy, the role of the campaign handlers – is a complex story that is only starting to be unravelled (Pomper, 1993; Nelson, 1993). The aim of this chapter is to explore the outcome in the light of three broad interpretative frameworks that have been commonly articulated, based on changes in the Democratic social base, retrospective evaluations of the Bush presidency, and Perot's challenge to the party system.

In the first perspective, Clinton's victory has to be understood in the light of long-term trends in the social and regional base of voting support. In this view, Democratic presidential contenders have suffered a string of defeats since 1968 for two primary reasons. First, in recent decades structural change in post-industrial society gradually eroded the size of the traditional New Deal coalition. Social change, including the decline of unionized, blue-collar workers, the growth of the Sun Belt, and the expansion of the suburbs, all tended to benefit the Republicans. Second, the Democrats lost touch with their traditional voting base, focussing too much on divisive issues such as those of race and gender that appealed to certain party factions, but failed to strike a chord with the majority of the electorate. By an effective strategy of appealing to mainstream America on moderate "apple pie" issues, it can be argued, Clinton brought back many of the middle-income groups who felt the party had deserted them, and thereby expanded the Democratic base (Stokes and DiIulio, 1993). To examine this explanation, we can consider the social and geographic basis of Clinton's support.

Did Clinton win through an effective strategy or, rather, did President Bush lose? In the second interpretation, many feel the decisive factor in the election was the retrospective evaluation of the way Bush handled his term in office, particularly the economy. By failing to engage in domestic politics, or to appear seriously concerned about the state of the American economy, many believe the President lost touch with the public mood, and he thereby threw away his chance of a second term. In the cliché, "It was the economy, stupid." To examine this, we need to consider trends in presidential approval and evaluations of economic performance during Bush's period in office.

But what of Perot? It seems plausible that explanations based on traditional models of two-party politics are inadequate for this campaign. The last interpretation emphasizes that Perot was decisive for the outcome, by providing a halfway house for dissatisfied Republicans, who could thereby express disapproval of Bush without moving all the way into the Clinton camp. Further, by increasing interest in the campaign, it has been suggested, Perot helped reverse the long-term slide in participation (Clymer, 1992). Although common, so far much of the evidence for this thesis remains highly speculative. Therefore the purpose of this chapter is to explore some of the grounds for these interpretations, and to consider the ramifications for future elections.

The Social and Geographic Basis of the Vote

The first explanation suggests that a more moderate southern ticket was able to bring the Democratic Party back in touch with middle America, by building an effective social and regional coalition. The 1992 election returned a Democrat to the White House for the first time in 16 years, thereby overturning theories of a Republican lock on the presidency. The "lock" thesis gradually became popular following the publication of Kevin Phillips's influential book *The Emerging Republican Majority* (Phillips, 1970), which spawned a lively debate (Shafer, 1991). The theory sought to account for the striking phenomenon that, from 1968 to 1988, the Republicans won every presidential election but one. The Carter victory in 1976 could be seen, in large part, as an exception due to Watergate. During these decades, Republican presidential candidates enjoyed on average a 10–point lead in the popular vote. If we average presidential support in 1968–88, we can calculate that the "normal" Republican vote was 53 percent compared with 43 percent for the Democrats (see Table 2.1). This lead was exaggerated by the winner-take-all system, so Republicans swept the board with 416 out of 537 electoral college votes. Based on normal vote analysis, the odds seemed stacked on the return of George Bush in 1992, with a predictable and unexciting contest.

This pattern of Democratic failure can be attributed to a series of particular circumstances: the unpopularity of successive Democratic contenders, the lack of experience of their campaign strategists, factionalism within the Democratic Party. On a longer-term basis, in its strongest version, the "lock" theory suggested social and regional trends had gradually eroded the traditional base of the Democratic Party in presidential elections. The classic New Deal coalition, forged during Roosevelt's 1932 landslide, consisted of European second-generation immigrant families in northern cities, African-Americans, organized labor, Jewish liberals, poor working-class whites, elderly social security dependants, and southern Democrats. During the 1970s and 1980s, the Democratic coalition was thought to be gradually fragmenting into contending and disputatious factions. Two trends, it was suggested, contributed toward this development.

Structural trends in post-industrial society – the flight to the suburbs, the fall in union membership, the expansion of the professional service sector, the layoff of blue-collar workers,

TABLE 2.1 *Presidential elections 1968–92*

President		Electoral college		Popular vote			
		% Dem.	% G.O.P.	% Dem.	% G.O.P.	% Ind.	% Lead
Nixon	1968	36	56	43	43	14	1
Nixon	1972	3	97	38	61	2	23
Carter	1976	55	45	50	48	2	2
Reagan	1980	9	91	41	51	8	10
Reagan	1984	2	98	41	59	1	18
Bush	1988	20	80	46	54	0	8
Clinton	1992	69	31	43	38	19	5
A.V. 1968–88		21	78	43	53	4	10

increased levels of education, the growth of the Sun Belt, new patterns of immigration – gradually transformed the composition of the electorate, and thereby eroded the size of the Democratic base. As shown in Table 2.2, over the last 40 years the proportion of blue-collar voters fell from almost half to less than a third (29 percent). Similar patterns of shrinkage are evident for the less well educated, union households, and those living in central cities. In counterbalance, there were some compensations in the increased proportion of black voters, who were almost all Democrats, and increased numbers of women voters, who tended to be more Democratic after the development of the gender gap in the 1980 election. Nevertheless in general, structural trends seemed likely to decimate core Democratic support if the party did not reach out to expand its traditional base. At the same time, *behavioral* trends such as weakening party loyalties, the rise of new issues, and ideological shifts, seemed to alter patterns of voting support within these groups, exemplified by the growth of blue-collar Reaganites.

Nowhere was the shift in Democratic strength at presidential level more evident than in the south, the heartland of the party after the Civil War. The once solid south was transformed in four decades from being one of the Republicans' weakest areas of presidential support into their strongest. Some suggested structural shifts were influential; the entry into the electorate of a younger generation of white southerners, the migration of elderly white northerners and Cuban exiles into the region, the urbanization of the "'po' white trash" subsistence farmers, and the long-term exodus of southern blacks to the northern cities (Wolfinger and Hagen, 1985; Petrocik, 1987). At the same time, political trends that moved the Democratic Party toward the left may have played an important role in converting conservative southerners into born-again Reaganites, notably Johnson's Civil Rights and Great Society initiatives (Black and Black, 1992, 1987; Brodsky, 1988; Grantham, 1988).

In contrast to the fortunes of the Democrats, the "lock" theory suggested the Republicans had forged an almost unassailable electoral coalition during the 1970s, consolidated and exemplified by Reagan's landslide victories in the 1980s. Key components of the coalition included "Moral Majority" southern white conservatives, anti-government and anti-tax populist midwest farmers, older traditional country-club Republicans in the Sun Belt west, and

TABLE 2.2 *Structural change in the size of voting groups*

	1952	1972	1992	Change
College	18	37	55	37
High school	48	48	32	−16
Grade school	34	15	13	−21
Professional	30	34	42	12
White collar	21	23	34	13
Blue collar/unskilled	49	43	29	−20
Non-union households	72	74	82	10
Union households	28	26	19	−9
Central cities	33	25	25	−8
Suburbs	31	33	44	13
Non-urban	36	42	30	−6
South	19	29	31	12
Non-south	81	71	69	−12
Black	4	9	12	8
White	96	91	88	−8
Women	51	55	53	2
Men	49	45	47	−2
Protestants	69	67	59	−10
Catholics	25	25	28	3
Jewish	4	2	3	−1
Other/no religion	2	5	10	8
	100	100	100	

Note: These are the proportions of voters in each group, not the proportions of the electorate or population.

Source: National Election Study, 1952–92.

the younger-generation professionals and small entrepreneurs in east coast cities. During the 1980s, under Reagan's leadership, there were inevitable tensions within the new Republican coalition, particularly rumblings of discontent among the "social" conservative leadership, but so long as it held together some believed the combination of social and geographic factors produced an almost unbeatable edge in presidential races. Yet 1992 refuted the theory; Bush left the White House with the lowest share of the popular vote of any incumbent president since 1912. Why? Did Clinton's middle-of-the-road appeal recapture the old New Deal coalition? Or did he manage to expand the Democratic Party's social and regional base?

Changes in the geographic basis of the vote

The geographic strategy of the Democrats was threefold: to break Republican control of the south with the first all-southern ticket since 1828; to expand the gains on the west coast evident in the previous election; and to capitalize on the economic recession affecting key states in the midwest, the rust belt, and New England. Yet they faced a discouraging track record; in 1984, Walter Mondale carried just one state; in 1988, Michael Dukakis won only ten. If we look at the state-by-state results in 1992, it is clear that Clinton did not experience an electoral college landslide (see Figure 2.1). Nevertheless, his support was coast-to-coast, winning major prizes from California (54 electoral college votes) to New York (33), with Ohio (22), Pennsylvania (23), New Jersey (15), and Illinois (21) in between. Clinton's success was far broader geographically than Carter's in 1976, and more efficient in translating popular votes into state gains. In 1976 Carter won 50 percent of the popular vote, and 55 percent of the electoral college vote, or a ratio of 1 to 1.1. In contrast, Clinton's 43 percent of the popular vote produced 60 percent of the electoral college vote, or a ratio of 1 to 1.6.

Since 1968, the south had become the strongest Republican base in presidential races, with particularly strong support among conservatives, whites, born-again fundamentalists, and Reagan Democrats. The Clinton–Gore ticket, from Arkansas and Tennessee, brought the major parties neck and neck in the popular vote (44 percent for Bush to 43 percent for Clinton), and split 11 states of the Confederacy in half. This remained the strongest region for Bush, who carried the major prizes of Texas and Florida (by a close 2–3 percent margin), plus North and South Carolina, Alabama, Virginia, Mississippi (with 50 percent of the vote, the best state result for Bush nationwide), resulting in 119 electoral college votes. Bush's support in this region was particularly strong among whites (49 percent of the vote), white born-again Christians (63 percent) and self-identified conservatives (66 percent). In contrast, Clinton made inroads by holding the home states of Arkansas and Tennessee as expected, and picking up Georgia (just) and Louisi-

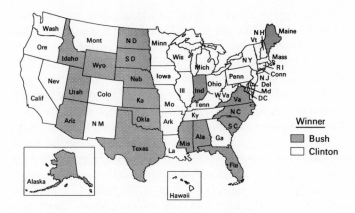

FIGURE 2.1   *Electoral college 1992 U.S. Election*

ana, gaining in total 39 electoral college votes. The south was not
critical to the outcome; even if Bush had taken every state in the
region, he would still have fallen short of victory. At other levels of
office, in the Senate and House, Democrats continue to hold about
two-thirds of all seats, and although the Republicans have made
some gains, the Democrats solidly control most seats in the state
houses and most governorships. Overall the outcome demonstrated
that neither side has captured the once "solid south." The
Democrats remained relatively weak in this region; they did not
restore the New Deal coalition, but nor did the "Republican
realignment" thesis hold water. Under the right conditions, the
south remains competitive for both parties.

Far more important strategically than the south, the Democrats
consolidated gains in the west, expanding their geographic base.
For the first time since 1964, the Democrats won every west coast
state. With 54 electoral college votes, California was seen as critical
from an early stage, and in 1988 Bush's victory had been wafer thin.
In the early 1990s, the Californian economy had been one of those
worst hit by the recession, with cutbacks in the defence industry, a
slump in the high-tech service sector, reductions in the state services
such as welfare and college education, and unemployment of 9.8
percent. The Los Angeles riots in the summer of 1992 further
damaged confidence, and reinforced the image of a society riven

by conflicting pressures from different ethnic groups, and which no longer could serve as the promised land for immigrants. Clinton established a 14-point lead in California, with further victories in Oregon and Washington on the Pacific coast, as well as Colorado, New Mexico, Montana, and Nevada in the Mountain West. In contrast, Bush had his largest lead in Utah, as well as winning Arizona and Wyoming, although this yielded a meagre electoral college dividend. Overall, Clinton won 40 percent of the popular vote in the region compared to Bush's 35 percent, while Perot achieved one of his strongest performances, with 25 percent of the vote.

In the midwest, the electoral college map divided, with Bush winning a north–south strip of six states from North Dakota to Texas, although again (with the exception of Texas) these sparsely populated states produced few electoral college winnings. The midwest had been badly hit by the slump in the early 1980s, and because of the labor shake-out they were less badly affected than some other regions by the recession in 1991–2. Ohio and Illinois had been hotly contested by all candidates, and both fell into the Clinton column, along with Michigan and Wisconsin. The north-east, badly hit by the recession, provided the strongest lead for Clinton over Bush (48 to 32 percent respectively). Some New England states should have been rock-solid Republican strong-holds: Vermont had only gone Democrat once before this century, in Johnson's 1964 landslide. Republican Maine was the President's family home, but the slump had badly affected sectors that had expanded during the 1980s, like tourism, the service sector, and high-tech computers. Only New Hampshire proved at all close; all the rest went to Clinton, including the prizes of New York and Pennsylvania.

Changes in the social basis of the vote

Therefore, the Democrats expanded their regional base. But who switched within these states? The strategy of the Clinton–Gore ticket, developed early in the campaign by the Democratic Leader-ship Council, and reinforced by the New York party convention, was to launch a strong appeal to middle-class, middle-of-the-road Americans, focussing on moderate issues like the expansion of college education, health care reform, job training, investment in infrastructure, and a stimulus package to produce economic growth, aimed at expanding the party's base. The Clinton–Gore ticket were seen as "New Democrats," progressive (concerned about global warming, AIDS, childcare) yet prudent (aiming to cut government and reduce the deficit), not just the old "tax-and-spend" liberals. Despite the Los Angeles riots, there was surprisingly little debate about race relations, poverty, drugs, homelessness, or the inner cities during the campaign. In contrast to 1988, Jesse Jackson played a modest role in the campaign, and indeed on some occasions Clinton seemed to distance himself in public from the African-American constituency. Women played a major role at the Democratic convention, and Clinton clearly came out in support of abortion rights and family leave, but the primary focus was the attempt to get more women into public office, rather than policies on affirmative action, positive quotas, or E.R.A. As a supporter of capital punishment, Clinton could not be branded, like Dukakis, as "soft on crime." The call to downsize defense spending and close bases was in tune with public opinion, with the end of the Cold War, symbolized by the fall in the Berlin Wall, which reduced the salience of defense issues. Did this moderate strategy succeed in bringing middle America back to the Democrats?

The analysis of group support during the last 40 years, shown in Table 2.3, shows that the Democratic base in 1992 remains a faded print of the classic New Deal coalition – Jewish liberals, low-income whites, African-Americans, Hispanics, union households, older voters. To interpret the overall long-term trends of gains and losses, the analysis can be divided into two periods coinciding with the previous table: 1952 to 1972, then 1976 to 1992. The results suggest the old Democratic coalition has lost some support among certain groups; whites (especially southern whites) who deserted in the mid-1960s, men, the young, union households, and Catholics who gradually lost their Democratic faith. Some of these groups have themselves been transformed; in the 1950s, "Catholics" usually meant Italian-Americans, Polish-Americans, and other ethnic groups from southern, central, and eastern Europe. In the 1990s, this group has become more socially and politically diverse, with the entrance of new Hispanic emigrés from central and southern America. In counterbalance, the Democrats have made gains among women, African-Americans, and older voters. The pattern demonstrates temporary fluctuations relating to the particular candidate: for example, the Catholic shift in support of John Kennedy in 1960, the overwhelming support among blacks for Johnson in 1964, and increased southern support for Carter in 1976. Overall, though, the general pattern is one of trendless fluctuations, and broad continuity over time, rather than a steady and consistent long-term erosion in support. We can conclude from this analysis that the structural shrinkage of the Democratic base has proved more significant than the behavioral shift among voting groups.

If we focus in more detail on the social profile of supporters for all candidates in the 1992 election, and changes in group support since 1988, the evidence suggests, contrary to speculation, the Clinton victory cannot be attributed to swings among key groups. The most striking observation is that the Clinton voters look remarkably like the Dukakis voters (see Table 2.4). Income proved a good predictor of voting support for Clinton and Bush, but changes in support were fairly consistent across all income groups; the Democrats made no inroads into the middle-class vote. In 1988–92, Democratic support declined by a few percent fairly evenly across most groups, with slightly heavier falls among self-identified liberals and Hispanic voters. There were no corresponding gains among self-identified moderates or conservatives. The only group who switched more substantially toward Clinton were Jewish voters, a relatively small group (4 percent), who may have been reacting to Bush's Middle East initiative rather than any positive appeal of the Democratic ticket. The Democrats continued to attract stronger than average support among African-Americans, Hispanics, older voters, low-income, union households, women, and self-identified liberals. The conclusion has to be that Clinton held the Democratic base, but failed to expand support beyond the party's traditional social constituency. The gains geographically were critical to victory. However, the explanation that as a "New Democrat" Clinton forged a new social coalition that could be consolidated for future electoral success receives no support from this analysis. The defeat of President Bush should not disguise the fact that, in the long-term, the Democrats remain stuck with a shrinking social base, while the Republicans have the advantage of a demographically expanding constituency.

TABLE 2.3 *Social basis of the Democratic presidential vote, 1952–92*

1952	1952	1956	1960	1964	1968	1972	1976	1980	1984	1988	1992	Average 1952–72	Average 1976–92	Diff
All	45	42	50	61	43	38	50	41	41	46	43	47	44	−3
Men	47	45	52	60	41	37	53	38	36	44	41	47	42	−5
Women	42	39	49	62	45	38	48	44	45	48	46	46	46	0
White	43	41	49	59	38	32	46	36	34	41	39	44	39	−5
Black	79	61	68	94	85	87	85	86	87	82	82	79	84	5
College	34	31	39	52	37	37	42	35	39	42	40	38	40	2
High school	45	42	52	62	42	34	54	43	43	46	43	46	46	0
Grade school	52	50	55	66	52	49	58	54	51	55	55	54	55	1
Union HH	61	57	65	73	56	46	63	50	52	63	55	60	57	−3
>30 yr	51	43	54	64	47	48	53	47	40	37	44	51	44	−7
30–49 yr	47	45	54	63	44	33	48	38	40	45	42	48	43	−5
50 +yr	39	39	46	59	41	36	52	41	41	49	46	43	46	3
Protestants	37	37	38	55	35	30	46	39	39	42	36	39	40	1
Catholics	56	51	78	76	59	48	57	46	39	51	44	61	47	−14
Republicans	8	4	5	20	9	5	9	8	4	7	10	9	8	−1
Democrats	77	85	84	87	74	67	82	69	79	85	77	79	78	−1
Independents	35	30	43	56	31	31	38	29	33	43	38	38	36	−2
East	45	40	53	68	50	42	51	43	46	51	47	50	48	−2
Midwest	42	41	48	61	44	40	48	41	42	47	42	46	44	−2
South	51	49	51	52	31	29	54	44	37	40	42	44	43	−1
West	42	43	49	60	44	41	46	35	40	46	44	47	42	−4

Source: 1952–88 Gallup polls; 1992 Voter Research and Surveys Exit Poll.

TABLE 2.4   *Changes in the vote, 1988–92*

	1988 Dukakis	1992 Clinton	Chg	1988 Bush	1992 Bush	Chg	1992 Perot
All	45	43	−2	53	38	−15	19
Men	41	41	0	57	38	−19	21
Women	49	46	−3	50	37	−13	17
White	40	39	−1	59	41	−18	20
Black	86	82	−4	12	11	−1	7
Hispanic	69	62	−7	30	25	−5	14
18–29yrs	47	44	−3	52	34	−18	22
30–44yrs	45	42	−3	54	38	−16	20
45–55yrs	42	41	−1	57	40	−17	19
60+ yrs	49	50	1	50	38	−12	12
Wt Prot	33	33	0	66	46	−20	21
Catholic	47	44	−3	52	36	−16	20
Jewish	64	78	14	35	12	−23	10
$15,000	62	59	−3	37	23	−14	18
$15–30,000	50	45	−5	49	35	−14	20
$30–50,000	44	41	−3	56	38	−18	21
$50–75,000	42	40	−2	56	42	−14	18
$75,000+	37	36	−1	62	48	−14	16
East	49	47	−2	50	35	−15	18
Midwest	47	42	−5	52	37	−15	21
South	41	42	1	58	43	−15	16
West	46	44	−2	52	34	−18	22
Lib	81	68	−13	18	14	−4	18
Mod	50	48	−2	49	31	−18	21
Con	19	18	−1	80	65	−15	17

Source: *New York Times* Exit Poll 1988; 1992 Voter Research and Surveys Exit Poll.

Evaluations of the Bush Presidency

The second interpretation rests on the familiar proposition: "Oppositions do not win elections, governments lose them." In this common view, it can be argued that what mattered were retrospective evaluations of Bush's performance as president,

particularly his handling of the economy (Campbell and Rockman, 1991; Duffy and Goodgame, 1992). As the conventional
wisdom about the election has repeated, "It was the economy,
stupid." To examine evidence for this, we need to consider trends in
presidential approval during Bush's period in office, evaluations of
his economic performance, and the relationship of these judgments
to voting support.

In mid-term, few anticipated that presidential popularity might
prove an electoral issue. After a low-key start, Bush maintained
high approval ratings for his performance in office compared with
other presidents at an equivalent stage in their administration
(Brace and Hinckley, 1992). Presidential approval in Gallup polls
for Bush averaged 61 percent throughout his administration,
slightly less than Kennedy and Eisenhower, but better than
Johnson, Reagan, Nixon, Carter, and Ford (Said, 1993). There
were strong rally-round-the-flag peaks; in March 1991, after the
Gulf War and fall of the Berlin Wall, Bush enjoyed approval ratings
of 89 percent, the highest rate ever recorded by Gallup polls in the
postwar period. During the summer and fall in 1991, the return of
George Bush continued to be thought plain sailing, which was
reinforced by perceptions of a weak field of Democratic challengers. Bush was expected to emulate Eisenhower in 1956, Nixon in
1972, and Reagan in 1984. In the postwar period, Ford was the only
Republican incumbent who failed to be returned for a second term,
and this could be attributed to exceptional circumstances (Watergate, the Nixon pardon, the O.P.E.C. energy crisis, and the
economic slump of the early 1970s). Bush may have had his
problems, but in mid-term he appeared more of a Reagan than a
Ford. As Carl Everett Ladd noted in a fairly typical assessment
before the early primaries:

> It can never be properly said, a year prior to an election, that an
> American president is "unbeatable." The public thinks and cares
> about the presidency too much for that. . . . Still, it's evident to
> everyone, including most Republican and Democratic strategists,
> that a president who more than 30 months into his tenure has the
> support of 70 percent of the public occupies a commanding if not
> unassailable position.

Yet, as Gallup polls reveal, from around September 1991 to
November 1992, President Bush experienced a consistent and

steady slide in his personal popularity; by the time of the election, only 34 percent expressed approval of his presidency, 20 points below Reagan's approval in the 1984 election.

What drove this dive? The most common explanation is public perceptions of the state of the American economy. Bush's rating on foreign policy remained fairly high, but evaluations of his handling of the economy slid rapidly from summer 1991 to election day. During this period, the objective economic indicators were sending mixed signals. Inflation and interest rates remained relatively low. The official level of unemployment was moderate (6.8 percent), not as severe as during the 1981–2 recession, nor as bad as the situation in most European countries. Much of the unemployment was concentrated in certain sectors, particularly the middle-class service occupations that had expanded so rapidly during the 1980s. Most of the models estimating the outcome based on a combination of objective economic indicators and presidential popularity predicted a Bush victory (Morin, 1992). On the other hand, economic growth was sluggish and uncertain, with G.D.P. up 1.9 percent per annum, industrial production static (+ 0.2), and retail sales slow (2.6 percent). The trade balance was in the red, while the federal budget deficit of $290bn. cast a constant gloom over Washington. Although not deep, the recession was prolonged; by the election, it had been going on for 15 months. Consumer and business confidence were low, reflecting a public perception of economic malaise, which did not seem to be being addressed with sufficient energy by the Bush administration. In early September an economic plan was waved about by Bush in a Chicago campaign speech to businessmen, but by and large his campaign seemed to be distracted by the character issue, criticisms of Clinton on the basis of the twin themes of "trust and taxes," and unable to offer a positive and clearly articulated solution to the nation's economic concerns. On many occasions, notably during the second debate, Bush seemed out of touch, disengaged, unable to grasp what all the fuss was about, and why people were so worried about their economic security.

Did economic perceptions and presidential approval influence the vote, as many suggest? First, if we look directly at ratings of the President during the campaign (Table 2.5), these confirm a strong relationship between approval for President Bush and final voting choice. Overall, almost all of those who eventually voted for Bush

(85 percent) expressed approval of the way he handled the job, compared with about a third of Perot voters, and 14 percent of Clinton voters. Given his record, with the democratic revolutions in central and eastern Europe, the end of the Cold War, Panama and the Gulf wars, there was more widespread approval of the way Bush handled foreign policy, expressed by almost all Bush voters, two-thirds of Perot voters, and almost half the Clinton supporters. On economic policy there was a familiar pattern; Bush voters were divided down the middle between praise and blame, while almost no Clinton voters approved.

The problem with interpreting this evidence is that these direct measures are open to rationalization; people may say they approve of Bush's record because they have already decided to vote for him

TABLE 2.5 *Approval of President Bush*

		Vote 1992		
		Bush	Perot	Clinton
Presidency	St. Approve	37	6	3
	Approve	47	29	11
	Disapprove	10	29	24
	St. Disapprove	5	36	62
	PDI#	70	−30	−72
Economic Policy	St. Approve	18	2	3
	Approve	34	2	13
	Disapprove	23	11	17
	St. Disapprove	26	85	68
	PDI#	4	−93	−70
Foreign Policy	St. Approve	69	35	18
	Approve	20	32	28
	Disapprove	6	13	19
	St. Disapprove	6	20	35
	PDI#	78	34	−7

Note: Q "Do you approve or disapprove of the way George Bush is handling his job as president . . . our relations with foreign countries . . . the economy?"

Source: National Election Study 1992.

TABLE 2.6 *Economic evaluations and voting choice*

	Vote 1992		
	Bush	Clinton	Perot
Sociotropic retrospective	−.34**	.31**	.03
Egotropic retrospective	−.11**	.09*	.01
Prospective	.01	.02	.02
R2	.16	.12	.01

Note: The figures are standardized Beta coefficients using O.L.S. regression.

Source: National Election Study 1992.

on other grounds. More indirectly, the impact of economic perceptions on the election can be analyzed by dividing survey items into three categories. *Sociotropic retrospective* evaluations relate to perceptions of the past performance of the American economy, usually during the year before the election. This includes concern over whether the levels of inflation and unemployment had got better or worse, perceptions about the national and state economy, and whether people believed the federal government's policies had made the economy better or worse. *Egotropic retrospective* evaluations relate to perceptions about personal and family economic circumstances during the previous year (direct pocketbook voting). People were asked whether their standard of living had improved or deteriorated, whether their income had kept up with the cost of living, and whether the economic policy of the federal government had made them personally better or worse off. Lastly, *prospective* evaluations concern judgments about future economic prospects, whether things are going to get better or worse, for the person and the country. None of these measures make any specific reference to the candidates or President Bush.

In the first simple model, the results of regression analysis in Table 2.6 confirm the conventional wisdom that concern about the performance of the national economy played a significant role in the election. The sociotropic (and to a lesser extent, the egotropic) retrospective evaluations proved to be significantly related to voting support for Clinton and Bush. In the more rigorous model in Table 2.7, controlling for party identification and self-identified liberal–

TABLE 2.7 *Model of voting choice*

| | Vote 1992 | | |
	Bush	Clinton	Perot
Party identification	.24**	.35**	.04
Lib–con ideology (self-identified)	.13**	.13**	.04
PRESIDENTIAL APPROVAL			
Approval President Bush	.24**	−.16**	−.15**
Approval Bush's foreign policy	.04	−.04	−.02
Approval Bush's economic policy	.06	−.11**	−.02
ECONOMIC EVALUATIONS			
Sociotropic retrospective	−.08*	.04	.06
Egotropic retrospective	.06	.01	.06
Prospective	.01	.02	.02
R2	.28	.33	.02

Note: The figures represent standardized Beta coefficients using O.L.S. regression analysis. *significant to a 0.005 level of significance; **significant to a 0.001 level of significance.

Source: National Election Study 1992.

TABLE 2.8 *Timing of voting decision*

	Bush	Clinton	Perot
Knew all along	12	7	0
Before conventions	7	12	3
GOP convention	2	4	0
Democratic convention	2	6	0
After convention	2	6	1
3–4 weeks before election	3	6	5
2 weeks before election	2	2	2
Last few days	3	4	5
On election day	2	3	3
Total % vote	34	48	18
N	556	780	295

Note: Q: "How long before the election did you decide that you were going to vote the way you did?"

Source: American National Election Study 1992 (Post).

conservative ideology, approval of the President and sociotropic retrospective evaluations continue to prove significant in explaining support for President Bush. However, the conventional wisdom needs two important qualifications. In the final model, prospective evaluations about the anticipated performance of the economy in the forthcoming year, and egotropic measures, proved insignificant. This is consistent with the common finding that concerns about the past performance of the national economy tend to prove more important politically than personal finances (Lewis-Beck, 1988; Fiorina, 1981). More surprisingly, none of the economic perceptions explain support for Perot. The results suggest Perot voters were not driven, as many suggest, by dissatisfaction with Bush's economic performance. The reasons for their support, and the electoral impact of Perot's candidacy, are important puzzles that therefore require further analysis.

Perot and the Challenge to Two-party Politics

So far we have considered the election as though it were politics as usual, but in one important respect it was not. The election symbolized the most serious challenge to two-party politics for 80 years. Just after the New Hampshire Primary in late February 1992, the idiosyncratic, opinionated, and cranky Texas billionaire Ross Perot announced on *Larry King Live* that he would run as an independent candidate, if placed on the ballot in 50 states. The declaration seemed almost off-the-cuff, accidental, unpremeditated. Yet it seemed to strike a chord. Throughout the campaign Perot played the political hokey-kokey, to the despair of party strategists and delight of reporters, building up a grassroots organization in spring, moving to front-runner in a couple of polls in May, before withdrawing in mid-July on the last day of the Democratic Convention (for reasons that have never become clear), then reentering again on October 1st. During the final month of the campaign, Perot spent an estimated $34 million on television, with $3 million alone on half-hour "infomercials" on all three major networks on the eve of polling. Overall, Perot spent an estimated $60 million during the campaign, slightly more than each of his rivals spent from official federal funds ($55 million each).

The volatility of the electorate, and the shock-waves Perot's candidacy caused to fluctuations in voting intentions, were demonstrated in the opinion polls. The pattern shows three phases in the campaign. During the first period, from the primaries through to the conventions, President Bush's front-runner status slides, until from May to July it appears a close three-way race with Clinton tending to be the underdog. In the second period, from mid-July through to September, following a moderate and united Democratic Convention, the withdrawal of Perot, and the G.O.P. convention in Houston captured by the conservative, Christian right, the polls rapidly propelled Clinton to a commanding lead. In the final month of the campaign, the race appears to tighten. After reentering the campaign in early October, Perot rapidly rose, at one stage gaining one percentage point a day, before he slowed toward the end. The average of the six final opinion polls estimated Clinton 44 percent, Bush 36 percent and Perot 16 percent, which proved close to the final tally.

In other countries in recent years, minor parties like the Greens in Germany, the Lombard League in Italy, and the National Front in France, have experienced considerable electoral volatility, with sudden swings in their favor during periods of government unpopularity and dissatisfaction with politics. "Flash parties" have arisen fast, and fallen as quickly, in the past. Populism in American politics, distrust of government, the search for simple solutions, and the appeal of straight-talking leaders to "get things done," is nothing new. However, in few stable democracies have individual candidates, lacking any organised national base or political track record, captured one in five voters across the country during a period of less than nine months. The fluidity of support this demonstrates in the dealigned American electorate is remarkable, and, it can be argued, disturbing. Traditional theories of voting behavior, rooted in party loyalties based on long-established social cleavages, cannot account for such a rapid rise.

The volatility of Perot's support is evident if we look at the self-reported timing of the voting decision (in Table 2.8). Most of those who voted for Perot (83 percent) decided in October, after he announced his reentry. More surprisingly, almost half of those who supported him decided to do so in the last few days or even in the polling booth. This last-minute surge was confirmed by the final pre-election opinion polls, which underestimated his support. Perot's 19 percent of the popular vote, or 19.7 million votes, is a remarkable result compared with previous third party candidates. The last one with serious support was Anderson in 1980, who got only 8 percent of the vote. As shown earlier (in Table 2.4), Perot proved weakest in the south, among blacks, women, and elderly voters, but overall he demonstrated nationwide appeal among most social groups. Perot managed his strongest performance in the Pacific Mountain states, such as Utah, Nevada, and Montana, as well as some states with a strong independent tradition like Maine, Alaska, and Kansas.

Third party candidates usually fade from national politics soon after the campaign: John Anderson in 1980, George Wallace in 1968, and Bob LaFollette in 1924 made no subsequent impact in presidential contests. In similar fashion, many expected Perot to pack up his tent and return to Texas after his moment in the sun. Instead, just when the Democrats and Republicans thought it was safe to return to politics as normal, his organization, "United We Stand, America," went on raising funds and mobilizing volunteers, while Perot continued to needle Washington, buying air-time for more "infomercials." Six months after the election, some surveys found more of Perot's than Clinton's supporters remained committed to their chosen candidate (Berke, 1993).

So was the shift to Perot decisive for the outcome? Many feel the 1992 election was characterized as usual by a deep mood of alienation with politics, encapsulated by the title of Germond and Witcover's book on the campaign: *Mad as Hell: Revolt at the Ballot Box, 1992* (1993). Some suggest Perot acted as a lightning rod for this mood. Perot may have attracted three constituencies: Republicans angry with Bush's broken promises on taxes; independents and non-voters without a political home; and Democrats unimpressed by Bill Clinton's performance. If support was even among these groups, then the net effect on the other candidates would have been neutral.

However, if Perot inflicted more damage on the incumbent, depriving Bush of a majority, he could thereby have allowed Clinton to win without the need to increase the Democratic share of the vote. To analyze this hypothesis, we need to see who switched to Perot, which other candidate they considered supporting, and whether they can be characterized as negative "protest" voters.

Who switched? Without a detailed panel monitoring churning in voting intentions at regular intervals from March to November, as Perot entered and exited from the race, the evidence is mixed. If we take retrospective measures – how people recalled voting in 1988 – these suggest that Perot inflicted the most substantial damage on Bush. The transition matrix of voting change in 1988–92 (Table 2.9) shows that out of every ten people who voted for Bush in 1988, five stayed with Bush, two deserted to Clinton, and two to Perot. In contrast, Clinton kept eight out of ten of those who voted for Dukakis in the previous election, losing only one in ten to Perot. To put this another way, about two-thirds of Perot's supporters came from the Bush camp in 1988. An analysis of vote by party identification confirms that Perot mainly damaged Bush. Out of every ten Republicans, President Bush held on to about seven, while one deserted to Clinton and two to Perot. In contrast, Clinton was far more successful in holding most (82 percent) of his Democratic base, and his gains and losses balanced out. Not surprisingly, Perot was stronger than average among independents, although they divided among all the candidates in roughly the same proportion as the general electorate. Despite dealignment and volatility, party identification continued to prove the strongest predictor of voting behavior for Clinton and Bush, as shown in the model developed in Table 2.7.

Therefore, retrospective evidence supports the thesis that Perot damaged Bush more than Clinton. However, if we turn to prospective measures – who else Perot supporters might have voted for – the evidence is more mixed, although these may be less reliable since they ask about hypothetical choices. If Perot had stayed out of the race in October, what might have happened? Respondents were asked about wavering; which other candidates they had supported at some stage during the campaign. Among Perot voters, about the same proportion said they had supported Bush and Clinton at some stage. Respondents were also asked in the campaign whether Perot had ever been their first choice. The results suggest that 19 percent of those who eventually backed Bush, and 23 percent who backed Clinton, said they once preferred Perot. Prospective measures therefore suggest that Perot's support would have been distributed fairly evenly among Bush and Clinton. Accordingly, it seems that these prospective and retrospective measures provide contradictory indicators, which cannot

TABLE 2.9   *Change in the vote, 1988–92*

| | 1992 Vote | | | |
	Bush	Clinton	Perot	
1988 Vote				
Bush	55	24	21	100
Dukakis	5	83	12	100
Didn't vote	30	51	20	100
PARTY IDENTIFICATION				
Republican	73	9	18	100
Independent	30	42	27	100
Democrat	8	82	10	100

Note: Based on the recalled vote in 1988 and party i.d. in 1992.
Source: National Election Study, 1992.

be resolved at this stage. On balance, the well-established retrospective measures, based on past vote and party identification, are probably more reliable indicators.

Did Perot mobilize new voters, especially those alienated with traditional parties? Against expectations, election day produced a reversal in the slide in voting participation. Turnout in the presidential election reached 55.9 percent of the voting age population, or 104.5 million citizens. This represented a marked increase from 1988 when 50.1 percent voted. Campaign events such as the debates generated increased public interest, and there seemed to be a revival in civic involvement through participation in talk shows, call-in radio programmes, and the post-bags of members of Congress, which indicate a significant revival in active civic involvement. What is less well established is whether Perot can be seen, as some like Curtis Gans suggest, as the catalyst for this development (Clymer, 1993). It is notable that reported non-voters in the 1988 election split evenly for the candidates in much the same proportion as the general electorate (see Table 2.9). Contrary to speculation, this suggests there was no greater tendency, according to this data, for Perot to provide a home for many new voters who had not participated in the previous election. Nevertheless, his role in the campaign may have increased participation and interest across the board.

It is commonly suggested that Perot benefited from the protest vote, tapping into the mood of discontent with "politics as usual" that many felt was evident in this election. Harris polls during the election found record levels of public alienation and dissatisfaction with government, challenging the legitimacy of American democracy. We can compare trends in confidence in government in 1964–92, and the relationship between cynicism and support for Perot, using the standard N.E.S. indicators. The results confirm the widespread perception that political trust took a further beating in this election; more people believed that many government officials were crooked, that government was run for a few big interests, that government could not be trusted, and that the government wasted a lot of the taxpayers' money. Trends, which had been on the upturn in the early 1980s, slid slightly again – although this tendency should not be exaggerated. Cynicism about government did not quite reach the depths plumbed in 1980 in the aftermath of Watergate, the oil crisis, the hostage crisis, and Carter's "malaise" speech. If we look at the relationship between confidence in government and voting behavior, the results indicate a significant (although fairly weak) relationship (see Table 2.10). Those who supported Perot were slightly more cynical than other voters across all indicators, but the difference was fairly modest. This confirms that Perot benefited more than other candidates from the mood of cynicism and alienation; and he proved significantly stronger among those who disapproved of President Bush, but this remains a far from complete explanation for his appeal.

Conclusions

Therefore, based on this evidence, we can draw some conclusions that seem appropriate in shaping our interpretations of the 1992 election. First, the Clinton victory was despite, rather than because of, changes in the social basis of the vote. Even with a more moderate ticket, the Democrats did not manage to reach out to middle America to build a new constituency among expanding social groups. Support for Clinton rests on a similar basis to the classic New Deal coalition built by F.D.R. 50 years earlier. There have been shifts within these groups, but the most important trend has been the long-term erosion in the size of the Democratic

TABLE 2.10   *Trust and cynicism in government, 1992*

	Bush	Clinton	Perot	Gamma
MANY IN GOVERNMENT CROOKED?				
Quite a lot	45	43	52	
Not many	46	49	42	
Hardly any	9	8	7	
PDI#	−36	−35	−45	.06
IS GOVERNMENT RUN FOR A FEW BIG INTERESTS?				
Benefit few	76	82	84	
Benefit all	24	18	16	
PDI#	−52	64	−67	.16**
CAN GOVERNMENT BE TRUSTED?				
Some of the time	67	69	78	
Most of the time	30	28	21	
Just about always	4	3	1	
PDI#	−63	−65	−77	.12**
DOES GOVERNMENT WASTE TAX MONEY?				
A lot	70	67	78	
Some	28	31	22	
Not very much	2	2	0	
PDI#	−69	−65	−78	.07*
SUMMARY TRUST SCALE				
Least trusting	49	51	64	
Moderately trusting	45	43	34	
Most trusting	6	6	2	
PDI#	−43	−45	−62	.16**

Note: Q: "How much of the time do you think you can trust the government in Washington?" "Do you think that people in government waste a lot of the money we pay in tax...?" "Would you say the government is pretty much run by a few big interests...?" "Do you think quite a few of the people running the government are crooked...?" The summary scale combines responses to the above. The Percentage Difference Index is the proportion most trusting, minus the proportion least trusting. A negative sign denotes lack of trust.

*significant to a 0.005 level of significance; **significant to a 0.001 level of significance.

Source: National Election Studies N.1651.

base. The outcome demonstrated that the Republicans do not have a lock on the White House, but nor did Clinton increase middle-class support. Clinton was elected with 43 percent of the vote, exactly the same as the "normal" mean share of the vote for Democratic candidates who were defeated in 1968–88.

This has important implications for future elections, as well as consequences for governance. One of the most striking recent trends has been the speed of Clinton's decline in popularity in the opinion polls within the first six months of office. After a brief honeymoon, presidential approval quickly plummeted, before appearing to bottom out, and possibly recover somewhat, in mid-summer. This can be attributed to particular events: the adminis-tration's handling of controversial issues like gays in the military, difficulties over key appointments like Zoe Baird, an inexperienced White House staff, the difficulties of tackling massive issues like the budget deficit and comprehensive health care reform. It may also be explained by more systemic factors: the aggressiveness of the new media, the breakdown of party discipline, the ongoing effects of economic recession, the inevitable difference between inflated campaign expectations and actual performance. But what needs to be stressed is that public approval of the President is low compared with other administrations at this stage of office, but it is similar to Clinton's share of the vote. In other words, we can speculate that the basic approval ratings may reflect the size of Democratic core support, with fluctuations around the mean caused by particular events. Insofar as public approval is critical political capital in Washington, this may have serious consequences for the effectiveness of the Clinton presidency.

The second major conclusion is that the analysis confirms that the election was, at least in part, a referendum on President Bush's handling of the national economy. Although the objective economic indicators were fairly mixed during the campaign, with the United States in a stronger position than many O.E.C.D. countries, the public believed that the American recession was continuing, and Bush was blamed for failing to put forward an effective programme to halt the slide. Concern about trends in the national economy during the previous year, and approval of the President, were significantly associated with voting support for President Bush.

According to the retrospective measures of vote switching, the main effect was a net transfer of support from dissatisfied Republicans toward Perot. In this sense, it does seem plausible to suggest that Clinton won in large part not by expanding his base, but because Perot opened the front door of the White House. If Perot continues to play a role in American politics, if confidence in government fails to be restored, if the American electorate continues to prove as volatile, this promises to add a highly unpredictable and unstable element to the dynamics of future contests.

3

Developments in Racial and Ethnic Politics

BRUCE CAIN

Twenty-five years ago, the focus of minority politics in America was almost exclusively on black–white relations. The central goal of the civil rights movement then was to end discrimination against African-Americans using a strategy that combined symbolic protest with litigation and political mobilization. Responding to the ferment of liberal activism and working with the bountiful resources of an expanding economy, Congress passed landmark legislation that aspired to eliminate inner-city poverty, ban institutional discrimination, and offer novel educational and commercial opportunities to African-Americans. African-Americans formed coalitions with liberal whites to elect black candidates to local, state, and national offices in areas where blacks had long been denied representation (Browning, Marshall, and Tabb, 1986; Sonenshein, 1990). On America's college campuses, the civil rights ferment led to the creation of new black politics courses that introduced a generation of students to the thinking of African-American writers such as Eldridge Cleaver and Malcom X, and to the history and culture of the African-American community.

Contemporary American minority politics is in transition from this earlier, more simple era of biracialism to a new one of increasing multiculturalism. While much of the south still conforms to a predominantly biracial pattern, black–white relations in a growing number of urban areas elsewhere constitute only one piece of a complex multiracial and multiethnic mosaic. As it was in the 1960s, discrimination against blacks and other racial and ethnic minorities is still a key problem today, but contemporary minority politics now also include such issues as immigration reform, language rights, urban enterprise zones, and inter-ethnic tensions. Multiracialism has also heightened group competition. Government programs conceived in the earlier biracial era have been expanded to cover Latinos, Asians, and nonracial groups such as women and the disabled. In some areas of the country, this has pitted the legitimate claims and interests of blacks against the equally legitimate claims of other groups at a time of declining economic resources and increasing public skepticism about the government's role in solving problems of poverty, inequality, and justice.

The transition from black–white biracialism to contemporary multiculturalism constitutes a new phase in the historical evolution of racial politics in America, an evolution that has always been shaped to a considerable degree by immigration policy and economic conditions. There have been two recurrent issues in the history of American minority politics: first, an assimilationist concern about absorbing large numbers of foreigners into the United States, and second, an egalitarian question about the relative conditions and opportunities for different racial and ethnic groups in the United States.

While in any period of American history both themes have been manifest, over time, their relative salience has varied. Assimilationist concerns, quite naturally, have tended to be more visible in periods of high immigration. From 1840 to the Depression, there was significant European immigration in the east and midwest especially, and significant Latino and Asian immigration in the west. The dominant group in the American population at the time was white, Protestant, and English-speaking. Certain elements of this population feared the impact of immigration upon American culture as they knew it and labor competition. The conflict between the dominant native-born population and new immigrants took different forms in various parts of the country. In the midwest, for instance, there were bitter conflicts over the creation of bilingual education for the German-speaking immigrants, and in many eastern states, inner-city Irish and Italian ethnic political machines fought for electoral control against suburban and rural native Protestant populations (Erie, 1988). In the west and southwest, state legislatures passed a series of laws that restricted the economic and educational opportunities of their growing Latino and Asian populations (Acuna, 1981). By the outbreak of World War II, increasingly restrictive immigration laws and the Great Depression had brought mass immigration to a virtual halt. With the supply of new immigrants shut off, social mobility and intergenerational assimilation eroded the differences between second generation Irish, Italians, Jews, and the white Protestant majority, and gradually lessened the national salience of assimilationist concerns (Wolfinger, 1965; Parenti, 1967).

As compared to assimilationist issues, egalitarian conflict during the nineteenth century was more focussed in the south than in the east, west, and southwest. Africans had been imported into the United States as slaves and relegated to a position of property. The Civil War emancipated them from slavery, but with the end of Reconstruction, African-Americans found themselves in a position of severe inequality relative to the white population. Since the immigrants were predominantly white Europeans and mostly resided in areas outside the south, the immigrant assimilationist issue was both geographically and intellectually distinct from the African-American equality issue during this period of American history.

The interruption of mass immigration and the lessening of assimilationist conflicts shifted the focus of minority politics in the post World War II period in a biracial direction. The migration of African-Americans into urban areas of the nonsouth after the war broadened the egalitarian issues of black–white relations in at least two senses. Most obviously, it widened the conflict from a primarily regional (i.e. southern) to a national problem: it was no longer just a problem caused by southern prejudice and discrimination. As African-Americans migrated out of the south for economic opportunities, they encountered both subtle and blatant forms of prejudice in other parts of the country and found themselves in new conditions of economic disadvantage. It became clear in the civil rights movement that the redefined egalitarian issues extended beyond legal and institutional discrimination to more elusive problems such as private prejudice and inequalities of opportunity.

As the dominant nonwhite group in America, blacks assumed leadership positions in the post-war civil rights movement and in progressive political alliances. They were the intended beneficiaries of Great Society civil rights and anti-poverty legislation. Indeed, as will be discussed in greater detail later, much of this legislation was modelled after and tailored to the African-American experience.

Other groups could claim these protections only by analogy to the black experience, but this has sometimes created problems because the experiences of different racial and ethnic groups are to some significant degree unique.

This phase in American minority politics began to change in 1965 with the termination of racial and ethnic immigration quotas. America entered a second period of extensive mass immigration that differed from the earlier period in several important ways. To begin with, a substantially higher fraction of the new immigrants were nonwhite, coming from Asia and Latin America. Secondly, whereas the immigrants in the earlier period took up residence in areas where blacks for the most part did not live, the newest immigrants moved into cities where African-Americans had resided since World War II. Thirdly, the legal protections and government programs that had been put in place to assist the African-American population were gradually extended to other nonwhites during the 1970s in recognition of past discrimination against them. The combination of these factors merged egalitarian and assimilationist issues in new and complicated ways.

In the nineteenth century, the vast majority of the immigrants were European and white. The discrimination and hostility they faced was the result of their foreignness – i.e., that they spoke different languages, practiced different customs, or worshiped different religions. Nonwhite immigrants (i.e. Latino and Asian) in the first immigration period constituted a smaller fraction of total immigration than today, were more severely discriminated against, and were eventually excluded as part of official immigration policy. The fact that a higher proportion of contemporary immigrants come from Asia and Latin America has widened the cultural/linguistic gap and exacerbated assimilationist fears, but the fact that they are also predominantly nonwhite has added an egalitarian dimension to the debate. In addition to thinking of themselves as different by virtue of being in a foreign land, *immigrants are more likely to think of themselves as different in the sense that they are nonwhites dealing with the prejudices of a majority white society.* This new construction of the earlier egalitarian conflict brings Latinos and Asians closer to African-Americans and constitutes the basis of a potential political alliance.

However, the egalitarian and assimilationist themes have also merged in a second way that serves to separate Latinos and Asians from African-Americans. The expansion of civil rights protections throughout the 1970s and 1980s to linguistic and ethnic minorities extended egalitarian logic to the assimilationist debate. It was now possible to speak of protecting *an ethnic and racial group's equal right to its distinctive language and culture.* Since this is not an interest shared with most African-Americans, it pits native-born blacks and whites against immigrant Latinos and Asians.

In short, the key new development in American racial and ethnic politics is the emergence of multiculturalism and its implications for the old civil rights coalition and its agenda. The remainder of this chapter will review the growth and extensiveness of multicultural-ism. Then we will examine the implications that this has had for the political strategies and interests of American minority groups. Finally, we will consider the problems that are caused when legal protections and policies forged in the biracial area are applied to new groups and in multiracial settings.

The Spread of Multiculturalism

The emergence of increasingly multiracial and multiethnic circum-stances in the United States is a function of several factors, but the most important one is immigration. The rate of legal immigration into the United States has increased every decade in the postwar period, rising from 1.7 immigrants per 100,000 residents in the 1960s to 3.1 in the 1980s. During the 1980s, 9 million immigrants entered the United States – 7.3 million legally (the largest number of legal immigrants in any decade in U.S. history, except for 1901–10) and an estimated 2 million illegally. The largest immigrant groups came from Asia (2.47 million), Mexico, and Central America (1.28 million), and Europe (593,000); and, specifically by country, from Mexico (974,000), the Philippines (431,000), China (341,000) and Korea (306,000). The vast majority of recent immigrants entered the United States for economic opportunities, but there were also 916,000 political refugees admitted during the last decade, the greatest numbers coming from Vietnam (303,916), Laos (132,140), Cambodia (109,345), and Cuba (105,699).

At the earliest stages of the post-1965 wave of immigration, the Latino immigrants, who were primarily Mexican, tended to take farm labor jobs in rural areas in southwestern states such as California and Texas. These rural workers were typically young male "sojourners" who left their families behind them, sent money home, and entered and left the United States periodically upon seasonal demand. Increasingly, however, Mexican immigrants in the 1980s began to find service and manufacturing jobs in urban areas. With the stability of nonseasonal work, the modal immigrant pattern shifted from young male sojourner to families with children taking up permanent residence in urban areas.

The pattern of Asian immigration since 1965 has been primarily urban and suburban, with the exception of some Indochinese political refugees residing in rural areas such as the Central Valley of California. The Asian immigrants have focussed on establishing small businesses, often with family employees. Since the start-up costs for businesses are lower in poorer neighborhoods, many of the Asian immigrant businesses are located near or in inner-city black or Latino neighborhoods. The fact that these businesses are family run and located in areas of high unemployment lays the groundwork for many of the inter-ethnic tensions that found such violent expression in the Rodney King riots. The Asian shopkeepers are driven by economic necessity to do business in ghetto areas with relatively cheap family labor, since they are competing in a market sector in which the odds of failure are much higher than the odds of success. At the same time, this strategy limits employment opportunities for the neighboring residents and contributes to the chronic ghetto problem of circulating more money out of the neighborhood than back in.

The pattern of economic forces attracting Asian and Latino immigrants into areas that were previously inhabited by African-Americans is quite common. For instance, the states that attracted the most immigrants in 1990 were, in order, California, New York, Texas, Illinois, Florida, New Jersey, Massachusetts, Arizona, and Virginia – all of which had comparatively large minority populations to begin with. Thus, some states (e.g., New York or California) became increasingly minority in composition, while others (e.g., North Dakota, Iowa, Maine, New Hampshire) remain relatively untouched by the demographic ferment of the last two decades.

In the aggregate, the 1990 census found that the white share of the total American population had decreased over the decade from

83.1 percent to 80.3 percent while the black share of the population increased from 11.7 percent to 12.1 percent , the Latino share from 6.4 percent to 9 percent and the Asian share from 1.5 percent to 2 percent. The geographic concentration of minority groups across the country is by no means uniform. Over half the blacks still live in the south, and the black population share is greater than or equal to 10 percent in only 17 of the 50 states (the same as in 1980). Fifty-five percent of all Asians live in the west, but only one state has greater than a 10 percent Asian population proportion (i.e., Hawaii at 58.3 percent). Seventy-five percent of all Latinos live in the south and west, but only eight states have Latino populations above 10 percent (up from 5 in 1980; see Table 3.1).

If we leave out Texas and Florida, the south is still primarily biracial – i.e., white and black. The mountain states, certain parts of the midwest and northern New England are still predominantly white, with only small concentrations of racial and ethnic minorities. Multiracialism is found mainly in the west (especially in the state of California with its 25 percent Latino, 9 percent Asian, and 9 percent black population, and in Washington), Texas (especially Dallas and Houston), Florida (Miami–Fort Lauderdale), New York, Boston, and Chicago. In other words, it is a growing trend in some, but not all, parts of the United States.

The Asian component of this mix, in particular, is still relatively small in all but a few areas. There is only one majority-Asian metropolitan area (Honolulu), and only one other (S.F.-Oakland-

TABLE 3.1 *Distribution of states by percent minority populations*

	≤10%	11–20%	21–30%	31–40%	41–50%	>50%
African-American						
1980	33	10	6	1	0	0
1990	33	10	6	1	0	0
Hispanic						
1980	45	3	1	1	0	0
1990	42	5	2	1	0	0
Asian-American						
1980	49	0	0	0	0	1
1990	49	0	0	0	0	1

San Jose) in which the Asian population share is over 10 percent (14.8 percent). While Asians own and operate businesses in urban ghetto areas, they tend to reside outside the ghettos in predominantly white cities and counties. Thus the most common pattern for Congressional districts with appreciable Asian population concentrations is Asian-white. Of the 27 Congressional districts with 10 percent or above Asian population shares in 1990, Asians were the largest racial group in only two districts, whites were the largest in 20, and blacks/Latinos were the largest group in none.

TABLE 3.2   *Distribution of Congressional districts by minority*
populations

	Majority	Plurality	Nonplurality > 20%	Nonplurality 10–19%
Black	17	3	65	78
Hispanic	11	6	39	48
Asian	2	0	2	23

In fact, there were only five Congressional seats in 1990 where each of the four major racial/ethnic groups – i.e., blacks, whites, Asians, and Latinos – constituted greater than 10 percent of the district population share. The more frequent patterns were biracial or triracial combinations of Latinos, blacks and whites, and in a majority of instances whites were still the largest voting group in the district. Prior to the 1991 redistrictings but after the 1990 census, there were 17 majority black Congressional districts and 68 others in which blacks constituted at least 20 percent of the population. Of those, blacks were the plurality population group in only three seats and Latinos in six, while whites were the largest bloc in 33. The same point about the continued importance of white voters holds for Congressional districts with sizeable Latino populations. There were 11 majority Latino Congressional districts in 1990, and 45 others with Latino populations of at least 20 percent. Blacks constituted 10 percent or more of the district populations in 21 of these districts, and whites had a 10 percent or greater share in all but three.

Clearly, there are a variety of racial and ethnic mixtures emerging in American political districts. Indeed, some of the uncertainty about what multiculturalism means in terms of politics and public policy stems from the variety of racial and ethnic combinations in different areas of the country. In a few Congressional districts, multiculturalism means the interaction of all four major racial and ethnic groups – i.e., white, black, Latino, and Asian. Moreover, more frequently it means a mixture of two or three racial groups and a variety of different nationalities.

Political Diversity and Multiculturalism

The presence of multiple racial and ethnic groups in itself changes the nature of race relations in the United States, but, in addition, the diversity of their circumstances and political attitudes further complicates the picture. The former is critical in understanding the strategies that are open to a group in the pursuit of political influence and power, and the latter to understanding how a particular racial and ethnic group defines its political interests.

It is instructive to compare African-Americans, Asians, and Latinos in terms of five key attributes – size, dispersion, cohesion, socioeconomic resources, and polarization against the group. The first two, size and dispersion, are critical variables in determining a group's electoral power in a district-based, first-past-the-post system. One obvious meaning of size is the population share of a particular racial and ethnic group. If a group's population share accurately reflects its share of voters, the former can be used as an indicator of a group's potential political leverage. Without knowing more about the particular electoral arrangements that a group has to work within, all that can safely be said is that the larger the population, the more potential voters, and hence the more electoral influence a group can potentially have. In an at-large system (i.e., a system prevalent at the local government level in which all representatives are elected at large), a group must constitute a majority in order to ensure that it wins representation if the voting is highly polarized along group lines. In a single-member district system, a group need only constitute a plurality (i.e., larger than any other group or coalition of groups) in the specific geographic area defined by a district's boundaries. For this reason, the type of electoral system employed in state legislative and local government elections has been a controversial issue in recent years – blacks and

Latinos have historically pushed for single-member district elections to replace at-large systems in order to lower the threshold of population needed to elect a representative of their choice (Karnig and Welch, 1980; Welch, 1990).

All of the above assumes that population shares accurately reflect voting shares, but that assumption breaks down in important ways for Latinos and Asians. In the United States, in order to be eligible to vote, a person must be 18 years of age or over and a citizen. A population that has a younger than average profile and a higher than average noncitizen component will have a smaller share of eligible voters than of population. If, in addition, the group possesses any or all of the characteristics of low voting populations – i.e. high residential mobility, low levels of education, low rates of home ownership – there will be a further drop in the ratio of actual to potential voters (Wolfinger and Rosenstone, 1980).

Consider the following example. In California in 1992, whites constituted 55 percent of the total population, Latinos 27 percent, Asians 10 percent, and blacks 7 percent. Eliminating those under the age of 18, the corresponding figures are 59 percent white, 24 percent Latino, 9 percent Asian and 7 percent black. Removing the noncitizens, the figures become 72 percent white, 12 percent Latino, 5 percent Asian, and 7 percent black. Finally, add in the socioeconomic biases that lead to a lower propensity to register and to vote, and the numbers for actual voters in the 1992 California election are 79 percent white, 10 percent Latino, 4 percent Asian, and 6 percent black. In other words, because there is a substantial gap between the population and voter shares for all minorities, and especially for Asians and Latinos, it can be misleading to judge potential minority electoral influence by sheer population numbers.

As discussed earlier, the white population share in the United States has been declining, but whites are still a majority or plurality in all states. California will probably become a majority minority state sometime during the next two decades. Even there, however, the white share of the electorate remains disproportionately high, and will remain so in the foreseeable future. The African-American population has grown slightly (primarily from net births over deaths rather than immigration), but is likely to lose ground to the faster-growing Latino and Asian populations over the next decade. The gap between eligible and actual black voters is significant, but it is not nearly as much of a handicap for blacks as for Latinos and

Asians. Latinos have become a sizeable minority in several states and cities, and even constitute a population majority in several Texas cities such as Loredo, Brownsville, and San Antonio. Moreover, their electoral influence is severely hampered by noncitizenship and a low median age. Asians are also growing fast, but, as we noted earlier, they are still less than 10 percent of the population on the mainland in all but California's Bay Area, and an even smaller fraction of the age-eligible voters. While Latinos and blacks are numerous enough to constitute the majority of voters in a scattering of Congressional and local districts, Asians are not numerous enough to constitute a voting majority in any Congressional or large local district seat in the United States outside Hawaii.

The second related variable is the dispersion of a minority group, which refers to a group's level of residential clustering. This is an important consideration in district-based representation systems, because a minority group must be clustered together in sufficiently large numbers to constitute a majority, or at least a sizeable plurality of a district, if it is going to control the electoral outcome in a given seat. It is possible for a group to be overly clustered or concentrated if, for instance, it constitutes 75–90 percent of the voters when it only needs 51 percent of the voters to control the district. In reality, over-concentration is a less prevalent problem for American minorities than under-concentration or dispersion.

Most typically, minority under-representation can be traced to the dispersion of minority populations over far-flung neighborhoods throughout a state or city, and the lack of any reasonably compact districting arrangement that would incorporate them into a district they can control on the basis of voter share. In this regard, African-Americans are ironically the political beneficiaries of the extreme residential and social prejudice they have had to endure. Residential segregation has created well-defined black neighborhoods in many cities that are sufficiently large and compact to constitute state and Congressional districts. More problematic are rural areas of the south, the focus of the Supreme Court's recent ruling in *Shaw* v. *Reno* (1993). The North Carolina legislature had drawn a sprawling, irregular district linking together disparate black rural and urban populations in an attempt to create a new majority black Congressional district that would meet the requirements of the Voting Rights Act and the approval of the federal Justice Department. Plaintiffs challenged the new district lines on the grounds that noncompact districting based exclusively on race was unconstitutional. The Court ruled that such a claim could be valid, and sent the case back to the lower courts for further consideration.

The dispersion problem is somewhat greater for Latinos and even greater for certain Asian groups. New Latino growth in the old historical barrio areas has usually been sufficiently compact to be reflected in redistricting, but movement during the 1980s into the suburbs, and continued farm labor migration into the rural areas of Texas and California, have been more problematic in this regard. The dispersion problem is even more substantial for Asians. The Japanese and Filipinos, for instance, tend to spread themselves over racially mixed or Anglo neighborhoods. The Koreans and Chinese, on the other hand, have moved into new enclaves of single nationalities rather than mixed Asian areas. As a combined racial group, Asians are rarely sufficiently large enough to constitute an influential voting bloc, but as specific nationality groups their potential electoral influence is yet smaller. Projecting into the next two decades, the high rate of Asian immigration and the lumpiness of Asian settlement patterns (i.e. that certain areas in the west and east are getting most of the Asian immigrants) might eventually create majority Asian population Congressional districts. Also, since Asian immigrants take half as long as Latinos to naturalize, they may be able to turn growth into political power more quickly (Pachon, 1991).

Size and dispersion control a group's electoral power, but coherence and polarization measure its political identity as a group. Coherence refers to whether a group has common interests/political views and whether it votes as a bloc. In this regard, it is important to distinguish between race and nationality. It is easier for a racial group to be united if it is not divided along national, ethnic, cultural, religious, or linguistic lines. African-Americans as a racial group are little affected by any of these differences. Aside from the relatively small Caribbean communities, the African-American population is largely homogenous with respect to religion (Protestant), language (English), country of birth (United States), and culture. The one difference that recent scholarship has focussed on is socioeconomic; however, divisions between middle- and working-class blacks tend to manifest themselves in primary races between African-American candidates, but in only a few other instances (Jackson, 1991) is there much difference between southern and nonsouthern blacks on measures of political attitudes, partisanship, etc. Most identify with the Democratic Party and are more likely than the rest of the population to favor a strong role for government (Welch and Foster, 1987, 1992; Gurin, Hatchett, and Jackson, 1989).

The tensions caused by nationality differences are sharper in the Latino community. The recent Latino National Election Survey discovered relatively high levels of national group identity as Mexicans, Puerto Ricans, and Cubans, but low levels of "panethnic" identity with such groupings as Hispanic or Latino. Moreover, the same study discovered that Mexicans, Puerto Ricans, and Cubans had little interaction with each other, did not feel that they had much in common culturally, and did not profess strong affection for each other. With the exception of the more conservative Cuban population, however, most Latinos did favor a liberal domestic agenda – increased government spending on health and crime and drug control, education, the environment, child services, and bilingual education, and, with the exception of the Cubans, Latinos identify with the Democratic Party by over a 2 to 1 margin (de la Garza *et al.*, 1992).

In sum, while there are real cultural and social differences between the different Latino groups, they are counterbalanced to some degree by prevailing similarities in party affiliation and issue preferences. Potential tensions and conflicts between the various Latino groups are also mitigated partly by the fact that the different nationality groups are geographically separated. The majority of Mexicans reside in the southwest so that even though they feel no special affinity for Puerto Ricans (who live primarily in the east) or Cubans (who live in Florida), this has little political consequence in the areas where Mexicans predominantly live.

While there has been no systematic national survey of Asian political attitudes to date, there have been a growing number of region-specific studies (e.g. Kitano, 1981). A survey of California Asians in the mid-1980s found some preliminary evidence of partisan and attitudinal variation across nationality groups. Japanese-Americans tended to be more closely affiliated with the Democratic Party, while the Chinese and Koreans were more evenly split between Democrats and Republicans (Cain and Kiewiet, 1984). More recently, a study of Asians in the San

Francisco–Bay area concluded that voting for Asian candidates divided along nationality lines. A popular Chinese-American candidate for Secretary of State was significantly less likely to get support from Japanese-American voters than their party registration alone would predict (Tam, 1992). This finding seems quite plausible given the legacy of past tensions between Asian nations, and the linguistic, cultural, religious, and socioeconomic differences between Filipinos, Japanese, Chinese, Indochinese and Koreans. Indeed, there is serious question as to whether the racial designation Asian, as opposed to the nationality classifications, will ever have political meaning in American politics.

Polarization, the fourth category, describes the degree to which other electoral groups support or oppose a particular racial or ethnic minority. The definition of a minority group's identity partly depends upon the commonality of its interests and attitudes, but also upon what other groups think about or do to them. The political identity of African-Americans, for example, was forged by racial prejudice and hatred directed against them by a significant number of whites. Surveys indicate that blacks are still more likely than other minorities to perceive discrimination against them, and to believe that it contributes to their economic disadvantage (Uhlaner, 1991). White voters are reluctant to tell survey researchers that they refuse to vote for black candidates, but experts in Voting Rights Act cases from around the country have measured systematic patterns of black–white polarization when black candidates run against white candidates (Grofman, Handley, and Niemi, 1992). On the other hand, it is clear that not all white voters are racially polarized and that white voting patterns have become heterogeneous and complex (Lupia and McCue, 1990).

Latinos and Asians report lower levels of perceived discrimination than do blacks and are less likely to say that it affects their economic circumstances (Uhlaner, 1991). However, the recent Latino National Political Survey shows that close to a third of Mexicans and Puerto Ricans perceived a lot of, and close to half perceived some, discrimination against them (de la Garza *et al.*, 1992). Moreover, Voting Rights cases in California and Texas have revealed a number of instances of racially polarized voting by whites against Mexican-Americans, but in areas of the country where there has been much new growth but no historical Latino presence, it is too soon to make any reliable determination about this. The evidence for Asians runs in the opposite direction. To date, Asian-American candidates have been extremely successful in winning Anglo votes at all levels. For instance, all three Asian Congressmen (two Japanese-Americans and one Korean-American) from California represent majority white districts. If polarization against a group reinforces its group identity, then it would appear at present that this type of reinforcement is much lower for Asians than for blacks and Latinos.

Finally, there is the matter of the relative socioeconomic status of the various minority groups in the United States. The African-American profile, despite important changes over the last 25 years, is still substantially disadvantaged. Some of these disadvantages lead to lower rates of participation, as discussed earlier. Over half of African-Americans, as compared to 31 percent of whites, are renters, and approximately a third as compared to a fifth of the white population have less than a full high school education. Lower levels of education and high mobility lead to, on average, lower rates of registration and voting, but the Jesse Jackson campaign, and the elections of Mayor Washington in Chicago and Mayor Bradley in Los Angeles among others, demonstrated that black participation can be high when the community is mobilized and motivated.

Aside from voting, another important means of influencing American elections is giving money. For obvious reasons, however, the African-American community has not been a major source of campaign funds. Thirty percent of African-Americans (as opposed to 11 percent of whites) live below the poverty line, and only 14 percent (as opposed to 32 percent of whites) make 50,000 dollars or more, the category from which most donations come. Lacking the necessary resources, African-Americans have had to follow primarily a mass voting rather than a campaign finance strategy. The political situation for Latinos is very similar to that for African-Americans in this sense. Sixty-one percent are renters and 49 percent have less than a high school diploma, compounding the problems of low participation caused by high rates of non-citizenship and low median age. Even so, like the African-Americans, mass voting strength is still their primary tool of political influence, because their low income prevents Latinos from being major players in the campaign finance world. Only 15 percent make above 50,000 dollars, a quarter live below the poverty level, and the median income for all Latino groups (except the Cubans) is over 10,000 dollars less than the white median.

The Asians are the most anomalous minority in this regard. Possessing the highest levels of education (only 18 percent have less than a high school degree and 43 percent have some level of college education) and the highest rates of home ownership (51 percent), one might expect relatively high levels of voter participation among their age-eligible citizens. However, this is not the case, and it represents something of a participation puzzle (Uhlaner, Kiewiet, and Cain, 1989). Asians, on the other hand, have become a major fundraising force in California, as one might expect from their relatively high median income (41 percent of Asians make over 50,000 dollars per year, with a median income of $42,245). It is possible that we may see Asians following the model of Jews in America, who have leveraged their resources into political influence that significantly exceeds their mere voting numbers.

The Political Consequences of Multiracialism

So far, we have established two points: first, that certain areas of the United States have become much more multiracial and multi-ethnic as a result of recent legal and illegal immigration patterns, and second, that America's new minorities are in certain critical ways different, and in others similar, in their objective circumstances. But what are the political consequences of the transition from biracialism to multiculturalism?

Most generally, one problem is that strategies that worked for African-Americans politically, and public policies that were designed for them during the biracial period of American race relations may not work as well for Asians, Latinos, or even for African-Americans in the contemporary multiracial and multi-ethnic environment. The key elements of the earlier biracial strategy were as follows: (1) mobilize potential black voters to maximize electoral influence; (2) lobby for more black majority districts in which blacks would have the controlling votes; (3) elect African-American candidates in these seats; (4) secure favorable policies by means of coalitions with liberal whites and other progressive groups in the Democratic Party, and (5) establish legal protections from Congress and the courts. All of these elements have in some way been called into question by developments in the 1990s.

The first element of this outlined strategy, voter mobilization, was the *raison d'etre* for the passage of the Voting Rights Act in 1965 (Thernstrom, 1987; Kousser, 1992). Southern blacks especially had extremely low registration and voting rates (i.e. between one-quarter and one-third of age-eligible blacks voted) prior to 1965. Literacy tests, poll taxes, and outright intimidation served to keep African-Americans from registering and participating fully in elections (Kousser, 1984). The Voting Rights Act prohibited these discriminatory procedures initially in the south and then subsequently in the rest of the country, resulting in a dramatic surge in black registration and voting in the late 1960s.

As a premise of empowerment, electoral mobilization is still important to the black community, although the experience of the last decade has tempered black expectations about how much influence they can have, and whether black candidates once elected are able or willing to do much to address the critical problems in the black ghettos of America. However, as a political tactic, it clearly is even more problematic for Asians and Latinos. Full electoral mobilization is impossible when a minority group has a large number of noncitizens and age-ineligible voters. At the very least, voter mobilization has to be extended back one step to the naturalization process – i.e., making sure that people who are eligible for citizenship take the necessary steps to become citizens. This may, for instance, require new tactics such as inventing techniques to facilitate the *en masse* naturalization of eligible minorities or putting more pressure on the Immigration and Naturalization Service (INS) to facilitate their handling of naturalization cases (Pachon, 1991). The important point, however, is that mobilization for Latinos and Asians is a more complex problem than simply getting people registered to vote.

The second element of the black political model was the creation of as many majority black districts as possible. This tactic evolved in the 1970s as African-Americans came to realize that unfair electoral arrangements, plus a determined white majority opposition, could mitigate the effects of black enfranchisement. The solution was to push for district-based systems and majority black districts wherever blacks were in a minority and a hostile white community was in the majority. In recent years, majority black districts became the desired goal of civil rights plaintiffs throughout the country, even when the evidence of white polarization against black candidates was ambiguous. Critics within the black community have pointed out that a districting strategy that assumes racial polarization when it does not exist may actually diminish black electoral influence, because it does not incorporate potentially sympathetic white voters in black majority districts (Swain, 1993).

Another complication is that as the black population has stabilized and the population of competing minorities has grown, the prospects of black political gains through majority black districting seem increasingly unlikely. Moreover, in some cities, because the Latino and Asian populations have moved into areas that were either formerly black or adjacent to black neighborhoods, the logic of majority minority districts may actually work against the interests of black representation. Specifically, the demand for new majority Latino or Asian districts may in the next decade require the disestablishment of some existing majority black districts. This issue was raised in the 1991 Los Angeles city and Los Angeles county redistrictings and in the 1993 Oakland City Council redistricting. In the LA cases, black incumbents represented areas with large and growing Latino neighborhoods. Latino activists wanted to remove the Latino areas and create a new majority Latino population district, but such a change would have forced either a reduction in African-American representation or the movement of African-American seats into white neighborhoods, altering the character and incentives of their representation in important ways.

The demands of Latino and Asian groups for more representation have placed African-Americans in an awkward political dilemma. On the one hand, many are understandably reluctant to employ the same logic and language used by white conservatives in the 1960s and 1970s when they opposed the electoral changes that brought more blacks to office. On the other hand, giving up black representation is difficult, particularly when many African-Americans feel that they have not yet realized most of the promises that electoral empowerment was supposed to bring. Latino and Asian activists are also discomforted by the tensions that these districting conflicts bring, particularly because they undermine inter-ethnic coalitions that are critical if minorities are going to be part of the governing coalition in federal, state, and local legislative bodies.

All of this is linked to the third component of black political strategy in the biracial period – the election of black candidates. Although the Voting Rights Act explicitly denies that there is a right to proportional representation and states that the purpose of the law is only to allow protected minority communities to elect a representative of their own choice, the informal goal of many minority voting rights activists during the past two decades has been to maximize the number of minority elected officials. Implicitly, the representation ideal has been both descriptive and substantive: descriptive in the sense that many believed that blacks could best represent blacks, Latinos could best represent Latinos, etc., and substantive in the sense that it assumed that minorities would be better represented in constituency service and policy if they had majority electoral power.

While there is some debate as to whether descriptive representation leads to better substantive representation (Swain, 1993; Thernstrom, 1987), the real difficulty in a multiracial environment is sorting out the validity and feasibility of various claims to descriptive representation. All democracies struggle with this issue to some degree. In European proportional representation systems, it centers on the exact formula used to calculate seat distribution and the threshold level needed to elect a representative to parliament. In Anglo-American systems that use single-member, first-past-the-post rules, descriptive representation can be facilitated or hindered by the districting process. But whereas the apportionment of seats to groups in P.R. systems occurs automatically by formula, the allocation in S.M.S.P. systems occurs by negotiation, without any fixed rules and at regular ten-year intervals. This turns out to be a recipe for bitter controversy.

Securing favorable policies by means of coalitions with liberal whites and members of the Democratic Party coalition was the fourth element in the post-1965 black electoral strategy. Having descriptive representation is of little value if a group's elected representatives are not part of the governing coalition in a given legislative body. A landmark study of minority representation in the Bay area showed that coalitions with white liberals were critical to the empowerment of blacks and Latinos in those cities (Browning, Marshall, and Tabb, 1986). Another study of the coalition that elected black Mayor Tom Bradley in Los Angeles and kept him in office for over two decades, found that Bradley's coalition depended heavily in the early years on support from the West Side Jewish community and East Side Latinos (Sonenshein, 1993).

But what will the component parts of urban coalitions be in the 1990s? Judging by commonalities in important political attitudes (e.g., faith in government's role in solving problems) and preponderant partisan dispositions (i.e. Democratic), blacks and Latinos would seem to have enough in common to be relatively stable coalition partners. However, as economic conditions in the United States worsened in the early 1990s, the divisive issues of immigration and bilingualism threatened to form a political wedge between them. Increasingly, black leaders worry that unrestricted immigration takes jobs away from native-born blacks and drains resources from states and counties that could otherwise be used to improve conditions in black neighborhoods. Similarly, as funding for schools competes with other services for scarce public revenues, blacks have questioned the wisdom of spending money on bilingual programs.

Coalitions with Asians have even greater uncertainties. To begin with, Asians, with the notable exception of the Japanese-Americans, are fairly evenly divided between the two parties. In addition, what little we know about their ideology and issue preferences suggests that Asians are on average more conservative than most Latinos and blacks. Add to all of this the recent tensions between Asian shopkeepers and their black patrons in New York and Los Angeles, and it would seem that a realistic assessment would hold out hope for coalitions between African-Americans and the more liberal elements of the Asian community, but certainly not with all or most Asians *per se*.

Perhaps the greatest uncertainty is in the behavior and attitudes of the liberal whites who served as critical coalition partners for blacks in the biracial era. To begin with, the percentage of whites who identify themselves as liberal has dropped to under a third (see Table 3.3) – in other words, there are fewer liberal whites to form coalitions with. Moreover, the agenda of white liberals in the 1990s is not as centrally focussed on racial equality as it was in the 1960s. Liberal whites are at least as much concerned with gender equality, the environment, gay rights, and abortion. By contrast, despite their liberalism on redistributive and economic issues, Latinos and blacks are not as liberal on social issues such as gay rights or

TABLE 3.3 *Party identification and ideology*

	White (1486)	Black (182)	Hispanic (125)	Asian-American (21)
Democrat (strong/weak/lean)	44	80	58	24
Pure Independent	12	12	13	8
Republican (strong/weak/lean)	44	8	29	68
Liberal (extreme/strong/weak)	27	37	22	33
Pure Moderate	30	38	36	38
Conservative (extreme/strong/weak)	43	25	42	29

abortion, and environmental issues tend to pit the pro-growth, job-creation interests of disadvantaged minorities against the pro-environmental concerns of middle- and upper-middle-class whites. The recent election of Richard Riordan, a Republican, to replace Tom Bradley, a black Democrat, may portend the difficulty in the 1990s of recreating earlier progressive coalitions. Mike Woo, his opponent, was unable to win the same high levels of support in the Latino and Jewish areas of the city that Bradley had depended on, while Riordan was able to put together a new conservative coalition based on the themes of more police and more autonomy for white neighborhoods over their schools.

Finally, in addition to the uncertainties multiculturalism raises about electoral strategies and future governing coalitions, it has also led to a number of public policy issues. The policy goal of African-Americans in the biracial era was to seek legal protections and enhanced opportunities from the court and various levels of American government. Since African-Americans were the largest minority, they were the primary beneficiaries of the civil rights legislation in the 1960s and of affirmative action programs in the 1970s and 1980s. That has now changed as these programs and protections have been extended to other types of groups – not only to Latinos and Asians, but also women, gays, the disabled, etc.

There are two consequences of this. First, the material benefits of affirmative action must now be shared. Public-sector departments in multiracial urban areas, for instance, not only have affirmative action guidelines with respect to African-Americans, but also for Latinos, Asians, and women. Inevitably, there are conflicts between these groups over the perceived equity of these policies. When the white police chief of Los Angeles resigned in the wake of the Rodney King riots, for instance, there was considerable tension between black and Latino activists over the appointment of his successor. Recent research into nineteenth-century urban politics suggests that such conflicts were prevalent then as well, and that Italian and eastern European immigrants found it difficult to dislodge the Irish from their positions in local government and politics (Erie, 1988).

However, an important difference between the conflicts then and now is in the role that the courts play in interpreting and enforcing these policies. As a matter of 14th Amendment doctrine, the use of racial categories is considered presumptively "suspect," and is permitted only when it serves a compelling state interest and is narrowly tailored to that purpose. In a series of affirmative action cases, the Supreme Court has attempted to find ways to allow racial preferment to be factored into public decisionmaking, but without condoning strict quotas. The deliberate murkiness of the doctrine leaves the protected classes without well-defined rights, and at the same time has fostered a belief among the majority white population that, regardless of court doctrine, there is racial preference in the law.

As discussed earlier, the extension of equal protection doctrine to linguistic and other minorities has multiplied the claims for protection, creating the difficult problem of sorting out the competing claims of different groups when there are no fixed guidelines. It has also weakened political support for affirmative action in certain quarters, because the assumption of an analogy between the condition of blacks that led to the policies in the first place and the condition of other minorities does not always seem valid. Should Asians be eligible to claim voting rights protection when Asian candidates have done so well in the past in winning white voter support? Should Latino immigrants be given preference in municipal hiring over native-born whites and blacks? These are the kinds of questions that will inevitably be asked in the 1990s as the country struggles to adapt biracial policies to a multiracial and multiethnic world.

4

American Political Parties: Growth and Change

PAUL S. HERRNSON

The 1992 elections presented both challenges and opportunities for American political parties. Record numbers of candidates ran for Congress and the race for the White House evolved into a spirited three-way contest. The parties were poised to play an important role in these elections as a result of some major changes they initiated in the previous two decades. During this period, the parties revitalized their organizations and increased their roles in election campaigns. Most of these changes were designed to increase opportunities for citizen participation in party activities or enhance the roles the parties play in the political system. Some political observers hoped that these developments would not only strengthen the parties, but result in the emergence of party-focussed campaigns similar to those waged in western European and other industrialized democracies.

Although American political parties are now stronger than they were in the early 1970s, they have not come to resemble their counterparts in the other industrialized democracies. Instead, they have followed a path of development that reflects the unique political, cultural, and historical circumstances in which they operate. This chapter analyzes recent changes in American political parties in an historical context. First, the parties' early development and decline are discussed. Then, the parties' organizational renewal and reform are examined. A discussion of recent party organizational developments and campaign activities follows. Finally, I speculate on the parties' future, focussing on the prospects for the development of party-focussed election campaigns similar to those associated with parliamentary democracies.

67

Emergence and Decline

For most of their history, American political parties were highly decentralized and without strong national organizations. They also lacked the class-based electoral support enjoyed by parties in most other democracies and were generally unable to muster the legislative votes needed to produce programmatic party government. There have been short periods of programmatic party activity in American history, such as the New Deal era. Most of these have followed electoral realignments and lasted only a few years.

Party organizations were, and continue to be, conceptualized as pyramid-like, with the national conventions at the apex, the national committees directly below them, the Congressional and senatorial campaign committees branching off the national committees, and state and local party organizations placed below the national party apparatus. Yet power is not, and has never been, distributed hierarchically. Power has traditionally been concentrated at the local level, usually in county-wide political machines. It flowed up from county organizations to state party committees and conventions, and then to the national convention. The national, Congressional, and senatorial campaign committees had little, if any, power over state and local party leaders or party members in office (Cotter and Hennessy, 1964).

The power of local party leaders came from their ability to handpick candidates, mobilize voters, and broker state and national party conventions. The patronage system provided local party leaders with the means to reward the largely uneducated immigrants who provided the votes and manpower needed to keep the parties' candidates in office. The ability to deliver votes and select delegates to party conventions extended the clout of local party leaders to the state and national levels. Politics during the parties' "golden age" (circa the turn of the twentieth century) were characterized by political bosses, graft, secret negotiations, and widespread voter fraud. Besides campaigns to capture the White House, party politics had little national focus during this period.

Although the Democratic and Republican national committees were formed in the middle of the nineteenth century, they had little continuity in their operations for much of their existence. Their organizational strength and activities waxed and waned with the demands of the presidential election. It was not until 1918 that the Republican National Committee (R.N.C.) assembled a full-time, year-round professional staff. The Democratic National Committee (D.N.C.) followed suit in 1928 (Cotter and Bibby, 1980). The parties' Congressional campaign committees were formed after the Civil War, and the two senatorial campaign committees were created in 1916, after the 17th Amendment to the Constitution transformed the upper chamber into a popularly elected body. None of these organizations possessed much clout with state and local party leaders or with the candidates they helped to elect (Committee on Political Parties, 1950).

The transition from a party-dominated system of campaign politics to a candidate-centered system during the early twentieth century further weakened the parties, taking its greatest toll on local party organizations, which had previously conducted most of the parties' campaign activities. The direct primary, new civil service regulations, and other reforms deprived party bosses of their abilities to handpick nominees and reward party workers with government jobs and contracts (see, for example, Key, 1958). Increased education and social mobility, declining immigration, and a growing national identity contributed to the erosion of the close-knit, ethnic neighborhoods that formed the core of the old-fashioned machine's constituency (McWilliams, 1981). The introduction of survey research, computerized voter files, and electronic mass media advertising provided candidates with the tools to conduct election campaigns independently of their party (Agranoff, 1972). Collectively, these changes deprived many local party committees of their bases of support, drove up the costs of campaigning, and transformed American electoral politics from a labor-intensive party-focussed system into a candidate-centered money-driven enterprise (Sorauf 1980).

Political Action Committees (P.A.C.s), or their predecessors, which had played a very minor role in elections prior to the 1970s, had become a major source of the campaign money needed to fuel elections in the 1980s. As a collectivity, P.A.C.s provided candidates with a far greater share of the campaign funds than did parties. In 1982, for example, P.A.C. contributions accounted for 30 percent of the money given to general election candidates for the House and 17 percent of the money given to candidates for the

Senate, making P.A.C.s the second largest source (after private citizens) of campaign contributions. Party contributions accounted for a mere fraction of candidates' war chests. In addition, P.A.C.s challenged parties in what are generally regarded to be traditional party functions, such as recruiting candidates, helping candidates devise campaign strategies, and mobilizing voters (Sorauf, 1980; Sabato 1981; Crotty, 1984).

Other signs of party decline were the fall-off in the number of voters who were willing to acknowledge they had a party identification or vote in support of their party's entire ticket. Partisan dealignment, split-ticket voting, and declining levels of political participation were by-products of the Vietnam War, Watergate, the civil rights movement, and the emergence of social–cultural issues that cut across traditional party lines (Nie, Verba, and Petrocik, 1979; Wattenberg, 1990). Generational change also led to the replacement of the strong party supporters who lived through the Great Depression and New Deal by partisan independents for whom these formative events were little more than ancient history (Burnham, 1970; Ladd and Hadley, 1975; Beck, 1984).

The decline in the parties' organizational strength and the disaggregation of their electoral bases contributed to the rise in individualism among candidates for office. Without a stable foundation of voter support in their communities or a local party apparatus to wage their reelection campaigns, members of Congress began to rely more on Congressional resources to insure their reelections (Mayhew, 1974). Others sought to create their own, personal organizations and followings (Agranoff, 1972).

Divided government also helped cause the parties' decline. The routine election of Republican presidents and Democratic-controlled Congresses gave neither party a clear mandate to accomplish its policy goals. For much of the period extending from the 1950s through to the 1980s, neither party could claim full credit for the nation's achievements – nor had to accept full responsibility for its failures. The politics of blame avoidance and the manipulation of political symbols were often substituted for more constructive approaches to problem-solving. Democrats and Republicans spent as much, if not more, time bashing each other as they did developing constructive policy alternatives. Campaigns became more negative as they become less policy-focussed.

Party Reform and Renewal

The Democratic Party's reform movement had its roots in a progressive struggle that sought to weaken local party leaders and make party activities more participatory. The reform movement made considerable progress following the tumultuous 1968 Democratic national convention. Protests on the floor of the convention and in the streets of Chicago sought to portray the nominating process as controlled by political bosses who were unrepresentative of the American people. The McGovern–Fraser Commission, and later reform commissions, opened up the process to rank-and-file party members, increased the size and demographic representativeness of the Democratic National Convention and National Committee, and adopted a written charter that included rules and procedures for governing major party activities. The reformers also instituted mid-term issue conferences, but these were discontinued by Paul Kirk after his selection as D.N.C. Chair in 1984. The reforms also led, unexpectedly, to the proliferation of presidential primaries and the lengthening of the party's candidate-selection process. The reforms had an indirect influence on the Republicans' candidate-selection process, as some state and local Republican committees voluntarily adopted similar reforms and others had reform measures forced on them by Democratic governors and Democratic-controlled legislatures.

In taking the power to select delegates to the parties' national nominating conventions away from party leaders and giving it to individuals who cast ballots in nominating primaries and caucuses, the reforms made it more difficult for long-time party "regulars" to attend state or national party conventions or play a significant role in other party activities. Party leaders found it difficult, and occasionally impossible, to reward the activists they had traditionally relied on to carry out critical election or organizational activities with a delegate slot, an appointment to some ceremonial post, or some other form of recognition (see, for example, Ranney, 1975; Crotty, 1983; Polsby, 1983).

The reforms also increased the abilities of issue and candidate activists, who had little history of party service (sometimes labelled "purists" or "amateurs"), to play bigger roles in party politics (Wilson, 1962; Polsby, 1983). They opened up party activities to newly organized groups, some of which gained control over local party committees and had a major impact on state party politics. Studies have shown that the new Democratic activists tend to be more liberal and the Republican activists more conservative than were traditional party "regulars" or party identifiers (Kirkpatrick, 1976; Miller and Jennings, 1986).

More extreme members of both parties have had some success in gaining control of their parties' conventions, and in nominating candidates for the presidency who represent their views. In 1972 the Democrats nominated George McGovern, and in 1980 and 1984 the Republicans nominated Ronald Reagan. Although both parties' nominees in the 1988 and 1992 elections were fairly moderate, liberal Democrats and conservative Republicans continued to influence those elections. Jesse Jackson won major concessions from Michael Dukakis in 1988 and Patrick Buchanan had a major impact on the Bush campaign in 1992. The activism of more extreme members of each party has at times made coalition building more difficult and harmed the campaigns of the parties' presidential nominees.

Nevertheless, the opening of the nominations process has enabled more people to participate in the political process. It has given women, blacks, and other minority groups that had been largely excluded from party politics in the past the opportunity to make their views heard. Moreover, the mobilization of the new activists caused many traditional party "regulars" to counter-mobilize, resulting in a reinvigoration of some party committees (Kessel, 1992; Edsall, 1993).

The impact that the reforms have had on the quality of the presidential candidates is a heavily debated issue. Some argue that the long-drawn-out nominations process, with its intense media scrutiny and requirement that candidates spend months politicking for votes in the far corners of the nation, has discouraged some of the nation's leading political figures from declaring their candidacies. Critics also claim that the process is more likely to result in the parties, and especially the Democrats, nominating outsider candidates who are ideologically extreme (Polsby and Wildavsky, 1984).

These critics believe that a process that maintains a larger measure of "peer review," such as the pre-reform system or the system the British use to select their prime ministers, would result in the selection of better, more moderate, candidates (Polsby, 1983). However, the nominations of George Bush, Michael Dukakis, and Bill Clinton indicate that qualified moderate, career politicians can win their party's nomination under the new system. The success of the "grassroots" campaign of independent candidate Ross Perot also suggests that a large group of voters would be hostile to any major party nominee who was selected under a nomination system that did not give rank-and-file citizens the opportunity to participate.

The reforms' effects on the distribution of power within the Democratic Party are more generally agreed upon. They have given the D.N.C. the power to require state party committees to conduct party activities in compliance with national party rules. This power has been upheld by a number of court decisions, including the US Supreme Court's decisions in *Cousins* v. *Wigoda* and *Democratic Party of the U.S.* v. *LaFollette*. The D.N.C., however, has retreated from strict enforcement of some party rules. For example, it decided to allow Wisconsin to return to the use of its open primary to select delegates to the national convention after forcing it to use a closed primary during the 1984 election (Epstein, 1986). A state that fails to comply with D.N.C. regulations can be denied seating and the right to partici-pate in the party's national convention. This power has helped to change the flow of power within the party apparatus. Power within the Democratic Party organization now flows in two directions: up from local and state party committees, and down from the national committee and the national convention. As a result, relations between Democratic national and state party organizations now bear a closer resemblance to the relations that exist between the federal and state governments. On policies concerned with political representation and participation, the decisions made by national institutions are given greater weight than the preferences of state and local majorities.

Party renewal changed the flow of power within the organiza-tional structures of both parties. Party renewal has resulted in the modernization of party committees that has enabled them to increase their roles in elections. It is a top-down phenomenon that has largely been driven by the parties' national, Congressional, and senatorial campaign committees. The most visible effects of party renewal have also occurred at the national level.

The renewal of the Republican Party followed the Watergate scandal and the trouncing the Republicans received in the 1974 and

1976 elections. The G.O.P. lost 49 seats in the House in 1974, lost the presidency two years later, and controlled only 12 governorships and four state legislatures by 1977. It also saw its support among voters drop precipitously.

The renewal of the Democratic Party followed President Jimmy Carter's landslide defeat and the Democrats' severe Congressional losses in 1980. The party lost 34 House seats (half of its margin) and control of the Senate. Unlike the party reform movement, party renewal was largely founded on a consensus developed in each party that the best way to revive their party's competitiveness was through organizational development.

The driving force behind party renewal was the changing needs of candidates. The new-style campaigning that became prevalent during the 1960s places a premium on campaign activities requiring technical expertise and in-depth research. Some candidates were able to run a viable campaign using their own funds or talent. Others turned to political consultants, P.A.C.s, and other interest groups for help. However, many candidates, especially nonincumbents, found it difficult to assemble the money and expertise needed to compete in a modern election. The increased needs of candidates for greater access to technical expertise, political information, and money created an opportunity for party organizations to become the repositories of these electoral resources (Schlesinger, 1985).

The changes that leaders of the Democratic and Republican parties instituted at their respective committees were heavily influenced by the basic candidate-centered nature of America's elections. Conscious of the fact that candidates, rather than party organizations, are responsible for waging modern election campaigns, party chairs and their staffs sought to create organizations that could assist their candidates' campaign organizations rather than replace them. Party leaders set out to develop programs to supplement their candidates' campaigns, not impose on them a party-focussed campaign.

The Federal Election Campaign Act of 1974 and its amendments (F.E.C.A.) also helped shape the parties' organizational renewal (Alexander, 1984; Sorauf, 1988). The F.E.C.A.'s contribution and expenditure limits, disclosure provisions, and other regulatory requirements make it virtually impossible for party organizations to dominate federal elections. Provisions of the law that place ceilings on the amounts parties can raise from individuals and ban contributions from corporate, union, or trade association treasuries limit the parties' ability to raise funds that can be used to help federal candidates wage election campaigns.

Provisions of the F.E.C.A. that prohibit presidential candidates who accept public funding from taking contributions from other sources, and place a ceiling on party expenditures made directly on the candidates' behalf, restrict party activity in their campaigns. In 1992, for example, each party could spend a maximimum of $10.3 million directly on behalf of their candidates as compared to the $55.2 million that was given directly to the candidates themselves.

The F.E.C.A.'s provisions for party activity in Congressional elections are less restrictive, but also limit the roles that the parties play in those contests. National, Congressional, and state party organizations are each allowed to contribute $5,000 to House candidates. The parties' national and senatorial campaign committees are allowed to give a combined total of $17,500 to Senate candidates; state party organizations can give $5,000. National party organizations and state party committees are also allowed to make coordinated expenditures on behalf of their candidates. These expenditures are made in cooperation with candidate campaign committees, giving both the party and the candidate a measure of control over them. Originally set at $10,000 per committee, the ceilings for coordinated expenditures on behalf of House candidates are adjusted for inflation and reached $27,620 per committee in 1992. Coordinated expenditure limits for states with only one House member are $55,240 per committee. The ceilings for coordinated expenditures in Senate elections vary by the size of a state's population and are also indexed to inflation. They ranged from $55,240 per committee in the smallest states to $1,227,322 in California. By limiting party activities in federal elections, the F.E.C.A. helped to insure that party renewal would reinforce the candidate-centeredness of American elections rather than encourage the development of party-focussed elections, like those held in other industrialized democracies.

Party Organizations and Campaign Activities

Party renewal has led to the institutionalization of national and many state party organizations, the development of programs to help develop state and local party committees, and the expansion of party activity in elections. As a result of their institutionalization, the parties have become fiscally solvent, organizationally stable, larger and more diversified in their staffs, and have adopted professional bureaucratic decisionmaking procedures (Herrnson, 1988).

Party fundraising has improved greatly since party renewal began. The parties have raised more money, from more sources, using more varied approaches than ever during this period. Figure 4.1 displays the tremendous growth in party revenues over the last nine election cycles. The Republicans, who began rebuilding their party first, have raised more money than the Democrats, but the gap started to narrow after the Democrats began to revitalize their party organizations after the 1980 election. Party fundraising clearly waxes and wanes in response to the presence (or absence) of a presidential election. It also responds to the popularity of the presidential candidates and the possibility that a party will win or lose control of the House or Senate.

Whether the Republicans will continue to raise more money than the Democrats is a difficult question to answer, but it seems likely they will. The greater wealth and homogeneity of Republican Party identifiers make it easier for them to give political contributions. The Republicans' ideology and long-term minority status also

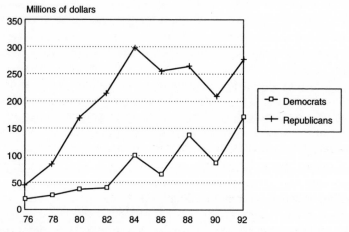

FIGURE 4.1   *Party receipts, 1976–92*

enable them to make negative, anti-government fundraising appeals, which are generally more successful than appeals to maintain the status quo (Godwin, 1988). Nonetheless, a strong leader and a coherent message are necessary ingredients to successful fundraising for both parties.

Most national party money is collected in contributions of under $100 through direct-mail solicitations. Larger contributions are raised at dinners, parties, and other traditional fundraising events, which experienced a revival in the late 1980s. Sometimes wealthy individuals, corporations, unions, or trade associations will utilize a loophole in the F.E.C.A. to contribute to a party organization's building fund or some other nonfederal, "soft money" account. "Soft money," which is raised outside of the federal campaign finance system, can be contributed in amounts in excess of the F.E.C.A.'s limits. However, it cannot be spent directly in conjunction with the campaigns of individual candidates for federal office. Parties use soft money to purchase equipment, strengthen local party organizations, broadcast party-focussed advertisements on television and radio, and finance voter registration and get-out-the-vote drives (Drew, 1983; Sorauf, 1988).

P.A.C.s account for a final source of party revenues. Many P.A.C.s contribute up to $5,000 per year to join a party "council" that receives briefings from administration officials, members of Congress, or other prominent party officials. The existence of these clubs is indicative of the symbiotic nature of the relationships that have developed between parties and many P.A.C.s (Sabato, 1984).

Their fundraising success has allowed the parties to invest in the development of their organizational infrastructures. They have purchased headquarters buildings, computers, and radio and television studios. They have also increased the sizes and professionalism of their staffs. In 1992, the D.N.C., the D.C.C.C., and the D.S.C.C. employed 270, 64, and 35 full-time staff, while their Republican counterparts had 300, 89, and 130 full-time employees (Herrnson, 1994). Committee staffs are divided along functional lines; different divisions are responsible for administration, fundraising, research, communications, and campaign activities. The staffs help party leaders formulate campaign strategies, target party contributions and services, and play a critical role in delivering these services to candidates (Herrnson, 1988, 1994).

The institutionalization of the national parties has enabled them to help renew state and local party organizations. The parties' national committees have hired regional political directors to assist state party leaders with fundraising, organizational development, and the formulation of realistic election goals and targeting strategies. They have made computer services available to state parties for accounting, fundraising, and analyzing survey data (Bibby, 1981; Conway, 1983; Conlon, Martino, and Dilger, 1984).

Computerized information networks make issue and opposition research, newspaper clippings, and other sorts of electoral information available to state party leaders and candidates. "Agency agreements," which enable the Washington-based party committees to make a state parties' share of campaign contributions and coordinated expenditures in Congressional elections, allow the state parties to spend their money on party-building functions and party-focussed campaign activities. As is the case with fundraising, the Republicans have enjoyed a lead in party building, but the Democrats have made significant progress in catching them (Herrnson, 1988).

National committee party-building programs have succeeded in strengthening, modernizing, and professionalizing many state and local party organizations. They have also altered the balance of power within the parties' organizational hierarchies. The national parties' ability to distribute (or withhold) party-building or campaign assistance gives them influence over the operations of state and local party committees. The D.N.C.'s influence is further enhanced by its rule-making and enforcement authority. Party renewal has made an important contribution to the development of a two-way flow of power within contemporary party organizations (Wekkin, 1985; Epstein, 1986).

Party reform and renewal have changed the roles that parties play in some elections. Parties are now more active in candidate recruitment, campaign finance, and the provision of election services than they have been at any time since their heyday at the turn of the century. Party involvement in presidential nominations is limited by party rules and customs, which are the legacy of the party reform, and the fact that there is no dearth of aspirants to the White House. Party committees write the rules under which presidential nominations are contested, but the selection of the nominees is largely in the hands of the individuals who participate in primaries, caucuses, and conventions.

The nomination process also reduces the roles that parties play in presidential general elections because presidential candidates enter these contests with the campaign organizations they assembled to compete in primaries and caucuses. These organizations and the subsidies they receive from the federal government provide successful nominees with most of the resources they need to campaign in the general election, leaving the parties to play a supplemental rather than central role in their elections.

However, the roles that parties play in presidential elections are far from unimportant. The national committees furnish presidential campaigns with legal advice, help with strategy, and give public relations assistance. Party opposition research and archives serve as important sources of political information. Moreover, the money the national committees spend directly on behalf of their candidates boosts the total resources under a presidential candidate's control by over 15 percent. In 1992, D.N.C. staff played a critical role in helping the Clinton–Gore campaign target voters and position Bill Clinton between President Bush and Ross Perot. The national committee also issued streams of communications on Clinton's behalf. The R.N.C. performed similar services for the Bush–Quayle campaign.

In addition, national parties can raise "soft money" for the purposes of financing party-building programs and voter mobilization drives in some states. In 1992, the Democratic national, Congressional, and senatorial campaign committees raised over $36 million and the R.N.C. over $51 million in "soft money," respectively. Most of these funds were distributed in accordance with the strategies of their presidential candidates. "Soft money" enabled the national parties to wage coordinated campaigns that supplemented, and in some cases replaced, candidates' voter mobilization efforts.

Party organizations are much more active in the recruitment of candidates for House, Senate, state, and local offices. Although they cannot simply select candidates for these offices, they have become more active in encouraging some candidates to run and discouraging others. Most recruitment efforts focus on competitive districts, but sometimes party officials will encourage a candidate to play the role of sacrificial lamb by running for an office that is almost certain to be won by the opposition party. Some of the most important party recruitment activity is conducted by the Congressional and senatorial campaign committees. Campaign committee staff meet with state and local party leaders to identify potential candidates and encourage them to run for office. They often use polls, the promise of party support, and the persuasive talents of party leaders, members of Congress, and even presidents to convince highly qualified individuals to run (Herrnson, 1988). A number of state parties carry out similar activities, but on a smaller scale (Cotter *et al.*, 1984).

The 1992 elections posed a unique set of recruitment-related problems for party officials. Congressional redistricting placed several House incumbents in the same election districts, placing party officials in a position to encourage some of the candidates to run in other locations. The parties succeeded in getting a number of House members to switch districts, but some – like Illinois Democrats William Lipinski and Marty Russo, and Louisiana Republicans Richard Baker and Clyde Holloway – refused to move and ran against each other. Lipinski beat Russo in the Democratic primary and Baker beat Holloway first in an open primary, and then in the general election. As these cases illustrate, increased party activity in candidate recruitment has not done away with the dominant pattern of self-selected candidates assembling their own campaign organizations to compete for the nomination. Nevertheless, it has influenced the pool of candidates who run for office, especially in competitive districts.

Party organizations play a larger role in Congressional elections than in presidential campaigns. They contribute money and campaign services directly to many Congressional candidates, and provide them with transactional assistance that helps them obtain campaign resources from political consultants and P.A.C.s. Most party assistance is distributed by the parties' Congressional and senatorial campaign committees to candidates competing in close elections, reflecting the committees' goal of maximizing the number of seats they hold in Congress (Jacobson, 1985–6; Herrnson, 1989).

During recent election cycles, the parties' Congressional and senatorial campaign committees made the maximum contribution to virtually every competitive House or Senate candidate. Most also benefited from a large party expenditure on their behalf. The parties were unable to make large coordinated expenditures in a significant number of close House races during the 1992 election cycle because redistricting greatly increased the number of competitive contests that took place. The Congressional and senatorial committees also created agency agreements that allowed them to make some of the coordinated expenditures that are allocated to their national and state committees.

In 1992, the G.O.P. spent over $9 million on House elections, over $2 million more than the Democrats. Republican committees also spent $20.8 million in Senate contests, over $8.2 million more than their Democratic rivals. These figures include contributions and coordinated expenditures made by all party committees. They do not include soft money expenditures. Republican spending was also better targeted than Democratic spending in House elections, as more Republican than Democratic money was spent in close House races. Both parties targeted their Senate spending very effectively. The biggest beneficiary of party spending in 1992 was California Senate candidate Bruce Herschensohn, who received a total of $2,478,144 in contributions and coordinated expenditures. This accounted for 24 percent of his total campaign spending. Barbara Boxer, who defeated Herschensohn, received a total of $1,761,082 from Democratic Party committees, accounting for 15 percent of her total spending (Herrnson, 1994).

Party assistance to Congressional candidates can also come in the form of campaign services. The national parties hold training colleges for candidates and campaign managers, and help many candidates hire reputable political consultants. They provide contestants involved in competitive contests, as well as some others, with assistance in polling, precinct targeting, issue research, campaign advertising, and other areas of campaigning requiring technical expertise or in-depth research. The Congressional and senatorial campaign committees assist candidates, particularly nonincumbents, with raising money from P.A.C.s and wealthy contributors who do not live in their states. Committee staff hold P.A.C. briefings, distribute mailings, fax messages, and spend countless hours on the telephone with P.A.C. managers in order to get P.A.C. money flowing in the direction of their most competitive candidates. National party endorsements, communications, and contributions serve as decisionmaking cues that help P.A.C.s decide where to invest their money (Herrnson, 1988, 1994).

Party campaigning in state and local elections varies by locality, but it has increasingly come to resemble party activity in Congressional elections. Legislative campaign committees in a number of states have begun to recruit candidates, make campaign contributions and expenditures, and distribute election services (Cotter *et al.*, 1984; Frantzich, 1989). A significant number of county party committees are also reasserting themselves in the electoral process (Gibson, Cotter, Bibby, and Huckshorn, 1985). This suggests that the party-building programs instituted at the national level have been successful in bolstering state and local party organizations.

In addition to the campaign assistance they deliver to candidates, the generic election activities that parties carry out benefit all candidates on the ticket, including those for state and local offices. Party-focussed television and radio commercials that convey a message to voters nationwide can increase a party's support in the polls. Party registration and get-out-the-vote drives can have a similar effect.

Conclusion

Party reform and renewal have made the parties more open, more responsive to political movements, and better able to assist their candidates with campaigning for elective office. As important as these changes are, they are limited. They have taken place within the confines of a decentralized, candidate-centered system of politics, and they have not resulted in the development of party-focussed campaigns like those that take place in most other democracies. Part of the reason for the limited scope of the changes are the narrow goals of the party leaders initiating them. Unlike many of the scholars who study American political parties and elections, few of the leaders involved in reforming, renewing, or revitalizing the parties wished to create a European-style, programmatic party system (Herrnson, 1992).

There are other reasons why parties in the United States have not, and may never, come to play as big a role in elections as their counterparts in other industrialized democracies. The separation of powers, bicameralism, federalism, and the further decentralization of state and local offices result in national, state, and local officeholders of the same party being elected by different constituencies. Single-member simple-plurality districts and other election laws also encourage individualism among candidates. The basic arrangements of American government support a candidate-centered election system that responds to local pressures. They discourage the formulation of cooperative, nationally focussed party campaigns.

The fundamental missions pursued by the parties contribute little to the development of party-focussed elections. The major objective of American party organizations is to help elect individual candidates, rather than to promote public policy (Epstein, 1986). The parties' organizational structures are largely decentralized, and party committees are primarily concerned with the election of candidates who run for offices within their jurisdictions. Relations among party committees belonging to the same party are deferential rather than hierarchical (Eldersveld, 1964). The dispersion of authority, the proliferation of party committees, and the differences of opinion that naturally flow from them, make it difficult for party committees to develop a consensus on issues, and even more difficult for them to campaign on one. They result in parties playing a supporting role in elections instead of becoming their major focus.

Lastly, historical circumstances and political culture contribute to the pragmatic nature of American parties. An overwhelming majority of Americans support the basic foundations of our current political, economic, and social order. The United States' heterogeneous population, large middle class, and lack of a feudal legacy provide little foundation for the ideological or class-oriented parties found in many other democracies (Hartz, 1955). Election outcomes typically depend on winning the support of voters who are located at the center of the ideological spectrum (Downs, 1957). Candidates have few reasons to campaign on ideologically focussed party platforms or adopt party positions that would be controversial in their districts. Political culture and electoral arrangements encourage candidates to associate themselves with middle-of-the-road positions, valence issues, local concerns, and to stress their personal traits.

The developments that have strengthened the parties in the last 30 years have made it easier for individuals to participate in party politics, encouraged new groups to become more involved in candidate-selection and other party activities, and changed the flow of power among the party committees. They have also enabled the parties to play a bigger role in election campaigns. Party money, campaign services, advice, and transactional assistance can be decisive in determining the outcome of particular elections.

Party activities in 1992, and in other recent election cycles, give some clues as to the future of American political parties. They will probably continue to develop as fundraising and campaign service organizations and to play an influential supporting role in many elections. Nevertheless, it is unlikely that party activities will become important enough to candidates for office to overturn the basic structure of America's candidate-centered election system. Unlike candidates for elective office in most democracies, candidates in the United States will probably remain responsible for securing their party's nomination and for conducting their own general election campaigns. The United States has not developed a system of party-focussed elections. Barring the introduction of major political reform, it is unlikely that it will.

5

Interest Groups and Policymaking

FRANK L. DAVIS

In the past three decades the number and activity level of interest groups has increased dramatically. Many argue that the role of interest groups has expanded as that of political parties has receded, making interest groups more important and political parties less important in the interaction of citizens with government (Loomis and Cigler, 1991). While defenders often paint interest groups as organizations dedicated to protecting citizens who would otherwise be overlooked in the workings of mass democracy, critics tend to portray them as conspirators out to hijack public policy for their own benefit.

Most current criticism of interest group influence grows from concerns regarding the representativeness of the interest group system and influence of interest group money. Those who question whether interest group activity accurately represents the concerns of the populace note that *some* groups – for reasons unrelated to the level of interest and concern among their supporters – have much greater difficulty sustaining group activity. Concern about the influence of interest group money is centered on the growth of wealthy interest groups' campaign contributions and their expanded use of paid advertising and professional lobbyists.

In this chapter I want to describe the distinctive role of interest groups, analyze their efforts to influence public policy, assess the degree of their impact on policymaking, and evaluate their role in legitimizing government decisions. Examples will include cases from the current debate regarding health policy. With health care-related problems threatening the medical and economic well-being of the nation, the area of health policy promises illustrative and timely examples. This discussion should provide the reader with a context within which to evaluate criticism of interest group influence.

Interest Groups' Narrower Focus

A decline in the impact of political parties and rise in the influence of interest groups has important implications for the way in which citizens are represented to government and the way in which government, in turn, is portrayed to the populace. Political parties and interest groups, commonly referred to as "linkage" institutions, are two major conduits of information and political pressure between governors and governed. Each links citizens with government in a distinct manner. Political parties are concerned with winning elections. To do this they must gain the electoral support of a large plurality of voters, necessarily creating coalitions with relatively diverse interests. Because of this, political parties often pursue policies of compromise and moderation. Each party strikes a conciliatory position among its constituents to insure against defections. In addition, with their aspiration to rule comes the responsibility to take stands on most of the issues on the current political agenda. So political parties tend to take stands – often somewhat equivocal stands – on a wide range of issues.

Since interest groups concentrate their efforts on influencing policy (as opposed to winning elections), they generally rely on motivating a smaller but more committed membership. They do this by staking out distinct, detailed, and decisive positions. As a result, interest groups tend to be more strident and less willing to compromise. To insure member support, most interest groups limit their advocacy to a narrow range of issues on which they can sustain general agreement within their ranks. An interest group that ranges too far from this formula may find that group members' solidarity is weakened, and as a result the group's influence is undermined.

Debates regarding health care policy illustrate the distinction between political parties and interest groups. Each sector concerned with health care – such as patients, physicians, nurses, hospitals, employers, insurance companies, health equipment producers, pharmaceutical manufacturers, and lawyers – has a different perspective. For example, physicians and other health care professionals worry about preserving the autonomy and incomes of those in their profession, insurance companies are fearful of being excluded from a role in a reformed system, pharmaceutical companies want to avoid the imposition of price controls, and trial lawyers are worried about preserving malpractice lawsuits.

Policy disagreements grow from these differences in perspective. While insurance companies and health care providers portray malpractice suits as a major culprit in the inflation of medical costs and advocate stringent limits on the financial awards in such cases, trial lawyers defend malpractice suits as the only realistic check on health care providers' malfeasance and as the best means of insuring just compensation for injured patients. Among health care providers, the interests of physicians may conflict with those of nurses, as status and/or pay for doctors may come at the expense of nurses and vice versa.

Even among sectors that appear to share common interests, disagreements arise. For instance, differences exist between nonprofit and for-profit hospitals. The greater the proportion of uninsured patients that nonprofit hospitals handle, the less threat these patients pose to the profits of for-profit hospitals, but the greater the burden they place on the resources of the nonprofit sector. Differences have also arisen between large and small insurance companies, and large and small business generally. A number of large insurance companies welcome reforms that would require insurance companies to establish networks of health care professionals because they have the experience and requisite resources to manage such networks. However, small insurance companies – short on the necessary experience and resources – fear being "squeezed out" by the larger firms under such a system. Mandating that employers provide health coverage is less of a threat for large businesses than for small ones, because most large businesses already provide such coverage, while for most small businesses it represents a new expense.

Because each of the major political parties' constituents have a variety of views regarding health care, party leaders speak in rather general terms about the nature of the reform they support. In its 1992 platform, the Republican Party declared its support for President Bush's health care plan. Bush's plan called for making care more affordable and providing access to a larger proportion of citizens, but avoided discussing specifics regarding changes in the delivery or financing of care. The Democratic Party platform also declared lofty goals, while at the same time providing sparse detail about how those goals would be achieved. In Congress, neither Republicans nor Democrats have unified around health care plans, and Democrat support for President Clinton's health care reform proposals is far from assured.

In contrast, literally hundreds of interest groups are involved in the health care debate. Virtually every perspective on health care is represented by at least one group. Patients are represented by consumer groups and labor unions; care providers by associations of physicians, nurses, and hospitals; those involved in health care finance by employer and insurance organizations; and other interests such as the likes of pharmaceutical and equipment manufacturers' organizations, and lawyers' groups. (See Table 5.1 for a partial list of interest groups involved in the health care policy debate.)

The positions of most groups can be clearly traced to the shared interests of their members. Consumer groups unanimously support patients' freedom to choose their physician. The American Association of Retired Persons is adamant about long-term care for older

TABLE 5.1   *Examples of interest groups involved in health policy*

Organisation	Membership
Groups representing patients	
Consumers Union	Consumers
Citizen Action	Consumers
American Federation of State County and Municipal Employees	Government workers
American Association of Retired Persons	Individuals 50 years and older
National Education Association	School Teachers
A.F.L.–C.I.O.	Union members of various professions
Health care providers	
American Medical Association	Physicians
American Academy of Family Physicians	Family Physicians
American Podiatric Medical Association	Podiatrists

American Academy of   Ophthalmologists
  Ophthalmology
American Dental Association   Dentists
American Chiropractic Association Chiropractors
American Nurses Association   Nurses
American Occupational Therapy   Occupational therapists
  Association
American Hospital Association   Hospitals and Hospital
                                administrators
Catholic Hospital Association   Catholic hospitals
Federation of American Health   For-profit hospitals
  Systems
American Health Care Association Nursing homes and hospitals
                                providing long-term care
Medical Rehabilitation Education Rehabilitation hospitals and
  Foundation   professional organizations
National Association of Psychiatric Private Psychiatric hospitals
  Health Systems

Health insurance companies
Health Insurance Association   Small, medium, and large
  of America (H.I.A.A.)   insurance companies
National Association of Health   Insurance agents
  Underwriters
Association of Independent   Insurance agents
  Insurance Agents of America

Pharmaceutical and medical equipment manufacturers
Pharmaceutical Manufacturers   Pharmaceutical companies
  Association
Health Industry Manufacturers   Medical equipment
  Association   manufacturing companies

Employers
National Federation of Independent Small businesses
  Business

Business
Chamber of Commerce   Small and large businesses
National Association of   Manufacturing firms of all sizes
  Manufacturers

Other interested groups
Association of Trial Lawyers   Trial lawyers
  of America
Distilled Spirits Council   Producers and marketers of
                                distilled beverages

Americans. The American Medical Association has strongly resisted price controls or any sort of restriction on health budgets. While the National Federation of Independent Business, representing small businesses, is adamantly opposed to requiring that employers pay for employees' health insurance, the Chamber of Commerce, with a mixed membership of small and large businesses (with many of the larger ones already providing employee health coverage), is willing to accept such a mandate. The Association of Trial Lawyers of America is working to preserve malpractice lawsuits. The Distilled Spirits Council is concentrating on opposition to financing health care with "sin taxes" on alcohol.

Variation in Involvement

Within a given policy area, some interest groups are more concerned and active than others. Such differences in commitment have important implications for groups' impact. The more central a policy is to a group *and* the more capable the group is of sustaining its effort over long periods, the greater and more consistent the group's influence is likely to be.

Estimating the impact of groups' concern for policy is relatively straightforward. For instance, groups whose principal concern is health care will devote a larger share of their effort and resources to influencing health care policy, while groups for which health care is a more peripheral concern will most likely dedicate a smaller proportion. Such groups as the American Medical Association, American Hospital Association, Health Insurance Association of America, and Pharmaceutical Manufacturers Association will direct most of their effort toward influencing health care policy. Groups like Citizen Action; the American Federation of State, County, and Municipal Employees; the American Federation of Labor and Congress of Industrial Organizations (A.F.L.-C.I.O.); National Federation of Independent Business; and Distilled Spirits Council will tend to direct a much smaller portion of their effort toward influencing health care policy.

While it is relatively straightforward to determine how central health care is to a group's mission, evaluating an interest group's ability to *sustain* effort is more difficult. To address this second aspect, it is helpful to understand why members join and support groups. The distinction between "private" and "public" interest groups provides clues to groups' likely persistence in efforts to influence policy.

Private Versus Public Interest Groups

Groups rely on an array of incentives to attract and retain members. These incentives can be classified into two categories: selective benefits and collective benefits. Selective benefits are those that can be provided or denied to specific individuals – such as access to periodicals, employment, and discount prices on insurance and other products. Collective benefits cannot be targeted at specific individuals; they are provided to groups of people or the entire population, and include benefits such as air quality, more effective national defense, and satisfaction in pursuing "good" public policy. Although most interest groups rely on a mix of incentives – providing some specific, material (selective) payoff and some psychic (collective) payoff for "good works" – each group has its own mix, and a group's relative reliance on each type of incentive has an impact on the group's behavior.

Private interest groups attract and retain members largely by reserving selective incentives for members. Interest groups that rely heavily on selective incentives are most common among corporations, professional associations, and labor unions. Among interest groups concerned with health care, for instance, pharmaceutical and insurance companies such as Pfizer and Aetna provide employment. Some argue that membership in the American Medical Association plays an important role in physicians' ability to practice medicine. Nonmember physicians, they contend, are ostracized both socially and professionally by A.M.A. physicians (Campion, 1984). Most professional and trade associations (for instance, associations of physicians, physical therapists, and hospitals) provide information of importance to professional practitioners in association newsletters. The American Association of Retired Persons attracts members with such incentives as insurance coverage, assistance in retirement planning, and discounts on auto rentals and hotel rates.

Public interest groups rely more on collective benefits such as members' commitment to the "cause" or policy. They seek collective goods, "the achievement of which will not selectively and materially benefit the membership or activists of the organization" (Berry, 1977). Public interest groups tend to concern themselves with such matters as consumer protection, environmental policy, civil rights and liberties questions, and general defense and peace issues.

Because one's commitment to a cause may be less consistent than one's concern with selective payoffs such as employment or professional contacts, public interest groups may face greater fluctuations in member support. As a result, public interest groups' involvement may expand or contract more as the visibility of a policy area waxes and wanes than is the case for private groups. In health care this is illustrated by the fact that private interests outside the health care industry, such as the Chamber of Commerce and National Association of Manufacturers, were active on health care issues long before consumer groups took up the cause. Citizen Action, for instance, had to persuade its membership that health care policy was important before it could gear up its effort on health care issues. For private groups, members need not be as committed to the cause, because they are motivated more by individual benefits than by the group's larger policy goals.

The inconsistency of member motivation may also lead public interest groups to greater financial insecurity. Many public interest groups depend upon funds from government, foundations, and other private sources to establish and maintain their organizations (Walker, 1983). An example of this is Families USA, a nonprofit advocacy group. Today, Families USA has 225,000 small, direct-mail contributors, but start-up expenses of $40 million were provided by wealthy benefactors, and the group continues to depend on funds from private foundations and wealthy individuals for a portion of its operating expenses. Some argue that this means that private interest groups will, in the long run, have greater influence than public interest groups.

Representativeness of Interest Groups

Recognition of variation in interest groups' ability to sustain activity in the policymaking process prompts concerns about how well the interest group system reflects opinion and interests within

American society. That is, is interest group activity an accurate reflection of citizen concerns, or are some citizens' interests over-represented and others' interests slighted?

The traditional evaluation of how well interest groups reflect opinion within the polity was grounded in pluralism (Truman, 1951). Pluralists presumed that those who wished to influence policy organized into groups. More widely held and intense concern resulted in more robust and active groups. Inactivity was a reflection of satisfaction or disinterest. It followed, therefore, that interest groups reflected the distribution and intensity of people's concern about government policy. The logical conclusion, then, was that interest groups accurately reflected citizens' concerns.

Bias?

Recognition of the dynamics of private groups, however, brought the pluralist perspective into question. The realization that membership could be motivated by a concern for individual (selective) benefits, as well as a preference for particular public policy options, implied that the distribution of selective benefits influenced interest group activity (Olson, 1965). As a result, the interest group universe could be expected to represent some concerns more effectively than others. Consequently, it could *not* be assumed that interest group activity accurately reflected people's policy preferences.

In general, some private interests would be more easily organized into successful groups than other private interest and most public interests. Differences in the ranks of the American Medical Association (A.M.A.) and consumer groups are examples. The membership of the A.M.A. alone accounts for over 50 percent (271,000) of all potential members; that is, of all (532,000) U.S. physicians. By contrast, the ten largest consumer groups are able to enlist a much smaller proportion – less than 3 percent (fewer than 7,000,000) – of all their potential members; that is, all (250,000,000) U.S. consumers. The difference in these groups' ability to mobilize support may be better explained by individual (selective) benefits provided by the A.M.A. than by a lack of support for consumer groups' policies. That is, the activity of these interest groups is not necessarily a clear reflection of the citizenry's concerns and preferences.

How Involved in Health Care are Interest Groups?

Health care also provides an excellent example of the dynamics of group involvement in the policymaking process. While interest groups become involved in health care for different reasons and to varying degrees, certain general patterns can be observed: (1) the more central health policy is to a group's policy concerns, the more attentive the group will be to health policy, and (2) the more consistent a group's ability to motivate members, the more likely it can sustain its commitment to a political struggle. Three categories grow from these two distinctions.

Those in the first category, *private interest groups with the greatest stake in the health care policy arena*, would be the most attentive and active in periods when health policy is of lower salience. When the policy area heats up, these groups are likely to become even more active and commit greater resources to meet the challenge of newly activated groups. In the area of health policy, groups like the American Medical Association, American Hospital Association, and Health Insurance Association of America fall into this category. Groups in the second category, *private interest groups whose major concerns fall outside of health policy*, will tend to become involved only periodically when their interests are more directly involved. Groups like the National Association of Manufacturers, A.F.L.-C.I.O., and Association of Trial Lawyers of America qualify here. The third category encompasses *public interest groups*. Their activity level is likely to fall more in periods of low salience (because of a lack of member commitment and interest) and rise more in level of activity and commitment of resources when their members become convinced of the issues' importance. Groups such as Citizen Action and Consumers Union tend to fit this description.

Subsystems Versus Issue Networks

As a result of these distinctive responses, different patterns of interest group competition emerge within policy areas. Political scientists have identified two: "subsystems" and "issue networks." The subsystem view describes a circumstance in which the public and most interest groups outside of the industry are inattentive. Subsystems tend to spawn "corporatist" strategies in which government officials cooperate with the most influential interest groups involved in the industry. Such a corporatist approach works quite smoothly because all of those involved – government policy makers, industry interest groups, and the "special" publics that are aware and active – accommodate one another's needs, largely "freezing out" less influential groups and pushing most of the costs on to those outside the subsystem who are largely unaware.

With such a corporatist approach, government policymakers may condone virtual self-regulation, with predominant interest groups setting the guidelines under which those involved in the industry must live (Peters, 1984). Examples of this strategy are the U.S. government's recognition of labor unions as workers' sole representatives, and its ceding of control over the licensing of practitioners to professional organizations – as with the American Bar Association's role in licensing lawyers (Hayes, 1978; McConnell, 1966).

The "issue network" view describes a circumstance in which groups emerge unexpectedly to play an important role in policymaking (Heclo, 1978). The number of active groups increases and the arrangements of groups that are more continually active in the policy area may be overturned. For example, "the enactment of new legislation in civil rights, environmental protection, consumerism, and safety" during the 1960s and 1970s resulted from the activation of a wide array of groups beyond those traditionally involved in these policy areas (Gais *et al.*, 1984).

Examples of both of these patterns can be found in the health care policy arena. During much of the past five decades, health care politics resembled the "corporatist" description of policymaking (Marmor and Thomas, 1972). According to Ron Pollack of Families USA, "in the past, health care debates have been dominated by those who make money [from the health care system] and disproportionately propagandize and get to Members of Congress" (Kosterlitz, 1993). When health care is of low visibility, most of the interest groups involved in health care policy tend to be those who have a major business interest in health care and that are more private (as opposed to public) in organizational character: groups like the American Medical Association, American Hospital Association, and Pharmaceutical Manufacturers Association, Pfizer Inc. (a pharmaceutical company), and the Health Insurance Association of America. The net effect of this pattern of involvement is that policy largely represents the preferences of what has been referred to as the "medical-industrial complex."

For limited periods, the health policy arena has resembled the "issue network" description, where groups from outside the industry have been active and influential. For instance, when health care for the elderly became an issue in the 1960s, a number of groups not usually involved in health policy – such as the A.F.L.-C.I.O., the American Association of Retired Persons, the National Farmers Union, and the National Association of Manufacturers – emerged as active participants in the health care debate (Marmor, 1973). Since groups from outside the industry traditionally have little influence on health care policy, they tend to voice dissatisfaction with standing policy and call for reforms when they do get involved.

When "outside" groups are activated, the standard strategy of interest groups with a perennial involvement in a policy area is to block action until the outside groups' and the public's attention decline. In this way, members of the subsystem avoid policymaking when the balance of power threatens their interests. Critics contend that this happened when President Carter attempted to "reform" health care in 1979. Members of Carter's administration charged that his health reform measure was blocked by hospital and other medical-related interest groups.

In the 1990s an issue network has again arisen in the area of health care policy. After years of dominance by the "medical–industrial complex," a diverse array of interest groups and the public at large are getting involved in health care policymaking. Consumer and labor groups are publicizing health care issues as never before, and a number of business groups outside the health care industry have embraced the need for change. In the face of such strong concern, interest groups traditionally involved in health policy – such as the American Medical Association – have abandoned their public position against reform and are putting forth their own proposals, trying to influence what appears an inevitable revision in the present system.

Resources, Tactics, and "Interested Publics"

Groups employ a variety of techniques to influence government policy. These include efforts targeted directly at policymakers and those aimed indirectly at officials through the agitation of interest group members and the public. Differences in the availability of resources lead interest groups to different tactics. Private interest groups generally have greater financial resources and a smaller corp of members. For this reason, they tend to rely more on "insider" tactics designed to make direct contact with governmental officials. Such efforts as employing professional lobbyists, running paid advertisements in newspapers most commonly read by government officials, and contributing money to candidates for elective office provide group leaders with firm control over the group's efforts.

In turn, public interest groups generally have more limited access to financing, a larger corp of members, and are often committed to a cause that can inspire broader public support. They are more likely to "go public" as such a strategy allows them to tap into their numerical strength. As a result, public interest groups are likely to rely more on "outsider" tactics, turning to the grassroots mobilization of citizens to contact and lobby government officials.

New technologies have been instrumental in the growth of public interest groups. Such tactics as direct mail, 800 and 900 number telephone lines, focus groups, and public opinion polls facilitate the mobilization of citizen support. Yet it should not be assumed that public interest groups are the major beneficiaries of these technologies. Effectively employing these tactics in successful policy campaigns is expensive. Some organizations are more capable of financing such efforts than others. There are signs that private groups may be employing these mechanisms to ever greater effect, and that it is these organizations, with their access to financial resources, that will be most capable of capitalizing on these new techniques.

Obviously, while the distinction between private and public can help in understanding interest group tactics, it should not be overdrawn. Generally, all interest groups want to motivate a high level of political involvement on the part of their supporters; and many private interest groups, such as labor unions and professional associations, have large memberships. Further, when the public's concern about a policy area rises and a large portion of the public becomes activated, public opinion will have an impact on the eventual policy. As a result, groups – both public and private in character – will publicize their case by trying to persuade the public of the virtue of their positions.

Interest Group Tactics

Efforts focussed directly on public officials generally fall under the headings of lobbying, advertisements in periodicals known to be widely read by government officials, campaign contributions, and court action. Pressure is brought to bear on officials indirectly by means of grassroots mobilization, influencing news coverage, and advertising in the mass media.

Lobbying

Lobbying is a traditional means of influencing government policy-makers, and involves personal contact with government officials. Lobbyists use a variety of arguments, from information about what is the best and most rational policy to what effect different courses of action will have on elected officials' support in the next election.

Professional lobbyists are hired for their experience and skills in contacting and persuading government policymakers. Many professional lobbyists have previously served in government and are now lobbying members of the institutions in which they served. Critics charge that some of these former government officials turned lobbyists are participating in a "revolving door" process, cashing in on their government contacts at the public's expense.

In addition, what may be called "amateur" lobbyists (interest group members who can make a persuasive case because of their commitment and familiarity with the group's cause) are assuming an increasing role. This type of lobbying may be a larger part of public interest groups' efforts, but private groups are also making extensive use of "amateur" lobbyists.

Advertisements aimed at government officials

Publications such as The *Washington Post*, *New York Times*, and *Wall Street Journal*, which are known to be read by a large proportion of government officials, offer interest groups an alternative channel of communication with policymakers. Robert Blendon of the Harvard School of Public Health pointed out that these advertisements "send a message to members of Congress about what it's going to look like in their districts . . . It's a warning" (Neus, 1993).

Purchasing advertisements, like hiring professional lobbyists, is expensive; hiring a public relations lobbying firm can cost $5,000 to $30,000 a month. A quarter-page ad in the *Washington Post* costs $13,204, and in the *Wall Street Journal* it is nearly $29,000. For this reason, these tactics remain more (though certainly not exclusively) the preserve of private interest groups.

Campaign contributions

Campaign contributions are probably the most controversial interest group tactic. Interest groups contribute funds through organizations – called Political Action Committees (P.A.C.s) – established specifically for the purpose of channeling campaign funds into electoral contests. An interest group's members and supporters provide funds to an interest group's P.A.C.; and the P.A.C.'s leaders, in turn, direct these funds as contributions to candidates on the interest group's behalf.

Since many interest group contributions are intended to insure access to officeholders, these funds go disproportionately to those candidates – predominantly incumbents – who are expected to win the election. On average, about 75 percent of P.A.C. funds are directed to incumbents, with the remaining 25 percent provided to challengers and candidates for open seats. Critics argue that this undermines the competitiveness of elections by increasing incumbents' already substantial advantages. A large campaign chest not only means that a candidate has sufficient funds to wage the next election campaign, but may also serve to frighten potential opponents away from the race altogether.

P.A.C.s associated with corporations, labor unions, and associations provide a large (and growing) share of candidates' campaign funds. As of the 1990 elections, P.A.C. money accounted for about 21 percent of Senate candidates' campaign receipts and 41 percent of House candidates' campaign receipts. For incumbents, the proportions were even higher: 24 percent for incumbent Senate candidates and 48 percent for incumbent House candidates. Private interest groups' financial advantage over public interest groups is strongly reflected in campaign contributions, with consumer and other public interest groups accounting for a relatively small proportion of P.A.C. contribution funds.

As the cost of campaigns has grown, candidates have increasingly come to depend upon interest group contributions. Critics contend that contributions provide interest group contributors with an unwarranted influence on policy. Even if this is not the case, and contributions only provide access to elected officeholders (as defenders claim), serious questions about the character of interest group influence persist. For instance, what advantages may accrue with greater access? Why would interest groups devote tens of millions of dollars to contributions each election period if they did not believe their expenditures yielded a significant return?

Appealing to the courts

Interest groups also appeal to the courts. The judiciary's insulation from electoral concerns can mean that court decisions may reflect considerations not found in the Congress's and president's deliberations. The judiciary, therefore, can provide an interest group with an alternative to the executive and legislative branches. As a result, the courts are likely to be an option more seriously considered either by the following groups: (1) those that have limited popular support or money with which to press their cases with the president or Congress, or (2) those that have exhausted their options with the other two branches. For groups with little support within the general public and limited financial resources, the courts provide an avenue in which such assets may be less important. Court action may also serve as a last resort for interest groups that have been unsuccessful with the legislative and executive branches, regardless of the group's access to political resources.

At the same time, court action may simply be an additional tactic, employed in combination with other efforts to strengthen a group's strategic position. Appealing to the courts can serve to publicize a group's cause, provide an additional avenue through which to press its case, and may increase pressure on other branches of the government to take a group seriously.

Publicizing public support

Alerting officials to public support can bolster an interest group's case. Groups may encourage members and supporters to send officials letters, postcards, telegrams, and faxes. This is most effective with elected officials, when the communication comes from constituents who will likely have a direct impact on the official's likelihood of reelection. Evidence of public support may also come in the form of demonstrations, rallies, or public opinion polls. Public support can be brought to officials' attention through lobbying contacts, advertisements, and in the form of news items carried by the media.

News coverage and mass advertising

Reliance on public opinion to bolster their case has increased interest groups' concern for cultivating public support. These efforts have been facilitated by the development of more sophisticated technology. Over the past few decades, interest groups have made ever greater use of new techniques. "Focus groups" of ten to twenty people, in which an interviewer explores reactions to policy arguments, allow interest groups to identify the most persuasive presentation of their case. Increasingly, public opinion polls are commissioned by interest groups both to identify the most effective means of presenting the group's case, and as a way of promoting the perception that the group's positions are widely supported.

Interest groups also pursue supportive news coverage. Toward this end, they suggest stories to news people, facilitate coverage of particular stories, and make news with public speeches, rallies, and other events. They also attract public support by advertising in media like television and general circulation magazines. This, in contrast to news coverage, gives the group complete control over the message. Computer-processed direct mail allows seemingly personalized contact with a large number of people drawn from lists of likely supporters, providing a means of attracting members and revenues. Groups can also advertise telephone numbers through which the public can obtain information or request messages be sent to their elected representatives.

Tactics in the Health Care Debate

The health care policy debate provides a number of examples. The public's current interest in medical care issues leads to the expectation that public opinion will have a stronger influence on policymaking than is the case in most policy debates. As a result, interest groups – both public and private – are placing greater than normal stress on efforts to persuade the public. At the same time, insider tactics are also quite evident.

A multitude of *lobbyists* are active in health care; over 750 health care organizations have registered lobbyists working in Washington. Private groups account for a much larger proportion of professional lobbyists' efforts. In addition to independent lobbyists, many public relations and law firms specialize in representing clients to the government. For instance, among pharmaceutical companies: Pfizer Inc. hired Michael S. Scrivner; the law firm of Patton, Boggs, and Blow is representing Smithkline Beecham; and the Pharmaceutical Manufacturers Association hired the Sawyer Miller Group to direct its effort. Aetna, a major insurance company, has hired a number of lobbyists including Black, Manafort, Stone, and Kelly; and the Duberstein Group Inc.

Evidence of the "revolving door" is also obvious in health care lobbying. The Health Industry Manufacturers Association hired Stuart Eizenstat's law firm to lobby on its behalf. Eizenstat is a prominent Democrat and former domestic adviser to President Jimmy Carter. Retired Republican Congressman Norman Lent is part of a lobbying firm employed by Pfizer. Another of Aetna's lobbyists, Ronnie Flippo, is a former member of the House Ways and Means (tax writing) Committee.

In the way of "amateur lobbying," a coalition of 20 consumer groups and unions turned out their rank-and-file members to make personal contacts in Washington with their senators and representatives. Among the groups involved in the effort were the public interest group Citizen Action; the Communications Workers of America; the International Union of Electrical Workers; the International Ladies Garment Workers Union; the American Federation of State, County, and Municipal Employees; and the Oil, Chemical, and Atomic Workers.

A number of interest groups are running advertisements directed at Washington decisionmakers. Pharmaceutical interests are particularly active. They are attempting to counteract criticism from members of the Clinton administration by stressing their expenditures on research and promoting the view that prescription drugs provide an inexpensive alternative to other forms of care.

Political Action Committees (P.A.C.s) associated with the health industry have a history of generosity. According to a study by Citizen Action, the Political Action Committees of the health and insurance industries have spent $153 million in House and Senate races since 1980. In the 1992 election, the medical, pharmaceutical, and insurance industries were represented by more than 200 P.A.C.s, and medical-related P.A.C.s contributed over $41 million to House and Senate candidates (according to calculations in *U.S. News*). Table 5.2 provides some examples from the 1992 elections of contribution totals for a number of P.A.C.s representing interest groups presently active in the health care policy debate.

The American Medical Association also utilized the threat of court action. Representatives of the group, fearful that they were being ignored by the President's staff, said the A.M.A. would sue if President Clinton's health care reform plan included price controls. The courts thereby provided an additional route through which the American Medical Association could press its case against price controls and served as a threat to the Clinton administration that ignoring the A.M.A. might provoke negative publicity and legal roadblocks.

Both private and public interest groups are heavily involved in mobilizing grassroots constituents. About 30 of the Pharmaceutical Manufacturers Association's member companies sent letters to their employees, retirees, stockholders, and vendors, in which the companies described consequences of price controls and urged that recipients of the letters write to members of Congress. The Hospital Corporation of America, a chain of 73 hospitals, distributed manuals (prepared by the firm's Washington lobbyists) to its 66,000 employees regarding how to work with local groups and write op-eds for local newspapers. Labor unions are particularly well suited to mobilizing members. The A.F.L.-C.I.O. plans to use phone banks, mailings, and personal contacts to mobilize its members in support of the Clinton administration's plan – if the plan conforms to the A.F.L.-C.I.O.'s position on health care reform.

Public interest groups, of course, are active in grassroots mobilization. Citizen Action got 1 million people to convey their

TABLE 5.2   *Examples of the campaign expenditures of health-related Political Action Committees for the 1991–2 election cycle*

PAC sponsor	Total contributions to candidates for federal office
Groups representing patients	
American Federation of state, County and Municipal Employees	$1,950,365
National Education Association	2,323,122
A.F.L.-C.I.O.	835,120
Health care providers	
American Medical Association	2,936,086
American Podiatric Medical Association	401,000
American Academy of Ophthalmology	801,527
American Dental Association	1,417,958
American Chiropractic Association	641,746
American Nurses Association	306,337
American Occupational Therapy Association	81,363
American Hospital Association	505,888
American Health Care Association	382,019
Health insurance companies	
Massachusetts Mutual Life Insurance Co.	278,088
National Association of Life Underwriters	1,371,600
Association of Independent Insurance Agents of America	590,798
Pharmaceutical manufacturers	
Pfizer Inc. (pharmaceutical manufacturer)	187,600
Glaxo Inc. (pharmaceutical manufacturer)	173,400
Eli Lilley and Co. (pharmaceutical manufacturer)	185,030
Employers	
National Federation of Independent Business	293,587
Other interested parties	
Association of Trial Lawyers of America	2,366,135
Distilled Spirits Council	67,901

sentiments on postcards to President Clinton's health policy task force and is employing volunteers in door-to-door canvassing and phone bank operations. The American Association of Retired

Persons has trained over 1,000 members to talk about health care at community meetings.

Groups are also actively trying to influence *news coverage*. The Health Care Leadership Council is having industry executives visit local editorial boards and Rotary Clubs. Consumers Union lobbyists are "talking up [their position] on drive-time radio shows in nearly 50 markets" (Kosterlitz, 1993). Families USA identifies stories for the news media to follow up and plans to put together a film documenting problems with the present health care system.

Consumers Union commissioned the Gallup organization to run a poll and released results to bolster its case. The American Association of Retired Persons released a poll it commissioned that showed strong support for long-term care. Advocates of a single-payer system also set up a 900 number "that individuals can call to request that postcards be sent to Members of Congress on their behalf for a charge of $2" (Kosterlitz, 1993).

Rx Partners, a coalition of seven pharmaceutical companies, is spending 2 million dollars for *advertisements aimed at the general public* to defend their role and oppose price controls on drugs. The Pharmaceutical Manufacturers Association undertook a multi-million dollar campaign aimed at convincing senior citizens that price controls on drugs would be detrimental to the quality of medical care.

A Coordinated Campaign

The Health Insurance Association of America (H.I.A.A.) provides an excellent example of how an interest group coordinates a number of tactics in a comprehensive campaign. With a recently retired member of Congress as its head, the H.I.A.A. (under the auspices of the "Coalition for Health Insurance Choices") financed focus group sessions, public opinion polls, advertisements, and an 800 telephone number in its campaign to preserve a role for the small and medium-size insurance companies it represents.

The Association employed a public relations firm to conduct focus groups and public opinion polls to identify the most popular way in which to present the H.I.A.A. proposals. Based on these findings, the Association funded 4 million dollars in advertisements in newspapers and on television featuring its policy preferences as part of a program aimed at preserving individuals' "right to choose" their doctor and insurance company. The advertisements also promised a pamphlet with more information to those who called a toll-free 800 telephone number. The number of calls to the toll-free line (34,000 in the first two weeks) was then presented to the news media as evidence of public support. To round out its effort, the Association undertook direct contact with officials – hiring a number of professional lobbyists – and spent over $285,000 in the 1992 elections.

Legitimation of Policy

The role of interest groups in influencing government policymaking is clear. What may be less apparent is the degree to which their policy positions influence citizen perceptions. Interest groups often assume a major role in citizens' evaluation of policy. That a group's policy stands are taken by its membership as guidance regarding the legitimacy of policy is not surprising. An interest group does, after all, profess to represent its members' interests. What is surprising is the degree to which interest groups serve a legitimizing function for nonmembers. Such a role is, however, not that difficult to understand. Individuals who are uncertain about the value of some policy may search for convenient cues, and interest groups' policy stands can provide such guidance. Nonmembers may trust the counsel of an interest group because of a perception that the group has expertise in a policy area or because of a group's role as protector of particular sectors of the populace. For instance, insurance companies' statements regarding public policy affecting insurance may be given weight because of the companies' extensive knowledge and experience with the topic. The American Association of Retired Persons represents not only its members, but the interests of older Americans in general. The American Medical Association's pronouncements regarding health care policy carry the weight of physicians' medical expertise *and* their reputation as "care givers" who are sincerely concerned with patients' needs.

Interest groups' influence with the public has been recognized by policymakers. An interest group's endorsement can provide an important boost, and condemnation a significant blow, to the political fortunes of proposed policy. Just as interest groups attempt to convince government officials to adopt the groups' policy preferences, government officials try to persuade interest groups to support the policy formulations prescribed by officials. While interest groups lobbied members of the Clinton administration on health care reform, members of the administration were courting interest groups' support for the administration's health care proposals. Representatives of the administration met with interest group leaders to reassure them that the administration's plan would benefit their members.

There are definite limits to the legitimizing authority of groups – both with their members and with the population at large. Dissension among labor union members is a good example. Many union members strongly disagree with the political outlook of their leadership and oppose a number of the group's policy positions (Schlozman and Tierney, 1986). As an example from the health field, note the American Association of Retired Persons' (A.A.R.P.) 1989 support for an increase in government fees to pay for new catastrophic medical coverage. The A.A.R.P. leadership's endorsement of the measure was not enough to convince a sufficient share of its members or older Americans generally that the measure was appropriate, and opposition among older citizens persuaded the Congress to rescind its action. The A.A.R.P., sensitive to this failure, has been more cautious in approaching the latest round of health care discussions. Interest groups can lose a great deal of clout if observers believe they have lost the confidence of their members and the public at large. Such a loss of trust would limit a group's ability to turn out support for measures it favors or opposition for those it dislikes.

Final Conclusions

The impact of interest groups on the American political system has been amply demonstrated in this chapter. What cannot be definitively addressed, however, is the value of interest groups in U.S. politics. Any institution's linkage of citizen and government will be imperfect. This is as true of interest groups as it is of political parties. Perhaps the most disturbing trend in interest group politics is the growing importance of money. Substantial treasuries are required to finance campaign contributions and to mobilize citizen support. Both of these factors provoke questions about whether more affluent interest groups have greater influence in the policymaking process. At the same time, interest groups constitute a major conduit of information, support, and influence between citizens and government. Ultimately, each student of American politics must decide for herself/himself whether interest groups contribute more to the problems or solutions in US politics today.

PART TWO

The Institutional Framework

6

The Presidency in the 1990s

JOHN HART

On April 29th, 1993, the *Washington Post* greeted its readers with a page-one banner-headline, "President Clinton's First 100 Days," followed by two lengthy reports on the President's performance in office, an extended editorial on the subject, and an opinion poll, all of which spread over more than two full pages of the paper. The first report, an analysis of the results of the opinion poll, was almost fatalistic in its tone. Under the heading, "Pessimism About Nation's Direction Is Growing Again Among Voters," it began: "The first hundred days of Bill Clinton's presidency have diminished public expectations that he – or anyone else in Washington – can do much to turn around a country that seven out of 10 voters think is going in the wrong direction. Whatever the voters may have believed last winter about what Clinton and the new Congress would do to fix the economy, reduce the federal deficit and put the country on a different path, they are noticeably more doubtful today" (Balz and Broder, 1993). The thrust of the second story was that President Clinton had lost his way. His policy agenda was seen as too ambitious and too broad-ranging, and distractions (like the issue of gays in the military and the Bosnian crisis) had deflected attention from his major economic policy goals and caused the White House to lose focus on the essentials.

The amount of space that the *Washington Post* devoted to this interim judgment on Clinton's record, after just three months and one week in office, will probably be inversely proportional to its longer-term significance. Presidents can adapt, circumstances are likely to change, and not even the meanest of critics could have expected President Clinton to have achieved the kind of goals he espoused in the 1992 election campaign within his first hundred days in office. Such artificial and interim judgments have little

110

significant value and, even if Bill Clinton turns out to be a one-term, failed president, it is doubtful that the causes of failure would be satisfactorily explained by the erratic ups and downs of his early days in the White House.

Ironically, the media are also aware of the flaws in this rush to judgment on the President's first hundred days. On the same day that the *Washington Post* had pronounced on President Clinton's performance, an editorial in the *New York Times* boldly declared that "the hundred days' test is, of course, fundamentally silly." The *New York Times* noted that the hundred days was a yardstick that originated during the presidency of Franklin Roosevelt (F.D.R.) and had been invented by journalists who were trying to come to terms with F.D.R.'s total domination of Washington politics during his first hundred days in office in the spring of 1933 (*New York Times*, 1993a).

Therein lies the "silliness" of contemporary applications of the hundred-days test. No president since F.D.R. has taken office in remotely similar circumstances. None of his successors faced anything like the enormity of the Depression of the early 1930s, and none took over the White House during a national emergency so clearly and unambiguously defined. Neither has any post-F.D.R. president had such a comparable level of public support for presidential initiative and leadership. As the beneficiary of a landslide victory in a realigning election, a strong coat-tails effect in the Congressional races, and as head of a political party that behaved as a "cohesive office-seeking team" (Pomper, 1992), F.D.R. enjoyed a political environment that none of his successors have shared, and most could only fantasize about. He exploited those circumstances skillfully, leading Congress to pass the legislation that made his one hundred days "a benchmark in presidential–congressional relations" and a model of how presidential–congressional relations ought to work (Polsby, 1986).

It was an exceptional model, in the literal sense of the term, but rather than being celebrated as an exception, F.D.R.'s first hundred days have come to be regarded as the norm. Presidents who have not been able to emulate his record are seen as falling short and, for most of F.D.R.'s successors, the hundred-days measure inevitably becomes the first mark of failure in their presidency.

The circumstances in which F.D.R. began his tenure in the White House were especially propitious for strong presidential leadership.

In times of crises, other branches of the government, and other powerful influences within the American political system, tend to stand back and let the president get on with the job. Public opinion also mobilizes behind the president in a crisis to give strong backing to leadership and direction in a way that rarely happens during less anxious periods. Support for the president often soars when the nation is in trouble, and presidential power is enhanced accordingly. But, in non-crisis times, the American polity is less enthusiastic about presidential leadership and less willing to give the president a free hand. In these more normal periods, the political system reverts to type and becomes what it was originally designed to be, a system of multiple centres of power, or, to be more precise, a system of multiple centres of opposition to power in which the president is frequently the target of opposition primarily because F.D.R.'s most enduring legacy is the expectation that it is the president who sets the agenda, points the direction, and leads the way.

The intense media focus on Bill Clinton's first hundred days serves to remind us just how much F.D.R.'s successors still have to live "in the shadow of F.D.R." (Leuchtenburg, 1983). However, at the same time, it also obscures important differences between the circumstances of F.D.R.'s presidency and those facing his successors. To put it succinctly, President Clinton was not the beneficiary of an economic depression, a realigning election, a landslide victory, a coat-tails Congress, a strong and responsible political party, and an overwhelmingly supportive public. Morever, unlike Clinton, F.D.R. did not have to operate within the confines of the post-Watergate presidency – an institution much more severely constrained in terms of power prospects and leadership potential than the presidency F.D.R. knew.

The Clinton Inheritance

The prospects for presidential power was the central theme of Richard Neustadt's seminal work on the presidency, first published in 1960 and now in its third edition (1990). Neustadt's argument is that the American presidency is an office of inherent weakness, not strength, where powers were no guarantee of power and where leadership could only be exercised successfully by presidents of extraordinary temperament and experience. In Neustadt's terms, F.D.R. was one of the exceptions who was able to make the presidency work. "No President in this century," Neustadt wrote, "has had a sharper sense of personal power, a sense of what it is and where it comes from; none has had more hunger for it, few have had more use for it, and only one or two could match his faith in his own competence to use it. . . . No modern President has been more nearly master in the White House" (1990).

Clinton and F.D.R. had much in common. Both were activist Democrats assuming the presidency after 12 years of conservative Republican leadership. Both were confronted by immensely difficult policy problems. Both had ambitious programs, and both were committed to changing the face of American politics. There are remarkable similarities in the tone of their inaugural addresses. F.D.R. spoke of "restoration," Clinton used the term "renewal." They both talked about boldness, hope, the need for action, and claimed that the American people, through the election, had mandated change in American government. However, F.D.R. would probably not have recognized the presidency that Bill Clinton inherited 60 years later.

The strength of the modern presidency that F.D.R. is credited with creating (Greenstein, 1970; Rose, 1991) began to be undermined incrementally even before his death in 1945. F.D.R. eventually encountered problems with Congress, with his party, and with his public popularity, and not even his personal magic was enough to ensure that he got everything he wanted. His successors got a lot less. The undermining of the modern presidency, however, really begins to accelerate from the time of Richard Nixon's tenure in the White House. The failure of the war in Vietnam and the scandal of Watergate combined to have an immediate adverse impact on the presidency. Those events ushered in a post-Watergate era in which subsequent presidents encountered significant new challenges to the scope of their power and found their office constrained by developments that had not been envisaged in F.D.R.'s time. Six such developments particularly constrain Bill Clinton's activist conception of the presidency:

(a) Statutory restrictions on executive power. The resurgence of Congressional authority and assertiveness in the 1970s led to a

series of statutory restrictions on the president's capacity to give direction to government in critical policy areas – areas in which pre-Watergate presidents usually had sufficient discretionary authority or encountered predictable Congressional deference. The best known of these are the War Powers Resolution of 1973 and the Congressional Budget and Impoundment Control Act of 1974, but there are also new statutory limits on presidential authority in the areas of arms control, arms sales, executive agreements, intelligence operations, foreign assistance, and international trade.

These provisions have not always worked as intended, but they have constrained post-Watergate presidents to a greater or lesser degree. At minimum, they force presidents to take note of political feelings in Congress, but they also have the potential to defeat presidents on major issues, or bring them perilously close to defeat. The existence of the War Powers Resolution, for example, forced President Bush, reluctantly, to seek Congressional support for the use of military force in the 1991 Gulf War, which he eventually received – but not without very substantial opposition (42 percent of the House and 47 percent of the Senate).

(b) The post-Watergate media. The media have changed quite dramatically as a consequence of the Vietnam War and Watergate, and that in turn has affected the power prospects for post-Watergate presidents. It began with what became labelled as Lyndon Johnson's "credibility gap" and was then compounded by Richard Nixon and the Watergate cover-up. A decade of managed news, deception, witholding of information, and outright lying made the media less reverential towards the presidency, far less willing to accept the word of the White House, and much more aggressive and critical in its reporting and analysis of presidential politics.

The cozier relationship that some pre-Watergate presidents enjoyed with the media has disappeared. It has been replaced by an adversarial relationship in which the White House press corps acts, in the words of one of Washington's most established political journalists, "as a group of contentious voyeurs trying to poke holes in the slick imagery that the President concocts and projects directly to the people through television" (Sidey, 1993). The coverage of what presidents do and say is much more extensive now than it was in the pre-Watergate days and is done more professionally by specialized White House correspondents, an ever-expanding White House press corps, and techniques of reporting that have become infinitely more varied, more visual, and potentially more damaging to contemporary presidents.

(c) The changed presidential nomination process. After its disastrous convention in 1968 and the subsequent loss of the White House, the Democratic Party changed the way in which it would nominate its future presidential candidates. Those changes were complex and their consequences profound (Polsby, 1983; Lengle, 1987). In essence, they opened up the nomination process (for both parties) and transferred the choice of party candidate from party leaders and elected officials to an amorphous mass of primary-election voters. They enabled outsiders, like George McGovern and Jimmy Carter, to contest and win their party's presidential nomination irrespective of the wishes of the party leaders whose role in the nomination process was considerably reduced. The effects of those changes were reinforced by the enactment in 1974 of major reforms in the financing of presidential campaigns, especially the public funding provisions which, in effect, democratized campaign funding and allowed outsider candidates a much better chance of accumulating the financial resources necessary to win their party's nomination. These developments have weakened that vital linkage between candidate and party, the consequences of which can be felt once the candidate becomes president and needs strong ties with party elites, particularly those in Congress.

(d) The budget deficit. Fiscal year 1969, which coincided with Richard Nixon's accession to the White House, was the last in which the budget of the United States was in surplus (approximately $3.2 billion). Since then, American citizens have had to live with a budget deficit that has grown at a staggering rate, especially during the Reagan–Bush era, and is the number one policy problem facing President Clinton. The anticipated budget deficit for 1993 of $332 billion is a very substantial restraint on an activist president who believes that government has a role in solving serious economic and social problems in the United States. Budget deficits of the current magnitude virtually rule out new federal spending and make cuts in existing expenditure a high priority for president and Congress.

(e) The legacy of divided government and Congressional reform. In only four of the 24 years between the elections of Richard Nixon and Bill Clinton have the presidency and both houses of Congress

been controlled by the same party. Thus, for 83 percent of the time during this period Americans have lived with "divided government." Political scientists have been arguing extensively about the causes and consequences of electing a president from one party and a Congressional majority from the other (Jacobson, 1990; Cox and Kernell, 1991; Thurber, 1991; Mayhew, 1991; Fiorina, 1992), and those debates are unlikely to be rendered moot by the fact that the 1992 elections produced "unified government" under the Democratic Party. Although, at this stage, there is no way of telling whether the Clinton victory has closed the most recent era of divided government or if it is merely a temporary deviation, concern about divided government continues to be highly relevant because of the legacy that such a lengthy period of institutional conflict has left, particularly for a Democratic presidency.

Until President Clinton's election, the Democratic majority in Congress had gone 12 years without having to deal with a Democratic president. Prior to that, there were four years of unified Democratic government under President Carter, whose relations with his own party in Congress were so tense and distant (Jones, 1988) that the Democratic majority got little practice in following the leadership of a Democratic president. One needs to go back to Lyndon Johnson's presidency to find the most recent example of unified Democratic government, where the Congressional majority was used to supporting presidential leadership. Unfortunately, from President Clinton's point of view, only 21 of the 258 House Democrats (8.1 percent) elected to the 103rd Congress served in the House during Johnson's presidency. Similarly, only five of the current 56 Democratic senators (8.9 percent) were there during the Lyndon Johnson years. The plain fact is that most of the current Democratic members of Congress have no experience of being led by a Democratic president.

Many of the current members of Congress, however, do have extensive experience of the institutional conflict that accompanies a sustained period of divided government, and this inevitably conditions the behaviour of legislators and how they deal with the administration (Cox and Kernell, 1991). Under divided government, leaders of the congressional majority are not obliged to expedite the president's program, powerful committee and sub-committee chairmen have a freer hand in shaping the policy agenda than they would when their own party occupies the presidency, and invididual members face even fewer problems in advancing constituency interests over national interests. Moreover, there is no guarantee that entrenched patterns of legislative behaviour will change merely because divided government becomes unified government overnight. Indeed, one of the major constraints facing President Clinton could well be the reluctance of the Democratic majority in Congress to relinquish the power, independence, and legislative freedom it enjoyed during the 12-year era of divided government when Presidents Reagan and Bush occupied the White House.

This era also coincided with the effects of the Congressional reform movement initiated by the post-Watergate freshmen class of 1974. In their revolt against seniority, Democratic reformers succeeded in dispersing power through the sub-committee structure and the revived party caucus. While presidents encountered difficulties in dealing with the entrenched oligarchy that ran Congress before the reforms took effect, the reformers made the president's task harder by weakening party leadership and increasing substantially the number of independent power centres in Congress. The Congressional barons are now more numerous than ever.

(f) The new world order. The collapse of communism in eastern Europe and the dismantling of the Soviet Union will have many repercussions for American politics and are likely to affect the presidency in two ways. First and foremost, they present an enormous policy challenge to the occupant of the White House to redefine the fundamental tenets of America's world role after almost half a century of remarkably stable and consistent foreign policy, in which the national interest was clear, broadly understood, and widely accepted. Bill Clinton defeated George Bush in "the last Cold War election" (Sigal, 1992–3), but, as the victor, he is now faced with the immensely difficult problem of giving some meaning and substance to that hitherto vacuous phrase invented by his predecessor, "the new world order."

The end of the Cold War also affects the presidency in an institutional sense, because it weakens a vital prop to presidential leadership and dominance in foreign policy, the threat to the security of the United States. For almost half a century, *national security policy*, has been a synonym for *foreign policy* and so much of what the United States has done in the field of international relations in the postwar years has been justified in terms of the threat of Soviet expansionism and the spread of communism.

That threat was also the justification for a lengthy period of presidential supremacy in foreign policymaking, during which time the president assumed leadership and Congress dutifully followed – a *modus operandi* that lasted until the late 1960s when the Vietnam War began to go wrong for the United States, and Congress began to lose faith in the idea that the president knew best. Since then, Congress has been, in the words of Richard Rose, "an awkward ally" of the president in foreign policymaking. "As congressional distrust of White House integrity has risen," notes Rose, "Congress is less and less willing to give unquestioning support to the President" (Rose, 1991).

During the post-Watergate years, there have been significant foreign policy differences between president and Congress, over Cyprus, Angola, Nicaragua, arms sales to Saudi Arabia, and the Gulf War, to name but a few (Mann, 1990), but the end of the Cold War and the declining threat to America's national security will probably encourage even more debate and more disputation over the direction of foreign policy. With U.S. interests less clearly defined, and the "new world order" more likely to revolve around international economics and trade rather than ideological conflict and the risk of nuclear war, presidents could well encounter greater difficulty in mobilizing support and exercising what the United States Supreme Court once unfortunately called "the very delicate, plenary and exclusive power of the President as the sole organ of the federal government in the field of international relations" (*United States* v. *Curtiss-Wright Corporation*, 1936).

The Context of the Clinton Presidency

The election and the mandate

None of F.D.R.'s successors have been able to win elections as convincingly as he did in 1932 and 1936, but all of them hoped to win well enough to create a mandate for their policy proposals and to convince other political elites, especially Congress and the media, that public opinion stands firmly behind the new leader. In this respect, President Clinton cannot take a great deal of satisfaction from the 1992 election results. In a three-way race, he won with just 43.3 percent of the vote, while his party suffered a net loss of ten House seats in the Congressional contests. And in only four of the 258 Congressional districts won by Democrats did Clinton gain a higher share of the vote than the winning House candidate (Cohen, 1993). This came at the end of a campaign during which serious doubts were raised about Clinton's trustworthiness and suitability for office, doubts that he was unable to dispel by election day and which ultimately clouded his victory (see Ladd, 1993). Moreover, voter dissatisfaction with the two major-party nominees resulted in a massive protest vote for an eccentric independent candidate, who withdrew from the race in July in slightly bizarre circumstances and then reentered in October. Ross Perot's 19 percent share of the vote was the second largest ever obtained by a non-major party candidate in U.S. presidential elections.

It should be noted that Bill Clinton was not the only president elected on a minority vote, nor is his 43 percent share of the vote the worst on record. Woodrow Wilson in 1912 and Abraham Lincoln in 1860 obtained an even smaller share of the vote and both, of course, had considerable accomplishments as president. Clinton's prospects will, as Everett Ladd has argued, be primarily by what he does in the White House rather than how he performed in the election (Ladd, 1993) but nevertheless one finds no resounding message of support in the 1992 election results, and there is not much in the nature of his victory to persuade Congress, the media, or the American public that this is a president who must have support to do whatever he thinks appropriate.

Analysts will argue about the meaning of the 1992 election, but some already see it as a classic case of retrospective voting. As Kathleen Frankovic has put it: "It was a referendum on the incumbent President – and George Bush lost" (1992). The problem for Bill Clinton then is how to claim a positive mandate from an election outcome that was essentially negative, in the sense of being a rejection of the previous president rather than an endorsement of the new one. If any mandate can be derived from election results, President Clinton's is a very ill-defined one and does little to ease his leadership problems.

Those problems stem from the fact that Bill Clinton presented himself as a leader who wanted to take America in a new direction. He campaigned strongly on the theme of change. He wanted to change the direction of public policy (away from the deadlock, drift, neglect, and mismanagement of the Reagan–Bush years). He wanted to change the direction of the Democratic Party (away from New Deal liberalism with its emphasis on big government and big spending). He wanted to change the politics of government in Washington so that "power and privilege no longer shout down the voice of the people," as he said in his inaugural address. Clinton's rhetoric, more than anything else, made change the theme of the 1992 election, but neither the rhetoric, nor the outcome of the election, were sufficient conditions for change, contrary to the exaggerated claims the new president made shortly after taking the oath of office. "The American people have summoned the change we celebrate today," he asserted in his inaugural speech. "You have raised your voices in an unmistakable chorus . . . you have changed the face of Congress, the presidency and the political process itself." Even allowing for the hyperbole that is now a staple ingredient of presidential inaugural addresses, there was little evidence to support Clinton's view that the American public had mandated sweeping change, or that the chorus was "unmistakable." The election turned on the economic performance of the Bush administration. The change that the voters summoned was the replacement of one manager of the economy with another. Beyond that, the message was not at all clear. All three candidates offered much the same: reductions in the budget deficit, reductions in public expenditure, and reductions in taxation. In the last week of the election campaign, survey evidence showed that almost as many voters thought Ross Perot was as well able to handle the economy as was Bill Clinton (Frankovic, 1993). At best, the 1992 election campaign identified the major problems. Specific solutions to those problems had been less well-defined and, in the longer term, that would create challenges for President Clinton. In government, he would have to move beyond his broad call for change to the much more difficult task of mobilizing public support for specific policy changes.

The policy agenda

Those policy changes were outlined by President Clinton in a speech to Congress just four weeks after his inauguration. It was an ambitious program, many aspects of which were likely to

encounter strong opposition from powerful interest groups or
from within Congress itself. At the core of Clinton's economic
policy was a plan to reduce the budget deficit by $500 billion over
four years through a combination of personal and corporate tax
increases and cuts in government expenditure. This was linked with
an economic stimulus package designed to reflate the economy by
"investing" (the new Democrat word for "spending") £30 billion to
create new jobs. In the same speech, President Clinton also
promised major reform of the health care system, welfare reform,
campaign finance reform, tougher regulation of lobbying, and a
national service program to enable students to pay back college
loans.

The difference between President Clinton and his two predecessors was summed up on one sentence in his speech to Congress. Just
a few minutes into his speech, President Clinton told his audience:
"Tonight I want to talk to you about what Government can do
because I believe Government must do more". Such views were
heresy during the Reagan–Bush years when the rhetoric of both
presidents emphasized their desire to get government off the backs
of the people and their belief that government itself was the
problem not the solution. Bill Clinton, on the other hand, believes
in government intervention, especially when major changes in
direction are called for, but his belief runs up against a polity that
has absorbed the Reagan–Bush rhetoric and become increasingly,
but selectively, suspicious of government activity and intervention,
particularly when it costs money. That suspicion has found a
comfortable home within the Republican Party and among the
more conservative members of the Democratic Party, reinforced, of
course, by the overriding need to reduce the huge budget deficit
which was, in large measure, a product of the Reagan–Bush years.

Leadership style

Given the weakness of President Clinton's electoral mandate, the
complete absence of any coat-tails effect in Congress, and the
difficulty of mobilizing support for his policy proposals, the
context of his presidency will, in large part, be shaped by his
conception of the presidency and his basic approach to governing
– or what, for want of a better term, might be called his leadership
style.

"A president ought to be a powerful force for progress," candidate Clinton told the Democratic national convention in accepting his party's nomination in July 1992. His commitment to change was a commitment to leadership, to do what all chief executives must do – give direction to government. However, post-Watergate presidents operate within a political environment that is structurally and culturally resistant to direction and leadership, and it will be interesting to see how far President Clinton's desire to lead is tempered by the structural and cultural impediments to leadership that he faces in Washington and beyond.

In many respects, President Clinton's leadership style is well-suited to the conditions he has inherited. During his pre-presidential years, as Governor of Arkansas, he acquired a reputation for being a conciliator and compromiser, a searcher for consensus. According to a profile of the presidential candidate published in the *New York Times* early in the 1992 election campaign, Clinton's conciliatory approach was fixed by his shock defeat in 1980 after one term as governor. When he returned to the same office in 1982, "the young Governor had discovered the dangers of pushing through an agenda ahead of public opinion and the risks of fighting the state's business establishment. As a result, he became much more sensitive to the vagaries of public opinion and much more adept in the art of accommodation." The article went on to note that, "Mr. Clinton's devotion to consensus has assumed near-legendary proportions in Little Rock" (Kolbert, 1992).

The Clinton leadership style is pragmatic, reflecting not only his personal predisposition, but also the recognition that post-Watergate presidents do not have a big stick to wield, save in the most exceptional circumstances, and cannot expect automatic support on all issues, even major ones. Inevitably, there will be occasions when the President, however reluctantly, must concede something in order to gain anything and there will be instances where direction will have to give way to acquiescence. On the other hand, there is some incongruence between being committed to major political change and a leadership style that seeks conciliation, compromise, and consensus, particularly so when the President faces such a fragmented, independent and leaderless Congress, a powerful special interest group system, an ultra-critical mass media, and fickle public opinion. So much of President Clinton's program will require a shift in direction from Congress and, to a large extent, the people it represents, that one might reasonably ask whether his commitment to change can be realized if he is so predisposed to compromise and conciliation with the very forces that must be overcome if the promise is to be translated into specific new policies and laws.

The Clinton Presidency: Problems and Prospects

President Clinton's early period in office provided a sharp lesson in the differences between calling for change in general terms and mobilizing support for specific policy changes. Almost immediately, the new President began to experience the constraints imposed by the post-Watergate presidency. Even before he had taken the oath of office he was forced to back away from his campaign promise of a middle-class tax cut because of alarming budget deficit projections. Then, in his first week in office, implacable opposition from a senior member of his own party in the Senate turned a minor campaign promise to rescind the ban against homosexuals in the military into a major confrontation and an unwanted crisis for the new administration. The President was forced to delay for six months his plans for ending the ban while a compromise was worked out that would satisfy Senator Nunn. By the first week of February 1993, the media were reporting resistance from House Democrats to the President's plans for reforming campaign finance. Later that month, there were the first indications that Clinton's economic stimulus package was in trouble. House Democrats refused to vote on the new spending proposals until they had first seen the President's deficit reduction plan. Ultimately, this was of little consequence because, in April, the stimulus package was defeated by a Republican filibuster in the Senate. In May, the House eventually passed the President's budget legislation, but it did so by the narrowest of margins (219 votes to 213), with 38 Democrats voting against the Bill, including 11 subcommittee chairmen, and not a single Republican vote cast in support. When the Bill went before the Senate in June, the proposed new energy tax, a major element of the President's deficit reduction package, was eliminated in the Finance Committee and the fate of the Bill on the floor of the Senate, minus the energy tax, ultimately depended on the casting vote of the Vice President, as did the final vote on the Bill in July.

The President also encountered opposition over foreign policy. When in April 1993 he indicated his desire for a tougher U.S. position on Bosnia, and possible military involvement in the form of air-strikes against the Bosnian Serb forces, the suggestion brought warnings from many members of Congress that such action might not be supported on Capitol Hill. It was enough to force President Clinton into a retreat. Limits to partisan loyalty, statutory restraints on presidential war-making powers, and confusion about U.S. interests in the post-Cold War era were among the reasons advanced to explain the Congressional opposition (see Doherty, 1993).

President Clinton's early difficulties were compounded by a hostile media and several errors of judgment on his part which played into the hands of the White House press corps. The troubles began in January, when it was revealed that the President's nominee for the post of Attorney General had broken the law by hiring an illegal alien as a domestic worker, and peaked in May, when the President decided to have a $200 haircut in Air Force One while it was sitting on the tarmac at Los Angeles airport supposedly tying-up air-traffic for an hour. Other embarrassments included the unjustified dismissal of staff in the White House travel office, the withdrawal of the President's nominee, Lani Guinier, to head the Civil Rights Division of the Justice Department after he had belatedly read and disagreed with her publications in law journals, and the clumsy selection process for a candidate to fill a vacancy on the Supreme Court. President Clinton was criticised for too much compromising, for faulty White House staff work, for being out of touch with the people who elected him, for poor judgment, indecisiveness, and incompetence. To make matters worse, he had to face the doom-and-gloom media assessments of his first hundred days in office.

These episodes, and others, had a cumulative adverse effect on President Clinton's approval ratings. At the end of February 1993, a Washington Post-A.B.C. News poll showed that 60 percent of respondents approved of the way the President was handling his job. By June, that figure had dropped alarmingly to 43 percent.

The problems encountered by President Clinton during his first six months in the White House may revolve around three critical aspects of the post-Watergate presidency. One presidency may differ from the next – leadership style, election mandates, political circumstances, party strength in Congress, and a host of other factors make Bill Clinton's presidency distinctive – but all post-Watergate presidents are likely to encounter problems with Congress, with the media, and with public opinion, and must necessarily attempt to manage each as best they can. While the ingredients of successful presidential leadership are inevitably elusive, success or failure will, in large measure, turn on how the President copes in each of these arenas.

Managing Congress

For presidents like Bill Clinton who wish to initiate new policies and bring about significant change in American politics, Congress is an obstacle that they have to confront with imperfect and inadequate resources. The impediments to presidential initiative and direction are well known: the weakness of party organization and party leadership in Congress, the relative strength of constituency interest on Congressional voting, the seemingly entrenched pattern of incumbency-protection behavior among members of Congress, and the role of political action committees in Congressional election campaigns that gives special interests a big advantage in manipulating the outcome of legislative battles. They present a formidable problem for any activist president.

What resources does a post-Watergate president have available to overcome these impediments? Mostly, the traditional ones. They can sell their policy initiatives to the public (although it is not always the case that national support for presidential policies translates into pressure on individual members of Congress). They can try to persuade wavering legislators (sometimes arguments on the merits of policy can prevail). They can offer inducements such as patronage, pork-barrel projects, and other government largesse (although there is never enough to satisfy Congressional demand and the enormity of the post-Watergate budget deficit further limits the usefulness of this device). They can cajole, they can plead, and they can compromise (although too much bargaining and compromising is now exploited by the post-Watergate media to cast the president as weak and indecisive).

One also ought to look at party as a resource for presidents in their dealings with Congress, even though party strength in Congress is rarely a useful predictor of support for the president on any given issue and "the decline of party" pervades so much recent analysis of American politics. However, the fact that the current president's party also controls the House and the Senate is significant for Bill Clinton in one important respect. The party in the majority organizes Congress and manages its agenda and, when unified government exists, it is almost always the case that the president's agenda will become the agenda for Congress, even if Congress subsequently treats that agenda harshly. Deference to the president over agenda-setting, which coexists with a post-Watergate resurgence of Congressional independence and fragmentation of Congressional authority, may perhaps be explained in terms of the increasing incapacity of Congress to set its own agenda, but, whatever the cause, it allows the president to set the terms of the argument and, in any political battle, that is a major resource. Indeed, in the longer term, assessments of President Clinton's performance might well focus on his skill in changing the agenda of American politics rather than his wins and losses on key votes in Congress.

Beyond that, party may be marginal to a post-Watergate president. Little can be done to prevent legislators voting against their own president if they are determined to do so, nor can party leaders effect retribution afterwards. Indeed, President Clinton's problem may not just be that party loyalty in Congress is weak, but that after more than a decade of divided government and a "reformed" Congress, attitudes toward leadership are hardening and party loyalty may not even prick the consciences of some members of Congress (Healey, 1993; Merida, 1993).

Of course, not all post-Watergate presidents fit the activist mold. Gerald Ford and George Bush, for example, were conservative presidents primarily concerned with preserving the status quo and resisting changes initiated by Congress. For them, there exists a mighty resource in the president's power of veto. During the post-Watergate period, particularly in the period of divided government, the veto has taken on greater significance as "a means of systematic policy control over the legislative branch" (Fisher, 1993). Of the 29 regular vetoes cast by President Bush during his four years in the White House, only one was overridden by Congress.

Managing the media

The adversarial relationship between the president and the media is as old as the presidency itself, and presidential reactions to media reporting have ranged from the private complaints of George Washington to the systematic harassment of journalists by the Nixon administration (Edwards, 1983). The post-Watergate period has been particularly significant, not only because of the effect of the Vietnam War and Watergate on the way the media reported the presidency thereafter, but also because of the high priority, in terms of time, staff resources, and personal effort, given by presidents to counter the ability of the media to mediate between themselves and the public.

Post-Watergate presidents have been innovative in developing strategies and tactics to manage the media. The 1992 presidential election campaign was particularly rich in new approaches, many of which Bill Clinton has already carried forward into his presidency. During the campaign, he skillfully exploited new media opportunities for presidential candidates by bypassing the mainstream political media (specialist political correspondents, television evening news, the "hard news" Sunday morning interviews like N.B.C.'s *Meet the Press* or C.B.S.'s *Face the Nation*) and utilizing more popular media like "chat shows," breakfast television programs where the questioning tended to be softer and the atmosphere less confrontational, audience-participation shows where he could respond to ordinary voters directly, M.T.V. through which he could reach younger voters, and local television stations via satellite link. This strategy gave him access to target audiences through a format where his message was less mediated than it would have been in the more conventional political media. As Philip Meyer (1993) has remarked, "historians of the twenty-first century may well decide that the 1992 campaign marked the time that the diversity in channels of political communication began to approach the diversity of political interests in American society."

A number of these new campaign techniques have been transposed to the White House to allow the president to go over the heads of the Washington press corps directly to the people. The "electronic town meeting," where the president responds to questions from a studio audience at a local television station, has been one favored device. New technologies have also been exploited to strengthen direct communication with the public, such as the installation in the White House of computer electronic mail so that the public can receive copies of presidential statements, speeches, and press releases, and also respond with their comments and opinions.

New technology is likely to lead to new varied White House communications strategies, although, whatever the means, the purpose will always be to reduce the risks of mediation by "inside-the-Beltway" journalists, analysts and pundits. Clinton's "talk-show presidency" (Kurtz, 1993) quickly disturbed the Washington press corps, which responded with a barrage of ultra-critical reporting during what was traditionally the President's honeymoon period. President Clinton's staff exacerbated matters by their open hosility to the traditional media and by an unwise decision to restrict the access of accredited White House reporters to the Press Secretary's office. By May of 1993, the media's war with the Clinton presidency had become a major media story itself, and the President was forced to take steps to improve the relationship, which included replacing the White House Director of Communications. However, even correctives like these are unlikely to change the fundamental nature of the President's relationship with the media. It is inherently an adversarial one, although with endless scope for new forms of adversity.

Managing public opinion

More than 30 years ago, Richard Neustadt highlighted the immense importance of public prestige to a president's power prospects. Along with professional reputation, wrote Neustadt, "the prevalent impression of a President's public standing tends to set a tone and to define the limits of what Washingtonians do for him or do to him" (Neustadt, 1990). Managing public opinion thus figures prominently in the activity of post-Watergate presidents, but it is as difficult a task as managing the Congress and managing the media. The way the public views the president is, according to Neustadt, "actually a jumble of imprecise impressions held by relatively inattentive people," but the ever-increasing number of opinion polls, the simplicity with which they translate "imprecise impressions" into stark percentage figures of approval and disapproval, and the prominence that the media give to poll findings, mean that presidents are never unaware of how they stand with the public.

Inevitably, more and more presidential attention is directed toward activities designed to enhance their public prestige which, they hope, will force politicians in Washington to support their policies. Samuel Kernell has labelled this approach to presidential leadership "going public," a strategy that has now become routine in presidential politics (Kernell, 1986).

The post-Watergate period has coincided with a substantial increase in systematic scholarly research on presidential popularity (Brody, 1991; Edwards, 1983; Kernell, 1986), which, in itself, is partly a response to the increasing importance of public opinion in the conduct of the presidency. "Going public" offers post-Watergate presidents a way around the obstructions they encounter in Washington, but it is a strategy that can have its problems, as President Clinton quickly found out.

One of the problems, like many aspects of the post-Watergate presidency, stems from the legacy of Franklin Roosevelt. A classic, and early example of "going public" was Roosevelt's famous "fireside chats," but the novelty of the public appeal wears off when it is used too often, and today there is little that is novel in a president appearing on television. So much so, that when President Clinton decided, in mid-June of 1993, to hold his first televised prime-time press conference, two of the three major television networks refused to broadcast it and the third cut off his broadcast after 30 minutes. It was Clinton's intention to use the press conference to counter a run of negative media reporting and an alarming decline in his public popularity by focussing on the successes of his administration, but media executives made a prior judgment that there would be little news value in anything the President said (Ifill, 1993), and there was not much the President could do about that. Not only did the media defeat the President's purpose by not screening the event, but the good news message was lost in the press the following day when many newspapers focussed instead on the story that the President had been spurned by the media.

There are other pitfalls with a "going public" strategy, especially when a President's performance ratings are declining. The risk is that presidential policies and actions are interpreted primarily as public relations exercises designed to boost presidential popularity.

For example, two days after President Clinton's decision to order a missile attack on Iraq's intelligence headquarters in late June 1993 in retaliation against the Iraqi attempt to assassinate former President Bush, a *New York Times* editorial questioned whether the missile attack was "intended to divert public opinion and bolster support for the President" (*New York Times*, 1993b).

President Clinton also found out that "going public" successes may not last very long. A two-hour nationally televised program, in which the President responded to questions from an audience of children, was seen as a public relations triumph. It coincided with a highpoint in his performance ratings, which began to slide just a few weeks later when other events began to have a counter-effect on public opinion.

Presidential attempts to manage public opinion and increase their popularity have met with varying success. Ultimately, however, one stark fact stands out. All post-Watergate presidents have left the White House with their public popularity lower than when they entered it.

Institutional support

The input of the president's staff can be particularly important in creating the conditions that make the Congress, the media, and public opinion respond positively to presidential leadership. Indeed, the growth of White House staff activity in these "liaison" or "outreach" functions has been a noticeable feature of the post-Watergate presidency. The president's institutional staff support, itself another legacy of F.D.R. (Hart, 1987), has given presidents the capacity to do things they could not possibly do on their own and, in the absence of the kind of leadership conditions that F.D.R. enjoyed, the staff is an even more vital resource to post-Watergate presidents than it was to F.D.R.

Contrary to the hopes of many critics (Hart, 1987), the power of the presidential staff has not been curbed in the wake of Watergate and the Iran-Contra affair. Bill Clinton, like all the post-Watergate presidents, has continued to centralize policymaking responsibilities in the White House with, in most cases, departmental secretaries playing a supporting role, and has expanded the capacity of the "outreach" staff units (Congressional relations, press, communications, public liaison, political affairs, intergovernmental affairs) to develop and implement the administration's public relations strategy. However, as the presidential staff has grown in size and become more specialized in its work, so too has the capacity of the staff to damage, rather than enhance, the power prospects of the president.

Aside from the disasters of Watergate and Iran-Contra, both directly attributable to the abuse of White House staff power, all post-Watergate presidents have experienced problems with their staff to a greater or lesser degree, usually in the form of senior White House staff antagonizing the very presidential constituencies they were meant to win over. Thus, while depending on their "outreach" staff to help win support for their policies and goals, post-Watergate presidents also need to be particularly alert to what seems to be a propensity for staff to magnify the president's problems with key presidential constituencies. In this respect, President Clinton moved quickly, and certainly faster than some of his predecessors, in correcting early and damaging staffing problems.

There is little reason to expect any significant change in the role of the White House staff in the 1990s. The centralization of power in the White House is well entrenched now, and strongly encouraged by post-Watergate presidents themselves. There is more uncertainty about the capacity of the staff system to help or hinder a president in the future, but the record to date is not good and one recent analysis of the institutional presidency has questioned the capacity of presidents to manage their staff. As John Burke has shown, effective staff organization and management is just as complex and difficult as the president's other major tasks (Burke, 1992).

The Post-Watergate Presidency and Presidential Leadership

The post-Watergate presidency is not in every respect different from the pre-Watergate presidency. President Nixon's predecessors were also constrained and limited in what they could do, and even strong presidents, like Franklin D. Roosevelt and Lyndon Johnson suffered defeats in Congress, were criticized by the media, and saw their popularity ratings decline. What changed in the post-Watergate era were the nature of the constraints and the degree of difficulty in surmounting them. Presidential leadership is a more daunting task now. The leadership skills required of contemporary presidents seem to be more intangible and elusive, and the resources for leadership vary according to changing conditions and circumstances. Presidential leadership is altogether less predictable.

Political scientists who study the presidency are more skeptical about the possibilities for presidential leadership than they were even a decade ago, and also quite pessimistic about the potential for presidential success. "Presidents must largely play with the hands that the public deals them," says George Edwards. "They are rarely in a position to augment substantially their resources. They operate at the margins as facilitators rather than as directors of change" (Edwards, 1989). Richard Rose has identified a "no-win theory" of the presidency emerging in some of the current literature (1991), and Aaron Wildavsky (1991) entitled a collection of essays *The Beleaguered Presidency*.

Although political scientists are moving away from heroic-leadership models of presidential power and from what Mark Peterson (1990) has called "the presidency-centered perspective" on American politics, public expectations about the president's ability to lead and give direction to government are still rooted in a previous age, seemingly fixed by the legacy of Franklin D. Roosevelt. Presidents are expected to solve the nation's problems and are held accountable when they do not. As Jon Bond and Richard Fleisher (1990) have pointed out, voters have rejected the incumbent president or his party in five of ten elections between 1952 and 1988 (six of eleven if one includes 1992), yet in Congressional elections they consistently reelect incumbents at an average rate of 90 percent. Such high expectations, fed by media reporting of the presidency of the kind mentioned at the beginning of this chapter, persist notwithstanding evidence showing that the public also recognizes that the president's job is now much more difficult than it was and that the media is more critical of presidents than ever before (Edwards, 1983). This may well be the biggest anomaly of the post-Watergate presidency. It adds to a president's leadership difficulties and compounds the problem by encouraging those who aspire to the presidency to satisfy high expectations by promising more than is realistically attainable and then suffering media criticism and decline in popularity when those expectations are not met. The post-Watergate president's lot is not a happy one.

7

Congress in Crisis . . . Once Again

ROGER H. DAVIDSON

"Americans are especially fond of running down their congress-men," observed Lord Bryce in the nineteenth century. Political pundits and humorists have always singled out Congress for special attention, finding in its foibles ample material for ridicule. Serious critics, mainly scholars and journalists, fault Congress for its disorder, inertia, and corruption. Journalists zestily take members of Congress to task for their perquisites, their junkets, their money-grabbing, and even their sexual exploits. Legislators themselves often promote Congress's shabby public image by posing to constituents as gallant warriors contending against its evils: such legislators "run for Congress by running against Congress" (Fenno, 1978).

In the 1990s, public unrest erupted into what can only be interpreted as a crisis of governance. One member of Congress called it a massive "civic temper tantrum." Few institutions escaped public criticism. A little more than a year after concluding the Gulf War in an orgy of national pride, President George Bush was turned out of office; successor Bill Clinton's public-opinion "honeymoon" hardly survived the wedding night, amd his job rating remained perilously low. Yet of all public institutions, Congress seemed to bear the largest share of public scorn. By spring 1992, only 17 percent of those questioned in a national survey approved of the way Congress was doing its job, whereas 54 percent approved of their own representative's performance. Both figures were all-time lows (Morin and Dewar, 1992). This exceeded the usual level of Congress bashing, and was reminiscent of the intense public unrest and reformism that marked the late 1960s and early 1970s. It reflected not only disgust at scandals and distrust of politicians, but also a growing feeling that the government was working poorly and that the nation itself had strayed off course.

Governing elites reacted with panic and confusion. In such a hostile atmosphere, Congress was unable to counter demands for reform coming from all directions. Scandals forced the House of Representatives to close its "bank" (payroll office) and reorganize its administrative arrangements. A new Joint Committee on the Organization of Congress was launched. Lobby-control laws were passed, and campaign finance Bills were seriously debated. Procedures for handling ethics complaints were reexamined. A staff compilation in September 1992 described 184 proposals that had been advanced in 11 different categories (U.S. Congress, 1993). Some of these suggestions were well worth considering. Others, mainly cosmetic, failed to address the underlying problems. Still others – including some of the most heavily publicized ones – threatened to emasculate Congress's constitutional prerogatives.

Sources of Crisis

The surface causes of public unrest were not hard to discern. Economic stagnation – manifested in miniscule growth and widely reported job layoffs – lay close to the heart of the discontent. Fissures in the social fabric – racial, ethnic, religious, even sexual – contributed to a new suspicion that the nation had become uncontrollable and perhaps ungovernable. The end of the Cold War brought only fleeting satisfaction: losing the menace of the Soviet's "evil empire" also meant losing a certain spirit of purpose and unity.

The crisis of the 1990s was peculiar, however, in its apparent absence of any coherent political, partisan, factional, or even institutional agenda. Weariness and frustration caused by 12 years of divided party control of the White House and Congress were targeted by many critics: "gridlock in Washington" became a popular soundbite during the 1992 elections. However, American voters have become notorious ticket-splitters with mounting disregard of party labels, and although the 1992 elections left the Democrats in charge of the two branches, the result was hardly a mandate for party government.

To be sure, complaints about Congress's structures and procedures were numerous, and compelling arguments were advanced for revision and realignment: nearly 20 years had elapsed, after all, since the last wave of structural innovations. House Republicans in particular had a lengthy wish list of proposals. The co-sponsors of the Joint Committee on the Organization of Congress cited overstaffing, committee overlaps, budget strife, breakdowns in communication between the chambers and between the branches, lack of policy integration, and too much partisanship. Yet, unlike past reformist eras, consensus was lacking concerning the preferred direction of change.

Equally unclear was the extent to which organizational defects had caused, or contributed to, the current discontent. Representative Lee Hamilton, D-Ind., noted that "Congress increasingly seems bogged down and unable to tackle the main issues that Americans are concerned about – from jobs and crime to health care reform" (U.S. House of Representatives, 1992). Few would disagree with that judgment, but faulty organization is at best an accessory rather than a root cause of policy stalemate.

Whatever the professional assessment of reformism, the agitated general public seemingly wanted change at all costs: they demanded, "Don't just stand there, do something!" Congress receives low marks from the public at large. Public approval of the institution rises or falls with economic conditions, wars and crises, scandals, and waves of satisfaction or cynicism. Congressional approval also often parallels public approval of presidents. Although extensively reported in the media, Congress is poorly understood by the average citizen. Partly to blame are the size and complexity of the institution, not to mention the twists and turns of the legislative process. Despite the presence of a large press corps containing some of the capital's most able journalists, neither the reporters nor their editors and producers can convey in the mass media the internal subtleties or the external pressures that shape lawmaking.

In contrast to Congress as an institution, most individual senators and representatives are given at least passing marks by their constituents. If voters believe that elected officials as a class are rascals, they do not typically feel that way about their own elected officials, nor have they shown much desire to "throw the rascals out."

This dichotomy is one more reminder of the "two Congresses" phenomenon: its dual character as a collection of locally oriented politicians and as a collective maker of national policy. The tensions produced by this dichotomy are inevitable ingredients of Congress's current crisis.

Congress as Representative: Parochialism and Professionalism

American political thought holds that the legislative branch is uniquely the people's voice. "Here, sir, the people govern," observed Alexander Hamilton – who was himself suspicious of popular institutions. "This body," said a former member of Congress, "is a mirror in which America can see herself." Opinion surveys indicate that citizens expect their representatives to mirror popular wishes and serve local interests. Lawmakers are judged less on policy positions than on their service to their districts or states. How accessible are they? How well do they communicate with voters? Do they help in solving voters' problems? And do they have the ability to "bring home the bacon" in the form of federal contracts, grants, and facilities? "All politics is local" was the dictum of former House Speaker Thomas P. "Tip" O'Neill. Although national tides form the backdrop against which Congressional elections are fought, they are typically won or lost according to local issues, personalities, and campaigning styles. The aggregate of all these contests is a locally based legislature charged with addressing national problems and issues. Selection processes, in short, are part of the pluribus from which the unum must emerge.

Nowhere is localism more evident than in the recruitment of candidates to run for House or Senate seats. Although party organizations are always on the lookout for quality candidates (strategic politicians, as they are called by political scientists), party leaders no longer select and screen candidates as they once did. One freshman representative observed:

> You can look around the floor of the House and see a handful – twenty years ago, you saw a lot of them – today, you can see just a handful of hacks that are put there by the party organization, and there are very, very few of them left. It is just mostly people who went out and took the election (Bibby, 1983).

The vast majority of today's strategically minded politicians launch their own careers, lining up supporters and financial backing with or without local party support. Once common only in suburbs and other areas lacking strong party machinery, self-promotion is now the central attribute of American political careerism. Journalist Alan Ehrenhalt sums it up (1991):

> The skills that work in American politics at this point in history are those of entrepreneurship. At all levels of the political system, from local boards and councils up to and including the presidency, it is unusual for parties to nominate people. People nominate themselves. Of all the inducements for launching a candidacy, the leading one is the likelihood of winning. And this depends primarily on whether the opponent is an incumbent or not (that is, an "open seat").

Constituency outreach

Incumbent legislators fashion distinctive ways of projecting themselves and their records to their constituents – what Richard F. Fenno, Jr., terms "home styles" (Fenno, 1978). The core ingredient of home styles is the image of trust: faith that officeholders are what they claim to be and will do what they promise. Another element is how legislators exploit their resources to explain and defend their performance in the nation's capital.

Home styles are conveyed in various ways: personal appearances, mailings, newsletters, telephone conversations, radio or television spots, and press releases. Indeed, legislators' success may be measured in how they allocate the perquisites of incumbency, including their staff, office, funds, and not least, their own time. One study found that the average representative made 35 trips home each year (not counting recesses) and spent 138 days there (counting recesses). Nearly a third of these representatives returned to their districts every weekend (Parker, 1980).

Staff aides extend senators' and representatives' outreach to their constituents. About 12,000 people serve in members' offices. Senators' staffs range in size from 13 to 71, depending on the state's population; the average is about 36. Representatives' staffs average about 17. Constituent relations are their most time-consuming job. This includes handling casework (requests for assistance), projects, requests for information, press relations, correspondence, and meeting with local voters and lobbyists. From a fourth to a third of these staff members work not in Washington, but in the home districts or states. Members of Congress have from one to six local offices in key home-state locations; more and more casework and voter contacts are handled there.

These constituent services pay off handsomely in support and votes. In a 1990 national survey, 17 percent of all adults reported that they or members of their families had requested help from their representative. Eighty-five percent of them said they were satisfied with the way their requests had been handled; seven out of ten felt the representative would be helpful if asked in the future. "Pork barreling and casework," remarked Morris Fiorina, "are almost pure profit' (Fiorina, 1989).

The "incumbency party"

The most important fact about House and Senate elections is that in most cases incumbents run for reelection and that they usually prevail. Since World War II, on average, 92 percent of all incumbent representatives and 75 percent of incumbent senators running for reelection have been returned to office. In an average election year, 50 to 70 House seats, and sometimes a few Senate seats, are uncontested. (In 1992, there were only 17 uncontested House seats and none in the Senate.) Reelection rates tend to be high and turnover rates low. Short of a major scandal or misstep, it is difficult to topple a House incumbent – and nearly as difficult to dislodge a senator.

In 1992 a dramatic concurrence of factors – economic recession, political unrest, and Capitol Hill scandals – conspired to produce the largest turnover in two generations. Yet even in the anti-incumbent year of 1992, when many challengers were emboldened to try for office, incumbent casualties resulted more from retirements (many involuntary) than from electoral defeats. Seven out of every ten senators and representatives who took the oath of office in January 1993 were returnees from the previous Congress; and the newcomers were not, by and large, amateurs: 72 percent of the House freshmen in 1993 had held prior elective office, compared with 68 percent of the returning members.

Why are incumbents so formidable? For one thing, they enjoy resources for promoting support – through speeches, statements, press coverage, newsletters and mailings, staff assistance, and constituent services. Equally important is money to wage an effective campaign and to scare off potential opponents. The average Senate campaign today costs millions of dollars, and House campaigns cost hundreds of thousands. Million-dollar House contests are not unknown. Nor does the fundraising cease when the ballots have been counted and the election won. Senators and representatives devote an inordinate amount of time and effort begging for money.

The average House member enjoys official perquisites valued at well over a million dollars over a two-year term – with six-year terms, senators have resources between $4 million and $7 million (Dwyer, 1991); and although incumbents need less money than nonincumbent challengers, they receive more from outside sources that view them, rightly enough, as better "investments" than their opponents. Incumbents spend, on average, from two to four times the money that challengers do. In 1992 they captured eight out of every ten dollars given by Political Action Committees (P.A.C.s). Most incumbents, in fact, finish their campaigns with a surplus – money that can be hoarded for future races, flaunted in public in order to scare off potential opponents, or dispersed to needier candidates (sometimes in exchange for support for, say, leadership posts).

What has been termed "incumbency advantage" has raised fears of an entrenched, arrogant cadre of professional legislators. Scandals involving Congressional perquisites have fed these suspicions, as have well-funded right-wing campaigns to limit legislators' terms of office by law or constitutional amendment. (The states, several of which have adopted term-limit plans for their legislators, are presumably forbidden to extend such limits to federal office-holders – a question to be resolved by the courts.)

Despite the built-in advantages enjoyed by professional politicians, one must not exaggerate their causes or consequences. Nonincumbents and even "amateurs" can and do win with good timing and attention to certain guidelines: run for an open seat, or against an official who has lost touch with the electorate, or in a year of voter restlessness. Blame the officeholder for "the mess in

Washington," and be prepared to spend money (even if it's your own) to minimize the incumbent's edge in visibility.

Member turnover remains significant. Even in years when few members are ousted from office by the voters, a goodly number leave Capitol Hill voluntarily – to retire, run for another office, or follow other pursuits. In 1992 a combination of voluntary retirements and electoral defeats brought 14 new senators and 110 new representatives, the highest turnover since 1948. As the 103rd Congress convened, 68 percent of representatives and 48 percent of senators had achieved their posts during the preceding decade. Natural processes of membership renewal, in other words, have by no means halted. Nor is high turnover *per se* – whether by steady increments or by massive partisan realignments – required to make Congress a responsive institution. In fact, representation is the leading task for most lawmakers and their staffs, who devote the bulk of their efforts to cultivating and communicating with their constituents.

Congress as Lawmaker: Organizational Fissures

Almost alone among the world's representative bodies, the U.S. Congress strives also to write its own legislation and monitor the vast governmental apparatus. Its powers, as enumerated in the 1787 Constitution, are undeniably expansive. In modern times, it has protected these powers largely by dividing its workload (into standing committees and sub-committees), by developing strong and subtle leadership mechanisms (largely party-based), and by generously expanding its expert staffs. The committee system dates from the early nineteenth century. So does strong party leadership, although it has recently resurfaced after a prolonged hiatus. The staff apparatus is a post-World War II phenomenon. These innovations have enabled lawmakers to deal with executives on a competitive footing, if not always an equal one.

The committee system

Congress has retained its active legislative role by dividing its workload, delegating to its committees (and even sub-committees) the detailed tasks of writing, revising, and overseeing laws. At first, *ad hoc* committees were designated to write Bills after an issue had been thrashed out on the floor. However, by the third decade of the nineteenth century, sets of permanent (or standing) committees had been created by each House to deal with recurrent topics and recommend legislation to the whole body.

Today, virtually all legislation originates or is shaped by committees and their sub-committees. Most Bills and resolutions that are introduced are automatically referred to the relevant committee having jurisdiction over the matter. Nearly all measures considered on the House or Senate floor have been considered in committee and reported out with a favorable recommendation. It is difficult, particularly in the House of Representatives, to bypass a committee that refuses to report a measure. "Congressional government is committee government," wrote Woodrow Wilson in 1885. "Congress in session is Congress on public exhibition, whilst Congress in its committee-rooms is Congress at work." This contrasts sharply with parliamentary bodies, whose committees are normally weak and whose deliberations center upon the full chamber.

By any standard, the House and Senate committee apparatuses are complicated: the 103rd Congress (1993–5) boasted some 251 formal workgroups – standing, select, special, and joint committees and sub-committees of those bodies. (This does not include seats on party committees or task forces, boards, or commissions of various types.) The Senate had 20 committees, and these in turn had 87 subcommittees; the House had 23 committees with 117 sub-committees. There were also five joint committees (with eight sub-committees) – not to mention the many temporary panels, boards, and commissions. Despite recurrent efforts to streamline the system, the committees display formidable resilience and autonomy.

The most important distinction among standing committees is between authorizing and fiscal committees. Most of the standing committees are the former; they draft the substance of policies (subject, of course, to the chamber's approval) and undertake oversight of executive agencies to ascertain how the policies are being carried out. The appropriations committees draft Bills (again subject to approval) empowering agencies to spend money for programs, while the revenue committees (House Ways and

Means; Senate Finance) draft revenue Bills to pay for the programs. Congress in 1974 erected a complex internal budget process by which it sets guidelines (proposed by House and Senate budget panels) regulating revenues and expenditures that are intended to be followed by all the committees; income and outgo levels are supposed to be brought into balance by reconciliation Bills.

Senators and representatives seek out committee assignments that will further their career goals: reelection, public policy influence, and leverage within the chamber. Especially coveted are seats on the most prestigious committees – those dealing with spending (Appropriations), taxing (House Ways and Means, Senate Finance), internal scheduling (House Rules), and foreign policy (especially Senate Foreign Relations). Individual lawmakers, however, often harbor special goals related to their experiences or electoral needs; farm-belt members gravitate to the Agriculture committees, western-state members to the Interior panels (public lands), and so forth.

Committee assignments are recommended by special panels of the four Congressional parties (that is, House and Senate Democrats and Republicans) and then ratified by the party caucuses. As far as possible, party leaders try to fulfill members' wishes in giving assignments. They pay special attention to the needs of new members and of members from competitive districts, who need help in ensuring their reelection. In filling seats on the top committees, party leaders are often lobbied to honor regional or ideological factions within the party. Under pressure from lawmakers who want as many assignments as possible, the sizes of committees and the numbers of assignments per member has risen in the past generation. There are now some 4,100 seats on Congressional committees and sub-committees. The average senator holds 11 assignments – three to four full committee seats and seven to eight sub-committee seats. The average House member holds a total of six seats – two committee and four sub-committee seats. Committees and sub-committees have become too large for deliberation. The average House committee now has nearly 40 members, the average Senate panel has 18. Even sub-committees have grown in size – to an average of 18 members in the Senate, 13.5 in the House. Once assigned to a committee, members normally have a right to be reappointed and to advance by seniority – that is, according to their terms of uninterrupted service on the committee. This is the celebrated "rule" of seniority, which is neither a rule nor a formal requirement. The seniority system contains conflict by providing for automatic selection of committee leaders, and it fosters professionalism by discouraging transfers from one committee to another. It enhances Congress's independence because it forces presidents to deal with committee leaders whose posts are virtually untouchable. Critics of seniority charge that it squanders the talents and energies of younger legislators by postponing their leadership duties; that it puts leadership in the hands of old and sometimes feeble members; and that it further insulates power within the two houses, making concerted party control very difficult.

Reforms adopted in the 1960s and 1970s chipped away at seniority prerogatives. First, committee rules limit the power of chairmen and provide remedies for curbing arbitrary behavior. Second, the party caucuses ratify all committee assignments, including chairmanships; several chairman have been rejected by their party, precedents that encourage all chairmen to remain responsive to their members' wishes. Leadership posts are now spread quite broadly. In the 103rd Congress (1993–5), majority-party (Democratic) senators held an average of two committee or sub-committee chairmanships; in the House, half of all Democrats served as committee or sub-committee chairmen.

Committees have enormous control over the legislative agenda: nine out of every ten bills that are introduced and referred to a committee go no farther in the legislative process. It is important to observe, moreover, that many committees are unrepresentative of the chambers as a whole. They tend to attract those legislators who are most intensely interested in the committee's subject matter, and those whose background or constituency demands predispose them to favor the policies and programs handled by the panel. This can tilt committee decisionmaking in favor of major programs or clienteles.

The role of committees in relation to their chambers and the political parties has engendered lively scholarly controversy. Three theories have been advanced (Maltzman, 1993). One is the institutionalized logroll perspective, which portrays committees as biased, autonomous units that are able to dominate policy outcomes within their jurisdictions. The committee system is a locus of institutionalized parochialism and logrolling that is rarely overturned in the parent chambers. Second, the chamber-dominated perspective sees committees as primarily agents of the chambers that created them. In their deliberations, committees constantly take into account the full chamber's preferences, aware that the chamber can amend or reject committee reports or, if necessary, abolish or restructure the committees. Finally, the party-dominated perspective views committee members as agents of the party caucuses that selected them. All members benefit from their party's electoral success, which in turn depends on the caucus's ability to articulate and enact a party platform. Thus, the parties appoint loyal members to committees and punish those who ignore their party's demands.

In fact, no two committees work in exactly the same way; "committees differ from one another" (Fenno, 1973). Each has a unique external environment; internally, each is a unique mixture of members, ideologies, and decisionmaking styles. Committees respond to the moods and procedures of the larger chambers. Those dealing with technical subjects have greater leeway than those dealing with subjects of broad popular appeal. Committees differ in the extent to which their jurisdictions must be shared by rival committees. Some committees are arenas for intense interest-group struggles; others are relatively ignored by lobbyists. Some committees deal with aggressive executive-branch agencies; others face weak or divided agencies, or none at all. Many committees or subcommittees have firm alliances with executive agencies and relevant pressure groups, forming one leg of the so-called "iron triangles" or subgovernments that dominate so much of domestic policymaking.

Leadership and management

Given the rampant individualism of American politicians and the well-known weaknesses of their political parties, it may come as a surprise that the parties manage the legislative process in Congress. They organize the two chambers, supply their leaders, shape the legislative agenda, and superintend the scheduling of business. Partisan control, of course, hinges on the size of the parties' ranks in the two bodies. The majority party (at least 51 senators or 218 representatives) organizes the respective houses. The party's size and unity determine how effective its control will be.

Recent political history has given the two parties quite different roles in the two chambers. Democrats have since 1930 controlled the House for all but four years (1947–8, 1953–4), often by lopsided majorities. Accordingly, Democrats maintain a tight grip on the House and its operations; the chamber's rules give the majority leeway to control committee and floor agendas. The frustrated, often bitter, minority Republicans, with slim hopes of taking over, are often reduced to the role of watchdogs and critics. The Senate, however, is a less partisan body. Party margins since the 1980s have been slim, with both parties in the majority at one time or another (Republicans 1981–6; Democrats 1987–90). Individual senators of either party command deference and influence; party members must often "cross the aisle" to forge winning coalitions behind measures.

The House of Representatives has a tradition of vigorous leadership. The Speaker, cited in the Constitution, combines the duties of presiding officer with those of a party leader; historically, forceful Speakers like Henry Clay and Thomas B. "Czar" Reed in the nineteenth century, and Joseph G. "Uncle Joe" Cannon and Sam Rayburn in the twentieth century, bent the unruly chamber to their agendas through procedural skills and the force of their personalities. After the 1910 revolt against Cannon's arbitrary power, the speakership declined and committee leaders moved into the resulting vacuum. A gradual rejuvenation of the office in recent years led to the brief, tumultuous tenure of Jim Wright (1987–9). Wright resigned five months into his second term as Speaker; although charges of unethical behavior precipitated his downfall, it was his intense partisanship and aggressive tactics that emboldened his enemies to attack him. Wright's departure was a personal tragedy, but it was not a repudiation of the strengthened speakership.

In the Senate, strong leadership is the exception rather than the rule. Only in the twentieth century did visible party leaders emerge, and even then they were no match for the powerful House Speakers. The conspicuous exception was Lyndon B. Johnson, who as majority leader (1955–61) worked with the Senate's conservative clique to dominate the chamber as has no leader before or since. Johnson was, as ever, *sui generis*; but his success mirrored the prevailing power structure and the conservative character of the 1950s.

Party committees and functionaries in both chambers perform a range of activities that members find useful. These include:

organizing the party, making committee assignments, scheduling business, collecting and distributing information, promoting members' attendance for important floor votes, maintaining liaison with the president and key executive officials, persuading members to act in accord with party policies, and aiding members and would-be members with campaign advice and fundraising. Members' increasing willingness to have party leaders perform such services is a calculated matter of convenience and self-interest: in today's labyrinthine legislative environment, individual lawmakers find it difficult to attain their objectives without the leaders' good offices. Out of faithful stewardship to the scattered goals of the 100 senators and 435 representatives, party leaders have gathered an impressive array of prerogatives.

Parties are the most stable and significant groups on Capitol Hill. Although party discipline is lax, party loyalty runs deep and is the leading determinant of voting in the two houses. Indeed, party-line voting in Congress was higher in the 1980s than at any time since the 1930s. While party voting remains below the customary standards under parliamentary systems, by U.S. standards the present levels of partisanship are quite remarkable. Elected lawmakers, in fact, are more reliably partisan than their constituents – whose declining party loyalties comprise one of the leading trends in American politics.

Paths to the Present Crisis

In recounting the recent history of Congress, at least three distinct periods, or eras, can be identified. The first was an era dominated by a conservative coalition (roughly 1937–64); the second was an era of liberal activism (1965–78); and the third is an era of contraction, or fiscal restraint (1979 to the present). In the first period, extending roughly from the second Roosevelt administration through the mid-1960s, Congress was dominated by an oligarchy of senior leaders – sometimes called "the barons" or "the old bulls." Whichever party was in power, Congressional leaders overrepresented safe one-party regions and reflected the limited legislative agenda of the bipartisan conservative coalition that controlled so much domestic policymaking. In that period, neither Presidents Franklin Roosevelt (1933–45) nor Harry Truman

(1945–53) made much headway with the domestic agendas; Dwight Eisenhower (1953–61) had only modest legislative demands to make. Few members of today's Congress survive from that bygone era. As memories of this era fade, however, there survive anecdotes and stories, some apochryphal, about the exploits and foibles of the old bulls – among them Speaker Sam Rayburn (D-Tex.), Ways and Means Chairman Wilbur Mills (D-Ark.), Senate G.O.P. Leader Everett M. Dirksen (R-Ill.) and, most of all, Senate Majority Leader Lyndon B. Johnson (D-Tex.).

The cozy domains of the barons were eventually pulled apart by what one commentator has called the "power earthquake" of the 1960s. The boundaries of the reform era are somewhat imprecise. The process of change began in earnest after the 1958 elections, which enlarged the Democrats' ranks by 16 senators and 51 representatives, many of them programmatic liberals. The election results had an immediate impact in both chambers. The reform era reached its climax in the mid-1970s, with a quick succession of changes in committee and floor procedures, and in 1975 the ouster of three of the barons from their committee chairmanships. The underlying cause of the upheaval was a series of unmet policy demands pushed by urban and suburban voting blocs as well as minority groups. The spirit of the era was reflected in the popular "movements" that surged into prominence: civil rights, environmentalism, anti-war, and consumerism. Proximate causes included reapportionment and redistricting, widened citizen participation, social upheaval, and technological innovations in transportation and communications.

Internally, the resulting changes pointed Congress in the direction of a more open, participatory legislative process: more leverage for individual lawmakers, more dispersion of influence among and within the committees. More leaders existed than ever before, and more influence could be exerted by nonleaders. More staff aides were on hand to extend the legislative reach of even the most junior members.

The reform era was an expansionary time in terms of Congress's workload. It was the era of "The New Frontier" and "The Great Society," witnessing a host of landmark enactments in civil rights, education, medical insurance, employment and training, science and space, consumer protection, and the environment – not to mention five new cabinet departments and four constitutional amendments. Legislative activity soared in those years by whatever measure one chooses to apply – Bills introduced, hearings, reports, hours in session, floor amendments, recorded floor votes, and laws passed. The processing of freestanding Bills and resolutions became the centerpiece of committee and sub-committee work.

In recent years, Congress again faces an environment that departs in significant ways from that of previous eras. The advent of what economist Lester Thurow calls the "zero-sum society" no doubt lies at the root of the changed political atmosphere. A sluggish economy combined with a costly and relatively impervious system of entitlements and, after 1981, tax cuts and program reallocations, turned the "fiscal dividends" of the postwar era into today's "structural deficits." Meanwhile, it became intellectually fashionable to repudiate the notion that governmental intervention could solve all manner of economic and social ills. Disenchantment with the results of 1960s and 1970s government programs, many of which had been shamelessly oversold to glean support for their enactment, led to widespread demands for a statutory ceasefire: divestiture, deregulation, privatization, and delegation to states and localities.

The advent of zero-sum politics is popularly associated with the administration of Ronald Reagan, who took office in 1981 with the pledge of cutting taxes and domestic aid and welfare programs. Reagan's election was, to be sure, interpreted at the time as a sea change in American politics; certain of Reagan's policies – especially the 1981 revenue cuts and the repeated threats to veto new domestic spending – contributed to the constriction of the legislative agenda. However, deteriorating economic conditions and shifting attitudes had already propelled President Carter in some (though not all) of these policy directions by 1979–80 (the 96th Congress). The altered environment had already produced a dramatic decline in legislative workload. Had Carter been reelected in 1980, it is probable that he, and Congress, would have travelled farther along the road toward zero-sum politics.

In the 1980s, the president and Congress became fixated on resolving fiscal and revenue issues, rather than designing new programs or establishing new agencies in response to constituent needs. In the domestic realm, the emphasis was on reviewing, adjusting, refining, or cutting back on existing programs. "There's not a whole lot of money for any kind of new programs," remarked Senator Thad Cochran (R-Miss.), "so we're holding oversight hearings on old programs ... which may not be all that bad an idea." Accordingly, individual members were less tempted to put forward their ideas as free-standing Bills or resolutions. Such new ideas as were saleable were more apt to be conveyed in amendments to large-scale legislative vehicles: re-authorizations, continuing appropriations, debt limits, or reconciliation Bills.

The 1980s environment reversed the previous era's liberal activism. Government revenues were curtailed by lagging economic productivity, exaggerated after 1981 by tax cuts and program reallocations. Few new programs were launched, and few domestic programs were awarded added funding. Although the public continued to expect Congress to take action to solve problems, there was vocal sentiment for cutting back "big government" and reducing public-sector deficits. Faith in governmental activism plummeted in the wake of criticisms of waste and ineffectiveness in government.

The results of what some observers call "cut-back politics" serve to define the characteristics of the post-reform Congress: (1) Fewer Bills are sponsored by individual senators and representatives. (2) Key policy decisions are packaged into huge "mega-Bills," permitting lawmakers to combine their initiatives and escape adverse reactions to individual provisions. (3) Techniques of "blame avoidance" are employed to protect lawmakers from adverse effects of cutback policies. (4) Non-controversial "commemorative" resolutions are passed into law – nearly half of all laws produced by recent Congresses. (5) Driven by budgetary concerns, party-line voting is at or near a modern-day high on Capitol Hill. (6) Leadership in the House and Senate is markedly stronger now than at any time since 1910. Today's leaders benefit not only from powers conferred by reform-era innovations of the 1960s and 1970s; they also respond to widespread expectations that they are the only people who can, and should, untangle the legislative schedule.

Conclusion: The Two Congresses Problem

The conflict between members' local constituency bases and Capitol Hill's centralizing institutions reemphasizes the duality of

Congress's role. The two Congresses problem manifests itself in public perceptions and assessments: citizens look at the Congress in Washington through different lenses from those with which they view their individual senators and representatives. Citizens regard their own legislators as agents of personal or localized interests. The institutional Congress is viewed as a lawmaking instrument and judged primarily on the basis of citizens' overall attitudes about politics and the state of the nation. The same dualism appears in media coverage: Congress is covered by independent-minded reporters for national media outlets, whereas individual members get more of a free ride from understaffed local media.

Congress struggles to maintain its prerogatives by crafting its own legislation and monitoring the governmental apparatus, yet many people question whether, realistically, Congress can retain meaningful control given the complex, interdependent character of current problems.

Moreover, members' pervasive parochialism militates against the coherent resolution of pressing issues, much less anticipation of future problems. Nor is unified party control the answer to the problem. President Clinton and his Democratic majority on Capitol Hill struggled to prove that they could govern, but parochial interests rendered that majority illusory. The President's initial budget, bent out of shape by compromises, passed by a whisker in the two chambers; and other issues, like health care and the North American Free Trade Agreement (N.A.F.T.A.), left the President's party even more divided. More than party control of the two branches, the underlying dualism of Congress – buttressed by ubiquitous interest-group activity – is the real source of "gridlock" in U.S. public life.

8

The Supreme Court and the Constitution

GILLIAN PEELE

The Supreme Court has an ambiguous relationship with the wider American political system. On the one hand, its power to interpret the constitution places it above the routine political fray. On the other hand, the Supreme Court's decisionmaking , and indeed the whole of the legal system, is suffused with political controversy. Appointments to the federal courts, especially to the Supreme Court, the character of the Supreme Court's docket, the jurisprudence of the court, and the administration of justice are all areas where the law and politics meet.

The extensive political powers of the courts in the United States – and most notably the power of the Supreme Court to review Congressional legislation – also raise difficult questions for democratic theory and administrative practice. Some of these questions concern the legitimacy of the Supreme Court's role. By what right do nine non-elected, non-accountable, justices set aside the preferences of elected officials and develop public policy in ways that reflect their own ideologies and values? How far in dealing with conflicts that have reached the courts should judges pay attention to public opinion, whether expressed through the election returns, so beloved of Mr. Dooley, or through the opinion polls? What notice should the Court take of the position of the other branches of federal government – of presidential policy and of legislative intent?

Other questions concern the competence of the courts to shape an ever-expanding area of public policy. To what extent are judicial proceedings appropriate for determining social policy? Have judges the expertise to weigh expert evidence on the merits of rival school districting or electoral redistricting plans? How should the courts weigh scientific evidence? – a question recently before the Court in *Daubert* v. *Merrell Dow* (1993). Are the courts capable of supervising the implementation of the policies they mandate? Is the judicial decision, couched as it is in the language of rights, an appropriate vehicle for the expression of policies that need review and reassessment?

These questions have been recurrent ones in American political debate and in scholarly discussion (Horowitz, 1977). The different permutations of political sympathy between the Court, the president and Congress, as well as shifts in the federal-state balance, interact with a changing agenda of constitutional issues to give these questions a perennial interest. Yet the advent of the Clinton presidency focussed renewed attention on the structure of the legal system and the role of the judiciary far beyond that which would normally be expected even in the excitement of a new administration. The election of a Democrat to the White House signalled a break with a period in which Republican Presidents Reagan and Bush had tried systematically to use the judicial system to promote conservative values. This goal had been pursued through a variety of methods, including the appointment of ideologically sympathetic judges, the strategic use of litigation by the Department of Justice, and the promotion of a distinctive theory of constitutional interpretation, based on the doctrine of original intent (Levy, 1988; Schwartz, 1988).

The Republican approach to the courts over the period 1981–92 reflected a more general feeling that the jurisprudence of the Warren Court (1953–69) and of the Burger Court (1969–86) had given judges too much discretion in interpreting the constitution, and that legal institutions had accumulated powers that properly belonged with elective institutions. The idea that the judiciary had become "imperial" acquired widespread credibility. Conservative criticisms focussed both on the substance of Supreme Court decisions and on the procedures by which they were made. In particular, conservatives deplored Supreme Court decisions that had restricted state and police powers and that had endorsed bussing, affirmative action, and a variety of race-conscious remedies to compensate for discrimination and inequalities in American life. Procedurally they objected to the broad interpretation of the Constitution to yield new constitutional mandates. The landmark abortion case – *Roe* v. *Wade* (1973) – aroused their particular fury, since it combined a markedly liberal interpretation of the constitution (based on a right to privacy that was not in the text of the constitution) with a result that was morally contentious. The "clash of absolutes" (the right of a woman to control her own body versus the right to life of the fetus) generated deep and extensive political and religious conflict within the United States, conflict that helped to fuel the new right in the late 1970s and divided the Republican Party in the early 1990s (Peele, 1984; McKeegan, 1992). Equally important, the abortion issue had the effect after 1973 of polarizing opinion about the role of the Supreme Court and about constitutional interpretation (Tribe, 1990).

Critics of the Reagan–Bush years inevitably therefore looked to the new administration to reverse what they saw as the packing of the courts with conservative appointments. They wanted Clinton to make a series of liberal judicial nominations from sympathizers attuned to the role of the law as a protection for minorities. Pressure groups, especially those concerned with civil rights, women's issues, and the poor, wanted a speedy reversal of Republican legal policy – not just because the courts were an important arena for advancing the agendas of such groups, but also because of the symbolic importance of the courts in the ideological battle. For the 12 years of the Reagan and Bush administrations, these groups had seen the "rights revolution" that they had helped initiate stalled and even rolled back; and they had seen both the federal government and the legal system (which had over the 1960s been associated with the protection of minorities) become hostile to their conceptions of public policy.

Clinton had himself made his views on legal issues clear in the campaign, saying that he wanted on the federal bench only men and women who had a "demonstrated commitment to the individual rights protected by our Constitution, including the right to privacy" (*American Bar Association Journal*, October 1992).

It would, however, be a mistake to see the Clinton administration as being likely to try to restore the role of the judiciary and the administration's legal policy to what it was prior to the Reagan election victory of 1980. For by 1993, the American legal and constitutional climate had changed in ways that made such a reversal impossible.

First, the Supreme Court, and indeed the whole of the federal judicial system, had been profoundly affected by the concerted efforts of Republican presidents to leave a permanent mark on the personnel of American justice. By 1993, 69 percent of all federal judges had been appointed by Presidents Reagan and Bush. The Supreme Court itself epitomized the Republican achievement. Apart from Chief Justice Rehnquist, the Court in January 1993 was composed of no fewer than five Reagan–Bush appointees (Sandra Day O'Connor, Antonin Scalia, Anthony Kennedy, Clarence Thomas, and David Souter). Of the other three justices, Byron White (a Kennedy appointment) was hardly a liberal and Harry Blackmun and John Paul Stevens, though pragmatic in approach, were Nixon and Ford appointments. Of course, as has been frequently pointed out, justices do not always reflect the views of the presidents who appointed them and justices do not always agree (Abraham, 1992). However, the Rehnquist Court was a Supreme Court that had been deliberately created by presidents anxious to turn the institutions of the judiciary to the right and to imprint their conservative values on the nation's constitutional deliberations (Savage, 1992). It would take time to alter the composition of the Supreme Court, let alone that of the federal judiciary as a whole, even though there were a number of federal judgeship vacancies pending when Clinton took office.

Secondly, the constitutional agenda had changed in a way that was as difficult for Democrats as for Republicans. Although the Clinton administration is generally more sympathetic to such causes as racial and gender equality than the Republicans were, the question of how best to translate those preferences into constitutional law is by no means easy. The contemporary issues facing the Supreme Court in the Clinton era divide Democrats as much as they divide Republicans and Democrats, and defy easy ideological analysis. Affirmative action presents a good example of this new complexity as the courts wrestle with the constitutionality and justice of giving preferences to one group of Americans over another on the grounds of race, seniority, gender, or other classification. However, there are equally difficult new questions on the agenda such as the right to die and rights of surrogacy.

Thirdly, Clinton's margin of electoral victory had been narrow, and his mandate accordingly seemed shaky. Moreover, although he faced an overwhelmingly Democratic Congress, it was not a Congress that felt itself to owe him any debts. On paper, the absence of divided government presented better opportunities for coherent policymaking. In practice, the Clinton administration faced a political situation in which he would have to fight to maintain the initiative, and certainly could not assume that Congress would rubber stamp either his policies or his personnel.

The Clinton Administration and the Department of Justice

The substance of American constitutional law and the enforcement of constitutional rights are profoundly shaped by the attitudes of the officials appointed to key legal posts within the administration and by the character of the bureaucracy working within the Justice Department. Indeed, there have been a number of significant recent studies that have devoted scholarly attention to posts that have hitherto been neglected in the study of American government (Clayton, 1992; Salokar, 1992). Many of the legal officials of the Reagan and Bush administrations became extremely controversial because of their association with the desire to turn the clock back on the civil rights revolution of the 1960s. Reagan's three Attorneys General – William French Smith, Edwin Meese III, and Richard Thornburgh – were all associated with a controversially conservative approach to legal administration, and Solicitor General Charles Fried acquired a degree of notoriety after a well-publicized book on the Solicitor General's office alleged that under Fried the office had become so politicized that it had lost its independence and its legitimacy (Caplan, 1987). Fried's own account emphasized the democratic legitimacy of adjusting legal priorities to reflect a change of administration (Fried, 1991).

The point at issue between supporters and opponents of the Reagan–Bush approach to legal issues was by no means straightforward. How far did an incoming administration have the right to change its approach to legal issues to reflect its own partisan concerns? Are the legal officers of an administration primarily servants of that administration, or are they in some sense different from other political personnel? Is it realistic to expect a new president of a different party to his predecessor to try to restore a degree of neutrality to the administration of justice, or should he dismiss the idea as naïve and move quickly to place his own partisans in key positions?

Clinton's choice of Attorney General was closely watched as a clue to his views on these questions. It was also closely scrutinized by civil rights groups, who hoped that both in substance and symbolically the new president would take the opportunity to begin the process of reversing the Republican ideological crusade.

Beneath the surface of symbolism there was also an important political and administrative agenda for the person appointed to head the Department of Justice. The G.A.O. transition reports had identified a series of management problems within the D.O.J., and there were inevitably budgetary problems in this as in other areas of domestic policy.

Clinton's first preference for the post of Attorney General was a woman – Zoe Baird. The nomination of a woman to head the Justice Department was significant not just because of Clinton's desire to create a cabinet that reflected America, but also to register the progress of women within the legal profession. Whereas women lawyers had long experienced substantial discrimination against them, in Clinton's generation they had moved to a position of full equality; this was reflected both in their numbers at law schools as well as in prestigious law firms. Women's groups such as the Fund for a Feminist Majority had lobbied hard for more executive posts to be given to women, and Baird's nomination caused Eleanor Smeal to praise Clinton for "taking a chunk out of the glass ceiling for women in political leadership."

The effect of Clinton's desire to confirm women's "coming of age" in the legal profession was, however, almost entirely ruined by the revelation that Baird and her husband had hired two Peruvians with no work permits for domestic duties. Moreover, she had paid no taxes on their salaries. Clinton, after a campaign in which he had pledged to uphold the highest ethical standards in government, was forced to withdraw the nomination.

The affair – coming as it did so early in the life of the administration – was a public relations disaster. It highlighted the problem of child care for working professional women, but also exposed the way some professional women got round the problem by breaking the law. It also exposed a degree of hypocrisy within the administration, since it became widely known that male members of the cabinet had used illegal immigrants for domestic help. The botched nomination harmed Clinton's reputation for competence, since quite clearly this factor should have been known before the nomination became public.

The damage was compounded when a second female nominee – Kimba Wood, a New York federal judge – was also forced to withdraw when it was found that she too had avoided paying social security taxes on her domestic help. The "nannygate" affair made President Clinton look faintly ridiculous and created an impression of inadequate staff work and mismanagement within the administration. Also, it infuriated the women's groups that the nominations had been designed to rally.

Finally, a third female candidate – Janet Reno, the chief prosecutor from Miami – was found to fill the Attorney General's slot. Unlike the previous nominees, she was single and had an unblemished record in all respects including the hiring of domestic help. Ironically, by the end of Clinton's first year in office Reno had to appoint a Special Prosecutor to investigate the collapse of an Arkansas property company (the so-called Whitewater affair) and the President's role in it, a decision that underlined the continuing sensitivity of the Attorney General's role.

The efforts to find a 'suitable' Attorney General marred the early days of Clinton's presidency and created an image of poor control and sloppy background research that continued to haunt him well after the appointment itself was made.

Other high-ranking posts in the Justice Department followed more slowly. In April 1993 Clinton announced a group of new appointments including, as Solicitor General, Drew Days III, a lawyer who had served in the Carter administration's Justice Department.

The Clinton administration was deeply embarrassed, however, with the attempt to fill one other very sensitive post in the Justice Department. The post of Assistant Attorney General with responsibility for the Civil Rights Division had been viewed as a crucial bellwether for the direction of policy in this area. Under Reagan, William Bradford Reynolds had used it to mount a major counter-offensive against the intellectual assumptions of civil rights policy since President Kennedy and had so offended critics that the effort to promote him to the position of Associate Attorney General was blocked by the Judiciary Committee. In the Bush administration the cynical nomination of an obviously unqualified black Republican, William Lucas, was rejected by the Judiciary Committee in an early example of Congressional assertiveness against Bush (Peele, 1992).

Clinton's nominee for the civil rights division was Lani Guinier, a female law professor of mixed race and a personal friend. Unfortunately Guinier, as an academic, had left a "paper trail," which was seized on by conservative activists anxious both to preserve the achievements of the Reagan–Bush years and to gain revenge for the 1987 rejection of the Robert Bork nomination to the Supreme Court. Guinier's academic articles explored the problem of minority empowerment through the use of cumulative majorities and other procedural devices. Although her views were put forward in an academic context, it was relatively easy to portray her policy goals as the imposition of quotas. Certainly, in addition to offending Republican attitudes, the nomination also deeply troubled conservative southern Democrats who were sensitive to the issue of quotas.

Although the nomination was announced publicly, once the right had seized the initiative on the nomination, support for it on Capitol Hill drained away. Guinier herself was bitter at the way the nomination was handled, and at Clinton's withdrawal of support before she could effectively defend her views. Clinton on this occasion looked doubly weak – first because he did not go into battle behind his nominee, and secondly because he argued that he had not read the views of his candidate. Civil liberties groups were also outraged that at the first hint of controversy on an issue of concern to them, Clinton had caved in to conservatives within his party.

Some of the blame for the fiasco was attributed to the White House counsel Bernie Nussbaum. Nussbaum owed his position as White House Counsel to his reputation in the world of corporate law and to his personal friendship with both Bill and Hillary Clinton. However, there emerged doubts about his political acuteness as the series of mishandled nominations and controversies broke over the new administration. In March 1994 Clinton replaced Nussbaum with Lloyd Cutler who had been called in by Carter at a crisis period of his presidency. The appointment of a shrewd Washington insider was symbolic though it was less clear whether it would work.

The Composition of the Supreme Court

Clinton's first year gives a clue as to the kind of judges he wants to see on the bench. Like his immediate predecessors, he recognizes the long-term impact of all judicial appointments. Indeed, as Clinton commented in August 1993, there were few things that he would do that would have more lasting effect than the appointment of federal judges. When Clinton came to office in January 1993, there were just over 100 vacancies in the federal judiciary; by December 1993 he had nominated 48 new judges, 18 of whom were women and 14 of whom were black or Hispanic. The level of minority representation in his first-year judicial nominees far surpassed not only that of Reagan and Bush's first-year nominees, but also that of Carter's. Moreover, although the right had predicted that the effort to produce diversity on the bench would lead to mediocrity, over 75 percent of the nominees achieved an A.B.A. "well-qualified rating" (again a higher percentage than that achieved by his three presidential predecessors).

It has already been noted that Clinton on coming into office faced a Supreme Court that was conservative in character and that had been chosen almost entirely by Republican presidents. It was, however, likely that he would be able to make at least one nomination to the Court. Both Byron White (aged 75 in 1993) and Harry Blackmun (aged 84 in 1993) were elderly and had served a long period on the Court. In fact, Byron White's intention to retire was announced in March 1993, thereby giving Clinton a chance to weaken the conservative grip on the Court, and to keep his campaign commitment to appoint a "pro-choice" judge with an expansive view of the Bill of Rights.

Whenever a vacancy occurs on the Court there is speculation about who might be nominated. In this case, the speculation was especially intense given the time – 26 years – that had elapsed since the last Democratic nomination had been made to the Court. Somewhat surprisingly, the administration appeared to have no clear strategy for filling the vacancy. The prolonged and public nature of the process of choosing the nominee was damaging to Clinton, who appeared to lose control of the timing of events.

There had of course been much speculation earlier about who might be nominated to the Court by Clinton if a vacancy were to occur, and several names were mentioned both in the campaign and over the three months between the announcement of the resignation and the nomination of a replacement. Early bets were on Mario Cuomo, the Governor of New York (cited by Clinton as a possible future justice in the campaign), and on Richard Riley, the Education Secretary and former governor of South Carolina. Both withdrew themselves from consideration. Other frontrunners were Judge Stephen Breyer, the chief judge of the First Circuit Court of Appeals. Breyer was interviewed by Clinton, but seemed not to form any close personal understanding with the President. Another political candidate – Bruce Babbitt, the former governor of Arizona who was Clinton's Interior Secretary – was dropped after environmental groups lobbied heavily to keep him in place at Interior (see Chapter 14, John Francis).

In the end – but the decision was not finally taken until June 1993 – Clinton chose a very well-qualified woman: Ruth Bader Ginsburg. Ginsburg had been a 1980 Carter appointee to the Washington D.C. Court of Appeals, a court with the largest amount of regulatory work coming to it and from which Supreme Court nominees Thomas, Scalia, and Bork had come. At 60 she was older than might have been expected, given the recent preferences of presidents for appointing young judges who could make a long-term impact on the court system. On the other hand, she manifestly had judicial experience, and as a woman who was Jewish she also added to the representativeness of the Supreme Court. She was, however, far from being an ideological liberal. Rather, she was a centrist who had exercised a swing vote on the Court of Appeals and her nomination seemed likely to reinforce the emerging center on the Supreme Court if she aligned with justices such as John Paul Stevens, David Souter, and Sandra Day O'Connor.

In one respect, the Ginsburg nomination was very much in keeping with Clinton's personal philosophy. Ginsburg had long been a committed defender of women's rights, including the right to abortion. She had, as Clinton mentioned in his announcement of the nomination, been the lead lawyer in numerous sex-discrimination cases in the late 1960s and 1970s (Biskupic, 1993). Although she supported the basic right to an abortion, Ginsburg was apparently critical of the legal analysis involved in the *Roe* v. *Wade* decision. This criticism made her more difficult to classify on any constitutional litmus test, and it was a mark of the shifting jurisprudential tide that, while wedded to mainstream civil liberties, particularly the sanctity of the First Amendment, she was also critical of the extent to which some recent Supreme Court decisions had preempted the role of state legislatures.

Inevitably, the nomination did not please everyone. Clinton's choice meant that he had certainly not picked an unequivocal liberal to balance the ideological conservatives placed on the Court by his Republican predecessors. Clinton stressed the need for a judge who could build consensus and heal ideological divisions, despite the arguments for balancing the conservatives with a radical alternative viewpoint.

Doubts were inevitably expressed from the pressure groups on the right who had come to use the courts as systematically as liberal pressure groups had once done (Epstein, 1985). Thus Wanda Franz, of the major anti-abortion coalition – the National Right to Life Committee – argued that "a majority of Americans" did not want a pro-abortion litmus test for the Supreme Court, but that Clinton had used one. (Opposition to the use of attitudes to *Roe* v. *Wade* as a litmus test for potential judges was frequently voiced by conservatives after Clinton's election, although they had approved the use of such a test in the Reagan–Bush years.) Thomas Jipping of the new right group "Coalitions for America" queried whether enough was known about Ginsburg's record and archly asked whether Clinton knew more about her views than he had about those of Lani Guinier. On the liberal side of the spectrum, civil liberties groups were reserved in their response. Gregory King, of the Human Rights Campaign Fund, a gay rights group, questioned her restriction of privacy rights for gays in the military and others raised more general questions about Ginsburg's stand on access to the courts, on privacy rights, and her leadership capacity.

The mood of Congress was nevertheless supportive. As the press predicted, her confirmation was achieved without much controversy. This was in stark contrast to recent Supreme Court confirmation hearings that had been highly controversial. (The length of time from nomination to confirmation for all judges had risen substantially over the 1980s and early 1990s.) In the case of Reagan's unsuccessful nomination of Robert Bork, Congress and the nation had been absorbed in a major debate about judicial philosophy because of Bork's record as a highly articulate conservative jurist. In the case of Bush's nomination of Clarence Thomas, the confirmation process had been made especially controversial by Anita Hill's allegations of sexual harassment and personal misconduct. The Thomas nomination had generated much debate about the adequacy of the Senate's confirmation procedures. Some regretted the extent to which candidates for the judiciary were subjected to what Senator Hatch had called "an ideological inquisition" and suggested a return to older procedures that did not probe nominees' attitudes to contemporary cases. Others, however, thought the procedures too lax, and underlined the extent to which Thomas had been able to dodge questions about his attitude to the abortion issue and to affirmative action, and had been treated far too leniently in relation to the Hill allegations (Simson, 1993). In 1993 the Senate changed its confirmation procedures slightly. The normal procedure is for the Judiciary Committee to take six weeks to review a candidate's background, then to hold two weeks of hearings on the nomination. The Judiciary Committee vote takes place a week later, and there is a vote by the full Senate a week after that. The kind of charges that emerged in the Clarence Thomas nomination led the Senate to introduce the device of a closed hearing to consider such personal testimony and to receive any background information prepared by the Federal Bureau of Investigation. Although this change was made in time for the Ginsburg confirmation, the character of Judge Ginsburg meant that there was little need for it. It remains to be seen how the process will work for Clinton's second nominee to the Supreme Court (Stephen Breyer).

The Judicial Role

One purpose of confirmation hearings is to examine the character and background of the nominee in an effort to ascertain whether any factors make them unsuitable for office. Hearings also allow questioning on policy, and in recent years, where judges are concerned, the judicial philosophy of nominees has come under extensive examination.

There are various ways in which the judicial philosophies debated within the United States can be characterized. All relate to the linked issues of how the judges should interpret the constitution (and, to a lesser extent, statutes), and thus indirectly address the issue of the role of the judiciary within the American democratic system. Lawyers and political scientists describe these debates rather differently, and indeed bring rather different assumptions to their study of the Supreme Court. Political scientists often draw a very sharp distinction between what they call the legal model and the political (or attitudinal) model of judicial decisionmaking (Segal and Spaeth, 1993). By focussing on how judges actually decide cases, rather than how they justify their decisions, political scientists usually give greater weight to policy goals and judicial outcomes than to legal criteria such as the need to resolve legal conflicts or eliminate doctrinal ambiguity.

There is, however, an important body of research that shows the extent to which legal and policy considerations are interlinked, and suggests that at the level of the Supreme Court the judges' agenda and their attitude to it is very much shaped by technical legal criteria. Certainly this has been recognized as an important factor in the Supreme Court's agenda setting – the crucial process of deciding which tiny group (about 150) of the 5,000 or so petitions for certiorari, the Court will hear in any term (Perry, 1991). Judges may have policy preferences and they may be highly predictive of voting behavior, but they also have been socialized into a role that demands a certain style of argument and attention to the needs of a legal system which has its own internal logic.

Constitutional scholars tend to use a different vocabulary to distinguish between the approaches of judges. The primary distinction that tends to be used to discuss judicial philosophy is that between interpretivists and non-interpretivists. Interpretivists come in a variety of forms, but whether they adopt a liberal or strict approach to the construction of the constitution, they all see the constitutional text as relevant to their decisionmaking. Non-interpretivists, on the other hand, are more concerned with the morality of the law and contemporary conceptions of justice than with any attempt to locate legal decisions or rights in the constitution. Although the academic debate has been fierce, within the judiciary almost everyone would fall into the interpretivist camp. The most prominent non-interpretivists, such as Ronald Dworkin and Michael Perry, are academics rather than practitioners.

Among interpretivists, the most strident debate in recent years has been between those who believe judicial interpretation can and should be based on the original meaning of the text, and those who deny the possibility and wisdom of constraining constitutional interpretation in this way. This is not the place to explore the flaws of the original intent doctrine; suffice it to say that its advocates – such as Robert Bork and Edwin Meese III – have found it particularly attractive because of the extent to which it appears to limit lawmaking by judges, even though, as has been pointed out, liberal judges such as Hugo Black have used a similar methodology to achieve radically different ends from those favored by conservatives (Wellington, 1990).

Congressional hearings inevitably probe the nominee's conception of the judicial function. Ginsburg's rather scholarly and technical approach, however, enabled her to side step much of the debate. When asked about her approach to the interpretation of statutes, she emphasized that Congressional statutes should be interpreted as Congress intended; but she argued that not all statutes were the same. Some, such as the Civil Rights Act and the Sherman Anti-Trust Act, were "broad charters" where the spirit as much as the letter of the law was significant. Such a distinction would of course suggest a much broader discretionary role for the judge in deciding cases than one that tied her to the text (*New York Times*, July 23rd, 1993). It also suggested a willingness to depart from the Rehnquist Court's increasing tendency to read statutes narrowly, and to refuse to infer anything not explicitly mandated by Congress. One example of this approach was the Court's 1992–3 decision in relation to a class action suit about the treatment of Haitian refugees. In *McNary* v. *Haitian Centers Council* it was decided by 8-1 that when the government officials capture immigrants on the high seas and return them to Haiti, this action does not violate domestic or international protections for people fleeing persecution. The Court believed that if Congress had wanted to protect foreigners who were fleeing persecution but had not yet reached the United States, it should have spelled that out clearly in statutes.

The Conservative Legacy

From the appointment of Anthony Kennedy to the Court in 1988, the conservatives could effectively control it (Savage, 1992). It should be noted, however, that the conservatives were not always consistent, and David Souter and Sandra Day O'Connor sometimes broke ranks with their more conservative brethren. In 1992–3 Kennedy, Scalia, and Thomas, according to one analysis, voted with Rehnquist about 90 percent of the time, while O'Connor and White voted with him about 80 percent of the time. Souter voted with Rehnquist 75 percent of the time. Even the more liberal justices Blackmun and Stevens, who dissented, most often voted with Rehnquist about 60 percent of the time (Biskupic, 1993). Thus the appointment of Ginsburg is not likely to shift the character of the Court much, although it will strengthen the moderate center.

The Court's handling of its agenda in the 1992–3 term (which overlapped the first six months of Clinton's presidency) underlines the effect of the Court's political character on some substantive policy areas and suggests the way the Court may be expected to relate to the Democratic-controlled Congress and to the presidency.

In terms of inter-branch relationships it should be noted that the Court is unlikely to generate the kinds of conflict seen in the New Deal period. By 1993 the Supreme Court had ceased to take the lead in advancing or restricting constitutional rights, and appeared to have moved from an activist to a consolidatory stance.

To say this does not mean that the conservative constitutional agenda has disappeared; rather, it means that the process of advancing conservative values will be piecemeal and incremental. The 1992–3 term confirmed some important trends in the Court's approach. For example, there appears to be a continued effort to strengthen the hands of police and prosecutors and to limit the rights of suspects in criminal cases. Thus in the 1992–3 term, the Court decided that a police officer may seize drugs and other contraband felt through a suspect's clothing in a search for weapons (*Minnesota* v. *Dickerson*). One commentator has made the point that the conservative Rehnquist court is reluctant to hear appeals from convicted prisoners, but willing to take appeals from states that have lost their prosecutions at a lower level in the judicial process (Savage, 1992).

This trend in the Court's jurisprudence had become particularly apparent in relation to death penalty cases where the Court has successfully reduced the avenues for further appeal even where new evidence is available.

To some extent, this denial of access reflects concern about overloading the Court. From the period of Burger's Chief Justiceship, the Court had been exercised by problems of overload although the more radical remedies (such as another layer of appeals) were not implemented, and some studies cast doubt on the extent of the problem (New York Judicial Project). However, the more conservative court had also become irritated with the endless opportunities for appeal thrown up by the operation of a dual system of courts.

Refusal to hear death penalty appeals also reflects a harsher approach to law and order issues, manifested earlier in Supreme Court decisions that decided that neither the execution of a juvenile nor the execution of a mentally retarded man were constitutionally prohibited (*Stanford* v. *Kentucky*; *Penry* v. *Texas*).

Another important theme that was continued in the Court's 1992–3 term concerned the constitutionality of using classifications based on race to promote equality. In two important voting rights cases, the Supreme Court allowed a degree of freedom to states that many civil rights groups considered at best confusing and at worst dangerous. Thus in an Ohio case (*Voinovich* v. *Quilter*), the Supreme Court unanimously decided that a state which wishes to concentrate its black voters into a single minority Congressional district did not first have to show that minority voters had previously been discriminated against. In that case, black groups felt that the 1990 reapportionment exercise (which in Ohio had been controlled by the Republican Party) had been devised in a way that diluted black strength and advantaged the Republicans. In *Growe* v. *Emison* (a Minnesota case), the Supreme Court again unanimously strengthened the role of the states in redistricting plans by affirming that where both federal and state courts are involved in the redrawing of legislative and Congressional districts, the federal courts must defer to state courts. The states were thus given more power to draw voting maps.

The most controversial voting rights case of the 1992–3 term, however, was *Shaw* v. *Reno*, a North Carolina case in which five white voters challenged the constitutionality of a redistricting plan that created a strange, snake-shaped, legislative district. The district had been drawn up with the aim of strengthening the black vote. In this case, the Court (by a 5–4 margin) allowed the white voters to challenge the districting plan on the grounds that the district thus produced was "bizarre" in shape and appeared to separate voters on the basis of race. The Supreme Court said that state officials trying to justify a district drawn to boost black or hispanic representation must demonstrate a compelling reason for it to meet the constitutional guarantee of equal protection. Justice

O'Connor opined that "racial gerrymandering even for remedial purposes" could "balkanize" the United States into competing racial factions and threatened to carry the country "further from the goal of a political system in which race no longer matters."

Redistricting decisions are supremely complicated, since they involve considerations not just of racial equality but also of partisan fairness and incumbency. The problem after *Shaw* v. *Reno* was that it was difficult to know what standards would pass constitutional muster. Inactivity by the courts could incur the wrath of the federal government; but equally, too interventionist an approach might also lead to constitutional censure. The Court, it should be noted, offered no guidelines of its own about how compact a district had to be, or indeed about the principles it would apply in districting cases. Certainly the decision appeared to throw much of voting rights jurisprudence into disarray and to invite further challenges to district plans. Frank Parker, speaking for the Lawyers Coalition for Civil Rights, stated that the decision would be very damaging for the future of equal voting rights; and many other civil rights groups thought that the five white complainants should not have been allowed to sue, since they had suffered no specific injury as a result of the redistricting.

Under Reagan, the Justice Department had tried to limit intervention in the electoral process to situations where an intention to discriminate could be proved. This reflected conservative skepticism about the need for governmental intervention to remedy accidental inequalities as well as their general dislike for using group classifications to promote minority interests. The hostility to group-sensitive remedies was of course most pronounced on the right in relation to affirmative action programs – i.e., programs designed to give an advantage to members of minority races. Increasingly, however, the right became hostile to many of the legislative efforts to eliminate discrimination – whether in the workplace, in the educational system, or in the wider polity.

In 1988–9 the Court had handed down a series of cases designed to make it more difficult for an individual to prove discrimination, decisions that were in part reversed by legislation (Peele: 1992). One case in 1992–3 showed the Court again attempting to make it more difficult for claims against an employer to succeed, an effort that doubtless pleased business, but was less welcome to civil liberties groups. Thus in *St. Mary's Honor Center* v. *Hicks*, the Court declared that a fired worker does not automatically win if he proves that a company is lying in its defence of a job discrimination claim. There still needs to be direct evidence of bias.

Two continuing themes of the conservative movement since the late 1970s had been the need to overrule *Roe* v. *Wade*, which had provided a constitutional right to an abortion and the need to reverse a run of Supreme Court decisions that had effectively banned prayer, and other religious expression, from the schools. Cases that provided the Supreme Court with an opportunity to review the abortion decision and the approach to the separation of Church and State were regularly before the Court in the 1980s and early 1990s. Yet, although the sympathy of the Court was clearly more pro-life and more pro-religion than before, the changes made by the Court stopped short of a fundamental overthrow of earlier precedents.

Abortion

In the abortion dispute, the Court had acknowledged a right to an abortion in 1973, but then restricted the right of access to it in a series of further cases. However, despite urgings from the then Republican Department of Justice, the Court did not reverse *Roe* v. *Wade*. Instead in *Planned Parenthood* v. *Casey* (1992), the Court used a framework outlined by Sandra Day O'Connor which abandoned the trimester framework set out in *Roe*. Although *Casey* allowed the states to regulate all abortions including those in the first three months of pregnancy, and allowed them to ban them altogether once the fetus had become viable, the Court continued to acknowledge a woman's right to an abortion prior to viability. Regulations made by the state should not unduly interfere with the exercise of that right.

This approach seems likely to produce a consensual position for the Court for the foreseeable future, leaving the judiciary with few substantive abortion disputes to resolve and transferring major responsibility for abortion policy to the states.

Church and State

In another group of cases, the Supreme Court addressed the difficult issue of the constitutional separation of Church and

State. Conservatives had come to power in the 1980s advocating prayer in schools, and anxious to overthrow the barrier between Church and State. In fact, the Supreme Court had not gone nearly that far, though it had sought where possible to lower the wall of separation. Three 1992–3 cases revealed the Court's willingness to be more sympathetic than before to religion. In *Zobrest* v. *Catalina Foothills School District*, the Court (by five votes to four) declared that public schools may provide a sign-language interpreter for a deaf child who attends a religious school. What was significant about this case was that it was the first time the Court had authorized a public employee to participate directly in religious education. It is worth noting that there was speculation as to whether the outcome of this narrowly decided case would have been the same had Judge Ginsburg been on the Court at the time.

In two other cases, the Court was similarly sympathetic to the exercise of religion. In *Lamb's Chapel* v. *Center Moriches Union Free School District*, the Court unanimously decided that a public school district (which allowed the use of its property to other groups) could not prevent an evangelical church group from using its facilities after school hours to show a film about family values. The Court reached its decision on first amendment grounds, and said that such a use did not entail an excessive entanglement with religion because it could not be said that the school was sponsoring the film as it was after school hours. In a similarly unanimous decision in *Lukumi Babalu Aye* v. *Hialeah*, the Court decided that a Florida city ban on animal sacrifice did infringe the constitutional right to the free exercise of religion. Although the Court did not, as Scalia would have liked, actually abandon the three-pronged *Lemon* test for determining what constituted an improper entanglement of Church and State, it had seemed to adopt a more tolerant approach than hitherto to interaction between religious and secular activities.

Conclusion

The Court must always expect to find that its agenda will contain issues of deep political controversy. Many of these issues defy definitive resolution, not least because of their inherent difficulty and the divisions within popular opinion. How far the Supreme

Court thinks it proper to address those issues will vary from generation to generation, though not even the most conservative Court would find it easy to pick its way around all political thickets. Although the Clinton administration is likely to make some changes to the Supreme Court, in the short term at least the Court will retain its cautious and conservative character, interpreting the constitution narrowly and initiating few new path-breaking precedents, and leaving more discretion to elective bodies at state and federal level.

Whether and how those elective bodies will take advantage of the constitutional freedom thus given them remains to be seen. What can be said with some confidence is that even if the Court manages for the duration to reduce its political involvement to some extent, it will not succeed in vacating the center of the political stage for very long.

9

Reinventing the Federal Government

MARTIN LAFFIN

The election of President Clinton, a president interested in issues of public management, has been widely interpreted as creating a favorable climate for reform of the federal government. Indeed, within two months of his inauguration he established the most extensive review of the federal government since the 1930s, under the direction of Vice-President Al Gore (Gore, 1993). Concern over the performance of the federal government has been growing over recent years in Congress, within the civil service, and among the public. Departments and agencies continue to be widely criticized for continued mismanagement and practices conducive to abuse and corruption. Of course, while there may be a broad consensus – across the bureaucracy, the two parties, Congress, and the White House – of the pressing need for reform of some sort, achieving consensus on the precise nature of reform is likely to prove difficult.

The success of Osborne and Gaebler's *Reinventing Government* (1992), which even briefly displaced Peter Mayle's *A Year in Provence* in the Washington bestseller lists, is an indicator of a groundswell favoring reform both inside and outside the bureaucracy. The National Performance Review, or the Reinventing Government Initiative, has used *Reinventing Government* as a blueprint for the reform of the federal government.

Reinventing Government, together with other recent more scholarly books (Barzelay with Armajani, 1992; Behn, 1991), presents the case for giving public-sector managers greater discretion to act less like "bureaucrats" and more like "entrepreneurs". The advocates of "entrepreneurial government" or a "post-bureaucratic paradigm" are critical of the traditional model of government bureaucracy based on command-and-control accountability. In their view, the traditional bureaucratic model rewards adherence to authority and rules, while containing disincentives for initiative and risk taking. The result is that government bureaucracies have become rigid and inflexible, elevating attention to due process rather over results.

In contrast, the entrepreneurial government or post-bureaucratic model stresses that the function of government should be to steer – that is, set policy, select service deliverers, and monitor performance – not to row, or actually deliver the services. Wherever possible, service delivery should be carried out by the market or delivery organizations responsive to the customer. Meanwhile, public-sector organizations should be reformed to focus on objectives or missions (what the organization should really be achieving) rather than adherence to bureaucratic rules and procedures, stressing results rather than procedural niceties, and monitoring performance rather than rule compliance. These changes will free public managers to take an entrepreneurial, flexible, and less risk-adverse approach to problems.

The aim of this chapter is to introduce the federal government through these two perspectives – the traditional bureaucratic model, based on command-and-control accountability, and the post-bureaucratic or entrepreneurial government model, based on a slimming down of federal functions and greater discretion for public managers. In practice, as will be seen, the need for agencies to adapt to changing circumstances tends to push them toward the post-bureaucratic model, while the political demands for greater responsiveness, especially from Congress, pull them back toward the bureaucratic model. Thus the dominant model in the federal government remains the bureaucratic one, though, as will be seen, the politics of divided government creates opportunities for many public managers to act as "political entrepreneurs." Accordingly, this chapter asks what are the key challenges facing the federal government? What is its role in the federal system? Are the power brokers in Washington ready to adopt this "new" vision of government?

The Challenges of the 1990s

The calls for government reform reflect the dramatic economic, social, and political changes affecting American society. Many agencies are having to rethink their roles and missions during a period of rapid national and international change. Defense is having to consider new scenarios and devise new strategies in the post-Cold War world. Departments like Commerce and Agriculture are widely seen as failing to keep pace with a rapidly changing U.S. economy at a time when Americans have never before been so pessimistic about the capacity of their economy to maintain its international competitiveness. According to the 1992 Government Accounting Office Transition Series reports, these departments continue to provide services more appropriate to the 1950s than the 1990s. Commerce has not updated its data collection and advisory activities; and Agriculture continues to be focussed on farmers' traditional commodity concerns, while ignoring the new demands of international competitiveness, and the new possibilities of biotechnology and trade (Barr *et al.*, 1993).

Despite these tremendous challenges, never has the federal government seemed so ill-equipped and poorly resourced to respond to such challenges. Any significant increases in expenditure are unlikely until the snowballing federal deficit is brought under control. Early in its term, the Clinton presidency proposed massive savings of $108 billion over the next five years, involving a 12 percent cut of 252,000 in the civilian federal workforce (Gore, 1993). Thus the Clinton presidency has not switched the federal government back into a 1970s growth mold; in terms of resource constraints, the 1990s resemble the financially strapped 1980s for the major domestic departments. Consequently, federal agencies face the challenge of working harder, with fewer resources, in striving to meet the new challenges.

Neither do Americans themselves favor a large increase in government spending or the role of government. The trust and esteem in which government has been held has steadily slipped since the 1950s. Recent scandals within the federal government have fuelled this trend – Irangate, a succession of defense procurement scandals, and by the Department of Housing and Urban Development (see later). The National Performance Review and the G.A.O. 1992 Transition Series reports have highlighted major management failures, such as Interior's failures to collect mining royalties and other sources of revenue available, and the Department of Education's substantial losses through failures to screen applicants for student loans.

The political environment of the federal government has also created new challenges. Fewer departments and agencies enjoy cozy "iron triangle" relationships with major interest groups and Congressional committees, relationships once widespread in the federal bureaucracy. This lost "world of establishments" (Heclo, 1989) has been replaced by a more uncertain, unpredictable, and fragmented political world, in which Congressional oversight behavior has become particularly worrisome for federal managers. Meanwhile, successive presidents, responding to the heightened expectations of the office, have sought to tighten central control over the bureaucracy.

In summary, one set of environmental pressures are pushing public managers toward some fundamental rethinking of the missions and role of their agencies; while another set – resource constraints, a new Congressional politics, and tightening central controls – limit the prospect for major change.

The Role of the Federal Government

In the 1980s, federal employees increasingly think, plan, analyze, evaluate, and dispense funds. Others, by contract or agreement, carry out federal policy (Levine, 1992).

To a great extent, those others are state and local governments. As Levine implies, the devolution of service delivery functions to the other levels of government has already made considerable progress. The Reaganite governing philosophy, stressing that services should be delivered by the lowest level of government possible, created considerable impetus toward devolution. During the Reagan years, public expenditure actually increased slightly (Schwab, 1991), but the domestic departments and the states lost heavily as expenditure shifted from discretionary programs toward mandatory programs, particularly Medicare and Social Security, and Defense; Reagan eliminated just two big federal programs, General Revenue Sharing and Urban Development Grants, while tripling the federal deficit. That impetus toward devolution has been maintained under Clinton, with the National Performance Review proposing to consolidate federal grants into a smaller number of broader and more flexible programs.

The case for devolving responsibilities to state and local governments has strengthened as these governments have acquired a new respectability. During the 1980s they demonstrated considerable capacity to innovate in policy and are at the cutting edge of public management reform. Indeed, the inspiration for *Reinventing Government* derives from achievements by state and local government – in fact, the book cites very few examples of good management practice from the federal government. Thus the traditional liberal Democratic justification for tight federal control of grants to the states, based on a view of the latter as both socially backward and managerially incompetent and even corrupt, has lost much of its plausibility.

Nevertheless, devolution does involve serious difficulties and complexities. The separation of steering from rowing is more than simply applying a simple, managerial logic. Federal agencies have developed extensive monitoring functions for good reasons – in response to past abuses, Congressional mandates, and expectations of national uniformity. The problem with delegating program authority is that at least 50 other governments have to be brought into enacting policy, increasing the variations in levels of service delivery and regulatory enforcement across the nation. Such a problem occurred under Reagan, where the delegation of environmental program authority to the states led to wide differences in the ways in which firms in the same industry were regulated (Waterman, 1989).

In practice, too, Reagan's New Federalism too often degenerated into "shift and shaft" federalism as the administration devolved programs to which it objected, assuming that the states would allow them to wither away. The particular problem now facing President Clinton is how to bridge the bottom-up "reinventing government" approach, advocated by Democratic governors impatient with the rigidity of the federal government, and the top-down, mandatory approach of the Democrats in Congress (Galston and Kamarck, 1993).

The Structure of the Federal Government

The federal government contains a remarkably diverse collection of organizational types – executive departments, independent agencies, commissions, and boards. This diversity reflects the ways in which federal government organizations have accumulated functions and responsibilities, more as the result of political deals and historical accident than through an overall master plan. As Moe remarks, "American bureaucracy is not designed to be effective" (1989).

Most federal activities and responsibilities are conducted through the executive departments, each headed by a cabinet secretary. The departments supervise a wide range of other agencies and bureaus that report formally to them. Many departments resemble large holding companies rather than the classical pyramid-shaped department. For instance, the Departments of Health and Human Services, Agriculture and Interior consist of a group of semi-autonomous agencies, in which the majority of their staff work, that actually deliver the services. Many of these agencies are run by powerful individuals backed up by professional associations. For example, in Health and Human Services, the various Institutes of Health enjoy considerable autonomy, as over the years they have acquired their own lobbying networks. In many cases the agencies collected under a departmental umbrella have conflicting or competing missions. For instance, the political leaders of a department like Interior have to devote much of their time to disputes among its agencies.

The allocation of functions among departments is a management consultant's worst nightmare, as what department does what is the legacy of past political battles and compromises. Thus the Department of Agriculture has become a significant player in the social policy field as it has acquired the federal food stamp program, a function it is likely to retain as long as the farmers retain their political clout.

By no means all federal government activities are organized in or through executive departments. Many activities are administered by independent agencies and commissions. These semi-independent entities have usually been established to distance them from Congressional or, more usually, presidential control. These types of organization are mostly found in the regulatory area where authority is delegated by Congress to an independent agency. The usual justification for the semi-autonomy of these regulatory agencies is to limit the opportunities for either the White House or Congress to intervene in favor of special interests.

Some of these agencies are headed by a single person, charged with the responsibility for oversight, for example, the E.P.A. administrator. Other agencies are headed by commissions and boards, the members of which are usually appointed for a fixed term by the president with senate confirmation. A few heads are even appointed on contracts longer than presidential terms to ensure their independence.

Career civil servants identify with their agency rather than any wider entity. There is no cross-departmental esprit-de-corps across the civil service as in the British civil service. As most career civil servants work in a department or agency, and often just one part of it, for most of their careers, they develop close links with clientele groups and the specialist press and especially with Congress, usually at Congressional staff level.

Largely as a result of the division of powers, federal departments and agencies are considerably less secretive than their European counterparts, particularly Whitehall. Compared with European civil servants, American civil servants do not value anonymity. Indeed, they conduct much of their work in a blaze of publicity – clientele groups and specialist publications know a great deal about the internal politics of agencies; the E.P.A. for example, even has a commercially published newsletter (*Inside E.P.A. Weekly*), which covers events within the Agency.

Federal departments and agencies are classic examples of the traditional bureaucratic model. This model is reinforced by the Administrative Procedures Act 1946, intended to check unreasonable use of bureaucratic discretion. The Act establishes standards of fairness against which the actions of federal agencies can be judged either through formal process of rule-making comparable to legal proceedings, or an informal process of consultation. A.P.A. has been widely criticized as placing managers in a legal straitjacket and encouraging expensive and protracted litigation. In response to these criticisms, the Negotiated Rulemaking Act 1990 was introduced to encourage the greater use of alternative dispute-resolution procedures as an alternative to formal rule-making. The Act encourages agencies to negotiate with interest groups over the text of proposed rules and regulations prior to the notice and comment period provided for under the A.P.A., thus speeding up the formal rule-making process.

Presidential Leadership of the Federal Government

The president heads the executive, but in practice the president does not enjoy, usually to his deep regret, a command-and-control relationship with the federal bureaucracy. The pull of the centrifugal political forces (particularly of Congress and interest groups) on the bureaucracies is too great. Perforce presidential leadership of the bureaucracy has to be exercised through indirect rather than direct controls over the bureaucracy.

The major way in which the president can act to ensure a responsive bureaucracy is through the use of appointment powers. He can draw on a wide range of people in appointing his cabinet. The sole constitutional constraint is that cabinet members cannot sit as members of Congress (there are 18 cabinet members in total now that Clinton has added the E.P.A. administrator, the 14 secretaries plus the U.S. trade representative, U.N. ambassador, O.M.B. director; and there is also the vice-president). However, the task of populating the administration is as much an act of "political management" as it is of bureaucratic management. Presidents consider a wide range of criteria: representativeness, ideological or policy compatibility, personal loyalty, competence, and political credibility. Presidents Reagan and Bush stressed political responsiveness and looked for personal loyalty and, especially in Reagan's case, ideological compatibility (Newland, 1983).

In contrast, President Clinton has placed greater emphasis on representativeness to create a cabinet that "looks like America," and has assembled the most diverse (as well as the largest) cabinet in history (five women, four African-Americans and two Hispanics), and placed less stress on ideological compatibility. Indeed, he has built into his cabinet a political tension between the conservative Democrats, in the economic portfolios, and the more liberal Democrats, in the social policy areas. While he may have done this to moderate his image as a "high-tax, high-spending Democrat," he also had good reasons of political management to draw extensively on the Democratic political rainbow. For Clinton, unlike Reagan who won with a clear ideological message, has had to continue to placate both the right and left of his party.

The majority of cabinet members are usually far from being strangers to the federal bureaucracy and Washington. In Clinton's cabinet, two-thirds (12) of the 18 cabinet members have previously held posts with the government; four others have been members of Congress, and a further two Congressional staffers; the remaining four, without Washington experience, include two former state governors and two big-city mayors.

These top appointees have their nomination confirmed in Senate hearings, during which senators scrutinize their views and often their personal life. These hearings can be used by senators to veto or, more usually, expose any personal indiscretions and the ideological predilections of appointees. During the Reagan–Bush administrations, the majority Democrats in the Senate used their power to pursue such intriguing questions as to why Secretary of Commerce Mossbacher had 25 phones in his Houston home, including one in the wine cellar. The Republicans had their revenge when Clinton had to withdraw two nominations for Attorney-General after it emerged that they had employed illegal aliens without paying social security taxes.

Below secretary level, a new president makes almost 600 sub-cabinet appointments at deputy, under, and assistant secretary level. Again these appointees are subject to Senate confirmation, though the nominations are seldom contested. Yet deeper down into the bureaucracy the president makes further appointments to about 700 non-career senior executive service (S.E.S.) jobs; again, these appointees are outside the competitive career service and serve solely at the president's pleasure. Under the Civil Service Reform Act 1978, the president can appoint up to 10 percent of the general positions across the S.E.S., and up to 25 percent in any one agency (except for certain reserved positions any S.E.S., position can be converted to non-career status, but P.A.S. positions can only be created by the president with Congressional permission). The third category of political appointees are Schedule C appointments exempt from the competitive service on the grounds of their confidential or policymaking character; they have no line management authority and are mostly special assistants and secretarial staff.

The subcabinet political appointments are usually contested between the president's staff and the new cabinet secretaries. The White House is anxious to place presidential loyalists in key jobs to ensure that the presidential agenda is implemented and, in terms of political management, to ensure representativeness and pay off political debts incurred during the campaign; while the cabinet secretaries worry about building an effective team. President Reagan controlled this appointments process very tightly; Presidents Bush and Clinton loosened White House control and favored a system of mutual agreement (at least in principle), whereby the White House permits a secretary to veto its nominees and the secretary, in turn, is permitted to veto White House nominees.

Nevertheless, the success of secretaries in getting their own way over appointments at this early point in an administration is a good indicator of their power. What makes for a powerful secretary is a combination of factors – a major department is one source of power, the Secretary of Defense being more influential than the Secretary for Energy; another source is standing in the president's political party; another is the ability to mobilize key interest groups; and another is that vital resource of personal access to the president (some secretaries have easy access, others may find access very difficult).

The problem for the president is how to balance responsiveness against effectiveness. Appointing people who share the president's philosophy may not be enough to guarantee presidential control of the bureaucracy. Those people need managerial abilities, technical competence and, above all, political resources and skills if they are to implement the presidential policy agenda. Presidents and White House staff have frequently bemoaned the tendency of appointees to "go native" or be "captured" by their departments or agencies. Yet to be effective, from the White House viewpoint, an appointee must know what is going on in the agency, and the more they know what is going on, the more likely they are to see the agency's viewpoint and be less amenable to centralized control from the White House (Heclo, 1977; Pfiffner, 1988).

Presidents have also used the Office of Management and Budget (O.M.B.) to influence the bureaucracy. President Reagan used O.M.B. to reduce federal regulation, relieving business of what was believed to be excessively expensive and burdensome controls. During his presidency, the oversight role of O.M.B. was considerably tightened to ensure that departmental and agency rule-making (outside the independent regulatory commissions) was consistent with administration policy (Waterman, 1989). This O.M.B. role continued under Bush, with Dan Quayle's Competitiveness Council working closely with O.M.B. Consequently, O.M.B. came under considerable criticism for seriously delaying regulations proposed by agencies, particular those from the Environmental Protection Agency.

O.M.B. could equally be used by the president to lead in the implementation of post-bureaucratic reforms. Indeed, O.M.B. originally did have such a role in promoting government-wide management reform. However, during the Reagan–Bush years, O.M.B. largely lost its capacity to take such a leadership role, as its remit was focussed on tightening central financial controls (Moe, 1990). Clinton's willingness to rebuild this aspect of O.M.B.'s activities and reduce its oversight functions will be a significant indicator of his commitment to post-bureaucratic reforms.

Finally, the cabinet as a collectivity is unlikely to play a major reform role. Cabinet government is weak in the United States and the president relies much less on the cabinet than do prime ministers (Campbell, 1986). The cabinet is not a decisionmaking forum, nor does it perform a major coordinating role as in most governmental systems; it meets only once every four to six weeks, mainly for the exchange of information. Also, unlike the cabinet in Britain and other European countries, a number of non-cabinet appointees and officials attend cabinet meetings as observers, thus the proceedings have a more public air than would be the case in Britain. Partly for this reason, presidents rarely use the cabinet to build up a consensus on issues, and secretaries often have little interest in other portfolios. Secretaries are more likely to lobby the president in private than to bring disputes into cabinet meetings, with such informal access to the president being a scarce and highly valued political resource. However, the cabinet apparatus of the domestic policy council and working parties of subcabinet officials can be important in resolving inter departmental difficulties.

Neither does the cabinet have a major coordinating role among departments in fixing legislative priorities. Indeed, the degree of presidential or White House involvement with the legislative side of departments varies considerably, and often secretaries and their appointees are left to steer their legislation through Congress as best they can.

Congress and the Bureaucracy

Departments and agencies face demands for political responsiveness from Congress as well as from the president. Congress is significant for executive departments and agencies in ways that parliament is not for Whitehall. Firstly, appointed officials are obliged to enforce the law in line with Congressional intent which, given divided government, can be at odds with presidential intent. Secondly, Congress, as the "architect of the bureaucracy" (Wilson, 1989), must legislate any significant changes proposed by the president in the structure of federal organizations, giving it an effective veto over reorganization projects of any significance. Thirdly, departments and agencies have to justify their budgets during the annual appropriations process as well as obtain periodic authorization for their programs. During these processes, Congress can set limits on the numbers of top P.A.S jobs in an agency, and determine employee numbers, and even the staff numbers in each section of an agency, though it cannot determine who those employees should be nor force them to resign. Fourthly, Congress has the power to instigate special investigations and subpoena officials and documents in the pursuit of such investigations.

These extensive powers mean that even departmental secretaries neglect Congress at their and their department's peril. Indeed, studies of bureau chiefs indicate that they pay more attention to Congressional members and staff than to White House staff, interest groups, and the courts (Kaufman, 1981).

Members of Congress have many reasons for closely scrutinizing the activities of agencies. First, an innate suspicion and distrust of the bureaucracy, especially after many years of Republican control. This distrust dates back at least to the Nixon White House and particularly Watergate. For example, Congress started specifying staffing floors in appropriation Bills after the Nixon administration defied congressional intent by refusing to spend Congressionally appropriated funds and imposing cuts through O.M.B. ceilings on agency staff numbers (Fisher, 1989). Congressional distrust was further fuelled, during the Reagan–Bush years, by the Irangate scandal and the failure of agencies, like E.P.A., to carry out Congressional mandates. Secondly, tightened finances over recent years have meant that Congressional time is less absorbed in considering new policies, "when there is less opportunity to do new things, then fine tuning and correcting the old becomes more attractive" (Aberbach, 1990).

Thirdly, Congress exercises close oversight because it has the capacity to do so. Congressional staff now number over 31,000 and the number of committees and sub-committees has mushroomed. For example, the number of committees to which the Department of Defense reports tripled between 1973 and 1988; in 1988, 14 full committees and 43 sub-committees held hearings on Pentagon issues, while some 30 committees and 77 sub-committees claimed some oversight responsibilities.

Congress is widely criticized for micromanaging the federal government. "Because of its right to authorize programs, appropriate funds, confirm presidential appointees, and conduct investigations, Congress can convert any bureaucratic decision into a policy choice" (Wilson, 1989). However, over recent years the nature of micromanagement has changed. Congress is less likely now than formerly to make specific administrative decisions, and more likely to place constraints on how those decisions should be made. Congressional micromanagement "increasingly takes the form of devising detailed, elaborate rules instead of demanding particular favours for particular people" (Wilson, 1989).

What are the implications of Congressional oversight for the proponents of entrepreneurial government? One significant danger is that excessive Congressional oversight, or Congressional micromanagement, makes administrators excessively risk adverse. As Kettl observes:

> The result is not so much paralysis as administrative sluggishness. Checking and cross-checking slow down the administrative process. Administrators become more circumspect about making decisions, less likely to take chances that could improve production or save money, and more likely to avoid making decisions at all if they can be avoided (1992).

Moreover, risk-adverse behavior can encourage even more micromanagement, Kettl goes on to point out, as tardy program implementation prompts members of Congress to set up yet further investigations to find out why.

Are Congress and executive agencies locked into an escalating spiral of micromanagement and risk-adverse administrative behavior? One perspective is that micromanagement has developed out of a mutual distrust between the two branches of government. Consequently, the remedy must be to restore that trust, as a recent National Academy of Public Administration (1992) report has argued. For "agencies that maintain trust with their oversight, committees can be expected to retain substantial discretion and relative freedom from legislative intervention" (Fisher, 1989).

Another remedy might be for Congressional oversight to move down the post-bureaucratic path by focussing on performance rather than compliance issues. Already Congress has moved in this direction by passing the Government Performance and Results Act in July 1993. The Act requires that at least ten agencies launch three-year pilot projects to develop annual performance plans that specify measurable goals. In addition, at least five pilots will also test "managerial flexibility waivers," exempting them from internal federal regulations if they meet higher performance targets – that is, by performing more effectively they will be able to earn exemptions from some administrative requirements. After five years, all agencies must begin to devise detailed annual performance plans in the light of the experience from the pilot projects.

Inspectors General

One important reform initiative taken by Congress during the 1970s was the creation of statutory inspectors general. As government spending rose, Congress became increasingly concerned about waste, fraud, and abuse. In 1978, Congress obliged all major agencies to appoint inspectors general, accountable to Congress, whose role is to ferret out and prevent fraud, waste, and abuse within their agencies and among contractors.

The record of inspectors general is mixed. A few have been assertive and drawn attention to major abuses within their departments. Others have been much less inclined to criticize their own departments when abuses occurred. For example, the Department of Housing and Urban Development IG was slow in alerting Congress to the abuses within the Department during the 1980s, and when he did he used such indirect language that his warnings were overlooked (Light, 1993).

The main criticism of inspectors general is that they have defined their role too narrowly. They are policing compliance to rules rather than seeking failures in the administrative systems that make fraud, abuse, and waste possible (Gore, 1993; Light, 1993). In this way they are reinforcing the traditional bureaucratic model, with its stress on risk-adverse behavior, and deterring more entrepreneurial behavior.

The Management of Federal Departments

> On one hand cabinet members owe their loyalty to the president who appointed them and who can remove them at his pleasure. On the other hand, cabinet members have constitutional duties to the law and congress as well as dependencies on the career bureaucracy and their clientele groups (Pfiffner, 1988).

Cabinet secretaries, bureau chiefs, and other top appointees must have a "juggler's disposition" (Kaufman, 1981), caught as they are between the two institutions of representative democracy. The White House expects them to develop the president's policy agenda, winning support for that agenda and overseeing its implementation. Yet they must also devote time to maintaining political support, not just that emanating from the presidency, for their agency – negotiating with and lobbying Congress, meeting with pressure groups, travelling around the country to visit other levels of government, and so on. To give an extreme example, the Department of Defense spread research contracts for the Strategic Defense Initiative (Star Wars) around 42 of the 50 states, even cultivating an international constituency by offering contracts in several western European countries (Smith, 1988).

The existence of sources of political support other than the presidency weakens agency responsiveness to the president. Those agencies or departments with strong political support in Congress or from an interest group are much more likely to act independently of, or even contrary to, presidential wishes than those agencies dependent on the president for political support. These latter agencies must substitute presidential support for group support to survive, giving the president political leverage over them.

Inside their departments, secretaries have direct line responsibility for the management of their departments (in Westminster-model terms, they combine the functions of ministers and permanent secretaries). The typical pattern is for the deputy secretary to take responsibility for the day-to-day management of the department. Below that level, departments are generally organized into programmatic or policy areas and staff (budget, administration, etc.) areas grouped under assistant secretaries. Their role, like that of the secretary, combines external political and internal line management responsibilities. They operate in a highly political environment and, in selling departmental policies, have extensive contact with Congressional members and staff. At the same time, they must be able to mobilize the career civil service around those policies and ensure their implementation.

The managerial authority of secretaries and agency heads is seriously compromised by their limited ability to reorganize their agencies. Whereas in British government programmatic responsibilities are frequently moved around within departments as priorities and resources shift, in federal departments such reorganizations require the cooperation of the appropriate Congressional committees. On one level this means that reorganizations involve extensive negotiations, usually with more than one Congressional committee or sub-committee, especially as reorganizations often affect the allocation of responsibilities among Congressional sub-committees. On another level, the necessity of negotiation with Congress opens up opportunities for interest groups to have their say in the process. Groups scrutinize any reorganization proposals intensely, acutely aware of how organizational structure conditions the exercise of power. Furthermore, they may conspire with any careerists affected by the reorganization proposals. These machinations only too often mean that the top political leaders of a department, and senior careerists, can be tied up in negotiations for months, and even then see a proposed reorganization lost in the black hole of a Congressional sub-committee. Consequently, they try to work with existing structures if at all possible.

In many departments the greatest challenge for appointees is how to control the agencies and bureaus nominally reporting to them. Often to the frustration of their nominal superiors, agency heads can act independently of the supervising department, using their political relationships with Congressional committees and interest groups to maintain political support. Where possible, bureaucrats and their agencies "appear to allocate benefits strategically in an effort both to maintain and to expand their supporting coalitions" (Arnold, 1979). Agencies win friends in Congress with a helpful approach to constituents' case work, a highly valued aspect of a member's role, and by assisting members with information and advice to become experts in their policy area.

Bureaucrats as "Political Entrepreneurs"

From this discussion it can be seen that many senior federal managers, appointees, and careerists are "political entrepreneurs," rather than entrepreneurs in the *Reinventing Government* sense. In their cross-national study, Aberbach, Putnam and Rockman note: "American bureaucrats, to a degree unmatched elsewhere, are responsible for shoring up their own bases of political support. Fragmented accountability forces American bureaucrats to be risk takers and forceful advocates for positions they hold privately" (1990).

The American bureaucrats also reported less contact with their departmental heads than bureaucrats in any other country studied, because of their dependence on Congress.

Many conservatives, reflecting on the Reagan administration, have criticized bureaucrats for being successful political entrepreneurs. They argue that the Reaganite revolution was stalled by a career bureaucracy of closet liberals anxious to defend their bureaucratic empires. They blame the failure to achieve major Reagan commitments to cut back government, such as the abolition of the Departments of Education and Energy, on bureaucratic subversion (Rector and Sanera, 1987). They stress the strategies available to bureaucrats – the capture of appointees, prevarication, leaks to the press and Congress, and end-runs to Congress. As a remedy they insist that the preeminence of the presidency over the career bureaucracy must be reasserted and bureaucratic discretion and independence curtailed, particularly through tighter central controls and keener loyalty tests for presidential appointees.

The evidence casts doubt upon the conservative contention that bureaucrats are a major source of obstruction (at least, deliberate obstruction). One study of spending cuts in five federal agencies under Reagan concluded, "there was little, if any, footdragging by career officials in the implementation of policy" (Rubin, 1985). Similarly, a study by Ingraham (1991) concludes that policy "success" was attributable to joint action by political executives and high-level career managers, and that careerist commitment was vital in making policy change stick. Moreover, top career bureaucrats themselves have become more conservative during the Reagan years. Seventeen percent of senior civil servants were Republican under Nixon, but 47 percent under Reagan (Aberbach, 1990). Indeed, looking back over the Reagan years, some conservatives see the problem of change as arising primarily from the power imbalance between the presidency and Congress rather than bureaucratic resistance, particularly as the "micromanagement" of agencies by a Democratic Congress has grown (Crovitz and Rabkin, 1989).

The Role of Political Appointees

The number of political appointees has increased significantly over recent years. The number of presidential appointments requiring senate confirmation (P.A.S.) increased from 152 in 1965 to 527 in 1985; similarly, non-career S.E.S. positions increased by 13 percent from 582 in 1980 to 658 in 1985, while career S.E.S. numbers fell by 5 percent (N.C.P.S., 1989). During the Reagan administration, the number of non-career and schedule C appointments reached a peak of 2,361 in 1986, and under Bush this level increased slightly to 2,435 in 1991 (U.S.G.A.O. 1992b). Some agencies and departments have a significantly higher number of appointees than others – for example, the Department of Education has the highest proportion of political appointees of any other department relative to career staff; while, at the other extreme, a "non-political" agency like the U.S. Coast Guard has no political appointees.

Many commentators argue that the number of appointees or "in-and-outers" has mushroomed beyond the levels necessary to ensure effective political control. The Volcker Commission, in particular, argues that the numbers of appointees (in all three categories) should be fixed at 2,000 from a level of 3,000 (in 1988) (N.C.P.S., 1988). The Volcker Commission and others argue that the growth of political appointments has created leadership instability at the top of agencies and departments, weakened the corporate memory of agencies, and lowered morale among career civil servants.

First, the rapid turnover of appointees weakens leadership, according to the Volcker Report, as they typically remain in office on average for just over two years, and non-career S.E.S. appointees for 18 months, whereas 70 percent of career executives have been with their agencies for ten years and 50 percent for 15 years (N.C.P.S., 1988). In addition, new appointees, particularly in line positions, take about a year to become effective in a post. Moreover, excessive political layering between the top appointees and career civil servants confuses lines of command. Other commentators argue that rapid appointee turnover means that appointees have incentives only to pursue short-term projects rather than the longer-term health of their organizations (Heclo, 1987).

Secondly, the Volcker Commission contends that increased numbers of appointees are adversely affecting civil service morale and recruitment. In particular, the increase in non-career S.E.S. limits the career prospects of career civil servants, as political executives are occupying many of the top jobs (at deputy assistant secretary level) to which careerists can aspire (most deputy assistant secretaries are graded at the top of the S.E.S. band and earn the same as their immediate assistant secretary superiors – $112,000 in 1992 – but, unlike P.A.S. they enjoy the further perquisites of job security and pensions). Meanwhile, dynamic young people are likely to be deterred from joining a civil service where the top jobs are increasingly closed off to them.

In contrast to commentators like the Volcker Commission and Heclo, Moe argues that increasing politicization is inevitable given successive presidents' need to consolidate their control over the executive branch. According to Moe, the enormous expectations that are placed on the modern presidency "far outstrip the institutional capacity of presidents to perform" (1985). Consequently, presidents are compelled to use all the powers available to them, particularly those of appointment, to impose their will on the bureaucracy.

To adapt Moe's argument to the departmental perspective, appointees can be seen to have a key role as "political entrepreneurs" in mobilizing political support for their programs and organizations – a role that the Volcker Commission underemphasizes. On one level, as individuals they may bring essential political skills, (especially those who have worked in Congress or in party organizations) not otherwise present in federal organizations. On another level, they may have political resources valuable to their organization, and derived from those affiliations that assisted them to be appointed – that is, a strong party power base, relationships with powerful interest groups, powerful political sponsors, or personal access to the president. On yet another level, they are able to deal with and lobby members of Congress in ways that career civil servants cannot, given the legal restrictions on the latters' political activities and their unwillingness to compromise their political neutrality.

Indeed significantly, the growth in appointees has coincided with a growth in the size of Congressional staff. That growth should be seen as partly reflecting the development by executive departments of countervailing political capacities in response to the substantial increases in Congressional oversight activities and capacities.

Appointee–Careerist Relations

The relationship between political appointees and their career civil servants is critical. Appointees are dependent on their careerists for their expertise, experience, and knowledge of how to work the federal system. Indeed, appointees can create serious political difficulties for themselves by not requesting career advice; one appointee reported how his careerists "left my ass in one of the biggest slings in town by letting me redecorate the office" (Heclo, 1977). Moreover, transient appointees can only make change stick by winning careerists' commitment. Careerists have equally strong reasons to work with, rather than against, appointees. It is the appointees who have the political mandate, and even now most civil servants regard themselves as professional experts and stand apart from partisan politics. Even more importantly, careerists recognize that continued political support for their agency and programs often depends on the agency being able to field appointees able to act as skilled advocates and use political resources such as access to White House and Congressional channels.

It is important to stress that political appointees, particularly at P.A.S. level, have day-to-day managerial authority over their career civil servants. Under the Civil Service Reform Act 1978, agency heads have the ability to establish and fill S.E.S. positions (subject to budgetary constraints). Political executives enjoy considerable flexibility and discretion in staffing S.E.S. positions, careerists can be transferred to any position with 15 days' notice, except after a change of president or agency head when there is a 120-day cooling-off period. In addition, political executives can influence the behavior of careerists through the annual performance appraisals that determine the allocation of performance bonuses. Yet significant constraints on appointees' ability to manage do exist. Considerable safeguards are in place even for S.E.S. managers, overseen by the Merit System Protection Board, and dismissals and forced transfers remain very unusual.

Despite several dramatic breakdowns in the relationship, especially during the Reagan years, "The evidence is overwhelming that experienced political appointees, regardless of administration, party, or ideology, believe that career executives are both competent and responsive" (Pfiffner, 1988). Recent surveys suggest that there has been little systematic abuse of the career system. Few career S.E.S. members indicated, in surveys conducted in 1989 and 1991, that they had personal experience with abuses of the S.E.S. system such as "shelving," forced resignations, artificial reductions-in-force to get rid of S.E.S. members, or arbitrary demotions (U.S.G.A.O. 1992a).

The "Quiet Crisis" and Reinvigorating the Bureaucracy

During the mid-1980s commentators began talking of a "quiet crisis" in the civil service. The "quiet crisis" refers to the problems confronting a civil service "unable to attract, retain, and appropriately deploy people with the skills and motivation needed for the tasks government faces now and in the next century" (Levine and Kleeman, 1992). In part, according to these commentators, this crisis has been produced by the long-term stalemate between a Democratic Congress and a Republican presidency which stalled government management reforms. The Reagan years, too, left a demoralized public service as public service pay fell, career prospects declined, and program activism declined (Levine, 1992).

The Bush years did prove to be less difficult for career civil servants. Bush avoided Reaganite bureaucrat-bashing and expressed concern over the condition of the civil service. Interest in contracting-out declined and political appointees were less hostile to careerists. In 1990 and 1991 catch-up pay increases were agreed for the S.E.S. As a result, 78 percent of S.E.S. members were satisfied with their pay in 1991, compared with only 11 percent in 1989 (U.S.G.A.O., 1992c). In any case, pay is not that critical a factor in federal employment; one survey of S.E.S. members quitting found that three-quarters gave reasons other than pay (Lewis, 1991, citing a 1990 Merit Systems Protection Board survey), for civil servant morale and motivation depend also on working within organizations that have vital and relevant missions.

The 1980s proved a fallow time for administrative reform, with the last major reform of federal government being the Civil Service Reform Act 1978. The Act was intended to build a senior executive service as a high-quality, mobile and politically responsive group of generalist public executives at the top of the federal government. To facilitate movement under the S.E.S. system, grade and rank are attached to the individual rather than the position. Apart from a few career reserved positions, agencies can assign either career or non-career appointees to any position. The S.E.S. has increased mobility within agencies, but inter-agency mobility remains very limited. However, as mentioned earlier, it has strengthened political control by giving appointees greater personnel management powers.

The National Performance Review

The Reinventing Government Initiative or National Performance Review that reported in September 1993 contains a wide-ranging set of recommendations covering the whole of the federal government. Heavily influenced by the post-bureaucratic perspective, the Review is based on four key principles:

1. *Cutting red tape*: "shifting from systems in which people are accountable for following rules to systems in which they are accountable for achieving results." Proposals include: cutting federal regulations in half over three years, loosening federal regulations on state and local governments, streamlining the budgetary process and procurement, reducing the role of central agencies, and decentralizing personnel management to give managers greater personnel authority.

2. *Putting customers first*: "use market dynamics such as competition and customer choice to create incentives that drive their employees to put customers first." Proposals include: requiring regular "customer" surveys by agencies, eliminating government monopolies where possible to encourage a customer focus, and structuring market incentives to replace bureaucratic structures in some policy areas (such as job training).

3. *Empowering employees to get results*: "empower those who work on the front lines to make more of their own decisions and solve more of their own problems." Proposals include requiring agencies to focus on service quality, develop measurable performance objectives, decentralize decisionmaking, severely prune middle management, and hold top management accountable through performance agreements with the president.

4. *Cutting back to basics:* "effective, entrepreneurial governments constantly find ways to make government work better and cost less". Proposals including giving the president greater power to cut spending – especially pork-barrel projects inserted in legislation by Congress, eliminate obsolete field offices (such as Agriculture's 1,200 field offices), eliminate unnecessary subsidies, make greater use of user-pays for federal services, and improve program design.

Although the Review is dressed up in the rhetoric of entrepreneurial government, most of the specific recommendations make good sense in their own right. Few people now question that the federal government needs a thorough spring-cleaning of its operations and procedures. In particular, the vast accretions of regulations and special interest subsidies, that have long outlived their original purposes, are a heavy burden. These accretions have built up largely as a consequence of divided government and have remained, as under divided government no part of government, whether the executive or legislative branches, has had the incentive to review them comprehensively. Only now has the federal deficit made such a review an urgent matter.

Nevertheless, soon after the release of the Review, while lawmakers and bureaucrats were quick to endorse the general principles, they hesitated over specific proposals likely to affect their constituents and their agencies. Even such modest proposals as those to abolish subsidies for honey, wool, and mohair (the legacy of attempts to manage wartime shortages) and to eliminate $7 billion spent on "highway demonstration projects" (a useful source of pork for members of Congress) were dubbed wishful thinking in the media.

To succeed in implementing the Review, the administration requires Congressional cooperation. Unless members of Congress can be persuaded to abandon many of their cherished pork barrel projects, the administration will be quite unable even to approach the level of savings projected. Of course, members will have to risk alienating some of their clientele within the bureaucracy, who will surely appeal to them when reforms threaten them. Of course, the Review recognizes the problems in the executive-legislative relationship and calls for these relationships to be reinvigorated; however, it offers no guidance on how this is to be achieved.

In contrast, the bureaucracy is likely to prove more cooperative. Many senior managers favor the direction of change, particularly toward enhanced managerial authority. Middle managers have been less enthusiastic; the Federal Managers Association has questioned the Review's easy assumption of massive savings by cutting middle management. The three main unions representing rank-and-file federal employees have supported the review, which promises the unions a greater role in determining personnel issues through a new National Partnership Council (McAllister and Cooper, 1993).

The Review also endorses recent steps taken to move away from national civil service pay scales. It has long been argued that the government's national pay schedule overpays some workers in low-cost areas, but creates recruitment difficulties in high-cost areas such as New York and San Francisco. The Federal Pay Comparability Act 1990 provides for a move toward "locality pay" – workers' pay will be moved to that of comparable private-sector jobs in their locality for 1.5 million government workers in the general pay scale (GS 1-15) by the year 2004, a move supported by the unions and employee groups (McAllister, 1993).

Gore has stressed that the Review is not intended as a quick fix. In several places the Review acknowledges that cultural changes of the type proposed do take many years, and eschews top-down in favour of bottom-up reform. The Review itself is written in accessible and upbeat language aimed as much at federal employees as at top management. Reinvention Teams of employees and Reinvention Labs have been quickly established in departments to drive change from within. However, the application of the boilerplate language of "customer-focus," "strategic plans," and "measurable objectives" indiscriminately to all departments raises questions about how the new directions are to be implemented in practice.

Of course, a groundswell for reform did already exist within the federal bureaucracy. Indeed, some of the initiatives recommended in the Review were already underway. For instance, the 1988 "Productivity Improvement Program" was established to encourage agencies to adopt quality improvement programs and created the Federal Quality Institute. And a 1992 survey of federal installations indicated that 68 percent had introduced the approach or were considering doing so, though most had only introduced the approach over the last two years (G.A.O. 1992b).

The applicability of quality management and its value within the federal government has been questioned (for example, Radin and Coffee, 1993). The evidence so far suggests that quality management is most effective in federal installations where a definite "product" is produced, such as the Department of Defense logistics/distribution center and Internal Revenue service centers. The approach has made far less progress in departments or agencies where the notion of a "product" and "customer" is difficult to pin down, such as in the headquarters of the executive departments. In addition, many careerists feel that the major causes of poor organizational performance are essentially political and lie outside their control in Congressional micromanagement, the instability of political leadership, fragmented lines of authority and jurisdiction among agencies, poorly defined relationships with state government agencies, and low funding levels.

Third Party Government

The Review also proposes the greater use of non-government service providers, arguing that public services need not necessarily be directly provided by government agencies. The federal government has always made great use of the private and voluntary sectors to deliver services both to the federal government itself and to the public. During the 1980s, interest grew in the use of "third parties" or contracting-out. It held out the promise of more effective and efficient government with leaner, fitter agencies sticking to policy decisions, and the actual work of service delivery done outside government by other agents (Savas, 1987). The Reagan administration instructed agencies to make greater use of private contractors and O.M.B. compelled many agencies to use contractors in place of increased staffing.

The advantages of contracting-out are not always as clear-cut as many advocates maintain. Various scandals have erupted, highlighting the problems of effectively controlling contractors, particularly in fields where great uncertainty is associated with the nature of the goods and services provided. Defense, Energy, N.A.S.A., Housing and Urban Development, and E.P.A. have been especially susceptible to contracting problems. Defense has been embarrassed by reports of heavy padding of defense contracts by private contractors (Donahue, 1989). In the H.U.D. scandal, almost 2 billion dollars were lost through collusion in the contracting process between appointees and developers (Welfeld, 1992). The Rogers Commission investigating the 1986 *Challenger* space shuttle explosion concluded that the complexities of the subcontracting process had contributed to the disaster.

During the 1980s, contractor workforces increased substantially, yet the monitoring and oversight functions of agencies remained poorly developed and resourced (Morgan, 1992). Many agencies tolerated contractors who were clearly placed in situations of conflicts of interest. For example, the Department of Energy is spending almost $200 billion over 30 years to clean up radioactive and hazardous waste in the government's nuclear weapons production plants and provide safe working environments. However, it is using the same contractors not just to handle much of the hazardous waste clean-up, but also to carry out the assessments to determine what parts of the antiquated weapons production facilities can be salvaged and made safer. Clearly, the contractors are in a conflict of interest situation (Goldstein, 1992).

The use of contractors has also raised important questions about precisely what are the "core functions" of a government agency. These questions are well illustrated by the case of the Environmental Protection Agency, whose Inspector General raised questions about the vulnerability of the Agency on Computer Sciences

Corporation for the provision of essential services. The I.G. found that E.P.A. was heavily reliant on C.S.C. for most of its critical financial and other management information, and was performing "inherently governmental functions" (Office of Inspector General, E.P.A. 1992). Moreover, the Agency had inadequate in-house skills to monitor the contractor effectively, so would have been seriously handicapped if the contractor had withdrawn. Similarly, a Congressional committee was outraged on discovering that the Secretary of Energy's evidence had itself been written by outside consultants. Finally, N.A.S.A., with 37,000 contract workers and 26,000 employees of its own, has now actually initiated "Project Core" designed to convert many contractor jobs back into Agency jobs (Shoop, 1992).

Of course, many of these problems are the result of poorly designed arrangements for contracting-out. The E.P.A. problems emerged, at least partly, as the result of O.M.B. staffing ceilings applied to the Agency, forcing it to contract out activities in an unplanned way. Indeed, Osborne and Gaebler consider the problem as one that can be reduced by improved management information systems that will enable steering agencies to monitor rowing organizations more closely (1992). Other commentators, such as Donahue (1989), argue that contracting-out works best where the services involved can be clearly specified beforehand, the competition among providers is real, and the results can be monitored and evaluated effectively. Given that most government services do not fit this pattern, the potential for further contracting-out will be limited.

The Prospects for Change

The role of the federal government and of individual departments and agencies has never been so much under challenge. Rapid political, economic, and social change has been outpacing the capacities of departments and agencies to adapt their roles and missions to changed circumstances. Federal organizations have been severely constrained by Congress and, at least during the Reagan–Bush years, by central agencies. Thus the ability of federal agencies to adapt will depend on the extent to which the political leadership of federal agencies has the political commitment, measured in time and energy, and the political resources and skills to cultivate necessary Congressional support. In addition, White House support for such renegotiation of missions and roles will also be crucial.

The National Performance Review is an ambitious attempt to reform the federal government in an entrepreneurial or post-bureaucratic mold. Already there does appear to be considerable support for the direction of reform from within the bureaucracy and from other levels of government.

Yet the post-bureaucratic path will prove to be difficult. The federal government already makes considerable use of third parties in service delivery, but failures in contract definition and monitoring indicate that competitive government can create as many problems as it resolves. Indeed, contracting-out has been the major source of recent federal scandals which, ironically, have contributed to a lowering of the public standing of the civil service.

These scandals have fuelled the cleansing fires of Congressional oversight. Congressional enthusiasm for oversight has been a major reason for risk-adverse bureaucratic behavior. Again, such behavior will be perpetuated if Congressional oversight continues in the form of command-and-control accountability. Congress has been reacting to what it sees as failures on the part of executive government – particularly failures to carry out legislative intent and to prevent major abuses. Thus if the federal bureaucracy is to be reinvented, the Congress-executive branch relationship will first have to be reinvented.

10

Governing the American States

JOHN KINCAID

Contemporary American federalism is marked by a seeming paradox: federal dominance and state resurgence. The federal government exercises more power over more aspects of domestic policy than ever. Evidence includes the fact that more than 53 percent of all federal laws explicitly preempting state powers (i.e., displacing state law under the supremacy clause of the Constitution) enacted in the 205-year history of the United States have been enacted only since 1970 (U.S.A.C.I.R., 1992b). Similarly, 59 of 61 federal statutes imposing significant regulations (i.e., mandates) on state and local governments have been enacted only since 1960 (U.S.A.C.I.R., 1993b).

Yet the 50 states (and their 86,692 local governments) occupy the leading fiscal and administrative position in domestic policy. In 1991, the federal government spent $0.9 trillion on domestic functions; state and local governments spent $1.0 trillion. State and local revenues grew faster than federal revenues during the 1980s, and state and local governments had 15.5 million employees in 1991, compared to 3.1 million federal civilian employees. Today, moreover, most citizens view state and local governments more positively than the federal government (U.S.A.C.I.R., 1993a). States and many local governments are widely seen not as reactionary, but as competent, innovative, and fiscally responsible (Bowman and Kearney, 1986; Osborne and Gaebler, 1992).

Many state governments and economies are larger than those of most independent nations. California, for example, has the world's seventh largest economy. Indeed, a new facet of state and local governance is international activity (Kincaid, 1985, 1990). States have more offices in Brussels, Frankfurt, London, Tokyo, and elsewhere than they have in Washington, D.C. Why? Because most governors, as well as many state legislators and city mayors, believe that success in the global economy produces more jobs and revenue than all the financial assistance that can be expected from the federal government. Thus, in contrast to sizeable opposition in Congress to N.A.F.T.A. in 1993, 43 governors supported it.

Explaining the Paradox

If the states are so resurgent, why is the federal government so dominant? The main reason is that the federal government has established a significant regulatory role in most domestic policy fields. For example, federal jurisdiction over land and water was historically limited to federal lands and navigable interstate waterways. Stormwater regulations contained in the U.S. Water Quality Act of 1987, however, assert federal authority over all lands and waters upon which rain falls in the United States. Federal officials argue that they must prevent nonpoint pollution from damaging federal lands and waters. Yet, because states have independently elected officials and constitutionally independent powers, the federal system has absorbed and adjusted to the shocks of increased federal power in various ways.

First, power distribution is not necessarily a zero-sum game. Increased federal policy activity has been accompanied by increased state and local activity as all governments have broadened their involvement in society. Since the 1960s, for example, environmental protection has become a major function of the federal, state, and local governments (see Chapter 14, John Francis).

Secondly, the federal system is highly intergovernmental. Federal policies often require competent state and local implementation (Dilger, 1989). For example, Food Stamp benefits for the poor are funded entirely by the federal government, but states determine benefit eligibility, issue identification cards, and pay 50 percent of the administrative costs. The federal government funds 90 percent of state National Guard costs, but each state's units are commanded by the governor except when called into federal service by the president, as in the Gulf War in 1991 where Guard units played important roles. State Army Guards make up 59 percent of the active U.S. Army. State Air Guards provide, for instance, 92 percent of the U.S. Air Force's domestic continental strategic interceptors. Guard units, however, are deployed most often by governors (e.g., 337 call-ups in 42 states in 1991 for such purposes as 73 natural disasters, 53 search-and-rescue missions, and one civil disturbance).

Thirdly, the federal government endeavored to reform and strengthen state and local governments. From the public works projects (e.g., rural electrification) of the New Deal during the 1930s through to the War on Poverty and civil rights legislation of the 1960s and 1970s, federal officials employed grants-in-aid, loans, technical assistance, regulatory mandates, court orders, and public opinion pressure to intervene in every aspect of state and local governance. In turn, as citizens began to value the federal government as a progressive force, they pressed reforms on their state and local governments.

Fourthly, in many fields, such as environmental protection and individual rights, the federal government sets minimum standards. State and local governments can, and often do, set higher standards. In the famous criminal case featured in *Reversal of Fortune*, the Rhode Island Supreme Court excluded crucial evidence damaging to Claus von Bulow because that court has a stricter rule for admitting incriminating evidence into a trial than the "exclusionary rule" set by the U.S. Supreme Court. Many state courts adhere to the federal standard, but some states apply a stricter standard based on their own constitution.

Fifthly, states can occupy any domestic policy field not prohibited by the federal government. For example, corporations are chartered by states, not by the federal government, and most types of insurance are regulated by the states. States may also enter vacuums created by federal retreats. When Republican Presidents Ronald Reagan and George Bush were seen as lax enforcers of federal anti-trust and consumer-protection laws, many states strengthened their comparable laws, and state Attorneys General enforced them more vigorously. In part, this was a partisan response. The Attorney General is elected directly by voters in 43 states, and in 1989, for example, 62 percent of the Attorneys General were Democrats. Of the six largest states, five (California, Florida, Illinois, New York, and Texas) had a Democratic Attorney General.

Sixth, the federal system retains some dualism. The United States has a dual (federal and state) banking system, and both the states and the federal government tax and regulate the telecommunications and securities industries. The federal government is the primary regulator of cable television, but county and municipal governments can regulate some local cable matters if they follow federal standards. The federal government paid about 90 percent of the cost of building the 44,000-mile interstate highway system and 75 percent of the cost of primary, secondary, and urban roads, but state and local governments own and maintain these highways.

Thus, in various ways, the federal system has enabled state and local governments to become strong, modern governments despite expansions of federal power. Nevertheless, the system has become less cooperative and more coercive since the 1960s, because the federal government has sought to harness state and local capacities to its own policy ends (Kincaid, 1993a). This trend has been facilitated by the growth of interest-group pressure on the federal government, by changes in the political party system and electoral districting that have made members of Congress less dependent on state and local officials for electoral success, by unprecedented federal commitments to individual rights and social welfare, by budget deficits that induce the federal government to shift policy costs to state and local governments, by media attention focussed on Washington, by disagreements among state and local officials that allow federal officials to "divide and conquer," and by diminished citizen understanding of the federal system. For example, a key feature of American federalism is dual constitutionalism: the U.S. Constitution and 50 state constitutions. In a 1992 survey, however, only 52 percent of adults knew that their state had its own constitution (U.S.A.C.I.R., 1992a).

Origins of American Federalism

American federalism owes much of its cultural origins to the federal theology of the early Puritan settlers. The word "federal" comes from the Latin *foedus*, meaning covenant. The Puritans extended their belief in a human covenant with God to covenants between individuals to form families (i.e., marriage), between families to form congregations, between congregations to form towns, between towns to form larger jurisdictions, and so on. Covenant ideas were basic to the Reformed Protestant tradition (e.g., Baptist, Congregationalist, and Presbyterian) that significantly shaped American culture. Many communities were established by formal covenants, and this practice gave rise to written constitutions in North America (Lutz, 1980). This cultural foundation was reinforced by later secular ideas of the "social compact" developed by Enlightenment theorists, especially John Locke.

The actual federalism created by the Constitution of the United States, however, owes its origins largely to the political compromises required to create a strong union of 13 diverse, independent-minded states. When weaknesses of the Articles of Confederation (1781) seemed to jeopardize national security and prosperity, nationalists (who became known as Federalists), such as Alexander Hamilton and James Madison, advocated a stronger union. Among other things, the confederal government could not levy its own taxes, directly raise an army, or regulate commerce between the states.

These problems were remedied by the U.S. Constitution ratified in 1788. The people of the states delegated more, but still limited, powers to a new federal government: including powers to borrow and coin money, levy certain taxes and excises, regulate foreign and interstate commerce, issue patents and copyrights, raise an army and maintain a navy, declare war, and "make all laws . . . necessary and proper for carrying into execution the foregoing powers." This "elastic" clause allows broad interpretations of federal powers. In turn, some explicit limits were placed on both state and federal powers; states were required to give "full faith and credit" to each other's public acts; and states were prohibited from discriminating against out-of-state citizens.

The key innovation that transformed confederalism into federalism, however, was the authority of the new federal government to enforce its laws against individuals (*Federalist* 15). For example, the federal government prosecutes individuals for tax evasion. Hence, the Constitution, unlike the Articles, established federal courts with broad jurisdiction separate from state courts. This change shocked many Americans because it violated their understanding of federalism as purely confederation, and evoked fears of a distant central government exercising tyrannical powers. Opponents of the Constitution, known as Anti-Federalists, especially feared that the U.S. Supreme Court would foster centralization. As the price of ratification, Anti-Federalists who were open to compromise insisted on a Bill of Rights, which became the first ten amendments to the Constitution in 1791. The Tenth Amendment reserves to the states "or to the people" all powers not delegated to the United States or prohibited the states by the Constitution.

Dual, Cooperative, and Coercive Federalism

Scholars have divided American federalism into many historical periods (Elazar, 1990; Wright, 1988). Generally, most recognize dual and cooperative federalism, while the label "coercive" for contemporary federalism is subject to more debate.

Dual federalism was articulated primarily by the Supreme Court – first to protect federal powers from state encroachment and, later, to protect state powers from federal encroachment. This doctrine held that the federal and state governments occupy separate, indestructible spheres of policy power. Although Chief Justice John Marshall occasionally rallied the Supreme Court to expand federal powers from 1801 to 1835, the Court's dual federalism jurisprudence frequently blocked both federal and state policy action, especially during the era of *laissez-faire* capitalism from the 1870s to the 1930s.

The Congress and presidents, however, were less dualistic. They provided patronage, land grants, pork-barrel appropriations, and public works projects to state and local governments. Also, in 1832, for example, President Andrew Jackson vetoed a Bill to recharter the Bank of the United States, partly because states wanted federal funds deposited in their state banks.

The legal bulwark of dual federalism was the Tenth Amendment; however, as Americans confronted the urban–industrial era, World War I, and the Great Depression, dual federalism became less tenable. Politically, the doctrine was crippled by the election of President Franklin D. Roosevelt in 1932; judicially, it was abandoned by the Supreme Court in 1941 when it declared the Tenth Amendment a mere "truism" (*U.S.* v. *Darby*).

As opposed to a neat division of powers, cooperative federalism emerged to emphasize a federal–state–local partnership in which all governments in the system share powers and coordinate their actions to address domestic issues of nationwide importance. The emergence of such cooperation was signalled by President Theodore Roosevelt's convening of the first meeting of a president with all 46 governors in 1908. The purpose was to advance natural-resource conservation. Unlike Canada, the United States does not practice "executive federalism" in which the heads of the federal and provincial governments meet regularly to formulate policy. The most recent meeting of this type was President Bush's 1988 "summit" with 49 governors to forge national education goals. President Bill Clinton, who attended the summit as governor of Arkansas, reaffirmed those goals. Many governors and other state and local officials are urging Clinton to convene "a federalism summit" to address their concerns about federal coercion.

The 1908 meeting was significant for several reasons. It began to formalize a system of intergovernmental consultation that now encompasses virtually all federal, state, and local officials in dense networks of interaction. It also symbolized Roosevelt's insistence that his New Nationalism did not mean centralization. It triggered the formation of what is now the influential National Governors' Association, and it fueled efforts to strengthen the governorship. Early Americans, smarting from abuses of power by royal governors, had made most governors weak, preferring instead to empower their legislatures.

Unlike dual federalism, which emphasized federal–state relations, cooperative federalism soon treated local governments, especially big cities, as a full "third partner" in the federal system. Direct federal–local relations became important New Deal policymaking, and reached their apogee under President Johnson's Creative Federalism and President Nixon's New Federalism. Those presidents poured unprecedented amounts of federal money into local coffers.

In bypassing the states, however, they angered governors and state legislators. Local governments are legal creatures of their states; they are not mentioned in the U.S. Constitution. When President Reagan articulated his somewhat dualistic New Federalism in the early 1980s, he excluded local government and focussed on federal–state relations. Many mayors, therefore, supported President Clinton's election in 1992 and then requested federal money for 4,396 "ready-to-go" transportation and development projects neglected during the Reagan–Bush years. The President requested funds in his "economic stimulus package" in 1993, but when Congress rejected this urban aid, mayors expressed disillusionment with Clinton.

A key characteristic of cooperative federalism was the growth of grants-in-aid to states and localities. Although grants were developed during the nineteenth century, first as land grants and then, after the Civil War, as money grants, they did not achieve significance until the 1930s for three reasons. First, New Deal deficit spending to stimulate the economy, plus the need for the federal government to rely on state and local governments to implement programs, produced a flood of federal money for states and localities. Secondly, grants signalled the federal government's willingness to cooperate with state and local governments and, in turn, induced those governments to cooperate with Washington. Thirdly, federal taxation of personal and corporate income, as permitted by the Sixteenth Amendment (1913) to the U.S. Constitution, was a powerful revenue-raising device. Consequently, the most dramatic fiscal transformation of American federalism occurred during the 1930s. In 1927, federal spending accounted for only 31 percent of all own-source government expenditures, compared to 52 percent for local governments and 17 percent for state governments. The federal share increased to 50 percent by 1940 and 72 percent by 1952, then dropping to 65 percent in 1957 – about where it stands today. In turn, state and local governments became increasingly dependent on federal funds.

This dependence, however, exposed state and local governments to federal intervention through conditions of aid – namely, rules governing funding eligibility, management, and expenditures. Federal officials believe that conditions are necessary to ensure accountability for expenditures of federal tax dollars. At first, conditions were modest, but since the mid-1960s they have become more numerous and complex.

Cooperative federalism, therefore, began to give way to coercive federalism marked by unprecedented federal reliance on conditions of aid, preemptions of state and local authority, mandates, court orders, and other devices intended to ensure state and local compliance with federal policies. This trend intensified during the 1980s, despite President Reagan's New Federalism philosophy of enhanced state powers and reduced federal powers. Reagan signed more preemption and mandate Bills than any president in U.S. history (U.S.A.C.I.R., 1992b, 1993b).

Characteristics of Coercive Federalism

Contemporary federalism exhibits eight key characteristics.

Diminished federal aid to states and localities

Although federal aid to state and local governments increased from $7.1 billion in 1971 to about $204 billion in 1993, aid peaked in 1978 at 27 percent of state and local expenditures and 17 percent of federal outlays. In 1992, federal aid accounted for 22 percent of state-local outlays and 13 percent of federal outlays (U.S.A.C.I.R., 1993c).

Four principal factors account for this relative decline. First, the federal government has incurred annual deficits since 1969, which ballooned after 1978, creating a total debt of $4.4 trillion by 1993. Second, state and local own-source revenues increased by 106 percent in the 1980s compared to 92 percent for federal revenues. This state-local revenue growth – due mostly to tax increases and the economic growth of the Reagan years – has been restrained in the 1990s by the 1990–1 recession, sluggish economic growth, and resistant taxpayers. Third, the federal government increasingly requires state and local governments to implement unfunded policy mandates, such as the Americans with Disabilities Act of 1990. Compliance requires sizeable state and local expenditures.

Fourth, federal aid to local governments has dropped steeply. The federal contribution to 50 big-city budgets, for instance, fell from 18 percent in 1981 to about 5 percent in 1992 (although states increased aid to localities from $81 billion in 1980 to $183 billion in 1991). One reason is that President Reagan opposed federal aid to local governments. Hence, two major programs were terminated: General Revenue Sharing (G.R.S.) in 1986 and Urban Development Action Grants (U.D.A.G.s) in 1988. G.R.S., enacted in 1972, provided largely unconditional federal aid on a formula basis to the 50 states and 39,000 local governments. (States were cut from G.R.S. under President Carter in 1980.) U.D.A.G.s, enacted under Carter in 1977, had provided $4.9 billion for some 3,300 projects in distressed cities. Another reason for the aid decline is that big-city Democratic political machines collapsed by the mid-1970s (e.g., Daley in Chicago and Kenney in Jersey City), and by 1990 more than 50 percent of Americans lived in suburbs. Big cities were left with little political clout in Congress and the White House.

Aid to persons over places

Aid to localities would have declined anyway, however, because federal aid for persons (e.g., Medicaid and Aid to Families with Dependent Children) now outstrips aid for places (e.g., highways and urban renewal). In 1993, 62 percent of all federal aid to states and localities was dedicated for payments to persons, compared to only 32 pecent in 1978. Most of the 88 percent increase in state–local federal aid of the last six Reagan–Bush years was for payments to persons. Aid for persons consists mostly of entitlement programs for which states have primary administrative responsibility; hence 89 percent of all federal aid now goes to states. Medicaid, for example, is the nation's principal health-care program for the poor. The federal government provides states with 50 percent to 79 percent of the funds for benefits (depending on a state's per capita personal income). Medicaid amounts to 35 percent of all federal aid to state and local governments.

Various factors contributed to this shift. For one, some entitlements are on "automatic pilot" – spending increases without Congressional action. Second, Congress has expanded many programs, especially Medicaid. Third, entitlements disproportionately benefit the growing senior-citizen population. For example, the elderly and disabled represented 27 percent of all Medicaid enrollees in 1990, but received 70 percent of all Medicaid funds. Fourth, many strong interest groups, such as the American Association of Retired Persons, now compete with state and local officials for federal money.

Fifth, representation in the U.S. House has, in effect, shifted from places to persons (Kincaid, 1993). Before the Supreme Court's "one person, one vote" apportionment ruling (*Wesberry* v. *Sanders*, 1964), most House electoral districts conformed to local government boundaries, thus tying most House members to local and state government officials. By the early 1970s, all states had reapportioned under the new rule. In addition, the rise of direct primaries, personal campaign organizations, political action committees, and media exposure sharply reduced the electoral dependence of House and Senate members on state and local officials and party organizations. Hence, funding incentives for Congress shifted from places to persons.

Finally, the shift of aid toward persons conforms in principle, though less in practice, to the now classic theory of fiscal federalism (Musgrave, 1959; Oates, 1972) that redistributing income and resources to the poor is best carried out by the federal government (because it captures all taxpayers), while allocating resources for specific public goods and services (e.g., police) is best done by state and local governments (because needs and voter preferences differ across jurisdictions). Under cooperative federalism, attempts were made to direct more aid to poor places (e.g., central cities and Appalachia). However, the United States remains the only federal democracy lacking a fiscal equalization program to distribute funds among states to ensure a minimum level of service provision by all states.

As Congress spread funds to all districts, and as aid to poor places did not always help poor persons, pressure mounted to shift aid to persons. Reagan and Bush generally supported this shift, preferring, for instance, to fund vouchers and provide tax credits for low-income persons to obtain housing rather than funding public housing construction and local public housing authorities. Some Reaganites wanted to "cash out" the more than 100 federal welfare programs and simply mail checks to poor people so as to cut costs, weed out the "undeserving" poor and middle-class claimants, and decimate the federal–state–local "welfare bureaucracy" which, in their view, is populated with liberal Democrats. The Clinton administration is reviving public housing, but it is not likely to reverse the shift of aid toward persons.

Conditions of aid to states and localities

Under his New Federalism, Reagan sought to reduce conditions of aid by convincing Congress to consolidate 77 categorical grants into nine block grants in 1981 so as to give state and local officials considerable discretion in spending federal aid in broad policy areas (Conlan, 1988). Most block grants are for states (e.g., the Job Training Partnership Act and Social Services Block Grant). The major city program is the Community Development Block Grant.

Total federal grant programs fell from 539 in 1981 to 404 by 1984, including 12 block grants.

Congress's preference for conditions, however, is reflected in its funding of 578 categorical grants and only 15 block grants in 1993. About 90 percent of all the aid money was placed in the categoricals. Congress has also reattached many conditions to block grants. In 1993 President Clinton agreed to a proposal from governors and state legislators, which had been requested by President Bush, to ask Congress to consolidate 55 categoricals into flexible block grants.

States view Medicaid as the most fiscally onerous categorical program. In 1989 the 50 governors urged a two-year moratorium on enactments of conditions, but Congress added more. Because of aid conditions, as well as inflation and voluntary state expansions of Medicaid during more affluent years, Medicaid increased from 7 percent of state general spending in 1970 to about 17 percent in 1993. The three largest state spending categories are now K-12 education followed by Medicaid, and then higher education. Governors, therefore, strongly support federal health-care reform.

Federal mandates on states and localities

Federal mandates are legal requirements that state or local officials perform functions under pain of civil or criminal sanctions. Little or no federal money is provided for compliance. In late 1993, the National Conference of State Legislatures identified 132 Bills in Congress containing new mandates. The U.S. Conference of Mayors estimated that, on average, ten major federal mandates consume 11.3 percent of big-city tax revenues, and the National Association of Counties estimated that 12 major federal mandates consume 12.3 percent of county tax revenues. Mandating reflects a significant change in federal behavior. Before the 1960s, Congress limited its infrequent interventions mostly to conditions of aid and to prohibitions of certain state or local actions.

Environmental protection mandates, for example, are the most onerous for local governments, in part because they will pay about 88 percent of the costs of public protection (e.g., sewage treatment). A study by Columbus, Ohio, reporting that compliance costs for current environmental mandates will increase from 11 percent of the city's budget in 1991 to an average of 23 percent in 1996–2000

(Hicks, 1992), galvanized mayors across the country. State and local officials mounted the first nationwide protest, called National Unfunded Mandates Day, on October 27th, 1993. President Clinton issued an executive order on October 26th to restrain administrative mandating. Reagan and Bush, however, had also pledged to reduce mandates.

Local governments receive mandates from their state legislature as well. Furthermore, while most citizens support federal and state mandates in such fields as environmental protection, they often resist local tax increases or service cuts to pay for compliance. Hence, local elected officials feel that they subsist "at the bottom of the food chain."

Federal preemption of state and local authority

Preemption of state and local powers has reached unprecedented levels since the 1960s (Zimmerman, 1991). Of 439 explicit preemption laws enacted by Congress from 1789 to 1991, 233 were enacted after 1969 (U.S.A.C.I.R., 1992b). There is a larger, though unknown, number of implied preemptions – namely, non-explicit statutes interpreted by federal agencies and courts as preempting state–local powers. Although states won more preemption cases (51 percent) before the U.S. Supreme Court in 1970–91 than in 1930–69 (41 percent), preemption cases increased from 95 in 1930–69 (2.4 per year) to 232 in 1970–91 (10.5 per year) (O'Brien, 1993).

The 439 preemption laws cover commerce (176 statutes), health and safety (113), banking and finance (50), civil rights (33), natural resources (27), taxation (21), and miscellaneous (19). Examples include the Bus Regulatory Reform Act of 1986, which deregulated the industry and prohibited state regulation of bus companies; the Federal Energy Management Act of 1988, which displaced some state authority to regulate realistic-looking toy guns; and the Age Discrimination in Employment Amendments of 1986, which prohibited laws requiring mandatory retirement at age 70, with a seven-year delay for state and local police, firefighters, and college professors. Some preemptions also entail mandates, such as environmental laws requiring states and localities to enforce federal standards or stricter standards of their own. The Clean Air Act Amendments of 1990, for example, established strict new rules and deadlines covering urban smog, municipal incinerators, toxic emissions, and acid rain.

In addition to factors already cited as contributing to coercive federalism, the rise of preemption is due partly to the paradox of federal dominance and state resurgence. For example, as states improved their regulatory capacities while the federal government pursued deregulation under Carter, Reagan, and Bush, many businesses began to advocate federal preemption of state regulation. Governors have also urged preemption in the belief that uniform national economic and environmental regulation will make the United States more globally competitive. The European Community has criticized what it regards as the barriers and inefficiencies of crazy-quilt regulation and taxation by 86,743 governments.

Intergovernmental tax immunities

In the past, the federal government permitted many state and local tax immunities, but as federal expenditures and deficits have grown, it has intruded on state and local revenue bases. In 1986, for example, Congress eliminated deductions of state and local sales taxes from federal personal income-tax liabilities and placed restrictions on state and local tax-exempt bond financing. In 1990 Congress outlawed health-provider taxes being levied by states to help raise Medicaid matching funds. Congress also required certain state and local government employees to pay federal social security taxes. This will entail significant costs, especially for big cities and counties.

Decline of cooperative programs

The cooperative features of most major intergovernmental programs, such as Medicaid, have eroded in recent years. To mask deficits, for example, federal officials have delayed and reduced disbursements to the states from the highway, mass transit, and aviation trust funds and from the Employment Security Administrative Account for state unemployment insurance. The number of federal sanctions entailing state losses of federal-aid highway funds increased from two in 1965 to 15 by 1991. Also, in 1990, Congress raised the federal motor-fuel tax by five cents but, for the first time, did not dedicate the entire increase to highway aid. State legislators argued that while this increase would raise $25 billion for the federal treasury, it would reduce state gas-tax revenues by about $2.8 billion because of reduced gas consumption and voter opposition to state gas-tax increases.

Federal court orders

Federal court orders requiring state or local action or institutional change – especially in education, mental health, welfare, public housing, environmental protection, and corrections – is another salient characteristic of contemporary federalism. In 1989, for example, 41 states were under court orders to reduce prison populations or change correctional conditions. Court orders governing prisons have cost some states more than $1 billion. In another area, when Massachusetts faced a budget crisis in 1991, a federal court ordered the state to maintain funding for mental retardation services as decreed in 1975.

The origins of such orders lie primarily in the U.S. Supreme Court's application of the Bill of Rights to state and local government action through the Fourteenth Amendment (1868) to the U.S. Constitution. This amendment requires states to guarantee all persons due process of law and equal protection of the laws. Enforced briefly after the Civil War, the amendment became a major force for individual rights protection only after the Supreme Court ordered southern states to desegregate their racially segregated public schools "with all deliberate speed" (*Brown* v. *Board of Education*, 1955). This momentous precedent initiated a profound expansion of federal powers and, for several decades, attracted considerable public support for that expansion. Although the Court has retreated from aggressive rights protection since it struck down state anti-abortion laws in 1973 (*Roe* v. *Wade*), court orders remain common because of judicial precedent, citizen rights to sue state and local governments in federal courts, and new rights laws enacted by Congress to overturn conservative court rulings limiting rights.

In an ironic twist of history, most state supreme courts now participate in "the new judicial federalism" in which they can grant more rights protection under their state constitution's declaration of rights than the Supreme Court allows under the U.S. Bill of

Rights (Kincaid, 1988). For example, the Supreme Court recently ruled that police need not obtain a warrant to search trash placed outside one's home for public disposal. However, the New Jersey and Washington Supreme Courts have ruled that their state and local police must obtain warrants. Thus, while federal agents can search trash without a warrant in those states, the state and local police cannot do so, nor can they ask federal agents to conduct a warrantless search and then give them incriminating evidence to take into state court.

There has, however, been a significant federalization of criminal law since the 1960s. Criminal law, traditionally a state power, now includes more than 3,000 federal crimes (e.g., drug offenses), including crimes subject to capital punishment. Thus, a person convicted in federal court for a capital offense committed in one of the 13 states that prohibits the death penalty can nevertheless be executed by the federal government. Given federal-state differences in rights protection and sentencing rules, federal and state officials frequently tussle over whether to prosecute defendants in state or federal courts. At the same time, because of the costs of heavy caseloads, federal and state judges try to push cases into each other's courts. Increasingly, state and local officials also face charges in federal courts. For example, Los Angeles police officers who were acquitted in 1992 of criminal charges in a state court for beating a motorist (Rodney King) were later convicted in a federal court for violating King's federal civil rights.

With respect to their powers generally, state and local governments won only 39 percent of the federalism cases decided by the Supreme Court in 1981–89 (Kearney and Sheehan, 1992). Their losses might have been greater had they not established the State and Local Legal Center in 1983 to file *amicus* briefs in federalism cases. The most significant federalism case in recent decades was *Garcia* v. *San Antonio Metropolitan Transit Authority* (1985), in which the Court applied the U.S. Fair Labor Standards Act to state and local government employees, thereby overturning a 1976 ruling (*NLC* v. *Usery*) that blocked application of this Act on Tenth Amendment grounds. The Court opined in *Garcia* that the states cannot expect the judiciary to protect their powers from federal encroachment by invoking the Tenth Amendment; instead, they must protect their powers by lobbying in the national political process like any interest group.

In another important case (*South Dakota* v. *Dole*, 1987), the Court upheld a condition of aid requiring states to raise to 21 the minimum age for purchasing alcoholic beverages, or else lose a portion of their federal highway funds. Although the U.S. Constitution reserves to the states authority to regulate alcoholic beverage sales, the Court ruled that the drinking age condition is not unconstitutional because federal aid is voluntary; states need not accept it. Many states do ignore small-aid programs, but it is politically and financially impossible for states to jettison such major programs as highway aid and Medicaid, both of which had few conditions when originally enacted by Congress and accepted by the states. Hence, Congress tends to attach new conditions to these programs to induce desired state or local policy action.

Notes of dissent have been sounded by Justice Sandra Day O'Connor, who has attempted to defend state powers under the republican guarantee clause (Art. IV, Sec. 4) rather than the Tenth Amendment. In *Gregory* v. *Ashcroft* (1991), for example, the Court held that the Age Discrimination in Employment Amendments of 1986 did not preempt the Missouri Constitution's mandatory retirement age for state judges. O'Connor opined that the right of citizens to determine the qualifications of their chief public officials is fundamental to a Republican form of government, which cannot be abrogated by the federal government. However, this reasoning has been developed in only a few other cases; it has not carried any ruling favoring states; and it has not attracted majority support on the Court.

Conclusion

American federalism has been a dynamic system of governance; consequently, coercive federalism is not likely to be the last movement. However, the unprecedented centralizing trends of the 1970s and 1980s are not likely to abate in the near future. Although many state and local officials expressed confidence that President Clinton, as former governor, would restrain coercive federalism, Clinton did not come into office with a federalism agenda, and his New Covenant campaign slogan bore no relation to the covenantal roots of American federalism. The 1992 campaign was one of the few presidential campaigns in which neither candidate articulated a federalism philosophy.

Governors who have become presidents in the twentieth century have not restrained federal power in favor of state powers. Woodrow Wilson and the two Roosevelts expanded federal power. Contrary to popular wisdom, the only real-dollar decline in federal aid to states and localities since the 1940s occurred during the Carter years. Although aid was again cut in 1982 and 1987, funding increased by 38 percent during Reagan's two terms. Reagan, however, presided over the enactment of more mandates and preemptions of state and local powers than any president. His New Federalism produced no net devolution of powers to the states, although it produced some decentralization of federal program implementation through block grants and relaxed administrative regulation. Under Clinton, Vice President Al Gore's National Performance Review proposed more grant consolidations and more flexibility for state and local implementation of federal programs. However, the administration plans to establish performance standards and to hold state and local officials accountable for meeting those standards.

Much of the seeming devolution of the Reagan–Bush years was due primarily to the resurgence of the states and to the fact that most states had Democratic governors and legislatures. States became activist governments; they received a fiscal windfall from economic growth; and, in many cases, they filled policy vacuums created by Reagan–Bush policy withdrawals. As some observers put it, the legacy of President Johnson's Great Society was kicked out of Washington, only to be adopted by the states. Reagan, therefore, supported unprecedented levels of federal preemption, in part to short circuit state adoption of that legacy. Hence, contemporary American federalism is marked by the seeming paradox of federal dominance and state resurgence.

PART THREE

Public Policy

11

The Politics of Urban Policy

DESMOND S. KING

American cities face formidable difficulties. Most urban governments lack the fiscal and economic resources with which effectively
to address the unemployment, welfare, health, narcotic, infrastructural, educational, and public transportation problems they confront. Cities are home to a disproportionate number of America's
most disadvantaged citizens, those least well prepared for labor
market participation. The resolution of these problems requires a
significant federal role. However, despite the election of a Democratic president, it is improbable, for political and fiscal reasons
explained below, that a major federal program directed to cities'
needs will be formulated and implemented.

The Problems of Cities

Urban problems are most severe in (but certainly not confined to)
the oldest American cities of the midwestern and eastern areas.
Cities such as New York, Chicago, Philadelphia, Newark, Cleveland, St. Louis, and Detroit experienced the strongest growth in
urban poverty in the 1970s and 1980s (Jencks and Peterson, 1991;
Kasarda, 1985). For instance, in Detroit between 1970 and 1980
population declined by 20 percent, while poverty (defined as those
living below the poverty line) increased from 14.9 percent to 21.9
percent (Wilson, 1992). In New York, poverty grew during the
same period from 14.9 percent to 20 percent and Chicago's
percentage of households in poverty also reached 20 percent, rising
from 14.5 percent (Wilson, 1992). By 1986 the percentage of
unemployment in St. Louis had grown to 9.4 percent, from 5.4
percent in 1960 (Savitch and Thomas 1991). Between 1950 and 1986

220

the numbers in jobs dropped by 33.5 percent in Detroit, 39.1 percent in St. Louis, and 15.9 percent in Chicago; in Atlanta during the same period, jobs increased 6.6 percent (Savitch and Thomas, 1991). In New York, manufacturing employment was 30 percent of total city employment in 1950 but 10 percent in 1989, while employment in services grew from 14.6 percent to 31.8 percent over the same period (Mollenkopf, 1992).

Central cities are disproportionately populated by ethnic minorities and disadvantaged groups (Massey and Denton, 1993). Central cities are sharply differentiated, both ethnically and economically, from their affluent suburbs (Landis, 1987). During the 1980s the percentage of households with incomes below the poverty line continued on a downward trend in suburbs, while rising in cities. The population of central cities declined in the 1970s and 1980s, but the percentage of poor increased (Jargowsky and Bane, 1990; Ricketts and Mincy, 1986; Wilson, 1987). The racial division between central cities and suburbs overlaps with a class division: "the central city has become that part of the metropolitan area reserved for minorities, while suburban communities are reserved for Whites. The ghetto, instead of being dismantled during the 1970s, was reinforced. Urban society grew more separate" (Landis, 1987). Landis exaggerates the neatness of the division between race and central city-suburb residence, but his general thesis is accurate. These patterns were also racial: the percentage of black households in Detroit in poverty in 1980 was five times higher than that of white households. Twenty-five years after the Kerner Commission investigated the causes of the urban riots of the 1960s, the authors of a follow-up concluded that:

> in spite of the some gains since the 1960s but especially because of the federal disinvestments of the 1980s, we conclude that the famous prophesy of the Kerner Commission, of two societies, one black, one white – separate and unequal – is more relevant today than in 1968, and more complex, with the emergence of multiracial disparities and growing income segregation (Eisenhower Foundation, 1993).

Some cities, especially in the south and west, have grown in the last two decades, though often possessing relatively small black populations.

The riots that erupted in Los Angeles in April–May 1992 were testimony to urban problems and their scale. Cities were pushed off the federal agenda during the 1980s: neither the Reagan administration (1981–9) nor the Bush administration (1989–3) had any political reason to address the needs of cities. Electorally, Republicans are far less successful in central cities than in relatively wealthy suburbs and rural areas. Second, to tackle these urban problems would require the expenditure of significant public funds without any obvious political dividends for Republican politicians. During President Reagan's tenure at the White House, the Department of Housing and Urban Development (H.U.D.) was neglected and brought into disrepute through serious mismanagement.

The fundamental problem for most American cities at present is an insufficient revenue and employment base (Bluestone and Harrison, 1982; Gurr and King, 1987). Their economies are weak, no longer bolstered by manufacturing and primary employment cores; tax revenues have declined, and the demands for welfare and health assistance have expanded. The economic problems are familiar to those regions elsewhere in the world whose traditional sources of activity have declined. The establishment of local economic development strategies dependent upon business have failed to produce a level of employment (and hence revenues) sufficient to satisfy their needs. Furthermore, federal aid has declined (see Chapter 10, John Kincaid).

Between the 1930s and late 1970s federal grants-in-aid to cities consistently increased, receiving boosts during the 1960s under Johnson's Great Society program and the 1970s under the Carter administration when new programs were established (Wolman, 1990). Federal policy was also a recognized instrument with which to respond to urban problems, as Johnson's Model Cities program and Carter's counter-cyclical measures demonstrated. However, by the end of the 1980s federal assistance to cities had dropped by 25 percent in real terms, and even more draconian cuts were unsuccessfully pursued in Congress (King, 1992). Under Reagan's "New Federalism," states were beneficiaries of federal funds at the expense of city governments.

These economic difficulties are most damaging for the least well-educated residents of central cities. In his study of jobs in the central cities of Boston, Chicago, Cleveland, Detroit, New York and Philadelphia, John Kasarda found that between 1970 and 1980 jobs not requiring high school diplomas fell by over a million, while jobs requiring only high school graduation dropped by under 400,000 (Kasarda, 1989). The number of positions requiring university degrees increased by half a million. These trends interact unfavorably with race and class in American cities, limiting the prospects of those most in need of jobs. As Paul Peterson reports: "the annual earnings of young men between the ages of twenty-five and twenty-nine declined by 20 percent between 1973 and 1986. Among blacks the decline was 28 percent. Among those without a high school education the decline was 36 percent" (Peterson, 1991; Harrison and Gorham, 1992).

As a consequence of these trends, there is a significant mismatch between the jobs available in central cities and the skills of those who live in them. In particular, undereducated young black males lack the qualifications necessary for entry into the postindustrial labor market. By 1986, 15.7 percent of black high school graduates aged 20–24 had no experience of work, compared with 4.8 percent of whites; and among high school dropouts, the rates were 39.7 percent for young black men and 11.8 percent for whites (Markey, 1988). These trends have occurred as the labor market premium on holding qualifications has risen. Unfortunately, during the 1980s black participation in college and university education declined in percentage terms.

This mismatch thesis has been disputed by some scholars. As an alternative, some emphasize the rapid growth of low-wage jobs and the disproportionate concentration of black workers in these positions. Low-wage jobs are argued to accompany the growth of high-tech employment, but because of structural barriers and rigidities, (such as discrimination) within the labor market, black workers are over-represented in this sector (Fainstein, 1986–7). Discrimination, historic and modern, is crucial to this explanation. Certainly the difficulties of removing legacies of segregation are considerable (King, 1993; Lemann, 1991; Massey and Denton, 1993). Opponents of the mismatch thesis thus argue that these legacies constitute entrenched and formidable obstacles to the achievement of economic equality for black and Hispanic Americans. Furthermore, the persistence of discrimination, whether covert or overt, in such areas as housing, real estate practices, and zoning laws maintain the economic inequalities and racial imbalances between central cities and suburbs (Danielson, 1976;

Mills, 1987; Tobin, 1987). There is also evidence that racial biases persist in employers' hiring decisions, resulting in discrimination however indirectly or discreetly (Kirschenman and Neckerman, 1991).

The economic difficulties of central cities and growth of suburbs has led some experts to urge the federal government to increase transportation facilities between the two areas. In a report for the Urban Institute, a professor at Harvard University's Kennedy School, Mark Hughes, recently advocated this approach (Hughes and Steinberg, 1993). Hughes argues that:

> some of the most persuasive post LA riot rhetoric says give the poor a greater stake in their communities. That's the right incentive but the wrong geography. Why, after a period of 30 years of massive infrastructure investment in the suburban labor market should the Government try to replicate that success in the inner cities, where the jobs have been lost? (Barringer, 1992).

He cites successful studies in Chicago, Los Angeles, Philadelphia, Washington, and Detroit. The Hughes thesis is that, rather than creating jobs in cities, it is more sensible to concentrate upon strategies to transport residents to those suburban areas where new jobs have been created. This strategy is likely to be increasingly articulated and influential among Washington policymakers.

The Politics of the Cities

Cities have played a crucial role in integrating and assimilating immigrants into the American polity. Throughout the nineteenth century, as America's rate of industrial activity expanded, urbanization occurred rapidly. Manufacturing and service employment were concentrated in the large industrial cities in the midwestern and eastern areas, and later in the west. The populations of these cities were a mixture of old Americans, whose ancestors had been resident for several generations, and hundreds of thousands of immigrants, emanating principally from Europe. All European nationalities were represented, but most prominent, at different periods, were the Italians, Irish, Scottish, Germans, Jews, Russians, Poles, and Scandinavians. In the twentieth century, many of these ethnic groups have moved out of the cities. They have been replaced by black Americans migrating from the south, particularly during the 1940s, in search of jobs, and, more recently, by Hispanic and Latino immigrants from Latin America.

Assimilating these immigrants was effected through urban political machines run and controlled by local politicians. These latter earned colorful sobriquets such as "Honest John Kelly" in New York, and "Bathhouse John Coughlin" and "Big Bill Thompson," who were both in Chicago (Erie, 1988; Gosnell, 1968; Guterbock, 1980). Machines have been defined as:

a form of party organization that induces its members to participate primarily through the use of material benefits. Party workers are marshalled by the promise of jobs; voters are induced to support the party because they believe that they will be favored with government services if their party holds power; leaders contribute because they can advance to better positions if their party is electorally successful. A machine . . . will be staffed primarily by professionals (Jones, 1983).

Party machines developed in American cities for two reasons. First, the decentralized organization of federalism encouraged local grassroots politics, controlled by parties. Secondly, residence in cities was segregated strictly on ethnic bases. Precincts and neighborhoods were distinguished from one another by ethnic group. This arrangement enabled neighborhoods to vote consistently for the same candidate. In exchange for votes, party machines, organized locally in neighborhoods, provided material benefits and incentives, most especially jobs and contracts.

Extensively criticized for damaging the opportunities of those ethnic groups less well represented in machines and for addressing pressing social and economic problems on an individualistic rather than a collective basis, party machines were the principal target of urban reformers in the early twentieth century. These "progressive government" enthusiasts sought to limit the power of party machines by making city elections nonpartisan, introducing competitive merit-based examinations for entry into local government employment, and making elections city-wide rather than precinct-based (Haber, 1964).

In many cities these reforms weakened, but did not end, the role of urban political machines. Urban politicians often have fewer resources to distribute and their practices are more tightly regulated. Local party politics are also more marginal to the presidential nomination process. However, many ethnic and minority groups resident in cities continue to see urban machines as mechanisms through which their political interests can be advanced and their rights defended, in a way analogous to earlier ethnic groups' successes (Browning *et al.*, 1990; Mladenka, 1989).

As the trends outlined in the previous section suggest, the politics of race is pivotal to urban politics. Race is now a more powerful cleavage in urban politics than class and gender (Winant, 1993; Sonenshein, 1993). Mollenkopf's description of New York City conveys a sense of the new divisions:

> Whites disproportionately hold managerial, professional, and clerical jobs in construction, transportation, finance, advanced corporate services, education, and government. Blacks tend to hold clerical and service jobs in health, social services, and government. Latinos are concentrated in service and operative jobs in manufacturing, restaurants, and health services. In each of these groups, male white-collar workers are more likely to be managers or professionals and females to be clerical workers, while male blue-collar workers are more likely to be craftsmen and women to be operatives (1992).

This characterization could be applied in other large American cities.

Mollenkopf's profile underpins the "urban underclass" composed of groups of city residents whose access to, and participation in, the labor market is either marginal or negligible:

> While many people entered the labor market, the growth of female-headed families kept large proportions of blacks and Latinos out of it. Despite the overall prosperity of the 1980s, labor-force participation rates declined among both men and women and poverty rose. These poor families tend disproportionately to be native-born blacks, Puerto Ricans and Dominicans (Mollenkopf, 1992; see also Galster, 1992; Jencks and Peterson, 1991; and Ricketts, 1992).

Although the poorest families tend to be female-headed ones, black women often have more successful labor-market participation in large cities (through clerical and other service positions) than black men. However, where black women are also the heads of household, then this positive effect may be removed. Thus the ethnic, class, and gender bases of inequality are overlapping and multilayered.

The racial polarization between cities and suburbs is further demonstrated in the 1990 census. Davis reports that between 1970 and 1990 the white percentage of the metropolitan core population in New York dropped from 75.2 percent to 38.4 percent, in Chicago from 64.6 percent to 36.3 percent, in Boston from 81.7 percent to 58.0 percent, and in Dallas from 75.8 percent to 49.8 percent (Davis, 1993).

Cross-cleavages, and the sharpened central city–suburb dichotomy, have increased the possibilities for blacks and other minority groups to attain political power in large cities. This development is often termed the "new black politics," to signal black American politicians' decisions to seek change through institutional politics (Persons, 1991). By 1990, 293 American cities, most with small populations, had black mayors (Persons, 1992). Consequently, cities such as New York, Atlanta, Los Angeles, Cleveland, Birmingham, Detroit, Chicago, Seattle, New Orleans, New Haven, Baltimore, Gary, Durham, and Philadelphia all have or have had black mayors. Los Angeles' Tom Bradley, in the mayoral office for 20 years before retiring in 1993, has not relied solely on black or Asian supporters, forging a more broad-based traditional electoral coalition; demographically, black voters never constituted a majority of voters in Los Angeles. In most cases, however, black candidates have succeeded only when there is a plurality of black voters in the city.

Black mayors enjoy no secret panacea for the same problems facing white politicians (Persons, 1991, 1992). Urban crime, poor education, drug gangs, and insufficient funding force black politicians to adopt fiscally austere policies and to disappoint their voters' high expectations (Grimshaw, 1992; Keller, 1992). However, politicians representing minorities are at least able to facilitate a more ethnically accurate representation of city populations in local government and services (Mladenka, 1989). They have appointed black police chiefs (conflicts between the police and black Americans contributed to urban riots in the 1960s and to the 1992 Los Angeles riot) and expanded employment opportunities for black Americans in municipal government. Some black mayors attempted to foster businesses run by minorities through the targeting of contracts. However, such "minority set-aside policies" were greatly constrained by the Supreme Court's 1989 decision in *City of Richmond* v. *Croson* (1989), which held (by six to three) such practices to be unconstitutional. In this case, the city council in Richmond, Virginia, established the Minority Business Utilization Plan, which required all major contractors receiving city grants to subcontract at least 30 percent of the dollar amount to businesses run by minorities. The Court ruled that the Plan violated the 14th amendment's equal protection clause. In his concurring judgment, Justice Scalia held that because the Constitution is colour-blind, programs such as Richmond's are unconstitutional.

A crucial concern of city politicians is money. Faced with less federal fiscal assistance, declining revenue bases, and no reduction in demands for city services, urban politicians have been forced to make economic development a priority (National League of Cities, 1993). The success of Republicans in controlling the White House during the 1980s and the significant federal deficit signalled much less federal aid for cities (U.S. Department of Housing and Urban Development, 1982, Wolman, 1990). Politicians in cities have responded by forging public–private partnerships to facilitate development and are encouraging businesses to locate within their jurisdictions through the provision of incentives such as those associated with enterprise zones (where businesses are guaranteed low or no taxes for a fixed period and certain employment regulations are waived) (Keating, 1993; King, 1992a). These developments have resulted in conflicts about economic growth in many cities, as "growth coalitions," composed of politicians and business leaders, have succeeded in harnessing public and private funds to the cause of economic development (DeLeon, 1992; Logan and Molotch, 1987; Stone, 1989).

As a percentage of city income, federal aid has fallen by over 10 percent for most large cities since 1980. This trend accentuates cities' fiscal difficulties, particularly since the recession of the Bush years damaged urban revenue bases. Political scientist Ester Fuchs expects these trends to worsen: "the prospects for urban America in the 1990s are in many ways worse than they were during the Depression era. . . . Many cities are crumbling under an old, rapidly deteriorating infrastructure and have no money to make the necessary repairs." Furthermore, borrowing the money necessary to undertake repairs and capital investment has been made prohibitively expensive by Republican fiscal management of the federal budget: "interest costs will take up an incredible proportion of city budgets because the rates for municipal borrowing have tripled since the end of World War II, as cities must compete with the *federal government's insatiable appetite for debt*" (Fuchs, 1992, emphasis added). Modifications to conditions of issuing local government debt for public capital projects has also weakened urban finances. In the judgment of the National League of Cities 1993 analysis of city finances, most urban governments succeeded in balancing their budgets only by continuing to cut services and privatizing services (National League of Cities, 1993).

Cities not only lack the resources to improve infrastructure, but, in many cases have had to cut health and welfare services. This approach is mirrored by many of the states whose own profound fiscal difficulties encourage governors and legislators to cut rather than spend, or even maintain, social services and capital funding. California presents the most recent case of this phenomenon. Since California is the United States' wealthiest state, its fiscal difficulties portend hardship for other states (Graham, 1993).

Federal Policy and the Cities

The New Deal Democratic Coalition had as a core element urban blue-collar voters. Consequently, from the 1930s until the late 1960s, urban citizens' voting behavior mattered fundamentally to American national politics, particularly to the fortunes of Democratic candidates. From the late 1960s, changes in the demographics of urban America combined with a reformed presidential nomination system, which accorded increasing power to candidate-centered primaries, and eroded the traditional influence of cities. By the 1980s this erosion was almost complete. A Republican voting analyst, John Morgan, is reported as declaring of central cities during the 1988 election campaign that: "we don't need their votes any more" (cited in Edsall and Edsall, 1991). President Reagan and President Bush addressed urban questions neither in their electoral campaigns, nor in the White House. For Republicans, cities were centers of Democratic support whose declining populations could be ignored. In 1940, 32.5 percent of those Americans living in metropolitan areas resided in central cities and 15 percent in suburbs; by 1980 the figures were 30 percent and 44.8 percent respectively (Fox, 1985).

These developments were powerfully reflected in federal policy. Federal grants-in-aid to cities peaked in fiscal year 1978 and have consistently declined since. In the phrase of political scientist Caraley, in the 1980s "Washington abandoned the cities" (1992). Through the reduction of federal aid, the increase in the services devolved to city governments (most notably in health care where the AIDS virus has placed a huge cost and administrative burden on cities), and an economic policy based on freeing market processes, Washington policies in the 1980s have contributed to, rather than eased, the difficulties faced by cities. Thus federal funds for pressing needs in health care, welfare, homelessness, education, public transportation, and infrastructural renovation have not been forthcoming. In Caraley's judgment:

these cutbacks accelerated the drift of large cities, especially the older ones of the East and Middle West, into under-serviced, violence-ridden, crack-infested, homeless-burdened, bankruptcy-skirting ghettos. . . . [The] Bush administration's inability to maintain economic prosperity combined with its unwillingness to engage in traditional counter-cyclical spending through grants to city and state governments has brought many cities their worst fiscal and service crises since the Great Depression of the 1930s (1992).

The Reagan administration ended the community development block grant (C.D.B.G.) and the urban development action grant (U.D.A.G.) programs, and replaced the public-sector job creation program, Comprehensive Employment and Training Act, with the private-sector-based Job Training Partnership Act. These and other services, which provided federal assistance to address poverty and education needs in central cities, were crucial to city governments. Nor could cities rely on substitute funds from their state governments, either because the state lacked funds itself or because its legislators and governors were unsympathetic to urban needs.

The political and electoral bases of this shift in Washington's approach to cities are uncomplicated. Central city areas disproportionately support Democratic politicians, while suburban voters are equally disproportionate in their support for Republicans. These patterns have their origin in the 1960s and were consolidated in the 1981–93 Republican control of the presidency. The post-1968 Democratic Party was commonly perceived as the party of minorities, civil liberties, and big spending. The Reagan and Bush campaigns did their best to increase this perception.

Between 1968 and 1988 the rural vote declined from 34.8 percent to 22.2 percent, while the suburban vote increased from 35.6 percent to 48.3 percent (Edsall and Edsall, 1991). As Schneider has noted, the suburbs contained a majority of the U.S. electorate by the time of the 1992 election (1992). The political interests of these suburban voters differ from those of voters in inner cities in two significant ways. First, suburban voters provide much better services for themselves, either publicly or through private arrangements because they have the wealth so to do. Privatization in education (that is, independent and parochial schools) and in leisure facilities removes suburban voters' interest in maintaining public services. Edsall and Edsall provide a startling statistic: "in 1986 fully 27.5 percent of all black school children, and 30 percent of all Hispanic school children, were enrolled in the twenty-five largest central-city school districts. Only 3.3 percent of all white students were in the same twenty-five districts" (1991). Second, suburban voters have less need for federal programs than do their fellow citizens in central cities. However, since suburban voters now matter much more than city voters to presidential candidates, it is the former's preferences that are more likely to prevail. The Washington march, organized by the U.S. Conference of Mayors in May 1992, demanding greater federal attention to urban needs, produced indifference from the Bush White House.

The Los Angeles riots, leaving 44 dead, occurred six months before America went to the polls in 1992. Both Republican incumbent and Democratic challenger dutifully promised more attention to urban needs were they to be elected (Solomon, 1992). However, the riots exposed the paucity of the Bush administration's urban programs, reinforcing the widely acknowledged weakness of the President's domestic policy (West, 1992; Weir, 1993). A year later, and despite a Democratic administration, many analysts criticized the weakness of the Rebuild L.A. project and the inadequacy of federal funding (Davis, 1993; Graham, 1993). The scale of the urban crisis surprised those businesspersons associated with the restoration strategy:

> Community activists have for years criticized the federal government for its failure to come to the aid of the struggling inner cities. But what is most striking today is the extent to which their anger is now shared by businessmen, who never before came closer to South Central than a concert at the LA Coliseum (Graham, 1993).

The Clinton administration's approach to urban problems includes many of the measures – such as housing vouchers, work-welfare and empowerment – about which Republicans were enthusiastic (King, 1992a). Clinton's Secretary for H.U.D., Henry Cisneros, has considerable experience of urban problems having served as mayor of San Antonio in 1981–9, and then through running his consultancy Cisneros Asset Management (Suro, 1992). Senator Phil Gramm strongly supported Cisneros's nomination (reported in Sammon, 1993). As mayor of San Antonio, Cisneros was required to build bridges between the newly mobilizing Mexican-American citizens and the old power elite. His approach to urban development was firmly rooted in the traditional "pro-growth" style, and Cisneros successfully wooed large corporations to settle in San Antonio. This style was not without its critics, who argue that the benefits for industrialists are excessive compared with the indifferent benefits for the disadvantaged.

Cisneros has yet to unveil significant new programs. In his confirmation hearings before the Senate Banking, Housing, and Urban Affairs Committee, he defined H.U.D.'s mission as ensuring "safety and prosperity" in communities and ensuring a "liveable and steady supply of affordable housing. I come to this assignment as an advocate of cities, a skeptic of the status quo and a believer in experimentation, federalism and the need to provide people with hope" (in Sammon, 1993). However, in interviews conducted several months after his confirmation, Cisneros did offer new priorities. He singled out racism as a major problem in cities: "race is at the core of the problems which confront America's urban areas" (cited in DeParle, 1993). The H.U.D. Secretary identified shifting subsidized public housing from the central city to the suburb as a major component in tackling racism. This priority is being pursued in both Dallas and Detroit. Cisneros proposed offering fiscal incentives to suburban governments for locating public housing in their jurisdictions. The H.U.D. Secretary has also focussed upon homelessness by spending a night in a New York City shelter for the homeless (Dugger, 1993). Legislation drafted by H.U.D. to reallocate funds to support new programs in local community development, to help the homeless, and to increase public housing in the suburbs, was passed by the House of Representatives in June 1993.

Given the fiscal legacy of the Republicans, Cisneros's opportunity to develop new programs is limited. Accordingly, his programs do not yet differ greatly from those of his free-market predecessor Jack Kemp, and he has endorsed schemes such as enterprise zones and vouchers. The extent of the overlap is suggested by Kemp's enthusiastic endorsement of Cisneros' appointment reported at the Senate hearing: "if there is one man who was born to be H.U.D. secretary, it is Henry Cisneros" (cited in Sammon, 1993).

Enterprise zones became a major issue in Congress and in presidential–Congressional relations after the Los Angeles riots (Zuckman, 1992). After agreeing to an emergency urban aid Bill of $1.1 billion for Los Angeles and Chicago, the House then concentrated on a long-term initiative. No substantial policy emerged from this process, except a further commitment to the creation of enterprise zones in which capital gains and other taxation requirements would be eased. Enterprise zones were not only advocated by Republican H.U.D. Secretary Kemp, but were strongly supported in the House by Democratic representative Charles B. Rangel from Harlem (though they disagreed on the terms of such zones). Enterprise zones will not prove a panacea for the serious problems confronting urban America.

Conclusion

It is important to place the current problems of large American cities in historical perspective. Both the 1930s and the 1960s were perceived as periods of great crisis, and during the latter decade the appellation "urban crisis" was used widely and indiscriminately. The riots of that decade – which, unlike those in Los Angeles in 1992, were not confined to one city – led many commentators to pessimistic conclusions about urban America, despite the initiation of the War on Poverty and Great Society programs. However, a number of factors have changed, which give credence to the view that cities are at present in a crisis of exceptional proportions.

First, in both the 1930s and 1960s the federal government was activist, and willing to respond to specific needs identified with populations in central cities. Second, while health care and homelessness were problems at those times, both have become much greater. Federal construction of public housing units declined dramatically in the 1980s (King, 1992a) and the scale of public health care has been increased several-fold by the AIDS and crack-drug problems. Third, economic growth has stubbornly failed to lift many urban economies from low economic growth or to provide the service jobs familiar in postindustrial economies. The unwillingness of the Republicans to finance the programs in education and training required to create the opportunities for those now marginal or excluded from the labor market has contributed to the formation of the urban underclass. Fourth, one of the sources of grievance in the 1960s – the denial of civil rights and equal opportunities to minorities – has theoretically been addressed in federal policy (Button, 1989). However, the persistence of black and Hispanic American representation in the most disadvantaged and poorest groups in society suggests that the solutions to these problems are less straightforward than previously believed. Furthermore, the civil rights records of the Reagan and Bush administrations, through appointees to the Supreme Court and the Civil Rights Commission, marked a weakened federal role in the protection of minority Americans' interests. Programs associated with affirmative action aims declined. Fifth, the resources for a concerted program to address urban needs are unavailable. The fiscal legacy of the Republican era is too great to finance domestic programs of this sort. President Clinton felt compelled to appoint officials with fiscally conservative records (Bentsen at Treasury and Panetta at O.M.B.) to economic and budget positions.

This last factor constrains proposals for city revival analogous to the Great Society. One candidate here is the National Urban League's *Marshall Plan for America* (National Urban League, 1991). The League is a Washington-centered pressure group that works and lobbies on behalf of black Americans. Its "Marshall Plan" is not focussed exclusively on American cities, but urban problems are central to its agenda. In 1990 it advocated a similar plan solely for cities. The League interprets the U.S. economic difficulties as a function of declining international competitiveness, and advocates extensive investment in human capital as a remedy. This proposal is not incompatible with the Clinton stimulus package. The League's proposals are premised on redressing the educational and social disadvantages of black Americans:

> The urban centers in which African Americans remain heavily concentrated are also the areas in which their educational and skills deficiencies are most prevalent and pronounced; the urban centers having large African American populations are the areas that have seen the greatest degree of deterioration of our physical infrastructure (National Urban League, 1991).

Their recommendations focus on increased investment in education and training, particularly preschool programs for disadvantaged children, and vocational training.

Another set of recommendations come from the Eisenhower Foundation's report 25 years after the Kerner Commission, titled *Investing in Children and Youth, Reconstructing Our Cities* (Eisenhower Foundation, 1993). This report urges federal expenditure on the Head Start inner-city program, schemes for high-risk youth in cities through nonprofit grassroots organizations, and a range of measures specifically for central cities. These latter included extensive job training and placement work, national education reforms, welfare reform, health care reform, and drug prevention and treatment. Their proposals are costed at $150 billion over a ten-year period.

President Clinton is unquestionably more committed to helping those less well off in the United States than his two Republican predecessors. However, central cities did not feature directly in his election campaign and his attempts to ameliorate their economic, wealth, and health prospects will include few programs designed specifically for urban areas. Paradoxically, Clinton's strategy for recovery is focussed on national policies, as were the strategies of Reagan and Bush. Indeed, new H.U.D. Secretary Cisneros declared in his confirmation hearings that urban renewal would "depend on a resurgent American economy – a private sector that spurs investment and spreads prosperity to the ghettos and barrios of our nation" (reported in Sammon, 1993). But where the two Republicans stressed promoting economic activity and relying upon the nebulous process of "trickle-down" to aid cities, Clinton's national program is far more activist, including federal training and education schemes, and fiscal stimulus. These measures should assist residents in central cities, but on a long-term basis. Federal health care reform should also be beneficial in the long run.

In the short run, members of the urban underclass cannot expect programs designed specifically for them. Nor can city politicians turn their skills to lobbying for any new federal largesse in the form of grants. Clinton's electoral bases include the voters in central cities, but he will want to avoid alienating the blue-collar and middle-class voters won back from the Republicans. He will also wish to ensure that those Americans voting for Perot in 1992 do not return to the Republicans in 1996. As a consequence, his policies for central cities will feature only as elements of national programs and not as separate schemes.

12

Economic Policy

PAUL PERETZ

Introduction

The conventional wisdom about American economic policy during the last decade is that there was a basic continuity of policy through the conservative Reagan and Bush presidencies, and a sharp break to new economic policies under Clinton. Here I argue that continuity in economic policy under Reagan and Bush is more apparent than real, and that the Clinton administration, with a few exceptions, has followed in the path of the Bush administration.

Three things explain this seemingly odd result. One is that Bush and his advisers were far less rightwing than they sought to appear, and Clinton and his economic team have proved to be far less liberal than people initially expected. A second reason is that as fiscal policy has declined in importance and monetary policy has increased, power over the economy has moved from the president and Congress to the largely independent Federal Reserve Board, America's equivalent of a central bank. This has increased the stress on combatting inflation and reduced the stress on lowering unemployment, especially near election time. The third reason is that the major political shift did not occur when Clinton became president in 1992, but in Congress between 1982 and 1986. In 1982 there was a Republican majority in the Senate and a conservative coalition of Republicans and southern Democrats dominated the House of Representatives. By 1987 the Democrats had regained control of the Senate, and liberal and moderate Democrats generally prevailed in the House. After 1986, Congress was able to stymie most presidential attempts to benefit the Republican constituency, and was able to make some progress in reestablishing the more liberal Democratic agenda (Alesina and Carliner, 1991).

The 1980–86 Period

It is impossible to understand the policies pursued by Bush, Clinton, and the Democratic Congress of the post-1986 period without understanding the major changes in economic policy that took place in the first six years of the Reagan administration. In 1980, Democratic President Jimmy Carter was defeated, and President Reagan, a right-wing Republican, was elected to office. At the same time there was a change of power in the Senate, with the Republicans winning a majority. The House of Representatives continued to have a Democratic majority, but more Republicans were elected to it and many of the Democrats were afraid that if they did not support Reagan, their constituencies, which contained a majority of Reagan supporters, might reject them.

This change in the political equation led to a number of fairly major changes in economic policy. Most of these were variations on themes that are perennial parts of the Republican agenda. There was a tightening of monetary policy in the first couple of years. There were increases in spending for national security, there were cuts in welfare spending, regulatory spending, aid to cities, and spending on infrastructure (Palmer and Sawhill, 1982; White and Wildavsky, 1989). There were changes in the tax structure to make the tax burden fall less on the rich and more on the middle and working classes. While the continuing Democratic majority in the House of Representatives limited the size of some of these changes, especially on the domestic spending side, they nonetheless constituted a distinct lurch toward the Republican agenda.

The most important change, however, was a relative newcomer to the Republican quiver. It had been normal for Democratic presidents to institute tax cuts in recessions to spur the economy. Republicans, however, had usually opposed these as inflationary. For a couple of years before the Reagan victory in 1980, a group of right-wing Republican members of Congress (led by Jack Kemp) had been pushing the idea of a major income tax cut. On the economic side they based this on the dubious supply-side argument that this could lead to increases in work effort that would increase revenues. On the political side they argued that the tax cuts might usher in a permanent Republican majority. Under Carter, this proposal had been treated with the disdain it deserved by both the President and Congress. Under Reagan, however, this idea was taken up and pushed by the President. With his weight behind it, it was hard for members of Congress to stand against a proposal that would put money into their constituents' pockets. Despite the fact that virtually all serious economists on both the left and the right predicted that the cuts would lead to massive deficits, they were enacted and signed into law.

The economists were correct. Ever since the passage of this legislation, the specter of huge and increasing federal deficits has had major effects on economic policy, keeping up interest rates, restraining growth, and making the task of managing the economy more difficult. While there have been a number of small tax increases in the subsequent decade by all three presidents, the deficit continues to dominate the economic agenda.

The post-1986 Period

In 1986 the Democratic Party regained control of the Senate and began to lose its fear that the large Reagan electoral victories presaged a major move to the right in the country as a whole. In the subsequent period they were able to stalemate new Republican initiatives and begin to assert their own agenda. While observers are correct in calling this a period of divided government, the edge lay with the Democrats in Congress.

However, the huge deficits that were a legacy of the early Reagan period led to a sea change in Democratic policy. For most of the post-war era, reducing the deficit had been a Republican staple, while the Democrats liked to pursue spending and tax reduction policies that tended to widen the deficit a little. However, confronted with huge deficits, the Democrats began to change their emphasis. With large deficits in place, spending programs became much harder to enact, and it was much more difficult to put in place tax reductions to lift the economy out of recession. Gradually, key Democrats on the economic policy committees in Congress began to see solving the deficit as a precondition to pursuing their preferred policies.

The rest of the Democratic agenda, however, remained unchanged. The Democrats favored greater equality in the distribution of income. They favored regulation to deal with what they perceived as abuses by business. They favored spending programs to help minorities, the poor, and the sick. They continued to support the provision of public goods, such as education and mass transportation by government. They viewed taxes and reductions in defense spending as necessary means to pay for these ends. During the post-1986 period there was gradual movement toward these goals and away from the Republican agenda. This change was slow during the last two years of the Reagan presidency and the first two years of the Bush presidency, speeded up a little during the second two years of the Bush era, and accelerated with the onset of the Clinton presidency.

In the post-Cold War era there is no set of policy decisions more important than those made to ensure the health of the economy. When the economy is healthy, inflation is under control, unemployment is low, and growth ensures more goods and services for all. When the economy is not healthy, runaway prices, high unemployment, and lowered real incomes are ever-present dangers. There is an extensive body of literature that shows that when the American people come to vote for their president, the health of the economy is their primary concern. Most think that Presidents Carter and Bush would have been reelected if the economy had been healthier when they came up for reelection (Edsall and Dionne, 1992). There is also some weaker evidence to support the idea that members of Congress belonging to the president's party are hurt if the economy is suffering when they come before the people (Fiorina, 1992).

Because of this, there is considerable incentive for the president and members of Congress of the president's party to help the economy thrive. Government has two major tools to attempt this, fiscal policy and monetary policy. The term "fiscal policy" refers to changes in the amount of government spending or taxation. Increasing spending or decreasing taxation puts more money into people's pockets, most of which will be spent on private goods and services. These purchases in turn will lead to yet more purchases, stimulating the economy, in what is generally referred to as a multiplier process. If inflation is getting out of control and the government wishes to use fiscal policy to slow down the economy, it decreases government spending or increases taxes.

The other major tool available to government is monetary policy. By increasing or decreasing the supply of money, the government can affect interest rates. If interest rates are pushed down, people are encouraged to purchase goods such as houses and cars that are usually bought with borrowed money. When these goods are purchased, there is more money in the hands of those who produce them, setting off economic expansion. When interest rates are increased, on the other hand, demand is lowered for these goods, leading to economic contraction.

Using these tools is a little like walking a tightrope. Policy makers are always seeking to balance between the evils of expanding too fast, thereby increasing inflation, and the evils of too slow growth resulting in lowered incomes and increased unemployment. Further, because policy changes made today may not affect the economy for months afterwards, those making policy have to be able to forecast what the economy will look like in the future, making the balancing task more difficult.

The presence of a large federal deficit has made it much harder to use fiscal policy, and somewhat harder to use monetary policy. Increasing spending or decreasing taxes would have the effect of increasing the deficit. This in turn would lead to increased federal borrowing. Many believe that this crowds out private borrowing, pushing up interest rates, and slowing the economy back down again. The presence of a large federal deficit has led the Federal Reserve Board, the body in charge of monetary policy, to become afraid of accelerating inflation, making it more cautious about lowering interest rates.

The balancing task is made even more difficult by the complexity of the economic policy process. Unlike many other countries where both monetary and fiscal policy are in the hands of the executive, in the United States fiscal policy during most of the period in question was shared between a Democratic Congress and a Republican president, while monetary policy was in the hands of a semi-autonomous body, the Federal Reserve Board. While this system prevented radical and unwise policies, it also made coordination difficult. For much of the post-1986 period, Congress, the president and the Federal Reserve were not in full agreement on what needed to be done. This made it much harder for government to react to undesired developments in the economy.

Fiscal policy under Bush

In 1981–2 a major recession led to a huge reduction in inflation. The reduction in inflation allowed a long period of recovery and slow growth. From 1982 to 1990 the economy grew. Because there was a deficit, fiscal policy was basically expansionary. However, this was largely offset by the tight money policies followed by the Federal Reserve, which slowed the rate of growth and prevented inflation from reigniting. The economy was also helped by a huge flow of money from overseas that helped finance the deficit, without having to print money to cover it, and held down interest rates. The result was one of the longest expansions in the post-war period.

During the 1988 election, the economy was still expanding. Unemployment had declined from 9.7 percent of the workforce in 1982 to 5.5 percent in 1988. Real gross domestic product had increased by more than 25 percent over the same period. Predictably, candidate Bush spent much of his election campaign stressing the so-called Reagan/Bush prosperity. This record was sufficient to sweep Bush, generally regarded as a weak candidate, into the presidency.

President Bush was a much more traditional Republican than his predecessor. While Reagan had given lip service to deficit reduction, Bush and his generally conservative team of economic advisers were much more eager to reduce it. While the economy was a distant second to foreign affairs in Bush's personal preferences, he had always been a believer in balanced budgets, and had in 1980 accused Reagan of "voodoo economics" for proposing the package that led to the huge deficits noted above.

As has been noted above, by 1988 the Democratic leadership in the House and Senate was also beginning to accept the necessity of achieving deficit reduction. In 1986 Congress had passed the Gramm-Rudman-Hollings Act, which set deficit targets for the next five years with the target being zero in the fifth year. Automatic spending reductions were meant to take place if the targets were not met. However, Congress proved able to circumvent these rules, with the result that the constantly changing targets had little effect on Congressional spending. By 1988 it was clear to all parties that procedural changes were not going to help much. There was a need for a substantive agreement that would use some combination of tax and expenditure changes to cut the deficit.

The central problem was that Congress and Presidents Reagan and Bush were not in agreement about whether the deficit should be tackled with domestic spending cuts or tax increases. Democrats in Congress felt that domestic spending programs benefitting their poor and middle-class constituency had been cut heavily during the early years of the Reagan administration, and that further cuts should be avoided at all costs. They were willing to enact some cuts in defense spending, but felt that the problem had been created by cutting taxes on the rich too heavily and could only be solved by increasing taxes. President Bush felt that domestic spending was too high, especially for the rapidly expanding social programs, and that taxes placed a burden on business and the economy. However, he was not himself unalterably opposed to tax increases. However, during the election campaign, he had tied his own hands. "Read my lips – No new taxes!" had became the most memorable phrase in his campaign, and was seen as his major promise to the American people. This made it hard to immediately turn around and agree to new taxes after all (Woodward, 1992b).

In the first two years of the Bush administration, O.M.B. Director Richard Darman lobbied the President and other cabinet members to negotiate a deficit reduction package with Congress that would include both spending reductions and tax increases (Woodward, 1992a). Bush was also being lobbied by the Federal Reserve Board. Their message was that unless something was done about the deficit, they would feel forced to pursue tight monetary policies that prevent growth in the economy. By 1990 these pressures had prevailed. In the autumn of 1990 Bush finally broke his "no new taxes" promise and signed a deficit reduction package designed to cut the deficit by $42.5 billion in 1991 and $496.2 billion in the 1991–5 period. Around half of the 1991 savings came from taxes, divided between income tax and social security tax changes that hurt the better-off sections of the population, and a variety of consumption taxes that hurt the middle and lower classes. The other half came from the spending side, primarily from cuts in Medicare, farm support payments, and defense.

While this helped somewhat, it still left a huge deficit, which was increased further by the economic slowdown that began in 1990. The chances of further movement were reduced to nil by the Bush administration's reaction to public outcry over the breaking of the "no new taxes" pledge. "The President has made it clear that he was forced to pay the tax ransom once in order to save the economy. He will not be forced to pay it again" (Sununu in *Congress Quarterly Almanac*, 1990). Without further tax increases, further deficit reduction was virtually impossible.

But without deficit reduction, any attempt to use tax cuts or spending increases to deal with the economic downturn that began in 1990 would be seen by the Federal Reserve as inflationary, and was likely to lead to offsetting increases in interest rates. Although Boskin, Bush's chief economic adviser, did recommend some fiscal stimulus in 1991, and a small stimulus package was proposed to Congress in 1992, nothing was done. The effective result was that fiscal policy was ineffective through most of the Bush administration and, because the deficit reductions took effect just as the economy was moving into recession, may actually have helped prolong the downturn.

Monetary policy under Bush

With fiscal policy ineffective in reducing the deficit or stimulating the economy, a greater than usual burden was placed on monetary policy. However, while monetary policy was quite capable of restraining inflation during the long expansion, it was less suitable for dealing with the 1990 recession and its aftermath. Monetary policy is very effective in cutting inflation and producing economic downturns. It is less so in dealing with recessions. While increasing the quantity of money and lowering the interest rate makes it more attractive to invest and to buy goods such as houses and cars, in recessions businesses and consumers may be afraid to commit their savings to such purchases because they fear bankruptcy or being laid off. This means that even in normal recessions it may take quite a while before the economy responds to lower rates.

However, these normal difficulties were compounded by a number of special problems in the post-1990 period. One was overbuilding. During the late 1980s too much commercial and rental construction had taken place. With vacancy rates approaching 20 percent in some cities, even low interest rates were not going to spark new construction in these areas. In a similar vein, the regulatory excesses of the Reagan administration had led to considerable tightening on the qualifications for loan approvals. Many who wanted to buy a house could not qualify under the new guidelines. Toward the end of the period, high interest rates in Germany, sparked by the need to rebuild East Germany after reunification, and the Japanese economic crisis of 1992, helped dry up the flow of foreign money that had held down real long-term interest rates. More generally, new management techniques and computer technology were leading to permanent downsizing of large corporations, retarding any increases in employment.

On the political side, a decade of conservative Republican appointments to the Federal Reserve had made it even more than usually afraid of setting off inflation. They preferred to make a small change and wait to see its effect, rather than making big changes that would do more to increase employment. The Federal Reserve also regarded the failure of Congress and the President to take more effective measures to deal with the deficit as somewhat irresponsible. They felt that high interest rates were due as much to the fact that the federal government was competing with the private sector for the limited pool of available savings, as they were to the policies of the Federal Reserve.

The result was open warfare between Bush's economic advisers and the Federal Reserve (Greenhouse, 1992). In the first year of the Bush presidency, the Federal Reserve saw an opportunity to push inflation down to near zero (Berry, 1989). In pursuit of this aim, they increased the discount rate (the rate at which they lend to banks) and decreased the money supply. The lagged effects of this move, together with the oil price shock in the first few months of the Gulf War, were the principal immediate causes of the 1990 recession. While they had expected a slowing, their hope had been to engineer a "soft landing," a small downturn followed by a rapid rebound. However, this was not to be.

Once the recession had started, the Federal Reserve was slow to reduce rates. This was not entirely due to their obsession with lowering inflation. It was also because they had to walk a narrow tightrope between over-stimulation and under-stimulation. The Federal Reserve could only affect short-term rates. If these were reduced too rapidly, investors might come to fear future inflation, with the result that the crucially important long-term rates might actually increase. Thus the Federal Reserve needed to increase the money supply enough to lower interest rates in the short term, but not enough to make people expect that long-term inflation would increase.

However, most observers felt that even given this problem, the Federal Reserve was overly cautious in its interest rate reductions, seeing a danger of inflation where none existed and making many small changes rather than a few big ones (Merrifield, 1992). Partly as a result, the economic recovery was slow in coming, and growth in the recovery period was less than half the postwar average.

Fiscal policy under Clinton

The election campaign of 1992 was one in which the state of the economy and proposals to improve the economy were the dominant motifs. In the United States, economic contractions are normally short lived, and are followed by a period of rapid growth. The downturn of 1990 lasted longer than usual and was followed by a long period of anemic growth. As can be seen in Figure 12.1, even though growth resumed in the summer of 1991, growth was so slow that unemployment continued to increase through most of 1992.

Clinton's initial response to this situation was to promise to follow traditional Democratic remedies. While he paid lip service to

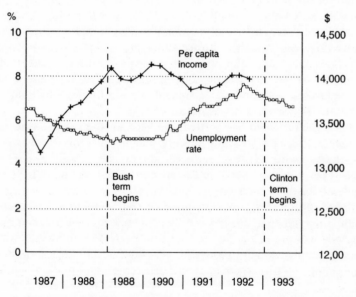

FIGURE 12.1   *Unemployment and real per capita disposable income, 1987–93*
Source: Council of Economic Advisers, *Economic Report of the President* (Washington, D.C., U.S. Government Printing Office, 1988, 1990, and 1993 editions). *Los Angeles Times*, October 9th 1993.

reducing the deficit, his primary emphasis for most of the campaign was on a middle-class tax cut and spending programs that would build the neglected infrastructure and retrain America's workforce. As the campaign wore on, however, his position began to shift. The unprecedented success of billionaire Ross Perot, who used his vast personal wealth to campaign for president on a program of reducing the deficit, made it important for Clinton to place more stress on deficit reduction. By the end of the campaign there was less stress on the middle-class tax cut and more stress on income tax increases for the wealthy, and reduced spending. However, even at the end of the campaign he was placing more stress on economic stimulus, and a vast new health program, than on the deficit.

By the time that Clinton took office in January 1993, the middle-class tax cut had been abandoned, and the huge investment in infrastructure and job training had been pared to a moderate $30 billion program in the first year, and a less moderate $169 billion over five years. In February, Clinton proposed a deficit reduction plan to cut around $500 billion over four years. Given that the projected deficit was $331.8 billion in 1993, this would not solve the problem, but would reduce it somewhat. Clinton proposed raising the money about two-thirds from tax increases and about one-third from spending decreases. On the tax side he proposed raising the top income tax rates from 31 percent, to 36 percent for those earning more than $140,000, and 39.6 percent for those earning more than $250,000. He proposed a general energy tax, and taxing 85 percent of social security receipts for those with incomes over $30,000. He also proposed tax credits for the less well-off, to ensure that the total tax burden for those earning $20,000 or less would not rise. On the spending side, Clinton proposed additional cuts in defense spending, selective cuts in domestic spending, and payment cuts to doctors and drug companies for the medical programs aiding the poor and the elderly. The package was not substantially different from packages that Congressional Democrats had been examining for the past two years, except that there was somewhat more emphasis on tax increases, and somewhat less on spending decreases.

The initial plan was to use the investment and infrastructure package to stimulate the economy early on, and then introduce the deficit package later when the economy was recovering and could withstand the fiscal hit. However, Congress had other ideas. The arcane rules of the U.S. Senate permit a minority party to filibuster (or talk to death) all Bills except budget Bills. Senate Republicans used this power to reduce, and then kill, the early stimulus package.

At this point, the Clinton administration was faced with a choice. Should it abandon what was likely to be an extremely difficult fight in Congress to pass the deficit reduction package, or should it retreat from this on the grounds that without the early stimulus package the deficit reduction package might drive the economy back into recession? Three things persuaded them to persist with the deficit reduction package.

One factor was the continued presence of Ross Perot. After receiving an unprecedented 20 percent of the vote, he was showing no inclination to act as a graceful loser. Instead, he was running programs on television about the continued importance of reducing the deficit and why the Clinton administration was not doing enough to solve the problem.

Another factor was the content of the Bill. Whereas President Bush's similar package had moved only a little toward tax equality, Clinton's package was aimed solidly at the rich. While taxes as a percentage of pretax income would fall from 7.8 percent to 7.6 percent for those earning less than $10,000, they would increase from 21.2 percent to 21.8 percent for those earning between $100,000 and $200,000, and from 20.9 percent to 23.8 percent for those earning over $200,000 (Cloud, 1992). Reversing the Reagan administration's tax giveaways to the rich was a goal that was central to Democratic Party values, and the necessary tax increases were much more palatable in the context of deficit reduction.

Perhaps most important were the arguments of his new economic advisers, Treasury Secretary Bentsen, and O.M.B. Director Panetta, two moderate Democrats recruited from the Congressional leadership. They argued that a deficit reduction package would not in fact lead to an economic downturn. While they agreed that tax increases and spending decreases would leave less money in people's pockets, they argued that this negative effect would be more than balanced by the effects of a deficit reduction package on interest rates. With lower deficits there would be less fear of inflation, and people would be willing to lend for the long term at lower rates. These lower rates in turn would stimulate the economy.

In Congress, the Bill was the focus of an intense struggle in which Republicans united against the package and conservative Democrats fought to make it conform more to their wishes. In the end, the Bill passed the Senate only when Vice-President Gore cast the deciding vote. Ironically, the major effect of all this conservative opposition was to make the Bill more liberal. Regressive energy taxes were stripped from the Bill, partly replaced by more progressive income sources, and partly by dubious spending cuts that many expected never to take place. In the end, however, the Bill was changed only on the margins, with most of the original measures passing. The administration estimated the final Bill would cut the deficit by $504 billion, lowering it from $332 billion in 1993 to $206 billion in 1997. A more realistic estimate by the Congressional Budget Office was that it would result in a $433 billion saving (Camia, 1993).

The passage of the Bill did indeed appear to lead to lower interest rates, with the 30-year Treasury Bill rate falling from 7.25 percent in January to 5.90 percent in October of the first year. A W.E.F.A. Group study commissioned by *U.S. News and World Report*, a generally conservative magazine, estimated that the deficit reduction package was responsible for as much as two-thirds of this fall and predicted that these changes would indeed lead to the deficit reduction package stimulating rather than depressing the economy (Hage, 1993; U.S. *News and World Report* August 20th 1993).

However, while the first year saw deficit reduction, many expected that later years might see increased spending now that Democrats occupied the House, the Senate, and the presidency. A particularly likely reason was the vast health Bill proposed by the Clinton administration, which would finally establish a national health service for all Americans. Over 200 billion of the 400 billion estimated cost of this service was to be paid for through cutting waste. This level of waste reduction would be completely unprecedented, and was seen as highly implausible by most experienced observers. Most thought that the program would instead lead to large increases in government spending, effectively undoing most of what had been achieved in the deficit reduction package.

Monetary policy under Clinton

Because the Federal Reserve usually is the most conservative part of the economic policymaking apparatus, it is normal for there to be more conflict between the Federal Reserve and the president when Democrats are in power than when Republicans hold the office. However, in the first year of the Clinton administration, relations between the Federal Reserve and the President were unusually amicable. There were two reasons for this.

One was the state of the economy. By the time that the Clinton administration came into office, a slow recovery had been in place for about a year and a half. A slow recovery could reasonably be seen as something that was in Clinton's interest. A rapid expansion might run its course before the next presidential election. A slow recovery should result in an economy that would still be expanding when Clinton came up for reelection in 1988. This meant that Clinton was much more willing to tolerate cautiousness on the part of the Federal Reserve.

The second reason was Clinton's deficit package. Bankers expect Republican presidents to push for deficit reduction. They were surprised and delighted to see a Democratic president and a Democratic Congress pushing for the same thing. Alan Greenspan, then Chairman of the Federal Reserve, was visibly lobbying for the Clinton package as it made its way through Congress, and Clinton declared himself opposed to moves by the House Committee on Banking and Housing to limit the independence of the Federal Reserve.

However, although relations between the Federal Reserve and the Clinton administration were much more amicable than those between the Federal Reserve and the Bush administration, the substance of monetary policy was little changed. Even as price increases fell to the 3 percent range the Federal Reserve continued to be worried about inflation and felt that so long as even minute growth was occurring, monetary stimulus should be avoided. While they did not increase interest rates for most of 1993, there was little or no interest in reducing short-term rates further to speed up the expansion of the economy.

International Trade

This discussion has concentrated on domestic economic policies, but it is impossible to ignore the international dimension of trade in the contemporary "globalized economy." President Bush made a major initiative in this area with the negotiation of the North American Free Trade Area (N.A.F.T.A.) with Canada and Mexico. He left this agreement to his successor to maneuver through Congress; and President Clinton did so successfully in perhaps the most astute political mobilization of his presidency to date. By gradually eliminating tariffs and other trade barriers in North America, this agreement will create an even larger trading bloc than the European Community.

The success of the N.A.F.T.A. accords was followed by the successful completion of the Uruguay Round of the General Agreement on Tariffs and Trade (G.A.T.T.).This was a world wide negotiation to eliminate additional trade barriers on agricultural products that have inhibited American farm exports. N.A.F.T.A. and G.A.T.T. represent the triumph of a free trade approach to international economics. This view prevailed despite pressures on the Democratic administration from unions for more protectionist policy, and despite a well-funded campaign by Ross Perot against N.A.F.T.A. The United States now seems determined to compete in the international market rather than retreat to its own internal market.

Policy Outcomes

Most economic policy over the 1986–92 period can be reasonably regarded as a series of struggles between a Democratic Party ensconced in Congress that sought greater equality of incomes, more domestic spending and tax increases, and a Republican Party controlling the presidency that wanted slower decreases in defense spending, decreases in domestic spending, less equality, and no tax increases. Because the Constitution gives more power over economic matters to Congress, and because the public holds the president responsible for the state of the economy, Congress has the edge in the struggle. Because of this, the 1986–92 period saw a slow erosion in the changes made in the first six years of the Reagan presidency, combined with unending stalemates.

The amount and composition of government spending followed a Democratic trajectory. In constant 1987 dollars, spending grew from $1,017 billion in 1986 to 1,180 billion in 1992. Defense spending fell from 27.6 percent of all outlays in 1986 to 19.6

percent of all outlays in 1993. In contrast, payments to individuals for such things as old age pensions, medical care, and disability insurance rose from 46 percent of all outlays in 1986 to 54 percent in 1993 (O.M.B., 1993).

The incidence of taxes also moved in a Democratic direction. Kasten, Sammartino, and Toder show that the tax burden on the poorest 20 percent of the population fell from 10.4 percent of their income in 1985 to 9.0 in 1993. They also show that the burden on the top 20 percent increased from 24.1 percent of their income in 1985 to 26.5 percent in 1993 (Kasten, Sammartino, and Toder, 1992). This redistribution was pushed even further by the tax changes in the Clinton deficit reduction package, referred to above.

However, both the incidence of taxes and the composition of government spending can reasonably be regarded as less important than the policies that determine the health of the economy. Here neither the Democratic nor the Republican Party can be said to have won. Rather, their continual struggles over fiscal policy handed over policymaking power to the Federal Reserve. And, while it is true that external circumstances and the excesses of the Reagan presidency were partly responsible for the slow growth of this period, it is probable that the Federal Reserve Board's cautiousness and conservatism and their strong anti-inflation bias also bears part of the blame.

The future, however, looks much more promising. With inflation now low and productivity improving, the most likely prospect is for slow growth until at least the next presidential election. Somewhat ironically, the cautious moves made by conservative Federal Reserve Board members appointed by Reagan and Bush helped Bush lose the presidency, and may well help Clinton to keep it.

13

Social Policy

B. GUY PETERS

After 12 years of relative neglect of social policy in the United States, Bill Clinton came into office pledged to making life better for the disadvantaged. The administration was pledged to reach this goal not through traditional Democratic "tax and spend" methods, but rather through more market-oriented programs, using workfare as much as welfare. While the commitments to new means of addressing social problems are in some ways laudable, they face enormous difficulties. Some of these difficulties are ideological and are bound up in the historical American resistance to strong government involvement in social policy. Other difficulties are related to the relatively weak American economy and the changing nature of work in the United States and other industrialized countries. The general trends appear to be in the direction of greater socioeconomic inequality and greater need rather than less, and government will be hard-pressed to stem that tide. That difficulty is, of course, exacerbated by the deficit problem. Social policy thus presents a significant challenge to the leadership and policy creativity of both Clinton and his administration.

The United States as a Welfare State Laggard

The conventional description of the social policy stance of the United States is that the country is a welfare state "laggard." Compared to other industrialized democracies, the United States provides rather sparse levels of social protection for the underprivileged. Further, many of the social programs that do exist tend to be means-tested, so that not only are the benefits rather meager, they are also difficult to receive and stigmatizing for the individuals who depend upon them. Although social security is a popular (and not means-tested) program for the elderly, even its benefits are limited and the program increasingly appears to be a means-tested program as more of the benefits provided to middle-class bene-ficiaries are subjected to taxation. Consequently, the middle classes tend to rely upon private pension and disability programs, rather than the public program, for full protection for their standard of living in old age or in the case of inability to work. Middle-class Americans thus have less reason for a vigorous political defense of those public programs.

There are several reasons behind America's restrictive approach to social provision. On the one hand, there is a pervasive cultural individualism and, with that, an attitudinal bias against social programs, and against government in general (Bellah, 1985; Cook and Barrett, 1992). This bias is especially pronounced in the case of "welfare" (A.F.D.C. – Aid to Families with Dependent Children), which is one of only a few programs on which the average American would like to see less government money spent. This cultural bias against government involvement with social policy is reinforced by the existence of a strong voluntary sector and private philanthropy that address at least a part of the real and perceived need for social services in the country. Citizens appear willing to contribute time and money to assist the very same people for whom they would oppose public assistance. Likewise, many of the poor appear more willing to accept private social services than to go on welfare or use other means-tested public benefits.

The relative success of the private sector in the United States has also contributed to the absence of support for the welfare state. During the immediate post-World War II period when Europe was implementing its welfare state programs, the American private sector was providing an economic bonanza for anyone willing (or able) to work. Those who did not participate in this bonanza were deemed to have only themselves to blame. In addition, whether because of the prevailing ideology or because of the need to compensate for the inadequacies of public-sector programs, the private sector itself began to provide many of the services delivered by government in other industrialized democracies (Rein and Rainwater, 1986). For example, most people who have health insurance in the United States receive it through their employer;

and private pensions are a larger source of retirement income for a substantial portion of the retired population than is social security.

Now that this extensive private-sector system of benefits has been created, it would be difficult for government to displace it. The resistance to proposed health reforms being offered by the insurance industry is but one example of the entrenched position of private-sector benefits and the difficulties of producing change. What is often forgotten in this discussion, however, is that private-sector benefits are heavily subsidized through the public sector. Benefits provided by employers for their employees are largely untaxed, although they amount to at least $200 billion of real income for employees. Also, the federal government has begun to insure the soundness of private pension schemes so that employees can be sure to receive the benefits they have been promised (and sometimes paid for) during their working lives. Tax breaks on individual retirement accounts make social security less valuable for prospective retirees. It is doubtful that private-sector benefits could be as generous, or as secure, were it not for the active involvement of the public sector.

Despite its relatively lower level of development, we should not dismiss the American welfare state entirely (Marmor, Mashaw, and Harvey, 1990). It does provide benefits to a very large number of people, and provides those benefits through a variety of programs, both based on social insurance and means-tested. Table 13.1 contains information on the major programs and the level of expenditure for those programs. Other than social insurance (including unemployment and workmen's compensation), the programs available are means-tested, with almost no general social assistance available. Even with the large number of people receiving these benefits, there are still a large number who do not receive social benefits that they might need and deserve. They do not apply for the benefits because of ignorance, because of pride, and because their irregular patterns of living make it almost impossible to establish the residence required for eligibility.

Although it began at a lower level, social welfare programs in the United States tended to fall even further behind those of other industrialized democracies during the 1980s. As a part of a widespread rethinking of the role of the public sector during that decade, the Republican administrations in office from 1981 to 1993 attempted to reduce public spending on social services and

TABLE 13.1   *Major welfare state beneficiaries and expenditures, 1990*

	Beneficiaries (thousands)	Expenditures ($millions)
Social security		
Retired workers	24,838	156,800
Disabled workers	3,011	22,100
Dependants	6,554	26,500
Others	5,426	42,700
Unemployment insurance	2,522	18,057
Means-tested		
A.F.D.C.	11,439	21,196
S.S.I.[1]	4,913	17,232
Earned income tax credits	33,693	5,902
Food stamps	21,500	17,702
School lunches	11,600	3,250
W.I.C.[2]	4,500	2,119
Medicaid	25,255	72,288
Energy assistance	5,800	1,641

Source: U.S. Department of Commerce, Bureau of the Census, *Statistical Abstract of the United States, 1992* (Washington, D.C., Government Printing Office, 1993).

Notes: [1] Supplemental Security Income.
[2] Women, Infants, and Children Nutrition Program.

to promote private-sector alternatives. Although social spending did not decline, and indeed increased by almost 200 percent in current dollars from 1980 to 1992, the benefit level for many recipients of means-tested benefits did tend to decline. For example, in just one year between 1991 and 1992 the real maximum benefit for A.F.D.C. recipients declined in 38 states and the District of Colombia (Shapiro, 1991). The holes in the "social safety net" became wider during the 1980s – despite promises to the contrary by the administrations – and more people slipped through them into the underclass. The number of people living in poverty increased, according to the official statistics, even though changes in the classification of poverty otherwise tended to reduce those numbers (Ruggles, 1990).

As will be discussed in greater detail below, the attack on the American welfare state was mounted through a variety of tactics, including attempting to reduce federal spending (or at least reducing the rate of increase in social spending), devolving program responsibility to states and localities, and tightening eligibility requirements. The net effect of these program changes was to exacerbate the existing inequalities in the country and to increase the number of people living at or below the official poverty level. These policy shifts accentuated the economic changes occurring in the United States and elsewhere, and made the impact of the global recession and the reduction in manufacturing jobs all the greater.

The Fundamental Problem: Inequality

The fundamental problem for social policy in the United States is the underlying social and economic inequality. Further, the experience over many decades indicates that this inequality is increasing, and may be likely to increase even more. Some 32.6 million people (12.7 million of them children) in the United States live below the official poverty line, and many others are faced with persistent economic insecurity. The lowest earning segment of the economy had a declining share of total income, while the upper decile had an increasing share during the 1980s. In all economies, social and economic inequality tends to be produced by the market and related socioeconomic processes, and public social programs are used to ameliorate that inequality. The market tends to produce rather high levels of inequality in the United States, and that inequality is continuing to increase as higher-paid manufacturing jobs are being lost through corporate restructuring, technological change, and foreign competition (Reich, 1991). Some of the socioeconomic inequality also is a function of the absence of public programs, especially a national health insurance program, that would alleviate some of the worst effects of earnings differentials. Further, many of the activities of government (especially the tax system) tend to benefit the middle and upper classes more than the lower classes, so that the net redistributive effect of public-sector activity in the United States is rather slight.

Americans are not prone to think in terms of social class, but rather tend to think more of race as the fundamental category of social stratification (Hacker, 1992). Nevertheless, there is certainly an underlying and significant degree of economic stratification in the country, and apparently a declining level of social mobility. With the rise of the large corporation and the decline of individual entrepreneurship, the opportunities for the able but poor person to become wealthy have declined. Likewise, higher education has become a crucial filter defining opportunities for young people. Despite the relative openness of the American education system, there is still a class bias reflected in the students who get to universities, particularly to the more prestigious universities. Social mobility and the dominance of the middle class are chief among the comfortable myths of American life, but are increasingly threatened by the reality of increased social and economic inequality.

We can think of social policies attempting to address three forms, or stages, of social and economic inequality in the United States. The first form, addressed rather successfully through social insurance, can be seen as a product of the life cycle, or of short-term economic dislocations. Retirement, disability, the loss of the primary income earner through early death, and somewhat later unemployment, have all been primary targets of social insurance programs. Rather than redistributing income across classes, almost all redistribution that occurs through social insurance has tended to be across the life of the covered individuals and their families. Soon after its adoption, social security also began to redistribute income across generations, as social security pensions became benefits for the elderly financed almost entirely through payroll taxes on the earnings of the younger generations still employed.

As noted, social insurance programs do not solve the income replacement problems of the middle class in retirement or disability. This is true even though their benefits are somewhat income-related; however, they do build a floor under employees and their families that can prevent abject poverty. These programs have their problems, including unequal treatment of women, high penalties for retirees who want to work part-time, a possible negative effect on capital accumulation, and a rather regressive revenue source. Despite these problems, social security and its allied programs are among the few real successes in the history of American social policy.

The politics of poverty

During the 1960s, primarily through the War on Poverty, social programs in the United States began to address a second form of inequality. Rather than being the product of the life cycle or of temporary misfortune, this form of inequality was persistent and tended to be transmitted from one generation to the next. The existence of this poverty was highlighted by books such as *The Other America*, although the underclass had existed for decades, if not for the entire history of the United States (Katz, 1993). The people living in this persistent poverty were supported at a subsistence level through a variety of means-tested programs, primarily Aid to Families with Dependent Children (A.F.D.C.), public housing, and more recently Food Stamps and Medicare. They were maintained in poverty, but little was being done to alter their lives or the future of their children.

The principal aim of the War on Poverty initiated by Lyndon Johnson in the 1960s was to break the cycle of poverty and to enable people to move out of deprivation. The principal tactics were to be education (Head Start), jobs and job training (Comprehensive Employment and Training Act and the Job Corps), as well as comprehensive attempts to alter the conditions and culture of poverty (Model Cities and the Office of Economic Opportunity). Although declared failures by several Republican presidents after the 1960s, and being largely dismantled by those presidents, some programs from the War on Poverty – most notably the Head Start program for preschool children – continue, and still attempt, to generate more fundamental social change than would be possible with most means-tested benefits. One of President Clinton's numerous campaign promises was to increase federal spending for Head Start. This promise is reinforced by Hillary Clinton's close personal attachment to the Children's Defense Fund, a major lobbying organization on behalf of Head Start.

As will be noted below, the goal of eliminating poverty is a formidable task given the extent to which existing social conditions and public programs tend to reinforce poverty and inequality rather than ameliorate it. There have been numerous political and academic debates over the root causes of American poverty, as well as how best to solve the problem. Other than for children and the elderly there is little sympathy for the plight of the poor and little effective support for programs that would do other than maintain them in that state.

Race is one of the factors complicating any attempts to address inequality. A significantly higher percentage of nonwhite Americans live in poverty than do white Americans (Table 13.2). Also, a substantially higher percentage of blacks and Hispanics receive A.F.D.C. than do white and Asian-Americans. The gulf between black and white America has arguably been increasing rather than decreasing since the 1970s. During the 1980s critics were able to argue persuasively (at least to those Republican administrations) that government programs were the source of poverty rather than a solution to the problem, and that only through individual initiative could people emerge from poverty (Murray, 1984). Some of the same was argued, albeit less effectively, about affirmative action programs and their impact on nonwhites. These ideological positions were used as justifications for a reduction in social spending and a decreasing emphasis on equal opportunity programs. The overlapping of race and poverty means that any attempts to deal with social conditions quickly become involved with other issues of

TABLE 13.2   *Poverty and program participation by race*

| | Poverty rate[1] | |
	Black	White
All persons	31.9	8.8
Children	44.8	15.9
All families	29.3	8.1
Female-headed families	56.1	37.9

| | A.F.D.C. recipients | |
	Proportion of population[2]	Proportion of A.F.D.C. recipients
White	80.3	38.4
Black	12.1	40.2
Hispanic	9.0	15.9
Asian	2.9	2.7
Other	3.9	2.8

Notes: [1] Proportion of population group living below poverty line.
[2] More than 100 percent because Hispanic may be of any race.

inequality and with issues of cultural politics that may be even more intractable than the social issues.

Other factors also complicate any attempts on the part of government to address the problem of persistent poverty. One is that many existing government social programs tend to lock their recipients into poverty and dependence rather than provide means to work their way out of that condition. In fairness, the persistence of dependence on programs is less than is often assumed, and many people do move on and off welfare each month; at any one time almost a third of A.F.D.C. recipients will have been on the program a year or less. Still, programs are not designed to make it easy for their recipients to make the move into the workforce. For example, A.F.D.C. tends to impose a very heavy "tax" on earnings by its recipients, so that above a very low threshold recipients lose two-thirds of any outside income as their benefits are reduced. Likewise, welfare recipients often will lose other benefits such as Medicaid, public housing, and possibly food stamps if they attempt to move off welfare and into the labor force. Also, social security taxes, and most state and local income taxes, are imposed on the first dollar earned, rather than being phased in. The Family Support Act of 1988 has ameliorated some of the problems of benefit loss for Medicaid, but other potential benefit losses persist if the individual goes to work. Given that most welfare recipients receive little more than the minimum wage without benefits if they do work, there are few incentives (other than pride) for them to seek employment.

The receipt of A.F.D.C. is usually dependent upon having children at home, although the Family Support Act enables adults without children to receive six months' support. Partly because of the emphasis on children as objects of support there is an ironic tendency of poverty to afflict women and children differentially. This, in turn, also means that poverty tends to be inherited. This inheritance can begin in the womb with poor nutrition, which then leads to low birthweight babies and premature babies that have a disproportionate number of health and learning problems later in life. The inheritance continues through disrupted families and the absence of effective role models of employment and success in education. It is also perpetuated by poor housing, poor neighbor-hoods, and poor education, with the children of poverty requiring extraordinary personal discipline and good fortune to escape that fate.

As well as children being present, being on welfare usually means that the father of those children must be absent. A.F.D.C. was originally envisaged as a temporary program for newly widowed or deserted women. Although it has now served as the major source of income for several generations of women and children, this idea was not part of the original conceptualization of the program. It has been almost impossible for government to adopt a program that would be less disruptive to family life, partly because of the strength of the prevailing ideology of self-reliance. Many people in the United States would find it difficult to accept the idea of their taxes being spent to support an able-bodied male who (at least in theory) could either himself find a job and support his family, or at least care for the children while his spouse worked.

Another factor in the delivery of social services that tends to complicate efforts to ameliorate poverty is that many social programs are delivered by state and local governments (see Chapters 10 and 11, Kincaid; King). Even if the programs are nominally federal and have federally mandated minima, they are administered locally and there are varying benefit levels and eligibility rules in every state. For example, an A.F.D.C. family of three in Alaska receives $924 per month, while a similar family in Mississippi receives only $120 per month. Some of this difference can be accounted for by differences in price levels, but by no means all.

Other public programs also tend to be affected by poverty and to reinforce existing inequalities. Education is an obvious example of one of these policies. In addition to the tendency of children from more affluent parents to do better in school, everything else being equal, than do students from less fortunate backgrounds, the manner of educational finance in the United States also reinforces poverty. Public education is largely a local function provided by over 14,000 school boards. The level of expenditures therefore is to a great extent a function of available local tax revenues. It is (relatively) easy for wealthy school districts to provide good educational facilities and to pay teachers well, while poor districts may have to impose very high tax levels in order to provide even minimal levels of education. This, of course, means that poorer students are likely to receive a lower-quality education and to have a diminished opportunity to escape from poverty. This inequality is being addressed through a number of court cases claiming equal protection under the 14th amendment, but the system of local finance (and hence inequality) is deeply ingrained in education. For example, the plan devised by the state of Texas to tax wealthy school districts to finance education in poor districts has raised a storm of protest and further legal action (Verhoek, 1993).

The financial aspects of education tend to disadvantage the children of the poor, but they are not the only problems in that policy sector. Teachers and school administrators tend to behave as if these children cannot, or will not, perform adequately in school. School buildings are not maintained, the worst teachers often are assigned to schools in poor neighborhoods, and these schools are not given equipment such as computers that might help the students learn. These deprivations, in turn, tend to mean that the children do not perform well and are not challenged to prepare themselves for higher education. One of the responses to this common pattern of behavior by school administrators has been for poor parents to attempt to take over and manage the schools themselves (Chicago), or to promote choice programs for their children (Milwaukee).

The tax system also tends to perpetuate socioeconomic inequality in the United States. Many citizens believe that taxes are progressively redistributive since they fund (among other things) social programs, but many taxes themselves are either proportional or even regressive. This is especially true of state and local government tax systems that rely heavily on sales and excise taxes. Many studies of state and local taxes have found that they differentially target the less affluent and that their regressive nature has been tending to increase. Even the social security tax that is directly linked to social expenditures is itself somewhat regressive. It is only charged on earnings up to a certain level ($55,500 in 1992), and is not levied on earnings other than wages and salaries. An affluent person receiving a large investment income will not have to pay any social security taxes on those earnings. Further, since social security tax is levied on the first dollar of income earned, it makes getting a low-wage job that much less valuable to someone who might otherwise receive welfare benefits. Again, this tends to make it more rational for a person to remain on welfare rather than attempting to move out of poverty.

In addition to the impact of government programs, other social conditions make escaping from poverty more difficult. One of the most important of these environmental factors is crime and drugs.

Although far from confined to the inner cities and poor minority populations, drugs and crime have wreaked havoc on the poor and underprivileged in American cities. For a group of people with few apparent economic opportunities and apparently little to lose, both selling and using drugs may not appear as incredible as it might for other people. With the drugs has come the crime that not only differentially victimizes the already poor, but also makes economic redevelopment of inner-city areas all the more difficult. The central position that drugs have come to play in inner-city neighborhoods means that attempts to bring them and their residents into the mainstream of social and economic life are made even more difficult than they already were. Not only are businesses reluctant to locate in these neighborhoods, but a large share of the potential entrepreneurial talent is diverted into illegal activities.

The "new poverty"

The United States, along with other industrialized countries, is now facing a new type of inequality. The second form of inequality described above was concentrated in the inner cities and among ethnic minorities, who often had relatively little experience in the labor force. This was the poverty of long-term unemployment and inadequate or nonexistent job skills reinforced by generations living on welfare. This new form of inequality, however, is affecting at least two different groups of people who might be expected to be able to support themselves adequately through the private economy. First, there are the many people who previously had been active participants in the labor force and who in some cases had been quite successful. As manufacturing jobs become less numerous, people with minimal education and no particular skills, who once could earn a middle-class income, find that this is increasingly impossible. Also, most corporations, in the name of enhancing competitiveness and productivity, have been eliminating middle management jobs, a trend made easier by the growth of office technology. Thus many people who believed they had a secure economic future now find themselves figuratively, if not literally, on the streets.

A second disadvantaged group emerging in the labor market are the working poor. For a significant segment of the population, the only work they can find is in jobs paying only the minimum wage and providing few if any benefits. Millions of people in the United

States work full time and yet receive no health benefits, and the number grows almost daily. The benefits that have been so important for delaying the development of the public welfare state in the United States are now available to a decreasing share of the working population. The American dream is becoming increasingly only a dream for a large segment of the labor force, while for those still employed in full-time salaried jobs the good life continues unabated.

It also appears probable that the market will produce even greater inequality in the near future. An increasing share of the jobs being created in the American economy are part-time and/or temporary positions, with low wages and few benefits. One indication of this trend is that the largest single employer in the United States is now Manpower, Inc., a temporary employment agency, with 200,000 more employees than General Motors. As well as a gulf between the employed and the unemployed, the gap between the declining number of people with full-time, salaried positions and those with part-time and/or minimum wage positions is increasing. An individual can work a full 40-hour week at the official minimum wage ($4.25 per hour) and still be in poverty. In addition, the real value of the average wage paid in the American economy has been declining, from $275 per week in 1980 to $256 in 1991 in constant 1982 dollars, so that even those earning that wage will find their standard of living increasingly under threat.

Even if the jobs being generated are not very good, a job is generally better than unemployment. It appears, however, that the economy may not be the engine for producing jobs that it has been in the past, even if higher levels of economic growth should return. Employers appear more willing to work their existing employees longer hours than to add new workers, given the potential costs of benefits involved in new hiring. Further, employers may not want to make any commitment to training or socializing new employees and may prefer to have temporary employees meet any fluctuations in the demand for work. Finally, international competitiveness is a major force driving firms to be leaner and to shed labor in favor of technology. In sum, firms have few incentives to create new jobs even if they are becoming more profitable, but rather have a number of incentives to keep their labor costs as low as possible.

There appears to be a need to address the long-term changes in the economy through social programs, but neither the target populations nor the dynamics of inequality are those to which the political system is accustomed. The new targets of social programs often would have to be middle aged and formerly middle class. These new members of the poor, or at least the relatively deprived, believed that they had prepared themselves for a secure economic future, but have found themselves unemployed and dependent upon social welfare or private charity. The real problem is that these economic changes appear to be permanent, so that short-term programs to tide over the newly unemployed, and the new poor, may not really help them that much. Those newly poor who lack a sound basic education may never be able to adapt effectively to the economic changes, so that longer-term programs of assistance and support may be needed. Likewise, those who will be able to make the shift into a new information-age economy will also need financial support and substantial additional training, if they are to be successful.

Several types of social policy intervention will be required to address the problems arising from these shifts in the economy. One is short-term, or perhaps even medium-term, direct social assistance. The individuals affected and their families need to be able to live at or above the poverty level before any other types of programs can be effective. For the working poor who have little or no job skills, some forms of assistance may be required for the indefinite future, and may be supplied through existing programs such as Food Stamps, Medicare, and (less widely available) subsidized housing. For the newly poor with more education and job skills, the involvement of education and training programs will be required to prepare these individuals for new occupations. This may be just the beginning of long-term cycles of training and retraining, since the job market is projected to change much more rapidly in the future than it has in the past.

Several factors will complicate the provision of this range of services to the newly poor, just as has been true for the services delivered to the more typical impoverished populations. Even more than the other services, this range of services will involve coordination of a number of programs and organizations. In addition to social service agencies and agriculture (food stamps), the needed range of services would involve education and labor market organizations. One of the persistent problems of the social services has been the coordination of the services available to people. The

Model Cities Program, for example, was designed in large part to ensure that residents of poor neighborhoods received the full range of services they should in an integrated manner. That program rarely worked as intended, and existing services for the poor often encounter coordination problems; there is little reason to believe that coordination would work better for this population.

Some of the same problems of family structure that afflict the traditional poor may also produce difficulties for the new poor. There might be no programs in effect like A.F.D.C. that tend to divide families, but the constraints of the market may produce strains on families now facing difficult economic times. These impacts may be felt even by families that are intact, i.e., with two parents. In particular, if parents can only earn a minimum wage, then often both must work full time to come close to making ends meet. Even for families who are earning the average wage in society, the declining purchasing power of that wage level may mean that both adults in a family will have to work. The United States has relatively little child care available, except that provided commercially, so that a good deal of income may be spent on child care.

In addition to the direct effects of inequality on social policies and the socioeconomic needs of members of society, there are a number of other, secondary, implications. These have a profound impact on public and private life in the United States, and the manner in which a number of other policies are conducted. Inequalities, other socioeconomic needs, and public policies at all levels of government reinforce each other to produce a cycle of poverty that tends to perpetuate inequality and poverty in the United States.

Reagan, Bush, and the loosening of the social safety net

The twelve years of Republican presidencies from 1981 to 1993 were a period during which what there was of a welfare state in the United States was dismantled. Few programs were actually terminated, but there were many changes that made the lives of the economically and socially disadvantaged even poorer. Some of the changes were subtle, involving alterations in the administration of programs; but even these had real effects on the outcomes for citizens. Others were more drastic and more obvious, with eligibility and benefits reduced. Given that the major social programs based on insurance principles are extremely difficult (politically and legally) to reduce, the Reagan/Bush cuts fell differentially on means-tested programs that benefitted the poor.

The Challenges for President Clinton

Welfare reform is but one of many pressing issues facing Bill Clinton. There is some comfort in the fact that almost everyone agrees that the existing programs, especially A.F.D.C., are not working, and that there is a need for a change. As he campaigned for office, Clinton promised (as had others before him) to end the "welfare mess" and to provide new solutions to the problems of persistent inequality. The problem is that there is no consensus on what the policy changes should be. Further, in the midst of other public problems such as fiscal policy, health care reform, immigration reform, and foreign policy, it is difficult for welfare reform issues to get the type of attention – either from the media or from official actors in Washington – to push through any comprehensive reforms of the system.

During the campaign, Clinton specifically rejected the stereotypical "old Democratic" approach to social problems. That approach was assumed to involve "throwing money at problems" and a willingness to maintain the underclass in some sort of reasonable existence regardless of the costs imposed on the public sector. The "new Democratic" approach was to emphasize individual responsibility rather than governmental support to deal with the problems of the poor. Welfare support would increase, but would be contingent upon the recipient preparing for work. Likewise, this new approach was to involve partnerships between the public and the private sectors, rather than relying upon government alone. Attempts would be made to involve industry in training program beneficiaries for new jobs and then would cooperate in providing jobs, initially subsidized by government. The basic concept is to make welfare a short-term measure to enable people to get back into the private economy, rather than a program that supports families generation after generation. Welfare and other transfer programs are to be supplemented by programs that would provide some publicly funded employment opportunities for young people until they are able to find jobs in the private sector. Again, this will cost money in the short term, but it is hoped that by teaching work skills and providing some positive reinforcement, these programs will pay for themselves in the long run.

The Clinton administration also faces significant challenges in dealing with the third type of social problem mentioned above – the loss of well-paying permanent jobs and their replacement by lower wage and/or temporary employment. These problems are being addressed through the Department of Labor, with Secretary Robert Reich as a vigorous advocate, rather than through the Department of Health and Human Services. This means that the emphasis will be on producing jobs and improving the quality (and wages) of jobs rather than on providing direct social welfare benefits. Still, this initiative, if funded, will require substantial amounts of federal money at a time when there are severe fiscal constraints on the federal government.

The fiscal constraints on government are affecting even the most basic level of American social policy – the entitlement programs such as social security. These programs account for almost one-quarter of all federal expenditures and have been increasing rapidly, given that the benefits are indexed and that the elderly proportion of the population has been increasing. The persistent federal deficit and the need to reduce federal expenditures (as an alternative to raising taxes) have forced a rethinking of the commitment to social security. There have been proposals to reduce the cost-of-living adjustments, and the rate of tax imposed on more affluent recipients will almost certainly increase as a part of the 1993 budget negotiations. Social security has been a sacred cow, but many politicians now see it as a potential sacrificial lamb.

Fiscal Restraints – the Mortmain of Reagan and Bush

Even if the Clinton administration has the political will to produce fundamental changes in social policy, the continuing federal deficit and the shortage of funds for federal programs would limit its ability to introduce reform. The deficit is the most persistent legacy of the Reagan and Bush presidencies, and it now places a mortmain on any creative policy actions by the public sector. Therefore, if the President is to meet his commitments to reduce that deficit, he either has to limit his creativity in social policy or increase taxes. An increase in taxation will almost certainly be necessary if any significant health care reform is adopted, but that program in itself will require entering a dangerous political thicket and the president may find few who are willing to join him on the trip.

Attempts at welfare reform would also be costly. In the short run, at least, most attempts to move people off the existing income maintenance programs through education, training, and/or job creation programs will cost more than the existing programs. The expectation is that in the long run these programs would actually be investments (a favorite Clinton phrase) that could save public money. They would save money by moving people off public assistance and into the tax-paying labor force, and should also reduce the intergenerational transmission of poverty. The difficulty is that the deficit is an overriding short-term problem for all politicians, so that coming up with the money to fund reforms will be difficult at present. In addition, programs to address the growing needs of the "new poor" will require even more money, and will be all the more difficult to finance in the current fiscal climate.

In summary, American government faces a continuing and growing problem in attempting to cope with social and economic inequality. There are programs on the books that will maintain the numerous poor in society at some meager level of existence, but these programs provide little hope for the future for those people and their children. Attempts at producing the long-term changes in the lives of the poor, implemented for a time during the Johnson administration, have largely fallen victim to apathy and fiscal problems. To the problems of the long-term impoverished have been added the needs of the newly poor, who also will require long-term, expensive programs to rectify their difficulties. All these problems are being faced by a government that is, if not actually broke, certainly in financial distress.

14

Environmental Policy

JOHN FRANCIS

In 1992, the election of the Clinton–Gore ticket confirmed for many observers the staying power and influence of environmentalism in American politics. Gore was widely regarded as one of the leading environmentalists in the Senate and the Democratic ticket was endorsed by major environmental groups throughout the country. The election indeed illustrated both the achievements of American environmental politics and the controversies that continue to impose serious limits on those achievements. Among the achievements is a remarkable and expanding body of environmental legislation that continues to be sustained by the courts, and is in large part renewed by Congress. Identification with environmentalist values is judged to be electorally productive. Popular interest in environmental concerns is substantial and enduring.

There are, however, also serious limitations to the influence of the environmental movement. There seems to be a considerable distance between the wide support for environmental values and the divisiveness that often characterizes substantive issues in environmental policymaking. There is nearly universal support for such environmental goals as the promotion of clean air and clean water, for the preservation of many species from extinction, and for the protection of great tracts of undisturbed land from development. There is widespread concern that air, water, and environmental quality are at risk, and that more should be done to protect them. However, consensus is often elusive on such specific questions as to who should pay for the clean-up of hazardous waste and how strict the standards should be for water conservation, for pesticide use, for automobile emissions, or for industrial pollution.

The Character of American Environmental Politics

American environmental politics are distinctive in two clear ways. First, approximately a third of the United States land area is under federal ownership (Johnston and Emerson, 1984). A good deal of this land is relatively undisturbed wilderness populated by a rich variety of species. Such extensive federal ownership is in some respects inherently controversial, but it also creates an identified area for controversy over environmental policy. Secondly, the political expression of environmentalism has not been transformed into the creation of an American version of the "green" political parties that have established a presence in European politics. Instead, in the United States an ever-expanding number of interest groups have taken the lead in environmental politics. The two main political parties in the United States serve as broad-based coalitions for candidate selection. Over the past two decades, environmental groups have played a particularly strong role in candidate selection within the Democratic Party (Galderisi *et al.*, 1987).

These distinctively American features of environmentalism set the political context for this chapter. A variety of environmental concerns characterize the contemporary American policy agenda and are likely to continue to dominate environmental politics in the years to come. These concerns include, first, the conflict over land use, particularly in relation to federal lands. A second concern is the apparently irreconcilable conflict between groups that seek to preserve species even at the expense of development, and groups that give priority to growth and jobs. A third concern relates to the multifaceted problems that arise from the widespread use of potentially harmful chemicals in food production and in other consumer products, and to the question of how to dispose of hazardous waste. Finally, there is the question of international activity in environmental issues, given that many of the problems facing the environment by definition extend beyond the borders of any single country.

The Expanding Range and Persisting Nature of Environmental Policies

Environmental politics are fundamentally about the interconnectedness of people and the world they inhabit. The politics of environmentalism in the United States has over the past four decades produced a politically potent mix of four sets of values (Hays, 1987). These long-standing values, when they combine in a particular issue area, reinforce one another and can prove a compelling political force. These values emphasize the need to limit the risks to health from pollution; there is a strong emphasis on the value of recreational activities such as hiking, boating and, more controversially, hunting or skiing, in natural settings. There is a strong emphasis on the preservation of natural beauty through the creation and preservation of natural parks and monuments and through restricting land use. And environmentalists emphasize the need to recognize the independent worth of nature, which they see as having a value regardless of any human use assigned to it (Leopold, 1970).

These four themes have been interwoven into American environmentalism over the past century. The use of natural resources became a politically salient issue in the last decades of the nineteenth century. The late nineteenth century in America saw the rise of the conservation and preservation movements (Hays, 1959). The preservationists promoted the national park system and argued for keeping some portion of the landscape undisturbed from the transformation wrought by economic development. An important aim of the preservationists was respect for natural beauty. The conservationist movement, on the other hand, offered a critique of existing resource use. Conservationists called for state intervention in order to provide for prudent management of natural resources for present and future generations. A broad acceptance of public health programs occurred at the same time as the conservation movement. The perception of urban life as unhealthy and the glorification of the values of fresh air and exercise associated with country life had been assumed for generations. By the late nineteenth century, however, the enforcement of standards governing sanitation and water treatment ensured that urban life was not necessarily hazardous to health.

In the 1960s questions of environmental health and beauty gained new prominence. The dangers of hazardous waste, of toxic accidents, of risks to the water supply and of general pollution forged new links among the environmentally conscious (Foss, 1987). At the same time, the critics of conservationism questioned the centrality given to human interests in the framing of policy for the use of natural resources. Many environmentalists adopted a perspective that was more ecologically-centered and less human-centered. This change of perspective in turn led to a more radical approach to issues ranging from the protection of endangered species to the protection of the ozone layer (Paehlke, 1989).

The expansion of the range of environmental issues has deepened the commitment of traditional environmentalist constituencies. New constituencies for environmentalism are also emerging, however. There is growing concern in impoverished urban areas that hazardous waste cannot be safely disposed of in cities. Environmental concern is growing among many groups that were traditionally assumed to put jobs above environmental issues, a growth that may produce even greater political influence for environmental groups in future.

Over the past two decades new issues have come on to the environmentalists' agenda – issues that go beyond the traditional concerns of local air quality, natural resource management, water quality, and land use. Increasingly, such issues as food labeling, military action (notably in the Gulf War), the North American Free Trade Agreement, transnational air quality, or waste disposal have linked environmentalist groups to a wide and diverse set of domestic and foreign policy problems.

There was once much skepticism about how long environmental issues would hold the attention of the American public which is often seen as primarily concerned with bread-and-butter issues. However, the steady interplay of the values of health, safety, and beauty, and a moral appreciation of nature, have together strengthened the political influence of environmental organizations over the last 30 years. If the location of a hazardous waste disposal site becomes an issue, if a landfill is discovered to be toxic and a danger to local residents, if a forest is judged to be threatened, if there is a decline in visibility in the landscape surrounding the Grand Canyon – then any or all of these incidents can reinforce the power of environmentalism in American life.

Yet alongside the continuing viability of environmentalism, there is a sense in which environmental politics is reactive and fragmented. To some extent, this fragmentation is a source of continuing richness and development in the environmental movement. On the other hand, it means that it is difficult to sustain the political coherence of the movement and direct it toward specific policy goals.

The Institutional Context

The effectiveness of environmental policymaking is the subject of much heated debate. Charges abound that American environmental policymaking is cumbersome, costly, and distorted in its implementation. These charges about environmental policymaking reflect criticisms of the whole American policy process. As has been noted throughout this book, the workings of the American political system and the efficacy of the decisionmaking process are profoundly affected by the divided governmental institutions and by the proliferation of political actors such as agencies and Congressional committees, as well as policy networks and organized interests. This complexity is further compounded by the existence of a federal system, and has produced a regulatory regime that is characterized by fragmented power and that is often driven, not by orthodox policymaking, but by litigation.

Of course, the conflicts over the specification of environmental policy can also be attributed in part to sharp disputes about values among Americans. Americans as individuals may possess apparently contradictory values, favoring the preservation of an undisturbed natural environment while at the same time demanding an ever-higher material standard of living. Some would say that the conflict is between conflicting ideological perspectives grounded in contending value systems. On one side of the debate are the postmaterialists, members of highly educated and economically better-off sectors of the population, committed to an environmentalist worldview. In contrast, the materialists, less welloff and less well educated, are committed to economic growth and seek in natural resource development the means to provide a higher standard of living for the nation (Milbrath, 1989).

The sharing of power between the states and the federal government, and between the executive, legislative, and judicial branches at *both* levels in the American federal system, has been an especially important factor in the evolution of American environmental politics during the past three decades. This multiplicity of powers, often reflected in uneasy accommodations, generates both opportunities and costs for environmental politics (Mann, 1986). The opportunities are found by groups concentrating on particular venues, such as the federal courts, in gaining access to the policymaking process. The costs begin to mount as groups seek to extend their influence by moving to include other branches of the federal government and the myriad agencies that have stakes in environmental policies. The fragmented nature of environmental decisionmaking is further reflected in the competing and entrenched bureaucratic, Congressional, and interest group constituencies, especially in the issue areas of land use, energy and air quality. The task of influencing policy become increasingly formidable when policymaking is extended to the states.

In the 1960s and 1970s environmental activists relied on successful litigation strategies in a number of critical areas. The role of the courts, although still important, has declined since then, and the last few years have seen much more attention devoted to legislative efforts to renew major environmental Acts concerning clean air and water, as well as initiatives in other environmental areas. In addition, the antipathy to regulation in both the Reagan and the Bush administrations has emphasized the importance of a sympathetic executive to promote environmentalist goals.

Among the lead agencies involved in environmental policymaking are the Environmental Protection Agency, the Department of the Interior, the Department of Agriculture, and the Food and Drug Administration (Clarke and McCool, 1985). Other actors include the Departments of Commerce, Energy, Labor, State and the U.S. Trade Representative. There are also numerous House and Senate committees and sub-committees active in environmental issues. The environment is a policy arena long characterized by powerful bureaucracies responding to their own powerful constituencies. One of the longest unresolved battles in the Washington bureaucracy is whether to merge the bureaus of Land Management and Forest Service. And the question of whether to elevate the Environmental Protection Agency to cabinet rank has been a long-running battle.

The division at the federal level among competing agencies is reinforced by the separation of powers. The question of the level of government at which an environmental decisionmaking responsibility should be located is thus controversial. During the 1960s and 1970s, environmentalists often pressed for locating decisionmaking power in environmental matters at the federal level, arguing that states were either unsympathetic to environmentalist agendas or lacked the bureaucratic sophistication and political will to achieve environmental goals (Davis and Lester, 1989). During the 1980s, when successive Republican administrations at the federal level were conjoined with many new state administrations with agendas and resources committed to environmental issues at the subnational level, there was new interest in the role of the states in environmental policy. It had long been recognized that if states adopted "higher" environmental standards than those articulated by the federal government, the tougher state standard would prevail when clashes occurred. Environmental groups began to form in large numbers even in states that had hitherto lacked such groups (Francis and Ganzel, 1984).

The advent of the Clinton administration has reopened the question of where Americans can expect to find new environmental initiatives. On such issues as reducing logging in national forests, restricting grazing on the public lands and protecting wetlands, the Clinton administration will often be taking up stronger initiatives than those found in many states, thus returning to the traditional model of an activist federal government that may be met with resistance from the states. However, in other areas the respective roles of "environmentalist" and "anti-environmentalist" will be reversed, in that the states will be found resisting what they regard as federally imposed risks to health and environment through the transportation and storage of highly hazardous wastes from one state to another. The continuing dilemma of how to handle growing quantities of dangerous waste encourages federal initiatives to compel the acceptance by states of designated locations for it. However, the states as well as local communities have become more formidable actors in environmental politics than they were even a generation ago. Thus, although there appears to be a widening consensus about the chemical risk to health posed by hazardous waste at both the federal and the state level, it also seems likely that under the Clinton administration any consensus that emerges in intergovernmental relations is likely to be shaped as much by the states as by the federal governmental agencies.

Institutionally, the Clinton administration has urged the creation of a federal Department of the Environment (see Chapter 9, Laffin). This would mean the elevation of the Environmental Protection Agency to the cabinet. It would also strengthen the number of environmental voices at the center of federal decision-making. More to the point, it would enhance the role of the Department as a center for collecting and disseminating information that would be likely to fuel controversy about environmental policy.

Political Parties, Interest Groups, and Environmental Politics

There is broad sympathy for environmental values among the public if these values are framed as general support for higher air quality, pure water, hazardous waste clean-up, and the creation of federal parks. When Americans are asked to choose between economic growth and values such as cleaner air or water, however, there is some reduction in the level of support for environmental values. There are also continuing divisions among the public about the formulation and implementation of environmental policy. When environmentalist values are expressed as trade-offs, environmentalist values are more prevalent among women, younger people, and those with greater educational attainment (Howell and Laska, 1992). It is among the younger age cohorts and the better educated that environmental groups have found their membership. There are, however, significant regional variations in environmental values. In the mountain states, environmental issues seem most likely to form a part of a total ideological perspective, largely as a result of the sharp debate over federal land ownership, water issues, and rapid economic growth.

The steady increase in groups seeking to influence public policy in the last three decades raises the question of whether such proliferation augments the political influence of these groups or dilutes their power. The proliferation of environmental groups has occurred both because of the formation of new groups (which have appeared in many parts of the country and on a transnational level) and because older groups have expanded their chapters. Indeed, it has been noted that environmental groups were among the fastest growing of all interest groups in the United States (Gais, Peterson, and Walker, 1984).

The era of rapid increase in environmental group activity has also been an era of expanding federal and state environmental legislation. Sometimes groups have worked closely with environmental agencies at both levels of government to facilitate new legislative initiatives. The great expansion of new groups led to significant changes in resource use decisionmaking in the 1970s and during the

Carter years (1977—81) a number of leaders of environmental pressure groups were appointed to high posts in the administration. Environmental groups suffered an abrupt change in their level of access during the Reagan years (1981-9). Although they initially felt threatened by the new administration, the period in fact confirmed their staying power in Washington. The Reagan administration appointed leading figures from commodity and industry groups to environmental positions as part of a direct ideological challenge to the environmental movement. Environmental groups, as a result of being able to define themselves against the Reaganite policies, were able to increase their membership dramatically. Moreover the environment was arguably the area of domestic policy where Reagan's policies were visibly least successful.

The Bush administration shifted markedly from a public anti-environment stance as Bush declared he would be the "environmental president." Bush appointed moderate Republicans (including some who had been active in the environmental movement) to natural resources and environmental agencies. The criticism of the Bush administration within the environmentalist movement was directed not at personnel, but at the lack of administrative initiatives and at the strong support given by Bush to deregulation. There was also an apparent abandonment of the policy of wetlands preservation. Generally, environmentalists came to see the Bush administration as having substituted symbolic statements for substantive policy commitment, a substitution all the more dangerous for its capacity to undermine the environmentalist movement itself.

Throughout the Bush administration, the relatively low price of energy meant that there was little pressure to expand energy development in the west. Many of the environmental conflicts revolved around hazardous waste issues, but another set of important issues involved the overcrowding of national parks, park management, and the role of private business concessions within the parks. The most deeply controversial issue, however, was the Endangered Species Act. Its divisiveness was exemplified by the debate about the threatened extinction of the Spotted Owl (Booth, 1992). To reproduce, the Spotted Owl required protection of its habitat in the old growth forests of the northwest, protection that would endanger the jobs of loggers in the region. The Bush administration tried to blame the Act itself and the uncompromising attitude of environmental groups for job losses in the northwest that had become politically sensitive for the Republicans. Bush called for major reform of the Endangered Species Act as a way of deflecting responsibility for unemployment there.

Probably the greatest environmental achievement of the Bush administration was the Clean Air Act of 1990.The Act sought to facilitate the adoption by other states of California's tough standards to reduce automobile emissions, and it sought to reduce emissions from plants in an effort to deal with the problem of acid rain. Environmentalists had been closely involved in the negotiations leading to the Clean Air Act, but parts of the legislation – notably those that relied on market forces to reduce overall levels of contamination and the relatively weak regulatory framework of the Act – drew sharp criticism from some groups.

Controversy is likely to intensify about the role of markets in environmental regulation. Reliance on markets suggests something of a moral compromise – that some pollution is acceptable if the overall quantity of pollution is in decline, a view not likely to be favored by those who take an absolute approach to environmental politics.

In region after region, when state legislatures and state parties are examined, it is apparent that Democratic legislators are distinguished from their Republican counterparts by their consistently greater support for legislation championed by environmentalist groups. Once in power, it is the Democrats (and this can already be seen as much in the Clinton administration as it was in the Carter administration) whose policies and appointments are influenced by the environmentalist movement. Indeed, the strength of the environmentalist movement within the Democratic coalition makes it the most powerful element in the party in some western states.

The absence of a green party – analogous to that found in many European countries – may puzzle some observers. The explanation is partly institutional. In the United Sstates, the two main political parties are regulated at the state level to facilitate popular participation in candidate selection. For groups wishing to play a role in the selection of office-holders, the threshold for participation in the established political parties is significantly lower than the cost of starting a new party. And of course for any new party, the likelihood of winning any meaningful set of offices is remote. From the 1960s, environmental activists gained a more sympathetic reception from Democrats than from Republicans. In the Democratic drought years of the 1980s environmentalist organizations in many western states supplied the volunteers and other resources needed to run campaigns. In some Congressional districts, environmental endorsement became a necessary, though not a sufficient, condition for securing the party nomination, and was seen as essential to lay the groundwork for an effective campaign (Galderisi *et al.*, 1987).

This partial incorporation of environmental groups into the Democratic Party, even though the Democratic party is rather porous, creates a set of expectations that go beyond the merely symbolic. Appointments by President Clinton have echoed those of Carter in the extent to which they have recognized the importance of environmentalist concerns. Bruce Babbitt, who has been made head of Interior under Clinton, was a popular governor of Arizona with a reputation as a successful negotiator between environmental groups and federal natural resource agencies.His early success at Interior may be measured by the opposition from environmentalists to the suggestion that he might be given a Supreme Court appointment (see Chapter 8, Peele). Carol Browner, the Head of E.P.A., was a former aide to Senator Gore and was director of environmental affairs for the state of Florida at the time of her appointment.

High expectations can also generate disappointments and protest. Certainly with the advent of the Clinton administration, environmentalists assumed that there would be substantive policy achievements, and where they have not been forthcoming (as when the administration withdrew its proposed increase in grazing fees on public lands, discussed below), the reaction has bordered on outrage.

The Western Landscape and the Recurring Question of Federal Land Use

Logging and grazing are two issues that are unresolved in American environmental politics. They certainly are not the only two unresolved issues, but they aptly illustrate the confluence of institutional and value conflicts that give environmental politics their durability and their intractability.

The background to the logging and grazing issues was the massive transfer of land to settlers as they moved westwards across the United States in the nineteenth century. The federal government carved states out of lands won by conquest or by purchase. Some lands were set aside by treaty as Indian reservations. For the vast majority of the holdings, however, federal policy was land disposal. The preferred methods of land disposal were either through the encouragement of agriculture (by allowing settlers to homestead 160 acres) or through the subsidy of a national transport network by making land grants to the railways. By the turn of the twentieth century, a significant amount of land was still left in federal hands: approximately one-third of the United States. The explanation in large measure is that homesteading was simply not feasible on the arid lands west of the 100th meridian – i.e., approximately west of the Rocky Mountains. Beginning in the late nineteenth century, federal policy gradually shifted toward retaining land – initially to preserve sites of natural beauty and for recreation. Later, national forests were established in the belief that the U.S. Forest Service was more likely to prove a prudent manager of the nation's timber reserves for future generations. Gradually, all remaining lands were retained in three broad managerial categories: park lands, forests, and public lands, – the last category embracing grazing lands, mineral lands, areas of beauty and lands that were once known as areas no one had wanted.

Recurring controversies over grazing and timber have dominated the western lands.The relationship between western cattle grazers and the Bureau of Land Management remains controversial. The extent to which national forests should be managed for commercial timber production is the central issue for loggers. Federal land-use decisionmaking has always been marked by controversy; but over the past three decades these controversies have widened. There has been renewed interest in locating minerals and fossil fuels on western lands, coupled with the vast rise in western-based recreation and the emergence of the environmentalist movement. The tensions between these developments have brought new meaning and new criticisms to the traditional federal land management doctrine of "multiple use-sustained yield."

The debate about whether or not multiple use is an appropriate land-use doctrine is multifaceted and emerges in the discussion of wilderness areas. Access is a particularly delicate issue, since increasing .the visitors to public lands has to be set against the need to preserve some areas of fragile beauty from mass tourism. The process of designating lands to be set aside as wilderness has moved slowly over the last two decades with protracted negotiations between state Congressional delegations and the federal agencies. Perhaps the classic illustration of land-use controversy is the conflict over grazing fees. In the arid regions of the west where ranchers came to own property, water was usually available. The practice developed of letting the cattle graze on the adjacent public lands. Over time, grazing permits were issued by the federal government to these ranchers. These permits really only make economic sense if the respective rancher owns adjacent private holdings. Critics have charged that the fees for cattle grazing are below the market rate and consequently involve the taxpayer subsidizing the ranchers. The ranchers are not the romanticized cowboys of the frontier, since the small ranchers have been marginalized as the grazing permits are disproportionately held by large corporations or quite wealthy individuals who live outside the region. Approximately half of the permits are held by 10 percent of the ranchers (Egan, 1993). A second criticism of current grazing practice is that much of the western landscape is ecologically fragile, and cattle grazing is causing serious damage to a good deal of the western rangelands (Hupp, 1992).

Demands to raise grazing fees have been seen by opponents as a threat to the ranching culture of the western lands and to the very tradition of cattle grazing (Gottlieb, 1989). From time to time, western ranchers and their supporters have fought either to have the lands privatized or to have ownership transferred to the states in which they are located, on the presumption that western states would be more sympathetic land managers than federal officials. Environmentalist organizations are depicted by western commodity users as peopled by wealthy and leisured individuals with little sense of the intergenerational commitment, work, and limited economic returns involved in raising cattle on public lands. In the views of both their supporters and critics, grazers are seen as economic "free riders." What is fascinating about the persistence of grazing controversies, however, is that the conflict involves a relatively small number of westerners – about 30,000 public range rangers – with a relatively small role in their local economies.

The rise of the environmental movement and its growing relationship with the Democratic Party described earlier, has put increasing pressure on Democratic administrations. These pressures became apparent under Carter, and have recently become evident under Clinton in demands to raise grazing fees and to reduce the size of the herds grazing on federal lands. Shortly after entering office, the Clinton administration argued that increased grazing fees would serve as a source of revenue in the 1993 budgetary proposal designed to reduce the federal deficit. The irresistible force of environmentalism ran up against the immovable object of the grazers. Ranchers argue that increases in the grazing fees would be more than they could pay and would drive them off the range. The Clinton administration backed away from raising grazing fees when western senators threatened not to support the budget if grazing fees were increased. In the aftermath of the budget bill's passage, the Clinton administration took the grazing fee issue up again and worked with a Congressional coalition to propose doubling the fee. The increase is judged by its supporters as modest but it has provoked anger in many western communities. Western senators led a successful filibuster against the proposed increase and at the time of writing the Clinton administration is exploring the option of increasing grazing fees by administrative means rather than by legislative action.

Logging

The northwest has long been a major logging center, and much logging takes place on federal lands. In addition to the challenge provided by the Endangered Species Act, there is criticism that logging practices permitted on public lands have contributed not only to a loss of beauty, but to an erosion of forests by the practice of clear-cutting large tracts of timber. A policy of selective logging would, in the judgment of critics, preserve the habitat of various species and maintain the aesthetic value of the forests. The northwest timber industry has been in decline in recent years for several reasons, not least competition from other parts of the country and the general difficulties of the construction industry. However, there is also the conflict between species protection and the logging of the old growth forests.

Environmentalist groups have deplored the logging of the old growth forests, especially because it threatens the Spotted Owl. Both logging firms and organized labor have bitterly objected to constraints that would damage an already troubled industry, especially given the need to stabilize the specialist logging communities in the northwest. The logging issue is a vivid illustration of environmental controversy between preservationists and those who see forests as resources to supply shelter for society and to support the logging way of life of generations from Oregon and Washington. To environmentalists, the old growth forests are to be cherished all the more as places of great beauty and as refuges for a wide variety of life, especially given the decline in forest area to about 10 percent of what it was 150 years ago. These sharp clashes of value have made policy compromise difficult. In the absence of any plan capable of protecting both the Spotted Owl and the timber industry, the Supreme Court imposed a ban on logging until such a plan could be devised.

The Clinton administration tried to fashion a compromise by allowing the maximum logging permitted under existing law. This amounts to 2 billion board feet a year, a level significantly below industry requests of over 3 billion board feet a year. The administration proposal permitted selective logging rather than clear-cutting as a means to sustain the industry. In addition, the administration offered a billion dollars a year in job retraining for loggers. The interest groups involved were disappointed by this proposal. The loggers argued that retraining was ineffective and – more to the point – stopped them from pursuing their preferred occupation. For environmentalists, controlled logging was still excessive and the selective cutting continued to threaten forests. The problem of regulating compromise is obvious. It remains to be seen whether being the agent of compromise is likely to be politically productive for the Clinton administration as it seeks to accommodate its coalition of organized labor and environmentalists, at the same time as promoting economic growth.

Toxic Substances

The chemical industry is probably the most compelling indicator of industrialization, just as steel was in the last century. Some 5,000 different chemicals are produced in the United States each year – chemicals that are used in nearly every stage of the food industry from the application of pesticides to the addition of preservatives (Schroeder, 1991). The health risk associated with this chemical usage has been highlighted by critics, who especially point to the scientific evidence of carcinogens found at different points in the food chain. The defenders of using pesticides and preservatives point out, however, that they make food cheaper and more widely available and argue that the risk is minimal.

The debate is to some extent about levels of risk; and there is little consensus about what levels of risk are acceptable. In the case of the link between cancer and chemicals, the courts have imposed their own restrictive interpretations on what levels of risk are acceptable. However, the absence of any widely shared understanding of health risk contributes to continuing political controversy given the widespread and continuing demand for chemicals. Indeed in some areas there appears to have been a growing acceptance of the risks of toxicity in such processes as dry cleaning, coal fire plants, and automobile use.

Transnational Dimensions

Environmental groups are becoming increasingly effective in environmental issues that transcend borders. Two recent issues that underline this trend to transnational organization are the issue of acid rain and the debate about the North American Free Trade Agreement (N.A.F.T.A.).

Acid rain became a domestic political issue in the United States, in part because of an alliance among the Canadian federal government, some Canadian provincial governments, some American states, and Canadian and American environmental groups. It was perhaps the first environmental issue to embrace domestic and foreign actors in a sustained fashion.

N.A.F.T.A. is an agreement to reduce tariff barriers between Canada, the United States and Mexico. American opponents of N.A.F.T.A. argued that it would encourage U.S. manufacturers to move to Mexico for cheaper labor costs and to avoid American environmental regulation. The fear of job losses sparked extensive union opposition to N.A.F.T.A.; but N.A.F.T.A. also raised concern among environmental groups who feared that the movement of manufacturing plants south of the U.S.–Mexico border would increase air and water pollution for both Mexico and the United States.

Three environmental groups – Public Citizen, the Sierra Club, and Friends of the Earth – brought suit in American federal courts, arguing that under the terms of the National Environmental Policy Act, N.A.F.T.A. required an environmental impact statement. N.E.P.A. requires an E.I.S. for any major federal action that significantly affects the environment. The statement must set out the environmental consequences of the particular federal action so that where adverse consequences are identified, Congress or the administration may intervene to review the undertaking. At the federal district court level, the environmental groups' arguments were accepted and the court ruled that an E.I.S. must be drafted before the treaty could be approved (Greenhouse, 1993). The Clinton administration appealed the ruling, pointing out at the same time that they were negotiating side agreements to N.A.F.T.A. dealing with job transfer and environmental regulation. The Federal Appeals Court overturned the lower court ruling and supported the Clinton administration argument. However, it is likely that such cases will expand in the future.

The implications of the court decision are interesting. The decision suggests a greatly expanded role for environmental groups in external affairs that had hitherto been regarded as the prerogative of government. The decision also demonstrates the capacity of environmental groups to intervene in the affairs of other nations.

Another illustration of the transnational dimension to environmentalist politics is the conflict between Canada and the United States over discharges from power plants that were making a major contribution to the acidification of rain and destroying forests and lakes all over North America. From the 1970s, the Canadian government had argued that there was a clear causal relationship between such emissions and the destruction of wilderness and recreational areas. The Canadians argued, moreover, that the source points of these emissions were disproportionately located in the United States, while the damage was disproportionately inflicted on Canada. Successive American governments argued that the scientific data was inconclusive and that more study was needed. By the mid-1980s, the Canadian government was working closely with environmental groups, who in turn collaborated with environmental groups in the United States In some cases, the groups belonged to the same transnational environmental organization. Their goal was to pressure Congress and the administration to be responsive to the Canadian concerns. Reliance on the interest group link was but one component of the Canadian strategy that contributed to the 1990 Clean Air Act's provisions addressing the problem of acid rain. The issue blurred domestic and foreign policy concerns in a remarkable manner (Francis and Macmahon, 1991).

To a certain extent, the channel of influence between environmental groups from Canada to the United States was reversed in the early 1990s, when Quebec sought to export electricity to be generated by the vast hydroelectric projects located in James Bay. The scale of the project troubled environmentalists and some of the inhabitants of the area, who feared environmental damage from it. The concern was taken up by American environmental groups. That opposition, along with changes in energy markets, persuaded New York and other states to cancel contracts for hydroelectric power from Quebec. The cancellations placed the project at serious risk of being completed without a market in which to sell the power produced (Verhoek, 1992).

Conclusion

Environmental groups have become increasingly important players in the American policy process and they have established a powerful role within the Democratic coalition. Yet, although there is much sympathy for the environmentalist cause, economic concerns set limits to that sympathy. The unresolved issues of environmental protection and economic growth have now become all the more urgent as American politics are increasingly affected by decisions taken beyond the United States' border. Whether the Clinton administration can find a way of resolving these problems without alienating vital parts of his coalition remains an open question.

15

Foreign Policy

PHIL WILLIAMS

Introduction

The end of the Cold War and the demise of the Soviet Union have brought the United States a new freedom in foreign policy. The disappearance of the structural imperatives of bipolarity as well as of a superpower adversary and a hostile ideology provide options that were effectively excluded during the period from 1947 to 1991. Furthermore, Washington is no longer susceptible to the "reverse influence" of allies whose major asset was the capacity to defect or collapse. Welcome as these developments are, however, they also pose problems. The implosion of the Soviet Union has robbed the United States of more than an enemy. It has also deprived Washington of a clearly defined role, of a coherent conceptual framework for approaching foreign and security policy, and of the influence that accrued to the United States as the only real source of countervailing power against the Soviet Union. The sense of direction and coherence in United States foreign policy will be difficult to restore as a result of domestic politics, economic concerns, and bureaucratic pressures. Indeed, in trying to manage its foreign policy through the remainder of the 1990s and beyond, the United States faces a double-whammy: "the issues have become more complex, posing greater challenges to the political system and the foreign policy process may be more fragmented and less able to cope with the complexity" (Deese, 1994).

Accordingly, the chapter sets out to do several things. First, it highlights the consequences of the end of the Cold War for American foreign policy. Attention is then given to the issues that have already begun to emerge out of a more fragmented and disorderly international system. Secondly, there is an analysis of the domestic problems the United States will face in its efforts to adapt to the post-Cold War world. Finally, the chapter offers an assessment of whether or not the United States is likely to succeed in reestablishing a coherent and effective foreign policy.

The End of the Cold War

The end of the Cold War was generally portrayed as a victory for American power. Yet there is a double irony here in that the end of the Cold War not only occurred against a background of growing concern about American decline, but also contributed to the loss of American influence (Kennedy, 1987; Nye, 1990). Throughout the Cold War, American leadership was founded on a comprehensive power base that was unmatched by any other single power, including the Soviet Union. Seemingly boundless economic capabilities, and a nuclear and conventional arsenal, endowed the United States with a capacity for global intervention that was both unprecedented and unsurpassed. Ironically, though, American influence depended not only on American capabilities, but also on Soviet capabilities: the more the U.S.S.R. tried to equal or exceed the military strength of the United States, the more it frightened other states, making them even more reliant on Washington for protection. States that were vulnerable to pressure from Moscow and dependent on the United States to deter Soviet efforts at intimidation, were reluctant to do anything that might encourage United States disengagement or abandonment. The long American tradition of isolationism combined with contemporary manifestations of this sentiment to fuel allied concerns and inhibit challenges to American wishes and policy preferences. This is not to suggest that allies such as France were acquiescent or that alliances were always harmonious. It is simply to argue that there were limits to dissent and that the ultimate dependence on the United States gave Washington a considerable reservoir of influence over allies and clients.

That reservoir has been seriously depleted by the demise of the Soviet Union. Military power that was used to protect against the adversary rather than for coercion of allies cannot easily retain its relevance when there is no longer a need for protection. The United States may have residual influence because of a reluctance on the part of some allies to break the psychological habit of dependence that developed during the Cold War. Yet this is a rapidly declining asset, as is perhaps most obvious in relation to the Federal Republic of Germany. With the end of the Cold War and subsequent unification, Germany is no longer a frontline state and has engaged in security cooperation with France to a degree that was inconceivable when Bonn was concerned about Washington's reactions to exclusively European security initiatives.

The difficulty for Washington is that this has opened a gap between the United States' self-image and the image of Washington held by its allies. The "Japan that can say no" is a product not only of Tokyo's increased economic power, but also of the absence of immediate security threats that require external protection. The end of the Cold War, therefore, has robbed the United States of its role and much of its influence. It has also left Washington without a policy framework for coming to terms with the challenges and problems of the post-Cold War world. There is no obvious successor to containment. Part of the problem, of course, is that the shape of the post-Cold War international system is itself somewhat indistinct. Assessments of this system vary from those who argue that it is essentially "unipolar" to those who see an emerging multipolarity (Krauthammer, 1991). These divergences reflect the lack of clear and obvious congruence between military power and economic power. They also reflect the continued question marks about the major actors.

The reaction to the Maastricht Agreement by several members of the European Union – as well as European ineptness in dealing with the Yugoslav crisis – has cast considerable doubt on the capacity of western Europe to emerge as a single unified actor on the world stage. The future of Russia remains equally uncertain, with reformers and conservatives still vying for the dubious privilege of trying to restore a semblance of order and efficiency to the Russian economy. Should the ethnic conflicts on the periphery of Russia tempt Moscow into efforts to restore regional hegemony, then the reintegration of Russia into the western state system would be seriously undermined. And although Japan has learned to say no, it is not clear whether it is also prepared to say yes to new responsibilities for upholding international order. The future of China is even more uncertain: while the combination of economic reform and political repression is clearly proving more effective than Gorbachev's efforts to start with political reform and hope that economic revitalization would follow, major question marks remain about China's future power and the orientation of its foreign policy.

In short, the end of the Cold War has ushered in a period of prolonged transition toward an unknown destination. The situation is further complicated by uncertainty about the United States' role – which magnifies the other uncertainties. The inability of the United States to define a new role for itself in a turbulent international system is likely both to compound and prolong the uncertainty. It seemed briefly during the Gulf Crisis that the Bush administration's enunciation of a New World Order would fill the vacuum. The New World Order concept, however, was too vague to provide much more than a brief legitimizing device for the war against Saddam Hussein. It also appeared to demand that America continue to play the role of world policeman, despite the fact that many Americans felt that domestic problems rendered such a role inappropriate.

The Gulf experience also underlined a basic lesson of the Cold War – that values and principles can best provide a basis for foreign policy when they are against something; they are a less effective guide in the absence of obvious and antithetical alternatives. It is much easier to define a role in terms of what one is against than what one is for. Attempts to implement foreign policy in terms of promoting democracy or human rights, for example – as the Carter administration discovered to its cost – are rendered problematic by the painful tradeoffs and awkward compromises that are central to efforts to cope with a complex international environment.

In sum, the United States has not only lost a role as superpower leader and protector, and a considerable amount of the influence that went with the role, but also lacks a framework of widely accepted judgments and assumptions to guide its policy through the mid- and late-1990s. Moreover, just as there was a natural congruence and resulting synergy among these three components during the Cold War, the change in all three elements makes the problem of adaptation much greater. The reformulation of United States foreign policy for the post-Cold War era has barely started, partly because it is not clear where to start, partly because of the difficulties of making sense of the post-Cold War world, and partly because of the growing preoccupation with domestic problems and the immediacy of foreign policy crises such as Bosnia and Somalia. Such crises have demanded a degree of attention that not only exceeds their intrinsic importance for the United States, but have also made it more difficult to think and plan for the long term. Dealing with what Dean Acheson once termed "the thundering present" has left little time or energy for the development of long-term policies and priorities by an administration that, even in its first year, appeared beleaguered by domestic pressures.

New Challenges and Issues

The challenges to United States interests and security in the post-Cold War world are far less immediate or dramatic than those posed by the Soviet Union. Nevertheless, events in the Gulf, Yugoslavia, and Somalia have already revealed that Wilsonian or Kantian visions of a peaceful world order have as little relevance in the post-Cold War world as they had in the late 1940s. It is not necessary to be nostalgic for the Cold War to recognize that its end did not signify the end of security problems for the United States or the international community.

There are several kinds of challenge that seem likely to arise. The most important, if also the most sensitive, is the need to manage relations with allies. The Cold War made static and comprehensive alliance systems the norm. Trading partners and security partners were synonymous. Inevitably, the partnerships became increasingly competitive in the realm of trade and economic policy; and even in the realm of security alliances they were characterized by disputes over burden-sharing or contributions to the common good – disputes that became increasingly troublesome as they converged with the more competitive economic relationships. In the final analysis, however, allies were allies and adversaries were adversaries.

This may no longer be the case. The end of the Cold War has removed much of the impulse toward cooperation among the major industrialized nations. While western Europe, Japan, and the United States are still bound together by economic interdependence, as well as by adherence to certain common values, the pressures for cooperation stemming from fear of a common enemy have disappeared. "The world is moving toward complex competition in which there are fewer permanent enemies and fewer permanent allies" (Schneider, 1992). With the security glue removed, the possibility cannot be dismissed that economic tensions among Japan, western Europe, and the United States will contaminate their relationship and undermine the cooperative links established during the post-World War II reconstruction and the Cold War. This is not to suggest that these nations will necessarily become enemies. Rather, in a world lacking the imperatives of bipolarity, alignments are likely to be much more fluid and more volatile than during the Cold War.

Closely related to this is the changed agenda facing the United States. At its simplest, this argument takes the form that traditional security issues are no longer preeminent, and that economic and trade issues have come to the fore. It is more accurate to argue that the old dichotomy between security and economic issues has broken down, and that the agenda now consists predominantly of issues that are neither exclusively security nor exclusively economic in nature. This is perhaps most evident in the challenge faced by the United States – and, indeed, other sovereign states – as a result of the rise of transnational processes and organizations.

There is also something of an irony here: in the 1970s and 1980s, transnational corporations were seen primarily as an instrument of United States power and policy; to the extent that they were a threat it was to the nations of the Third World which were unable to prevent or control economic penetration. Yet the more recent emergence of transnational criminal organizations (T.C.O.s) (most notably, the Colombian drug cartels) that export illegal drugs to the United States, suggests that the initial understanding of the transnational problem needs to be revised. These criminal enterprises achieve access – which is something that all transnational organizations want – not through negotiation with government but through circumvention of government restrictions (Huntington, 1973). Their actions challenge some of the most basic features of state sovereignty and highlight very dramatically the permeability of borders, whether to illegal commodities or to illegal aliens. T.C.O.s have emerged as part of what James Rosenau has termed a multi-centric world, composed of many kinds of non-state actors who are important not because of "their legal status, capabilities or sovereignty," but because of their capacity to initiate and sustain actions that are outside the bounds of state activity, and that challenge the traditional dominance of states. As Rosenau has noted, "Not all actors in the multi-centric world are caught up in the authority networks of the state-centric world. Some have managed to obfuscate, even elude, the jurisdiction of a single state" (Rosenau, 1990). Others have even managed to elude the jurisdiction of the state system as a whole.

The interaction between the state-centric and the multi-centric worlds, or between sovereignty-bound and sovereignty-free actors, is one of the most important features of contemporary global relations. The interaction is characterized by complex patterns of cooperation and conflict, in which the desire of states to exert greater control over their environment confronts the quest for autonomy on the part of the transnational organizations. And it is not certain that states have the capacity to emerge triumphant from this struggle. So far, the United States has been remarkably unsuccessful in its efforts to deal with the Colombian cartels, an outcome that suggests that the challenge posed by T.C.O.s could significantly threaten national and international security in ways that, as yet, are only dimly understood.

Another part of what some analysts have termed the gray area phenomena is the collapse of nation states (Manwaring, 1993). In different ways, both Yugoslavia and Somalia are examples of this. They provide what may become the archetypal dilemma for American foreign policymakers during the remainder of the 1990s: should the United States intervene in an effort to restore order in such situations even though it has no immediate interest at stake? What level of blood and treasure is worth expending as part of a general commitment to maintaining international order and humanitarian values? The way in which the Clinton administration has vacillated on the use of force in Bosnia highlights the difficulties of answering this question. Unfortunately, the comment by Charles Maynes that "people are upset by the problem and frightened by the solution" may well be increasingly applicable as more and more states become unglued (quoted in Doherty, 1993). The loss of authority and legitimacy can occur either because of incompetent government or because even competent governments can be over-whelmed by the dissatisfaction resulting from poor economic performance and the failure of nation-building. The aspirations of sub-national ethnic groups, the pressure of uncontrollable population movements, and the growing gap between the demands placed on governments and their capacity to meet these demands may well be leading to a fundamental long-term crisis for the nation-state.

A more familiar problem is likely to arise from states that move outward rather than implode. Rogue states that refuse to accept either the territorial status quo or even the rudimentary norms of international society are likely to remain a problem, especially if they are able to acquire weapons of mass destruction. Had Iraq had nuclear weapons, the calculus of risk before the effort to expel it from Kuwait would have been very different. Yet, proliferation of nuclear, chemical, and biological weapons may be impossible to stop. So long as non-proliferation regimes are imperfectly observed by potential suppliers – whether states or transnational corporations – it is only a matter of time before a rogue state acquires nuclear weapons. And even where a new nuclear state does not have ambitions for regional hegemony, the dangers of regional arms races are very real. In some cases, of course, nuclear weapons will be acquired because of insecurity rather than ambition. Even so, the acquisition of nuclear weapons by a state involved in a regional conflict is likely to have significant knock-on effects. At the very least, it will exacerbate the dynamics of the security dilemma in which one state's defensive actions are seen by others as threatening. The incentives for neighbors to acquire nuclear weapons of their own may also increase.

The counter-argument to all this is that the spread of nuclear weapons will enhance international stability (Waltz, 1981). In essence, the argument is that states that acquire these weapons will be transformed into inviolable sanctuaries. The inhibitions on resort to military force between nuclear powers are far greater than between conventionally armed states. The model is the United States–Soviet relationship during the Cold War. Yet this may prove difficult to replicate. Other states will not have the kind of economic and technological resources to develop the stabilizing features and safety mechanisms that were deployed by both Moscow and Washington. Moreover, even the superpower arms race was characterized by concern over strategic imbalances: although both the United States and the Soviet Union made great efforts to reduce the vulnerability of their strategic nuclear forces to surprise attack, they were constantly concerned about asymmetries in the strategic balance and the possibility that their efforts would be insufficient. Regional nuclear arms races are likely to be an even more fertile breeding ground for paranoia. In short, the result of the diffusion of nuclear weapons could be a series of destabilizing arms races and dangerous nuclear confrontations between states with little experience in the demands of crisis stability and the responsibilities of crisis management.

Partly because of its concern over this kind of instability, partly because of anxiety over the kind of state likely to acquire nuclear weapons, and partly because of the desire of a state to maintain its predominance, the United States has given a high priority to efforts to restrict proliferation. Yet once again, Washington faces both a policy problem and a policy dilemma. The problem is how to mobilize the international and transnational community in support of a stringent verification regime. The dilemma stems from the fact that even if the United States succeeds in this first objective, the regime is unlikely to be completely effective. Consequently, how much faith should be placed in a strategy of prevention as opposed to a strategy of mitigation? If nonproliferation efforts are unlikely to be completely successful, what actions can be taken to contain the potentially destabilizing consequences of the spread of nuclear weapons? And if the United States does try to enhance the stability of regional nuclear balances, perhaps through the supply of technologies that help states control their nuclear arsenals (for example, permissive action links), how can it do this without undermining the legitimacy and continued efficacy of the efforts to stifle proliferation?

Another set of potential problems concerns democratization of the states of eastern Europe and the former Soviet Union. The problems here are largely inherent in what has been termed "the dual transition." States that are attempting to move simultaneously toward both democracy and market economies encounter considerable difficulty. The political costs of the economic dislocations involved in reform make governments shy away from necessary but painful steps; yet the failure to reform the economy could well encourage a reversal to authoritarianism. Although outside financial aid or managerial assistance can facilitate the process, it is unlikely to be decisive. While the transition problem is both pervasive and long term, the United States has a particular interest in ensuring its success in Russia, where the possibility that the process will fail and that Moscow will revert to a hard-line, highly nationalistic foreign policy is a continuing cause for concern. Unfortunately, this is not something that the United States can influence except at the margin.

The other potential problem for the United States is China. Although the United States would like a cooperative relationship with China, certain aspects of China's policies – such as the domestic violation of human rights and the reluctance to constrain arms sales – tend to evoke mildly punitive responses from Washington. Even when these are largely symbolic, they make Beijing less rather than more willing to cooperate with efforts to uphold international regimes or maintain norms of behavior. Moreover, the long-term question about China – and it is equally relevant to Russia – is whether or not it will conclude that the long-term advantages of cooperation with the west are sufficient to make it abandon any plans for territorial revisionism.

What is most striking about these agenda items is their complexity and the inability of the United States, acting alone, to have a decisive impact on the outcome. The international environment has become simultaneously more complex and less amenable to American influence. The lack of familiarity with problems that are far removed from the Cold War is compounded by the inherent ambiguities and uncertainties surrounding these problems. There are few easy options in the post-Cold War era. The United States will not only encounter new limits to its power and influence, but find that its policies require inescapable tradeoffs and a high level of tolerance for moral ambiguity. The old patterns of leadership will have to be replaced by more subtle efforts to convince others that it is in their interests to do what the United States would prefer them to do. At the same time, the United States will find that influence and impact depend crucially on timing. Failing states, for example, need to be dealt with before they fail rather than after. Indeed, if efforts to deal with disintegrating states, regional conflicts, immigration and refugee flows, transnational criminal organizations, and other gray area phenomena are to have any chance of success, early warning is essential. Not only are the demands on intelligence and response capabilities much greater than during the Cold War, but the forms of intelligence have to change with greater emphasis on human intelligence than hi-tech intelligence, and greater willingness to overcome the preconceptions and wishful thinking that all too often encourage disregard of clear warning signals.

In addition, Washington will almost certainly discover that there is a greater need for strategies that hedge against both uncertainty and failure. The use of military power to deter and defend is unlikely to be appropriate to situations that are rarely clear cut, in which the line between domestic and foreign policy has become blurred, and in which there is a growing confluence between transnational criminal behavior and challenges to national and international security.

These challenges demand imaginative multilateral solutions rather than unilateral United States actions; new kinds of capabilities and bureaucratic structures; and subtlety and patience. Their successful management also requires that the United States policymaking system functions at least as effectively as it did at any time during the Cold War. The next section highlights a variety of considerations that suggest that this is unlikely.

The Domestic Context

The United States political system has several characteristics that militate against an effective response to the ambiguous, yet potentially very onerous, challenges of international order in the post-Cold War world. Perhaps the most important is the central paradox of the United States political system – the mixture of highly developed and regulated structures and an extremely disorderly process. It is also a political system characterized by the increased salience of institutionalized competition and conflict, the growing preeminence of domestic issues, a preoccupation with the short term, a tendency to avoid hard choices, and a distaste for ambiguity in international affairs. "The overall picture is one of an erosion of consensus, a fragmentation of responsibility, and a competition for influence" (Schneider, 1992).

To contend that the United States political system is ill-equipped for the conduct of foreign policy, of course, is neither novel nor startling. The system has long been characterized by a rampant pluralism that makes conflict over policy unavoidable, endemic, and debilitating. This is not really surprising in a nation built on diversity. As Warner Schilling noted in the early 1960s, many of the conflicts and debates over the direction of American foreign policy "simply reflect the diversity of opinion Americans are likely to hold

. . . regarding the state of the world and what America should do in it" (Schilling, 1962). In many respects, diversity is very healthy, and there are few observers who would advocate suppression of the political debate to achieve greater effectiveness in the conduct of foreign policy. At the same time, excessive conflict in the policy-making system can seriously undermine the American capacity to act decisively and to provide steadfast international leadership. And there are several developments that suggest that this is increasingly likely.

During the Cold War, the United States was able to overcome many of the impediments to an effective foreign policy stemming from the rampant pluralism and structured turbulence of the American political process. Without an external enemy to provide the impetus to mobilize national energies and resources, however, foreign policy is likely to be subsumed by domestic politics. Lacking what James Schlesinger described as "the magnetic north for calibrating its foreign policy," it is highly probable that America will hop from issue to issue without a clear sense of direction – a superpower without a cause (Schlesinger, 1993). Although such an approach provides an opportunity for a reassertion of pragmatism over ideology, it also places foreign policy at the mercy of domestic politics: Congressional sentiment, the vagaries of the public mood, the sensationalism of the media, the parochialism of pressure groups, and the myopia of bureaucratic politics will become more intrusive than ever before.

The implication is that establishing a consensus on foreign policy to replace the Cold War consensus will prove enormously difficult. During the Cold War, United States foreign policymaking almost invariably exhibited what Roger Hilsman termed a "strain towards agreement" largely because of a general recognition of the dangers inherent in policy paralysis (quoted in Schilling *et al.*, 1962). In effect, the Cold War was characterized by dual containment – successive administrations not only succeeded in containing the Soviet Union, but also some of the more debilitating consequences of the normal functioning of the United States political system. There were differences and conflicts to be sure, but bipartisanship (although never complete) endured from the 1940s to the mid- and late-1960s. Considerable value was placed on consensus, and the foreign policy debate revolved largely around proposals to fight the Cold War more effectively.

Fissures in this approach began to appear during the latter half of the 1960s as the Vietnam War undermined both the foreign policy consensus and a foreign policymaking establishment that had led the United States into a conflict that it did not fully understand, was not properly prepared for, and could never win politically. Consequently, it was not surprising that this establishment – which consisted of "relatively homogeneous, part-time pragmatic and mostly bipartisan Northeasterners" was "subsumed by a much larger more diverse elite of full-time foreign policy professionals" who are "far more political and ideological than their predecessors" (Destler, Gelb and Lake, 1984). These foreign policy activists tend to polarize debate rather than occupy the center, to offer destructive criticism rather than constructive proposals, and to intensify rather than defuse controversy over foreign and defense policy.

Even so, what Destler, Gelb, and Lake term "the unmaking of American foreign policy" was held in check by balancing mechanisms that helped to bring extremist policies back to the center and to ensure that even the polarization of debate was not excessively damaging. From the latter half of the 1950s onwards, United States policy toward the Soviet Union consisted essentially of two tracks – strength and negotiation. Although there was often controversy over the balance between these two components, the net result of public and Congressional pressure was usually to ensure that they were both present. When policy appeared to veer too far in one direction – *détente* and negotiation under Carter or strength under Reagan – public and Congressional pressure brought it back to the center. This helps to explain why Reagan's military buildup actually began under the Carter administration, while the Reagan administration, which was widely perceived as very hard-line, eventually presided over an unprecedented *détente* with the Soviet Union (Firestone, 1982).

In the post-Cold War era, the problems are greater and the balancing or countervailing mechanisms less effective. The loss of familiar terms of reference is likely to intensify the accretion of rival policy proposals, as competitive elites promulgate widely divergent values and highly disparate policy preferences about the appropriate U.S. role and responsibility in the post-Cold War world. The disappearance of external imperatives for action not only weakens the limits on policy conflicts, but also reduces the opportunities for correcting and balancing mechanisms to come into play. With no "clear and present danger" to mobilize against, no sense of urgency, and the complexity and intractibility of the issues on the foreign policy agenda, the foreign policy debate is likely to be characterized not by an effort to rebuild consensus, but by an entrepreneurial free-for-all. With professional policy elites competing for attention and influence in the market place for new proposals, it is highly probable that the foreign policy debate will be unstructured, and unresolved – except by default. The process itself will be "more fragmented, less autonomous, and more politicized than usual" (Schneider, 1992). It seems unlikely that widely accepted conclusions about the U.S. role or compelling prescriptions for a new policy framework will emerge. And while stabilizers can prevent extreme fluctuations of a two-track policy, they can do little to correct a policy characterized by drift, vacillation, and an *ad hoc* approach to global problems. Nor is the vacuum likely to be filled by a bureaucracy in which the pressures for competition and the tendencies toward conflict are also increasing. Bureaucratic politics and organizational rivalries are a result of a system in which "quasi-sovereign" departments and agencies with divergent institutional interests are compelled to compete for both resources and influence over policy (Schilling *et al.*, 1962). Even if fragmented bureaucratic structures are another familiar feature of the policymaking system, however, there are several developments that seem likely both to increase organizational parochialism and to intensify disputes over jurisdiction. The first is that with no critical issue compelling policymakers to provide direction and establish priorities, there are new opportunities for organizational imperialism. With everything up for grabs, influence and resources do not accrue to the timid. Second, if there are new opportunities for aggrandizement, there are also new dangers. Efforts to reduce the budget deficit and the consequent constraints on resources give interdepartmental rivalries a sharper edge: in periods of budgetary stringency, even comfortable rivalries take on a zero-sum quality. Third, the drive to reduce government initiated by the Clinton administration will only add to the determination with which institutions, agencies, and military services defend their central roles and missions. And more often than not, these roles and missions are related to traditional problems rather than those on the new agenda. The United States military, for example, has recognized the need for downsizing and for rationalization of resources. The base-force developed by the Bush administration was a sensible move in this direction. Yet it is striking that reduction has not been accompanied, to anything like the same extent, by a reconfiguration of forces for specialized new tasks such as peace enforcement.

This leads directly to another problem – which is that many of the new issues on the foreign policy agenda do not fit the traditional categories. These problems blur two familiar and long-standing distinctions – that between domestic and foreign policy, and that between economics and security. The first distinction has been eroded by phenomena such as transnational drug trafficking, which combines the problem of domestic demand with that of foreign supply. The second has been eroded by the growing linkages between security and economics, linkages that have been perhaps most evident in the strident debates over burden-sharing in American alliances. The difficulty, especially in the second case, is that the organizations and policymaking communities that have grown up to deal with these problems place them into discrete categories that allow for only partial and fragmented solutions. As Irving Destler noted, "The security complex and the economic complex tend to operate autonomously, with much interplay within each but relatively little between them" (Destler, 1994). So long as economic and security issues are dealt with in separate tracks, the United States will not be able to develop adequate responses. Simply because agencies and departments do not find new forms of cooperation palatable let alone congenial, however, should not prohibit efforts to promote interaction and enforce cooperation.

Part of the problem is one of restoring some semblance of balance to a process that traditionally has been dominated by the preeminence of security issues. The Clinton administration's decision to create a National Economic Council to parallel the National Security Council is clearly an attempt to move in this direction. Yet, as Destler has noted, this could actually perpetuate rather than overcome the bifurcation.

Efforts to integrate the activities of the two committees are unlikely to be effective, and it would make far more sense to have a National Policy Council that gives roughly equal representation to both security and economic specialists and explicitly sets out to overcome fragmentation and compartmentalization of issues

(Destler, 1994). Whether dealing with relations with Japan or with Russia, it is no longer appropriate to compartmentalize security and economic issues: they are increasingly inseparable aspects of the overall relationship. It is important that the tradeoffs between, for example, economic aid to facilitate the success of democracy in Russia, and military spending to hedge against a more assertive and nationalistic Russia, be considered explicitly and in a comprehensive analysis that is fully understood by key decision makers. In the absence of an overall coordinating committee of this kind, the various facets of foreign policy are likely to continue along their separate tracks until brought together by domestic or international crises.

A rational approach to policy coordination and integration is made all the more difficult by the broader context within which priorities have to be worked out. Although public opinion on foreign policy may be rather more stable than was once believed and the volatile swings of mood between the extremes of isolationism and internationalism a feature of the past rather than the present, media attention ensures a highly politicized and emotional context for playing out foreign policy debates. Issues are dealt with not on their merits, but in terms of the emotion or angst they arouse. It has been argued, on the basis of the war against Iraq, that "the techniques of effective news management can compensate for the decline of the old foreign policy establishment and the rise of domestic political forces" (Bennett, 1994). Yet, it is at least equally plausible that the increased pervasiveness of television in particular has exacerbated the undesirable consequences of other corrosive trends in the American political system, not least because of its importance in setting the foreign policy agenda. Lacking a role and a policy framework that would provide at least some criteria for determining the importance of international issues, challenges, and events, policymakers will tend to assess significance in terms of political salience: the more coverage given to an issue by C.N.N., the networks, and the press, the more important will it be deemed to be. In these circumstances, the agenda for action will be determined more by media attention than by the national interest. Moreover, even if public opinion is no longer characterized by volatile swings, attentiveness to particular foreign policy issues is likely to be ephemeral. This will place a high premium on policies with immediate or short-term payoffs. The difficulty is that many of the problems of the post-Cold War world are resistant to immediate panaceas or short-term palliatives. They require patience and determination, a willingness to make sacrifices and at least a medium-term commitment of time, energy, and resources.

This suggests another weakness of the American political system – the relatively short time horizons of the makers of foreign policy. A preoccupation with immediate payoffs is inherent in the four-year presidential term and the two-year terms of members of the House of Representatives. Nevertheless, it means that foreign policy priorities will often be determined by political expediency rather than assessments of the national interest. This could have one of two consequences: either neglect of foreign policy in favor of domestic issues and initiatives that promise to be popular, or an attempt to achieve short-run foreign policy successes at the expense of more important but long-term foreign policy needs.

There are several reasons for believing that the former option is more likely, and that increasingly foreign policy will be relegated to a position of secondary importance. First, there is likely to be some public disillusionment with the increasing messiness of the policy process. As William Schneider has argued, "The more foreign policy looks like politics as usual, the more likely Americans are to get turned off."

The diminishing opportunities for dramatic presidential initiatives and successes in foreign policy may be even more important. In the past, presidents have been able to act decisively in foreign policy, even when they have been stymied in domestic policy – it was the one area where there were opportunities for decisive and dramatic outcomes, where they were not mired down in the messiness of Congressional logrolling and compromise. This may no longer be the case. The kinds of issue on the agenda are not readily amenable to dramatic short-term initiatives that have immediate and obvious benefits. Failed-nation states, for example, present a series of potential quagmires in which it is far easier to get in than out, in which the prospects for successful action are limited, and in which the benefits to the United States are unlikely to match the sacrifices that will be required. In circumstances where the international arena may be as intractable as the domestic, presidents will tend to see risk rather than opportunity in interventionist policies. Moreover, even successful foreign policies and military actions overseas do not guarantee reelection if domestic needs are not met. Although foreign policy crises may still create a "rally round the flag" effect, this is likely to be a short-term boost at best. It could also turn into a liability, especially if a president fails to exhibit the same decisiveness in dealing with domestic issues as foreign policy challenges. This certainly happened to President Bush in the aftermath of the war against Iraq. As Sidney Blumenthal noted, "by mobilizing national energies for war, while maintaining passivity on the domestic front Bush prepared his own disintegration. . . . Foreign policy did not . . . offset domestic; instead, the contrast of command and fecklessness rapidly diminished him" (Blumenthal, 1992–3).

The relegation of foreign policy will also result from a pendulum swing toward restoring the primacy of domestic issues. During the Cold War the requirements of national security and global leadership were preeminent – and domestic needs were neglected. The result is that the United States faces an increasingly onerous and demanding domestic agenda. As former Secretary of Commerce, Peter Peterson, and James Sebenius have argued, "After four decades of the Cold War, failure to make progress on a 'domestic agenda' now threatens American long-term national security more than the external military threats that have traditionally preoccupied security and foreign policy failure to invest in productive capacity, research and development, and infrastructure; the crisis in American education; the exploding underclass, and other domestic problems may have greater direct impact" on American institutions and values than the threats from abroad "which have traditionally preoccupied the national security community." Part of their argument is that America has become "a choiceless society, substituting denial and rhetoric for meaningful action" (Peterson and Sebenius, 1992). The result has been a spiral of deficits and debts accompanied by decline in areas of public provision in such areas as health policy and social welfare. Underlying all these issues, however, are not only questions about the American economy and the extent to which America can reduce its budget deficit and reestablish its economic competitiveness, but also concerns about the prevailing patterns of governance.

One manifestation of this crisis of political structures is an institutionalized gridlock that characterized the Bush presidency and, in some areas, reduced policy to procrastination. Although Democratic control of both Congress and the presidency has partially alleviated the institutionalized gridlock, the Clinton administration has to deal with a Congress in which divisions within the Democratic Party loom almost as large as the split between Republicans and Democrats. It also has to confront parochial concerns, special interests, and an undisciplined pluralism in which conceptions of national interest are sacrificed to organizational self-interest, pressures for adaptation are resisted by departments and agencies preoccupied with institutional health, and policy proposals are evaluated almost exclusively in terms of sectoral impact rather than national well-being. In these circumstances, the prospects for a major redefinition of roles and responsibilities and a reinvigoration of U.S. foreign policy are minimal.

Implications for Policy

The synergy between the fluidity of the post-Cold War international system and the turbulence of the domestic political system and policymaking process seems likely to result in a foreign policy characterized by drift and indecision, sporadic and unpredictable interventionism, growing frustration with allies and adversaries alike, and an approach to foreign policy that owes more to emotion and expediency than to rational calculation. In an essay on the foreign policy process written over 30 years ago, Warner Schilling identified what he termed a "policy syndrome" derived from the autonomy of the actors in the policymaking process "and the resultant necessity for voluntary coordination among them" (Schilling *et al.*, 1962). He suggested that the process could end in stalemate and a failure to produce a clear policy; that it could be compromised by the need for accommodation; that it could be unstable as first one group of policymakers then another take it in different directions; that it could contain contradictory elements as different organizations and institutions pursue their own independent policies; that there could be a large gap between declaratory policy and implementation; that it could be blind to new problems or, even when they are acknowledged, still be too slow in responding; and that it could be leaderless and indecisive. The central argument of this chapter is that although most of these policy pathologies were held in check – even if they were not completely avoided – throughout the Cold War, they are likely to be much more obvious in post-Cold War foreign policy.

In fact, it became evident very quickly in the Clinton administration that overcoming the constraints and inertia of the political system, and doing something about the budget deficit and health care,would require difficult tradeoffs, painful compromises, and the rapid depletion of the political capital of the new President. In these circumstances, it was impossible for the President to engage in new foreign policy initiatives or even to try to establish a new sense of direction and priorities in foreign policy. Partly the result of particular circumstances, this is also likely to be the pattern for the future: without an external threat to act as a rallying point for the mobilization of national energies and resources, the pluralism and sectionalism of the United States political system, more often than not, will result in the kinds of policy outlined by Schilling. Facing situations where U.S. interests are not as immediately and obviously involved as during the Cold War, presidents will be castigated for being too active in foreign policy or for not being active enough, for ignoring crucial international problems, or for devoting scarce resources to foreign policy at the expense of domestic needs.

Unless the United States is able to define a clear role, establish a new policy framework, and recognize that influence can only be exercised through subtlety and skill, there will be a prolonged period of drift and indecision in foreign policy, at a time when international problems are magnifying, and the frequency of crises is accelerating. These crises may not be as compelling as were those of the Cold War, but they may be even more demanding.

It is also clear that they demand multilateral solutions. The United States has neither the will nor the capability to act alone. Unable to find or impose solutions to international problems through unilateral efforts, the United States needs to cooperate much more comprehensively than in the past with other leading states in the international community and to work through multilateral institutions such as the United Nations. Yet, even if the United States tries to redefine a role for itself as a facilitator rather than guarantor of international order, it will still encounter many frustrations. Multilateralism requires not only a broad consensus among the major powers on what needs to be done to maintain international order, but a commitment to peace keeping and peace enforcement in spite of the costs and casualties that might be incurred. Even if this is achievable internationally, it is not clear that it would obtain domestic support. Multilateral approaches would create some domestic resonance, involving as they do both burden-sharing and responsibility-sharing. The difficulty is that multilateralism is likely to satisfy neither those who want a more activist foreign policy, nor those who prefer disengagement from American commitments and abstinence from military intervention overseas. Senator Richard Lugar, for example, has claimed that "Multilateralism has become a cover for US retrenchment and the abandonment of leadership to the vagaries of international events" (quoted in Doherty, 1993). Others, too, see it as an abdication of U.S. global responsibility. On the opposite side, however, are those who regard multilateralism as a euphemistic rationalization for continued foreign policy activism. The "America first" strand of elite and popular thinking, in particular, sees the domestic problems facing the United States as a reason for eschewing international activism, whether unilateral or multilateral.

With no stable calculus of American interest, this debate is likely to prove both divisive and inconclusive. The juxtaposition of international fluidity and domestic fragmentation will make it extremely difficult, if not impossible, for the United States to develop either a clear role conception or a compelling policy framework for managing new challenges and resolving new dilemmas. Indeed, both the domestic incentives and the international opportunities for the Clinton administration to reformulate a new foreign policy framework and take decisive initiatives are relatively weak, while the inhibitions on doing this are very strong. The vacillation on Bosnia is in many respects symptomatic. It is a function partly of the Clinton administration itself, but also reflects the complexity of the issue and the shortcomings of the foreign policymaking process. The implication is that the United States will be unable to mobilize the energies and resources for the sustained and systematic international involvement that is essential for dealing with the messy problems of the post-Cold War era. Policy is likely to be leaderless, indecisive, and evasive of responsibility.

This is not to imply that there will be a reversion to isolationism. U.S. foreign policy will be characterized far more by drift than by insularity. The impulse may be there, but traditional isolationism is impossible in an interdependent world. Moreover, an isolationist policy would require a level of decisiveness that the political system is simply unable to generate. Rather than a decision to withdraw, therefore we are likely to see incremental reductions in international engagement, punctuated by occasional short-term interventions. What is likely to be lacking is a sustained long-term commitment to international order. This should not be surprising. The United States has a tradition of winning wars and retreating, to at least some degree, from the problems of the subsequent peace. Yet it is an approach that is likely to have long-term costs. Unfortunately, the politics that infuse foreign policymaking may permit no alternative. Foreign policymaking during the Cold War was very effective, but was also an aberration. Current trends suggest that De Tocqueville may have been correct in his belief that America lacked the qualities necessary for the effective control of diplomacy.

PART FOUR

Contemporary Issues

16

Health Policy: The Analytics and Politics of Attempted Reform

CALUM PATON

This chapter considers the problems of reforming American health care, looking at both the internal dynamics of the current major reform proposals, and the political environment that has shaped their reception and is likely to determine both the substance of any legislation in this field and the way it is implemented.

By now, the problems of American health care are well known. They consist primarily of gross inequalities in access to health care and of rising costs that continue to spiral out of control. Although the United States spends more on health care than any other industrialized country, there are vast disparities of access between different racial, economic, and geographic groups. For Americans *with* health insurance, the health care that is available compares favorably with that of other countries. For Americans *without* health insurance (and recent evidence suggests that approximately 31 million Americans fall within this category), the standard of health care is comparable with that found in developing countries. An analysis of infant mortality rates, a commonly used indicator of the quality of medical care, illustrates this point well. White Americans, 73.6% of whom have health insurance, have an infant mortality rate that is comparable with that in many western European countries. Black Americans, 37.7% of whom have *no* health insurance, have an infant mortality rate closer to that found in many Third World countries.

The soaring costs of medical care have several damaging features that have acted as a spur for reform. From industry's perspective, the costs of providing health insurance for employees is a burden that they feel disadvantages them in a competititive international climate. From the perspective of the individual, the cost of health care (particularly for catastrophic illness) can have devastating effects, since even the best medical insurance available will frequently be exhausted by such illness. Prolonged illness may well lead to financial ruin.

Although these features of American health care may seem to mark it out from other western societies, it should be noted that recent developments in both the United States and in Europe (primarily involving the use of markets and giving less attention to social equity than in the 1970s) have served to reduce American exceptionalism. Thus, although the United States has hitherto never been seen as a market leader in health policy, there are some arguments that suggest – descriptively rather than prescriptively – that things are changing. Like it or not, the inequitable pluralism of U.S. health care and its reliance on both private provision and private financing may represent the future as well as the past.

The Legacy

Prior to the 1960s, U.S. health care was largely in private hands, although not dominated to any significant extent by the laws of the market place. Nonprofit hospitals and autonomous "office physicians" predominated on what economists would call the "supply side" of health care; and most health care was privately financed. The 1960s reforms (primarily the creation of Medicare and Medicaid in 1965) introduced government financing, while leaving most provision in private hands. In the 1970s, weak and decentralized "indirect" planning structures were introduced in an attempt to rationalize provision and control costs before addressing the problems of inequality of access that so concerned liberals such as Senator Kennedy. The landmark "planning" Act was the National Health Planning and Resources Development Act of 1974. Federal legislation at this time also sought to encourage Health Maintenance Organizations (H.M.O.s), which were seen in the 1970s as part of a regulatory initiative rather than as part of a market initiative. H.M.O.s act as a special type of insurance company that directly owns or manages providers (hospitals, etc.) and therefore avoids the tendency of providers to pass high costs on to insurers.

In the 1980s, health policy was policy by default. The "Reagan revolution" in the 1980s tapped into a political and public mood at the time that suggested that planning did not work. There were one or two significant initiatives (at the technical rather than political or ideological level), such as the introduction of "Diagnosis Related Groups (D.R.G.s)." (D.R.G.s are groups of clinical conditions that are homogeneous as to their need for treatment and, by implication, homogeneous for cost. They are used as a regulatory tool that limits price increases by hospital.) However, the philosophy of the Reagan administration was to let market forces rationalize the system if they could. To some extent, this was wishful thinking. American health care has traditionally not been characterised by market discipline in provision, but by inefficient subsidy of fee-for-service medicine, operating through local monopolies (whether for profit or nonprofit), by the mechanism of third-party insurance. A *laissez-faire* approach was not likely to lead to the rationalization of the system. Market-oriented health reformers saw the need for competition in provision and, furthermore, also an end to traditional fee-for-service medicine in the private sector. Such market competition was – in the eyes of many reformers – to come through "Health Maintenance Organizations" (H.M.O.s), which would enrol patients and guarantee their health care for the year. (That is, H.M.O.s were a *special* type of insurance company that would *own their providers*, and end the tension between the provider and financier that led to spiralling costs when allied to rapacious consumer demand for everything available in health care, whatever the cost.)

By the end of the 1980s, it was clear that costs had not been rationalized at all – and that markets had only worked patchily and to a limited extent in controlling costs. Indeed, much of the research-based literature implies that for-profit corporations delivering health care were in fact more costly rather than less costly by comparison with traditional providers.

The Reemergence of Regulation

The decline and fracturing of the right-wing coalition that produced Reaganism led in health care to a reemergence of interest in regulation. It was never likely, however, that a recourse to the approaches of the 1970s would occur. The election of President Clinton in 1992 put squarely on the agenda the concept of "managed competition." The person credited with originating this phrase is Professor Alain Enthoven, Professor of Public and Private Management at Stanford University, and a health economist who had previously been a young Assistant Secretary of Defense under Robert McNamara in the early 1960s. Disillusioned by what he saw as the inefficiency of government, yet with a commitment to some version of social equity, Enthoven argued that managed competition was the best means of rationalizing the health care system while permitting (both fiscally and politically) greater equity than had hitherto been either affordable or seemingly politically possible (Enthoven, 1988).

The Main Proposal

Enthoven's latest proposal for reform has been devised in coordination with the so-called "Jackson Hole group," the name deriving from the fact that the group meets at the home of Paul Ellwood, a long-time health policy analyst and government adviser. The essence of the approach is to seek to combine greater efficiency in provision of health care with some degree of equity in purchasing on behalf of various stipulated populations (such as the poor). To this extent, Enthoven is a free-market economist who nevertheless sees a need for government regulation to ensure that specific "problems with the market" (market failure) are addressed in devising a meaningful reform. One such problem is "risk selection." Insurance companies will seek to exclude those in higher risk brackets such as the poor and sick (unless they are fully recompensed for the higher costs of care that such groups are likely to incur when properly covered). Managed competition seeks to minimize the incentive for health plans to select risk by establishing:

A single point of entry for all subscribers/citizens.
A standardised benefit package.
Risk-adjusted premiums.
Agreed standards for access to care, including tertiary care.

These stipulations are made in the context of rules to ensure coverage of all in a sponsored group. It is argued that small employer groups seeking health care for their workers need to be pooled into large purchasing cooperatives, in order to spread risk and achieve economies of scale in purchasing. Large purchasing cooperatives were also needed to acquire expertise and manage competition by allowing enough purchasing power *vis-à-vis* the power of providers. Large cooperatives would also offer choice to individuals who could change their medical plans.

The Jackson Hole group has proposed a *Health Insurance Purchasing Cooperative (H.I.P.C.)*, which would play the role described above – of pooling small groups of employers and also coordinating the purchase by government of health coverage for the disadvantaged in society. These *H.I.P.C.s* would contract what Enthoven calls Accountable Health Partnerships (A.H.P.s), which would in effect either be Health Maintenance Organizations or other organizations offering what is increasingly known generically in the health policy literature as "managed care." This last concept refers to the alleged need for care plans for specific diseases and conditions, to allow both cost-control and standardised "health planning" at the micro level within the hospital or community setting.

Accountable Health Partnerships can allegedly produce better care at lower cost, on the following principles. First, they are expected to produce loyalty, commitment, and the responsible participation of their physicians. Secondly, they will render compatible the incentives confronting doctors, the interests of patients, and the interests of society in high quality (yet economical) care. They will do this primarily by ensuring that the incentives of their enrolled physicians are directed to making them work within the budget of the organization that pays them.

That is, there will *not* be a split between the purchaser and the provider, in that the Health Maintenance Organization (a special kind of insurance company) will be the purchaser that also owns or directly controls the provider. If, however, by the purchaser we mean the H.I.P.C. operating on behalf of citizens, employers, and government, rather than the H.M.O. with the H.I.P.C. contracts, the purchaser/provider split remains.

Thirdly, the A.H.P.s will allegedly have an incentive to produce information systems adequate for the purpose of monitoring the effect of health care – what are known in the literature as health outcomes. They will study variations in clinical practice and increasingly move toward adopting cost-effective patterns of care. Fourthly, these organizations will in effect do a kind of decentralized health planning, in that they will match provision (for example numbers and types of doctors) to the needs of their enrolled populations. One particular need in the United States is to increase primary care at the expense of both secondary and complex tertiary care. Of course resources generally should be matched to needs of population served, – not just numbers and types of doctors.

Finally, and most prescriptively, such organizations will allegedly indulge in what has become the buzz phrase of "Total Quality Management" (T.Q.M.), which broadly means "do it right first time rather than rectify mistakes." This approach allegedly cuts costs and renders compatible both quality improvement and cost reduction.

In pointing to some current problems in U.S. health care not addressed by traditional private sector-based fee-for-service provision reimbursed by third party insurance, Enthoven and the Jackson Hole group can make common cause with more general critics of U.S. health care. First, inability to control costs, or even the rapid rise in costs, sits fair and square with gross inequity in terms of access to care by those who need it. The general inequality of access has already been mentioned, but in the United States this inequality has some highly specific features also. There is, for example, a lack of primary care and an excess of specialists. There is an excess of facilities even after "competition" has supposedly rationalized the system. There are wide variations in clinical practice, medical uncertainty, and a lack of data on outcomes; and there is a lack of preventive, promotive, and "social" care – in particular, a record on childhood immunization which, as Enthoven points out, in a debating point no doubt intended to sting his fellow analysts, produces a record worse than that of Cuba. (In fact, the comparison is somewhat unfair given Cuba's impressive record in health care for a previously underdeveloped country – at least until the collapse of Cuba's trading partners in the former Soviet bloc).

The Jackson Hole reform proposal thus seeks to set right the problems of the traditional fee-for-service system, consisting of solo practice and remote third-party insurance. The group considered the incentives of the traditional system to be wrong, not least because the existing system creates a costly adversary relationship between provider and payer. Other major defects in the existing system correctly identified by the Jackson Hole group plan are the absence of any planning forceful enough to match resources to population needs, and the financial separation of the various components of the traditional system prevents rational resource allocation.

The key question, however, is whether a "pro-competitive regulatory framework" designed to produce managed competition could put right such wrongs. The Jackson Hole prescription offers comprehensive care to enrolled populations, on the basis of percapita prepayment either by individuals or their employers – or by government on behalf of the poor. The proposal also puts providers at risk for costs and poor quality, and makes them publicly accountable to some extent in these realms. It is nevertheless very much an open question as to whether "managed competition" would in fact rationalize the U.S. health care system. However, it is significant that universal coverage for care is very much the *final* element of the Jackson Hole proposals.

It is certainly true that one of the major problems in U.S. health care, from the viewpoint of the economist, is that demand is "price inelastic." Where all expenses – however excessive – are tax deductible and where a lot of insurance policies involve " the employer paying all," then there is certainly little incentive to control costs.

When one adds to this the fact that existing benefit packages are not standardized, competition is even more difficult: the market is segmented and even H.M.O.s may not compete in that, for example, some will be renowned for good care in one specialty and bad care in another. The perfectly rational fear by consumers of exclusions "in the small print," whether in traditional medical insurance or in Health Maintenance Organizations, means that – in the absence of regulation – genuine competition by providers on an equal basis in the "same market" may be difficult to achieve.

To put it another way, neither consumers nor government may have adequate information on providers, in a segmented market, to allow effective competition. Thus the Jackson Hole proposals may contribute something to improving the prospects for a market in provision.

Furthermore, the proposal at least acknowledges that "risk selection" is a problem in health insurance. If insurers can discriminate among the population, they will seek to exclude "bad risks" (i.e., the poor, and sick) wherever possible. If insurers and the providers that they own (or contract with) are not regulated to "take all comers" on the basis of annual open enrolment and full reimbursement of the actuarially calculated costs of those they cover, then either the poor and sick will simply not get coverage or the insurers who cover them will increasingly run into financial difficulties. Consequences of the latter will be that either they will go bust, or will provide inadequate care for those they cover. In other words, there will be "poor H.M.O.s for the poor" – at best.

In summary, managed competition seeks to minimize the incentive for health plans to be selective on the basis of risk by mandating the following :

- A single point of entry (i.e., all the population to be covered through the regulatory efforts of H.I.P.C.s, in H.M.O.s or equivalent organizations).
- A standardized benefit package, albeit a minimalist one excluding many items of care.
- Risk-adjusted premiums, paid by government where necessary.
- Standards set for access to care (which may include "managed care" on the basis of clinical protocols that set out procedures and, by implication, expected costs for particular diagnoses within specialties.)

The Political Environment

It is difficult to foresee an *effective and equitable version of managed competition* being implemented in the current political environment; it simply challenges too many vested interests. Even if private insurance is able to adapt to play a significant role in the new financial/purchasing arrangements without subverting them in the direction of the traditional system (a very dubious proposition in any case), the fact that the Jackson Hole proposals do not call for a redistributive payroll tax will make it difficult to ensure that the needs of those hitherto excluded from the system are adequately financed and covered through any reform, even if fully implemented. It is of some significance that the name of Enthoven has been identified with tentative health care reform proposals throughout the duration of the Reagan and Bush administrations, as well as in the early days of the Clinton administration. Health care is not seen as an exceptional need that transcends income so much as simply another good to be purchased in a more cost-effective manner, in the eyes of mainstream "market" reformers. To expect the inequity of health care to be addressed without fiscal redistribution is to expect a lot.

Furthermore, there is no specific advocacy of the effective and comprehensive "group Health Maintenance Organization" as opposed to what are known as "individual H.M.O.s" which are more loosely organized and controlled, and that have, as suggested by research in the 1980s, a poorer record in cost control, let alone in promoting social equity. The aim is to keep coverage in the private sector and to ensure that there are "no free riders" – that is, to ensure that those who can pay (whether individuals or firms) do pay. The role for government is therefore a peripheral or tidying role.

The importance of the insurance industry in sponsoring Democrats as well as Republicans (such as Lloyd Bentsen, Treasury Secretary, when he was a Democratic Texan senator) means that replacing pluralistic private insurance with a quasi-public national health insurance, as in Canada, is effectively off the agenda. The insurance industry is now more powerful than the "doctor lobby." The American Medical Association is now more of a toothless tiger than it used to be when physicians were scarcer.

Toward the Clintons' Plan

It is arguably because Enthoven's earlier reform proposals have been mediated in a right-wing direction to produce the current Jackson Hole reform proposal, that a schism has opened up between "conservatives" and the "liberals" advising what was – in 1993 – the President's Healthcare Commission, headed by Hillary Clinton. Furthermore, liberal senators such as Howard Metzenbaum (Ohio) are opposed to "managed competition." Health reformers such as Jay Rockefeller (West Virginia) are concerned about equity.

The conservatives seek a pro-competitive regulatory framework in the context of weak proposals to increase social equity, and the liberals seek a greater role for government in pursuit of greater social equity as well as cost control.

While pro-competitive regulators admittedly argue for a Health Standards Board to define "the uniform and effective health benefits" that would be eligible for tax-favored coverage in the private sector and also an "Outcomes Management Standards Board" to ensure that information is available to help purchasers and H.I.P.C.s, these are in effect technical (albeit important) regulatory functions to ensure that money is not wasted in the marketplace.

In mainstream U.S. politics, the *choice* has recently been not really between the traditional system, managed competition and socialized health care, but between various fairly weak versions of managed competition as opposed to a traditional system. The question is, can the "Clinton Plan" (White House, 1993) go beyond traditional incrementalism in reconciling equity (a national health insurance) and cost-control?

Some prominent "market-oriented" health care analysts (such as Professor Mark Pauly of the Wharton School in Pennsylvania) have even argued for significantly less regulation than that inherent in the Enthoven proposals, let alone the Clinton proposals. Pauly argues that "risk selection" by insurance companies is an overrated problem; that the alleged crisis caused for companies' costs by health care coverage for their workers is also an overrated problem (on the grounds that it is simply an economic choice between higher wages and less health care, on the one hand, and lower wages and more health care, on the other); and that traditional regulation is not likely to succeed. As with many who embrace the right-wing version of public choice economics, it is argued by Pauly that the incentives for regulators to do the right thing are not evident. In other words, according to this perspective, in analyzing health care reform, we should be considering a narrow version of economic man.

The Clinton Plan, on the other hand, calls for:

- Guaranteed comprehensive health care benfits for all Americans.
- A series of geographically based, state-administered Health Alliances (from traditional fee-for-service medicine to H.M.O.s).

• Cost incentives to choose economical plans, but allowances for extra payments by individual.
• Fixed payments to health plans to control costs.
• Coverage at the same rate for all participants ("community rating") with purchasing Alliances adjusting payments to health
• plans (from their general revenues)to ensure that the more expensive, i.e., those who are more poor or more sick than average, are properly covered.
• A National Health Board to control and mandate standards for coverage quality and service.
• Allowance for large firms to set up their own Health Alliances.
• Incorporations of existing schemes (such as Medicaid and Medicare) in the new structure.

The Clinton Plan is a brave reform which – if implemented – would bring the United States "in-line" with Europe. It would combine aspects of national health insurance with aspects of *regulation* (or "managed") competition. It would allocate *partly* public resources to individuals' chosen health plans in a manner not entirely dissimilar to that in the Netherlands.

The major question at the time of writing is whether the usual pressures of American politics will destroy the radical nature of the reform? While the plan does not prohibit (even *traditional*) private insurance, it regulates it rigorously by U.S. standards. Currently, the American Medical Association is agnostic, seeing "good and bad" in the plan. As an episode in American policymaking, it is a fascinating development. Whether or not American *politics* responds, remains to be seen. On paper, the plan is, however, an attempt by the United States to follow Europe, rather than vice versa.

The "Oregon Plan"

The 1980s were a decade of inaction at the federal level concerning health care reform, although significant state initiatives to develop innovative patterns of delivery, and in some cases to increase equity, were beginning to occur during that time. (In 1993, for example, Oregon and Washington states were seeking to combine cost-control and greater equity.) Whatever version of health care reform is adopted at the federal level – and this includes the Clinton administration – it is likely that the effects of both Congressional behavior and any subsequent implementation throughout the federal system would render reform incremental rather than comprehensive.

The most significant change is likely to occur in terms of what is publicly covered for those populations depending upon government for their access to health care. Formal "rationing" devices such as the so-called Oregon formula are likely to increase in salience.

The state of Oregon has been developing various versions of its proposals, which in effect cover more of the poor for a smaller range of medical treatments and conditions. That is, allegedly on the basis of both expert definitions of which procedures produce "health gain" (better health status) and which do not, on the one hand, and popular participation in making hard choices, on the other hand, a schedule of allowable and non-allowable procedures as regards publicly financed health care is drawn up. The state's Medicaid program is then extended to include all those hitherto excluded rather than simply the traditional Medicaid population. This is rendered affordable, however, on the basis that previously reimbursable procedures will in some cases no longer be available through public finance.

On the one hand, this can be presented as a progressive proposal (supported by Clinton during the campaign in 1992), yet can also be presented as contributory to a two-tier system in that it is only the poor who are "rationed." (Vice-President Al Gore, during the campaign, opposed the Oregon approach.)

Conclusion

Significant changes in American health care are less likely to come in the 1990s from structural alterations than from changes to the role of the consumer. It is perhaps in this realm, to return to the introduction of this chapter, that the United States is a "market leader" rather than market follower. The role of the consumer is now much more part of the rhetoric, at the very least, in British and European health care than previously, partly as a result of U.S. influence. Furthermore, debates about "who should make the hard choices in a context of rationing health care" – the expert or the consumer (technocracy or democracy) – is a live one in the more publicly financed systems of Europe, where such decisions are at least more fairly and squarely social decisions. In the United States, however, such decisions tend to affect only those segments of the poor who are dependent on the public purse, and are an anathema to the bulk of the population.

One of the significant impetuses for national health care reform (which has been a non-starter in effect since the 1960s) has been the increasing discontentment, at a time of economic recession, of what Galbraith would call the "contented majority" (Galbraith, 1992). That is, middle-class people as well as working-class people have been losing their jobs and finding out what it is to suffer from insecurely held health insurance. The most likely political source of health care reform is to ensure that "the richer pay" – on the basis that, if they cease to be rich, they will still get coverage.

At bottom therefore, it is by giving the better-off a stake in what might broadly be called the social welfare system of the country that significant welfare reform in the United States may be achievable. To that extent, the U.S. health care system may therefore be belatedly catching up with Europe.

There is a problem here, however; if the aim is increasingly to ration expensive care, then one can ration on the basis of income or on the basis of access to services irrespective of income. If one chooses the latter, the poor may suffer for those excluded services for which they cannot afford to pay in the private sector. If, however, one rations on the basis of income (assuming that the U.S. political system is able to handle such a significant process in a coherent way), then one is in effect creating government finance or government programs on the basis of either a formal means test or on the basis of a sliding scale of income.

This removes the *"stake in welfare" for the better-off,* which is necessary to sustain "healthy" welfare programs in a society such as the United States, where the atypical social manners of the faddish politically correct sit uncomfortably alongside a highly inegalitarian and conservative political economy.

17

Women in American Politics

BARBARA BURRELL

Organizing collectively to elect women to office is a distinctive phenomenon of the second feminist movement. In the first feminist movement, the suffragists campaigned for over half a century to obtain the vote for women, so that they could have a voice in who the lawmakers would be. However, it appears that the suffragists were not concerned with women representing themselves. Either out of expediency or from a philosophy that viewed men and women as operating in different spheres of society, the suffragists did not publicly advocate the presence of women as officeholders. Many opponents of female suffrage inevitably regarded the presence of women in public life as degrading for their sex and for the political process.

But certainly there was interest in women taking a more active role in the political life of the nation after obtaining the vote. Twenty-three states elected women to the legislature or some other office in 1920. In its early years, the League of Women Voters kept records on the number of women seeking and winning elective office. Some states barred women from office holding. Feminists had to mount campaigns to acquire that right. As late as 1942, the Oklahoma constitution prohibited women from holding such offices as governor, lieutenant governor, and attorney general (Gruberg, 1968).

Achieving numerical representation for women in elective office has been a goal of the second feminist movement. In 1963, President Kennedy's Commission on the Status of Women issued a report in which it urged that more women be elected to public office: "Women should be encouraged to seek elective and appointive posts at local, state, and national levels and in all three branches of government." The Commission, however, rejected the proposal of one of its committees, the Committee on Civil and Political Rights, which had in effect asked for temporary discrimination in favor of women in appointive and elective office, so that they could achieve greater equity in leadership positions.

The National Organization for Women (N.O.W.), in its founding statement of purpose in 1966, called for action "to bring women into full participation in the mainstream of American society now" and called for women to run for office themselves. The National Women's Political Caucus, of course, was founded precisely for the purpose, among other things, of increasing the numbers of women in public office.

Not only have women's rights activists wanted to elect more women to public office, they have wanted to change governmental policies and enact new laws that would establish equity for women to improve their status – the substantive element of representation. The National Women's Political Caucus, for example, in its initial statement of purpose, pledged to oppose racism, sexism, institutional violence, and poverty. Thus feminists have had two complementary, but not always identical, goals. The election of more women to office should contribute to the passage of legislation that addresses the special concerns of women, they assumed, but not all women favor an activist government role to achieve equity. Primarily, feminists have worked to elect only certain women to office, those who share the goals of the women's movement. Women who will be endorsed by various women's rights organizations have had to advocate certain public policies, the principal one being support for women's right to choose to have an abortion (see Chapter 8, Peele).

The Range of Women's Organizations

N.O.W. and the N.W.P.C. are membership organizations which are involved in a wide array of activities. Indeed, N.O.W. did not make electoral politics a central arena of action for itself until after the Equal Rights Amendment failed in 1982 to be adopted by the requisite number of states to become part of the Constitution. These two organizations have been joined by other women's groups that have as their single purpose the election of more women to office and the affecting of public policy through that effort. Thus, since 1974, the Women's Campaign Fund has recruited, trained, and financed women running for office, and in 1986 it was joined by EMILY's List, whose goal has been to elect pro-choice Democratic women to national office. In 1991 Ellen Malcolm, the founder of EMILY's List, shared the List's strategy with Glenda Greenwald, so that she might create a Republican counterpart organization. The WISH List was the result that supports pro-choice (i.e., pro-abortion right) Republican women. Within both the Democratic and Republican parties, other efforts have been made to establish funds and committees in support of women's candidacies, but they have not been sustained.

How successful have these groups been in achieving their purposes of electing women to the national legislature? When the N.O.W. was founded in 1966, two women were U.S. senators and ten women served in the U.S. House of Representatives, 2 percent of the total Congressional membership. A quarter of a century later in the 102nd Congress (1991–2), two women sat in the U.S. Senate and 28 women served in the House, 5.6 percent of the total membership of the Congress. Among 25 established democracies, the United States was fourth from the bottom in the proportion of its members in the lower house of parliament who were women (Rule and Norris, 1992). The election of women to national offices has been a drag on the progress women have made in lower-level officeholding.

Women have been stymied in their quest for greater numerical representation in the U.S. Congress principally because of the factor of incumbency. Throughout the contemporary era most incumbents (those already holding the elected position) have run for reelection to the House and Senate, most incumbents have won reelection; and most incumbents have been men. The opportunity structure has not been kind to newcomers. Between 1968 and 1992, only 11 women obtained a seat in the U.S. House of Representatives by defeating an incumbent (three in primary elections). Male challengers have been just as unsuccessful.

Following the founding of the National Organization for Women in 1966, which in a sense marks the beginning of the second feminist era, women's access to political leadership positions was visibly enhanced. Women increased their presence as major party nominees for the U.S. House of Representatives fivefold over the course of this era. They have captured 471 Democratic and Republican nonincumbent nominations for House seats. (The number of women who have been nominees is somewhat smaller, as several women have received more than one nomination.)

In 1968, 19 women were major party nominees, including ten incumbents running for reelection, 2 percent of all potential nominees. In 1992, 106 women obtained their party's nomination, including 26 incumbents, but this number was only 12 percent of all possible nominees. (Since there are 435 seats in the House and the Democrats and the Republicans can each nominate one individual per district, potentially 870 persons can be major party nominees in any election year. The actual number is usually smaller because in some districts no one is nominated to oppose an incumbent, and even in a few cases an open seat nominee has faced no major party opposition in the general election. This was the case for Carrie Meek, who won the Democratic Party nomination in her Florida district in 1992 with 83 percent of the vote against two opponents and had no Republican opponent in November in this overwhelmingly Democratic district.)

Because it has been the minority party during this period, the Republican Party has had a greater opportunity to nominate women for the House than the Democratic Party. It had fewer incumbents seeking renomination and reelection. But Democratic women have taken greater advantage of available opportunities. Democratic women obtained 258 nominations compared to 213 for Republican women between 1968 and 1992. Throughout this period, Democratic women were a larger proportion of that party's nonincumbent nominees than were Republican women. The gap was most noticeable in 1992 when nearly twice as many Democratic as Republican women won nonincumbent nominations (53 to 27).

Two different visions of how best to recruit women to political office have been advanced. Eleanor Smeal and the Fund for a Feminist Majority have promoted one approach. The Fund's operating belief is that feminists should "flood tickets" with women candidates. The more women who run the better, regardless of how realistic their chances of being elected. Other groups have pursued a more strategic policy, targeting their efforts on those races deemed winnable. EMILY's List has been perceived as most prominent in the latter approach. Potential endorsees must pass a rigorous screening process with the bottom line being: can she win? (See Friedman, 1993.) These groups practice politics as the art of the possible. Their critics in the feminist movement call this practice the "politics of scarcity," which deters qualified women from running (Kaminer, 1992).

Open Seats

If women are to increase their numbers in the national legislature, they have to create a presence in those races where the opportunities for ultimate victory are perceived to be the greatest, namely in open seats where incumbency is not an issue. The number of open seats in an election year has varied from a low of 27 (6 percent of all districts) in 1984 to a high of 75 (17 percent) in 1992. In 1968, 37 districts had no incumbent running for reelection; five Democratic and three Republican women vied for their party's nomination in those contests. In 1992, 57 Democratic and 25 Republican women mounted primary election campaigns in the 75 open districts. A clear trend toward a greater presence of women candidates in these elections has occurred over the course of the feminist era. The proportion of women candidates per race in the early elections was 0.09 (1968–72), meaning that theoretically one in nine races had a female candidate. The figure increased to nearly one-quarter (0.23) in the 1974–8 elections, and climbed to one-third between 1980 and 1990. Women's presence jumped significantly in 1992 to 0.55. The proportion of women candidates per race in 1992 was 0.76 for the Democrats and 0.33 for the Republicans. The majority of Democratic races (55 out of 75) had at least one female candidate. Just over one-quarter of the Republican contests had at least one female candidate. Although women's presence has grown over time, in most of the election years the voters have not had the opportunity to vote for a woman candidate had they wanted to in a majority of the primary contests.

Women who have run in open seat primary elections, however, have done as well as male candidates. Female candidates' success rate equalled that of male candidates between 1968 and 1972. Women did slightly less well in the 1974 through 1978 period, and then went on to surpass the men in the 1980s (Burrell, 1992). Women open seat primary election contenders in 1992 did substantially better than their male counterparts. Forty-three percent of the women won compared with 26 percent of the men. Women polled an average 31 percent of the vote, compared with an average 23 percent for men in 1992. In recent elections, women candidates have also outpaced male candidates in the raising of early money to fund their campaigns in open seat primary elections (Burrell, forthcoming).

General Elections

In the general elections, both male and female incumbents have been overwhelmingly successful at achieving reelection, and both sexes within both parties have been equally unsuccessful in challenging incumbents. Sex has been a minuscule factor in the average percentage of the vote a Congressional nominee has obtained during this era. Women have performed as well as men at the polls.

In open seat general election contests, Republican female nominees have been quite successful, but very few in number. In the early years of this period the few Democratic female open seat nominees had a higher success rate than their male counterparts. Sixty-four percent of Democratic female open seat nominees won compared with 46 percent of male nominees. Their advantage then disappeared. Throughout the 1980s, these candidates had few successes. The year 1992 dramatically reversed this trend. Democratic female open seat nominees won 68 percent of their races against male challengers, and in four other races beat female Republicans for a 73 percent success rate. In 1992, 24 women were newly elected to the U.S. House of Representatives, four times as many victories as the previous high of 1974 when six women were newly elected. Twenty-one of the 24 first-term Congresswomen in 1993 had won in open seats. Women increased their proportion of House membership to 10.8 percent. In addition, four women were elected to the Senate for the first time, bringing its female membership to 6 percent.

Women's P.A.C.s have been instrumental in the campaigns of many recent female Congressional nominees. P.A.C.s are limited by federal law in the amounts of money they can contribute to a candidate. They can give up to $5,000 in a primary and another $5,000 in the general election. But EMILY'S List has pioneered a new method for increasing the influence and overall amounts of money a group can be credited with supplying to a candidate. In addition to its own donation regulated by law, a group can ask individuals to write a check to a candidate, but rather than sending it directly to the candidate, the check goes to the organization – which in turn bundles it with checks from other individuals and then gives the packet of checks to the candidate. In total, EMILY'S List contributed over $6 million dollars to women candidates using both the traditional P.A.C. route and the "bundling" procedure. Overall, in 1992, over $7 million dollars flowed to women candidates in federal elections from women's P.A.C.s.

Both P.A.C. money and bundled money have been criticized by campaign finance reformers and have been an issue in campaign finance reform proposals. EMILY'S List has come under fire for its practices in recent days, although one has difficulty seeing thousands of women bundling their money together to impact on elections as a corrupting influence on the political process. Women's rights organizations have not only formed P.A.C.s in order to contribute money to women candidates. They have developed recruitment strategies, organized campaign workshops for potential candidates and campaign managers, acted as consultants and workers on campaigns, and served as mentors in acquainting women candidates with other sources of financial support in the Washington community.

Evidence also suggests that women voters are voting disproportionately for women candidates. For example, in four of the 11 Senate races in 1992, when matching a woman against a man a gender difference of 10 percent or more was present with women more supportive of the female candidate. Gender differences were present in all of 11 races. This is part of a more general contemporary phenomenon. Polls have found women more supportive then men of a generic woman candidate over a generic male candidate. Democratic women candidates have especially attracted women's votes, which is part of a recent trend of women voters giving more backing than men to Democratic candidates (Smith and Selfa, 1992).

Policy Representation for Women

Women have brought very different experiences and voices to the halls of Congress. They have had distinctive stories to tell. When the Family and Medical Leave Bill was debated on the floor of the Senate in February of 1993, Senators Patty Murray and Diane Feinstein told how they had to quit their jobs when they gave birth (Clymer, 1993). U.S. Representative Carrie Meek also testified before a sub-committee hearing on the subject of paying social security taxes for household help. Speaking in support of the proposed legislation, she told her fellow representatives, "I was once a domestic worker. . . . My mother was a domestic worker. All my sisters were domestic workers" (Dowd, 1993). Single mother and U.S. Representative Barbara Rose Collins (D-Mi.) has introduced the Unremunerated Work Act, which would require the Commissioner of the Bureau of Labor Statistics to conduct nationwide time-use surveys of all unpaid work performed in the United States, and require the Commerce Department to include all unpaid work performed in the United States in its calculations of the gross domestic product. The surveys would have to include household work, work related to childcare and other care services, agricultural work, work related to food production, work related to family business, and volunteer work. Earlier, U.S. Senator Paula Hawkins (R-FL) had dramatically described the abuse she had received as a child before a Senate committee investigating the issue.

The activities of the Congressional Caucus for Women's Issues are one measure of that concern. The Women's Congressional Caucus was formed in 1977. In 1981, the organization changed its name to the Congressional Caucus for Women's Issues and admitted congressmen as members. Men, however, cannot hold Caucus office, serve on the Executive Committee, vote on policy matters, or elect officers. It is a bipartisan group with Republican and Democratic co-chairs. Each Congress it adopts priorities for that legislative session. Throughout much of its existence the Caucus has focussed on a compendium of Bills known as the Economic Equity Act (E.E.A.). Introduced into every Congress since 1981, it has grown and changed as parts of it have been enacted into law and new agenda items have emerged. During the 102nd Congress (1991–2), the E.E.A. focussed on development of job skills and creating new opportunities for women. Seven provisions of the E.E.A. became law in that Congress: legislation to help train and place women in nontraditional jobs; to provide assistance to employers willing to hire women as apprentices; to establish a glass ceiling commission; to expand eligibility for Pell

Grants students who are less than-half time, the majority of whom are women; to encourage women and minorities to enter the fields of math and science; to establish a microloan program to assist women, low-income and minority entrepreneurs in establishing small businesses; and to study whether women and minority businesses have fair access to insurance.

Added to the E.E.A. as priority omnibus measures in recent Congresses have been the Women's Health Equity Act and the Violence Against Women Act. The women's health initiative began in 1989 with a call for a G.A.O. study of the exclusion of women from medical research at the National Institutes of Health. Caucus efforts have resulted in the creation of an Office of Women's Health Research at N.I.H. The Women's Health Equity Act, as introduced in the 102nd Congress (1991–2) "seeks to improve research, services, and prevention of conditions affecting women."

The Violence Against Women Act would increase funding for police activities designed to reduce rape and domestic violence, establish services for victims of rape and domestic violence, and provide training for police, prosecutors, and judges in dealing with crimes against women. The Bill would also make gender-based violence a federal civil rights violation.

The issue priority of the Caucus that perhaps has received the most publicity and conflict in recent Congresses has been job leave for family members. The Family and Medical Leave Act was finally enacted into law as one of the first Bills of the 103rd Congress after an eight-year journey through the national legislature. The Family and Medical Leave Act mandates that employers of 50 or more workers provide them with up to 12 weeks of job-protected unpaid leave each year to care for a newborn or newly adopted child, for a seriously ill immediate family member, or in cases of the worker's own serious illness. These issues are representative of the major work women members of Congress have been doing to achieve greater equity for women in our society and to improve their status.

On December 7th, 1992, all of the 24 newly elected women in the House held a press conference setting forth their agenda for the 103rd Congress, including full financing for Head Start early childhood education programs, passage of a family and medical leave Bill, the codification of the Supreme Court abortion ruling in *Roe* v. *Wade*, and the extension of federal laws against sexual harassment to Congress itself. The women members of Congress thus indicated their desire not merely to "stand for women" and serve as symbols of what women can achieve; but also to act for women by setting the legislative agenda.

How much of their distinctive legislative agenda will actually be translated into public policy remains an open question. But in many ways the elections of 1992 marked a new stage in the ability of women to mobilize politically and to advance their policy concerns.

18

The Changing Media

TIM HAMES

The elections of 1992 highlighted a number of technological innovations and recent developments that have substantially altered the relationship between politics and mass communications in the United States. This chapter will illustrate these major new trends.

First, significant changes within the American media – especially television – have created a much more diverse industry. Second, there was a major reevaluation by the media of its own role in presenting American elections after the 1988 presidential contest. Third, the aforementioned changes in American television led presidential candidates in 1992 to run rather different media campaigns than they had in the 1980s. Fourth, after their post-mortem on 1988, the major American networks covered the 1992 campaign differently. Finally, the early experience of the Clinton White House indicates that they intend to take the new media methods gained while campaigning into their media operations in government.

The New American Media

From the perspective of political campaigning, the American media remains dominated by television, but a very different type of television from ten or fifteen years ago. As television has become the primary means by which most Americans receive news information, and as it is by far the chief medium for political campaigning, it inevitably dominates this chapter. The focus here will be centrally presidential. This is for two reasons. First, the media itself is heavily

335

White House based, more so than the separation of powers would strictly justify. This is partly because covering the activities of one individual is much easier for all branches of the media – but especially television – than examining a complex collective body such as Congress or a secretive and technical institution such as the Supreme Court. Secondly, as far as campaigning techniques are concerned, presidential contests have usually been the means by which innovations are made that are then borrowed and adapted in all other political contests.

There are plenty of other media outlets besides television, of course; the United States boasts 10,000 different magazine titles every week, some 1,800 newspapers appear daily, and there are over 10,000 licensed radio stations (and a large number of unregistered ones). However, except for very local political contests, the sheer size of most American states makes it inevitable that for gubernatorial, senatorial, and especially presidential contests, television is the premier means by which candidates both try and get news coverage ("free media" in the jargon) and advertise their campaigns ("paid media").

This vital importance of television is partly explained by the lack of a national press in the United States. With the exception of the distinctly middle-market *U.S.A. Today*, the size of the United States has precluded any newspaper being available in most American cities. It should be noted that new technology for transmitting newspaper material may make that less true in the next ten years. For the meantime, 98 percent of American cities have only one regular daily newspaper. A much smaller proportion of Americans claim to get most of their daily news information from newspapers rather than television than would be true in western Europe.

For most of the period since watching television became a majority pastime in the United States. (the 1950s), the medium has been dominated by three giant national networks – A.B.C., C.B.S., and N.B.C. – which produced "national" television programs and sold them to local television stations, the overwhelming majority of which were tied as an affiliate to one of the big three. In the 1980s this cozy and extremely profitable oligopoly was challenged by a number of new pretenders, largely created by technological change.

The first such rival was the video recorder, which gave viewers the option of using the television screen for something other than watching the output of the major networks. By 1992, two-thirds of American households possessed a VCR.

A new competitor to the big three was a rival channel, Fox T.V, owned by media mogul Rupert Murdoch. Although little more than an irritant to its competitors at first, Fox discovered a string of hit programs (most notably, *The Simpsons*) and by 1990 Fox owned and operated seven television stations with 140 affiliates (Graber, 1993).

More seriously still, the grip of the big three over local stations, especially in the area of news production, was slipping. The number of independent television stations increased from 120 in 1981 to over 400 by 1990 (Diamond, 1991). Those stations that remained linked to the major networks became increasingly independent in their behavior. Responding to consumer demand for more local news, they began to give that a greater proportion of total news coverage at the expense of the costly output from the big networks.

Furthermore, they began to gather "national" news for themselves. In previous years, the expense of maintaining separate Washington, D.C., or New York City offices just for news production had driven local television stations to buy the network output instead. Dramatic technological advances, especially the availability of relatively inexpensive satellite time and improvements in portable microwave transmitters, slashed transmission costs and increased the number of stations that could directly cover events in Washington, D.C. The local newscaster in the studio could now interview politicians or comment on news pictures from Washington bounced by satellite, and cut out the big network middleman. This has had a revolutionary effect on the balance of power between the big three and their affiliates in news presentation. As Doris Graber has put it: "Satellites have enabled many small stations to view the activities of the national government through the prism of local interests" (Graber, 1993).

An even more dramatic change has been the explosion of cable television. The proportion of households who have access to such T.V. has increased from 22.6 percent in 1980 to 60.6 percent in 1992 with over 11,000 cable systems supplying 57 million television households (Guskind, 1992). The cable phenomenon has had a devastating effect on all aspects of conventional television, but a particularly severe impact on the news departments. New and imaginative alternatives such as the Cable News Network

(C.N.N.) and C-Span have risen and transformed the nature of news television. C.N.N. has undoubtedly been the most high-profile. Launched in 1980 by magnate Ted Turner, the idea of a 24-hour news station based in Atlanta, Georgia, was initially ridiculed by the media establishment. By 1990, it had 18 overseas bureaus, was watched in over 50 million American homes, and had a further 200 million viewers in another 100 countries. Its well-publicized coverage of the Gulf War raised those figures even higher and confirmed the station's highly profitable status.

For the moment C-Span, which provides continuous coverage of Congress and other aspects of the federal government, remains mostly the preserve of political enthusiasts and represents only a modest threat to the mainstream newsgathers. Nevertheless, it is hooked into over 3,000 other cable systems, and has the technological capacity to reach an audience of over 40 million.

The impact on the big three corporations in general, and their news wing in particular, has been predictably catastrophic. From its position of comfortable power in 1980 when 90 percent of American televisions operating on any evening would be carrying an A.B.C./C.B.S./N.B.C. production, there has been a notable slump. That average is now much closer to 60 percent (63 percent in 1990) and can fall as low as 55 percent on some evenings. A falling market share has squeezed advertising revenues badly – cable now claims to get about one-quarter of all TV advertising – and profits have tumbled. This has had an obviously adverse effect on the companies concerned. The 1980s saw A.B.C. merge with Capitol City Communications (a company one-quarter of its size, but by then equally profitable), N.B.C. was taken over by electronics giant G.E.C., and C.B.S. fought off hostile takeover bids and witnessed numerous boardroom plots and coups.

The newsrooms have seen costs slashed as profits fell. Against this highly uncertain background, they prepared for the elections of 1992 with the memories of the 1988 campaign looming large.

The Press Post-mortem on 1988

When the press in general, and national television especially, looked back at how they covered the presidential elections of 1988, they felt a profound sense of unease and remorse over a number of aspects.

There were substantial misgivings over the media's creation of the "character issue," which had forced Democratic frontrunner Gary Hart out of the race over the issue of adultery and eliminated Senator Joseph Biden on the relatively trivial issue of his tendency to poach the public words of others. The unattractive sight of the press in full flight digging up aspects of the candidates' pasts with questionable links to their ability to govern was widely condemned.

More generally, the media believed it had allowed all presidential candidates (but notably the Bush camp) to run substanceless campaigns based on image and negative attacks on their opponents, reinforcing similar (and often distorted) television commercials that the press had failed to challenge. The 1988 campaign, it was alleged, had been dominated by news handlers or "spin doctors" who had succeeded in dazzling the media with their trickery. Television had allowed them to do this by shortening the coverage given to each campaign on the daily news (one source claimed the average length of story had fallen to ten seconds), which gave politicians the excuse to build their message around slogans or "soundbites." The excessive attention given to opinion polls – there had been 259 conducted by eight major organizations compared with 122 in 1980 – had also allowed the presidential aspirants to duck the issues (Mann and Orren, 1992).

In short, the media had been too obsessed by the question of "who's winning?" when its proper function, in its retrospective view, was to be a forum for public discussion of serious policy choices. It had, in the name of neutrality, allowed one candidate (Bush) to get away with outrageous and unanswered attacks on the other (Dukakis). The two national nominating conventions had been undiluted propaganda exercises for the parties concerned. The media had even allowed the primary focus for real issues – the presidential debates – to have their formula watered down so that they were little more than joint press conferences once again based on the war of soundbites.

Rightly or wrongly, the impression that television news had somehow failed its audience in the elections of 1988 became widespread, as did a determination that things would be done differently next time.

It was thus these two trends, a substantially changed television market, and a more assertive national news media, that faced presidential candidates in the 1992 elections, and that will probably figure highly in future political contests. They produced a substantially different media politics as a result.

The Candidates' New Media Strategies

The presidential campaigns of 1992 were not slow to notice the different television environment that the 1980s had created, and they made a very stark response to the opportunities offered by new technology and the weakened grip of the established networks over political reporting.

The traditional presidential campaign's media strategy had been based around gaining time on the national networks news programs or by soliciting support on current affairs programs through interviews or formal press conferences with (allegedly political heavyweight) representatives of the national press corps. As news coverage of a day's campaigning shrunk, this led to the promotion of the clever quip, attack, or comment called the soundbite, but it remained a message aimed at the viewing voter through the medium of national news programs.

This style of campaigning – much unchanged in many ways since the introduction of television – was substantially altered in 1992, and there is every reason to believe that the change is permanent. The initial revolt came from independent candidate Ross Perot, who announced his possible candidacy on a cable TV phone-in program and avoided the national news corps as much as possible during the remainder of his quixotic campaign. As a political novice with relatively few detailed policy positions, Perot knew he would get unsympathetic treatment from the serious news professionals. Indeed, once Perot moved from being an interesting fringe sideshow to leading national polls by June 1992, both the quality press and the television network news started to attack his supposed megalomania and raise questions about his character.

He was swiftly followed by Bill Clinton. Although Clinton had many friends in the Washington/New York press fraternity, his vicious pounding over allegations of extramarital affairs and evasion of service during the Vietnam War led him away from the traditional media strategy and to emulate Perot. Finally, the Bush reelection team decided they too would try a different media strategy. For all three candidates, the basic technique was the same. They gave less emphasis to dealing with the personnel of the major networks and more on reaching the voters directly through the new television outlets.

Cable television was swamped by presidential candidates. The C.N.N. television phone-in show *Larry King Live*, where Perot had announced his possible candidacy, received him several more times during the election. Perot also concentrated on other C.N.N. shows. Clinton especially, and Bush also, appeared with Larry King and gave greater attention to cable. Both Perot and Clinton bought cable television airtime to explain their policies, or appeared on cable-run "town meetings" where they would take questions from ordinary viewers in the studio. The Clinton campaign, counting on their man's probable appeal to the notoriously low-turnout young, took every opportunity to present him on M.T.V., a very popular 24-hour cable station based on music videos. One additional benefit for the candidates was that the hosts of such shows, and the ordinary voters they featured, tended to be far more deferential and less confrontational than professional news inter-viewers. It was, therefore, a much softer route for candidates to get their message across.

All three candidates, but especially Clinton, made themselves available to local television stations to be interviewed by the local newsreaders. Clinton's media team also offered tapes of campaign events Clinton had done during the day to local stations, which frequently aired them unamended. Once again local television presenters, like cable, tended not to ask aggressive questions, and allowed the politicians to get their message across. This strategy had the further asset that the campaign could decide what were the key states it needed to win and concentrate candidate interview time on them rather than wasting time aiming a message at millions of already committed voters and risking hostile interviewers.

When the candidates did appear on the national networks they frequently shunned the conventional news programs in favor of chatshows. Again, Ross Perot was the trail blazer, offering himself to all three breakfast television shows on a regular basis. Clinton swiftly followed, and belatedly George Bush held morning gather-ings with ordinary citizens for the benefit of breakfast viewers. Clinton carried this tactic even further by appearing playing his saxophone on the late night and ultra-cool *Arsenio Hall* chat show. When Bush suggested such behavior was unpresidential, Hall, an icon to many younger voters, ridiculed him at the start of his next show. Again, the interviewers were kinder than news interviewers would have been. Added to this, the campaigns believed, many voters who did not regularly watch the news every evening did watch this sort of television.

To some extent, the candidates' political commercials followed their wider media plans. Political advertising on cable, barely in existence in 1988, consumed an estimated 15 percent of campaign advertising budgets in 1992 (Guskind, 1992). The joy of cable for political operatives was its market segmentation. Clinton courted first-time voters on rock and roll stations; Bush pursued the Reagan Democrats via the country and western outlets. Both Bush and Clinton moved more of their conventional television commercials away from the national networks and toward local television stations in critical states.

To a modest extent, radio was revived as a political medium in the 1992 contest. For the first half of this century radio had been the premier political media outlet. The rise of television saw a progressive retreat for three decades. In certain smaller states (notably in the south and the upper mid-west) it had remained a useful outlet for political commercials, even during this period. Its recent revival has been the product of three factors: first, the introduction of the radio chat show where aggrieved citizens telephone their complaints and questions, which are often of a political nature. This has attracted both listeners and, hence, political aspirants, back. The second factor is the rise of highly political and deliberately controversial radio talk show hosts who have attracted a massive following. The most prominent of this breed is the ultra-conservative Rush Limbaugh, who uses his daily three-hour show to bash "feminazis" and other liberal targets. Limbaugh was awarded a place of honor at the 1992 Republican Convention and both George Bush and Dan Quayle appeared live on his program. Finally, the rise of speciality radio stations aimed at different ethnic groups and tastes (sports, varying types of music, etc.) has made radio an effective means of targeting political advertising in the same way that cable television has benefited.

The Media's Strategy to the Candidates

For all their good intentions that the 1992 campaign should not repeat the mistakes of 1988, the national networks' treatment of the opening phase of the campaign did not appear to be particularly distinguished. Yet again the Democratic frontrunner, in this case Bill Clinton, had his campaign rocked by constant investigation of the character issue, notably allegations by Ms Gennifer Flowers that she had been Clinton's mistress, plus the candidate's constant redefinition of exactly how he had come to avoid the Vietnam conflict. On this occasion, the frontrunner survived, and the network media drew back and questioned its own actions.

The 1992 election was treated differently by the mainstream television networks and there was something of a backlash after the draft-dodging episode in New Hampshire. The networks were less obsessed by the opinion polls than four years earlier. In part, this was because the New Hampshire primary had seen the polls badly misfire. Exit polls in the Republican contest implied that Patrick Buchanan had come within 10 percent of defeating President Bush, whereas the actual gap was 16 percent. On the Democratic side, the polls substantially underestimated Bill Clinton's 26 percent of the vote, allowing Clinton to argue that he, rather than Paul Tsongas who took most votes, had actually left New Hampshire the strongest. The summer polls saw wild swings between Bush, Clinton, and Perot, until Perot's withdrawal in late July catapulted Clinton into a 20-point lead and he never trailed in a national poll again.

The networks announced, with all due solemnity, that they would not be carrying ten-second soundbites, but would more fully cover candidates' policy statements. C.B.S. news stated that no story would be shorter than 30 seconds, but backtracked a little from that as election day grew closer. All three networks spent much more time analyzing the nation's problems and what the real issues were that the candidates needed to address, and less time on the "who's winning?" element. By and large, they stuck to this new approach. Television, along with many state newspapers, started analyzing campaign claims and political commercials and testing the truth of them. What impact this innovation had on either campaign managers or voters remains unknown. Coverage of the two national conventions, which had been slipping for some elections, took a further cut (Shafer, 1988).

Perhaps the best symbol of this new coverage was the presidential debates. The media publicly lobbied for the sterile formula employed in 1988 to be replaced, and were supported by Bill

Clinton's operatives. When Bush initially failed to agree terms for the debates, all three channels gave prominent coverage to Clinton's accusations of political cowardice. Ultimately, there were three presidential debates and one vice-presidential debate. The first followed the basic format of 1988, the second debate had the candidates sitting on stools and featured questions from the audience, the vice-presidential debate had a single question-master who allowed Vice-President Quayle and Senator Albert Gore, Jr., to interrupt and contradict each other in a free-flowing manner, and the final presidential debate also featured a single moderator, but with somewhat more formality.

Regardless of what the public thought of the content of these debates, their format was widely praised (not least by the television networks themselves), they drew huge audiences, and are unlikely to be abandoned in future contests.

The 1992 election thus led to the paradoxical result that just as fewer people were watching the three major networks' election coverage, and politicians reacted to that shift by deemphasizing the traditional news medium, the networks developed a more imaginative, policy-oriented, and critical approach to reporting presidential campaigns.

President Clinton's Media Strategy

Despite the turmoil for the major networks that manifested itself in the 1992 battle, they felt confident of remaining the preeminent means by which administrations displayed their policies in government. This belief that A.B.C., C.B.S., N.B.C., along with the *Washington Post*, *New York Times* and *Wall Street Journal*, represent a media elite that the White House is beholden to has already been tested under President Clinton. The Clinton team having won power by, in part, responding to changes in the American media, seemed inclined toward governing according to those changes as well.

Even before his inauguration, Bill Clinton hosted a two-day conference on the American economy in December 1992 that aimed for, and gained, substantial cable television exposure. After launching his economic program with the State-of-the-Union address of February 17th, 1993, Clinton and his cabinet headed for C.N.N. and local television stations to sell it rather than relying just on the national networks.

The new president's first televised cross-examining came through a "town-meeting" in Detroit, where he answered questions from the public rather than those from high-paid interviewers. He did not hold his first formal White House press conference until two months into office. Clinton officials have followed the pattern of 1992 by offering themselves to the breakfast shows, as well as the serious political programs such as *Face the Nation* (C.B.S.) and *Meet the Press*. Complaints about a photo-op presidency rapidly surfaced from the affronted networks.

On taking control of the White House, the traditional functions of the Press Secretary (as administrative assistant to the media and public spokesman for the president) were split in two. Dee Dee Myers kept the title of Press Secretary, but George Stephanopoulos (as Communications Director) was assigned to media briefings. Early clashes with the press over the search for a female Attorney-General who had paid the required taxes on legal babysitters (so-called "nannygate"), and the storm over plans to admit homosexuals to the military, led to complaints from the administration that the media had returned to its bad habits of short-termism and sensationalism.

Reporters complained of access to the Press Office being cut back and far less respect being given to the traditional media giants. These complaints were ignored by the administration as Stephanopoulos attempted to implement the new techniques learned during the presidential election to the art of governing. Relations soured further between the press and the White House as Clinton appeared to abandon the traditional news outlets. Ultimately this was a power struggle that the press were destined to win. In late May 1993, after a torrid month when relatively unimportant issues such as the President's $200 haircut and the botched attempt to replace the White House travel office with an Arkansas firm drove down Clinton's poll standings, Stephanopoulos was moved out of his post. His replacement was Washington insider and moderate Republican David Gergen.

The administration's strategy under David Gergen was much more traditional and respectful to the established media. The new media outlets were used by the White House, but much more cautiously. Hence after the President launched his health care initiative in September 1993, scores of radio stations were invited to broadcast news of it from the White House lawn. Vice-President Gore took his plans to reform the American bureaucracy to the breakfast shows, C.N.N., and the comedy show *Late Night with David Letterman*. Gore's highly successful televised debate with Ross Perot on the North American Free Trade Agreement (N.A.F.T.A.) took place via Larry King's show on C.N.N.. There have been signs of an improvement in media politics as a result of this more balanced stategy, but a great deal of early hostility still needs to be cleared.

Conclusion

The 1990s, symbolized by the elections of 1992, have seen important changes in the way politics and the media interact. The longstanding power and role of the big three national networks over television has been broken as local television stations have gained more autonomy, and new types of television, notably cable, have proved powerful challengers. Political campaigns, although perhaps slow to notice the importance of these innovations, have now done so vigorously. The wounded networks, at least in 1992, have shown signs of altering the way they cover the political process. The Clinton administration believes it can incorporate the new techniques of 1992 into at least some of its communications work for governing. These are very major changes that seem likely to affect American politics into the next century.

There remain uncertainties left by this chapter. It is unclear whether and how the orthodox media will combat the new competitors that have emerged. They might build on their reformed coverage and go up-market to outclass their opponents, or may feel obliged to follow the lighter style adopted by their rivals. Local and cable television may come to resent being seen as a soft option by campaigns and revise the way that they treat candidates. Even if they do, the continued increase in the proportion of households using such outlets may give political operatives little choice but to keep working with the new media. It is possible that some new technological innovation will emerge (high definition television perhaps) to shake up the media even more dramatically.

How far radio's recent renaissance can be taken is a fascinating question. One matter does seem certain: election campaigns have now reached such a level of professionalism that whatever trends become evident in the media, politics is likely to follow.

Part Five

Theoretical Perspectives

19

Visions of American Politics

CHRISTOPHER J. BAILEY

The primary concern of previous essays in this volume has been to describe and explain recent developments in American politics. Individual essays have shown how new problems and demands have replaced the old fears and imperatives of the Cold War to generate new stresses within the political system. Domestic issues suppressed by the imperatives of national security have bubbled to the surface and generated new demands for government action. Structural problems have become apparent in an economic system dependent for so long upon defense spending. A foreign policy designed for a bilateral world has become redundant. Ideological positions based on the need to confront communism have lost much of their meaning. Taken together, the essays seek to chart the changing landscape of American politics.

The focus of this concluding essay is not the content of American politics but the way that American politics is studied. Although a discussion of the manner in which political inquiry is conducted in the United States may appear to be arcane, the relevance and importance of the subject soon becomes apparent. First, knowledge of the means of political inquiry is essential if studies of the content of American politics are to be evaluated. Neither explanations of political phenomenon nor debates between professional academics can be properly assessed or comprehended without some knowledge of the approach to the study of politics being employed. Second, an examination of the dominant means of political inquiry in the United States reveals a great deal about the nature of the political system. Particular approaches to the study of politics become dominant because their biases are consonant with those of the prevailing regime. Explaining this consonance ". . . is a problem worthy of the attention of every political scientist" (Lowi, 1992).

Two purposes will be served by this essay: one descriptive; the other interpretive. The assumptions underpinning the dominant means of political inquiry in the United States will be detailed. Different approaches to the study of politics will be shown to have spawned different explanations of the same political phenomenon. The aim is not to offer a critique of the different approaches, but simply to elucidate various visions of American politics. Evidence will be generated as a consequence of fulfilling this aim to support the thesis that means of political inquiry become dominant because their biases are consonant with those of the prevailing political regime. The dominant approaches to the study of politics in the United States since the end of the Second World War will be shown to contain biases consonant with those of Cold War America. What the end of the Cold War might mean for the study of politics in the United States will be discussed in a final section.

Like others who have sought to characterize the myriad offerings of students of American politics, it is wise to offer two caveats at the outset. First, the process of characterization necessarily involves simplification. Some of the complexity and subtlety within the various approaches will undoubtedly be lost as a result of this process. The hope is that improved clarity of elucidation will compensate for such losses. Second, comprehensiveness is impossible in a piece of this length. Space does not permit a discussion of all the approaches to the study of politics that have been employed in the United States over the last century; nor is it possible to provide a comprehensive list of all the major works within a particular approach. It is not the intention to offer an abridged *State of the Discipline* (Finifter, 1993). The works that have been cited in the section "Visions of American Politics" have been chosen because they are well-known, and illustrate well the sort of vision that results from employing a particular approach to the study of politics. They are not necessarily the most important works in the field.

The Study of American Politics

Approaches to the study of politics in the United States have changed considerably since Columbia University established the first graduate School of Political Science in 1880. Normative approaches that trace their ancestry to the philosophical musings of Plato and Aristotle, and legalistic approaches that have their origins in the writings of British political theorists in the seventeenth and eighteenth centuries, have been supplemented at various times over the last hundred years or so by institutional approaches, behavioral approaches, and rational choice approaches: each approach offers a different perspective on both the content and means of political inquiry. Institutionalism dominated the study of politics from the early twentieth century until the 1930s. Behavioralism emerged in the late 1940s to become hegemonic by the early 1960s. The rational choice approach to the study of politics became dominant in the late 1970s.

Why particular approaches to the study of politics become dominant at different times is important and not well understood. The emergence of new methods of political inquiry is clearly linked to wider intellectual fashions. Developments in science, psychology, philosophy, sociology, economics, and other disciplines obviously have an effect on such an eclectic subject as politics. Too great a reliance upon the explanatory force of changing intellectual fashions, however, would be a mistake. Although changes in the intellectual *milieu* may help to explain the emergence of new approaches to the study of politics, they do not explain why particular approaches become dominant at different times. What is needed is some recognition of the symbiotic relationship that exists between the study of politics and the political world. The political world not only provides the substance of the study of politics, but also plays a role in promoting the subject through the funding of research and the appointment of scholars to peer review committees. Such patronage and funding is not value-free, but reflects "the needs and interests of state power as this is lodged in the minds and perspectives of career bureaucrats in the Executive Branch and on the staffs of major congressional committees" (Lowi, 1993). The result is a close consonance between the values of the regime and the dominant approach to political inquiry. Institutionalism flourished because its values were consonant with those of Progressive America; the values of the behavioral approach were consonant with those of Cold War America; and the values of the rational choice approach were consonant with the new conservatism of the late 1970s and 1980s.

The institutional approach

The origins of an institutional approach to the study of politics in the United States can be traced back at least to the work of Alexis de Tocqueville, and perhaps to the work of the Founding Fathers. In *Democracy in America*, first published in 1835, de Tocqueville provided a detailed analysis of American political life that went far beyond the description of constitutional codes, public law, and formal political structures that was the staple of the legalistic approach. Not until the dawn of the Progressive Age, however, did institutionalism replace legalism as the dominant method of political inquiry. In the first decade of the twentieth century, the nature of political inquiry was transformed as a result of two developments. First, intellectual fashions changed. The scientism of F.W. Taylor and the pragmatism of Thomas Dewey ushered in an era in which greater emphasis was placed on facts. Second, political exigencies demanded a new approach to the study of politics. Progressive Reformers within the newly founded American Political Science Association (A.P.S.A.) sought to promote an approach to the study of politics that was consonant with their own values and needs. Some observers have even argued that the A.P.S.A. should be regarded as part of the Progressive Movement (Somit and Tanenhaus, 1967; Seidelman, 1985).

Institutionalism was attractive to those within the Progressive Movement because it served the purpose of reform by highlighting the gap between an idealized conception of American democracy and the reality of political life. Leading advocates of the institutional approach argued that the purpose of political inquiry was to describe the political world as it actually existed. In *The American Commonwealth*, James Bryce declared that his purpose was "to paint the institutions and people of America as they are . . . to avoid temptations of the deductive method and to present simply the facts of the case" (Bryce, 1888, vol. 1). A few years later Bryce wrote in his book *Modern Democracies* that: "The time seems to have arrived when the actualities of democratic government in its diverse forms, should be investigated" (Bryce, 1921, vol. 1). What was needed, the institutionalists asserted, was a more accurate description of political institutions than had been provided under the legalistic approach. To meet such a need, students of politics were urged to collect more facts about government. Bryce in his address as President of the A.P.S.A. in 1909 told students to: "Keep close to the facts. Never lose yourselves in abstractions. . . . The Fact is the first thing. Make sure of it. Get it perfectly clear. Polish it till it shines and sparkles like a gem" (quoted in Somit and Tanenhaus, 1967). Although the institutional approach expanded the scope of political inquiry beyond the narrow focus of the legalistic approach, no systematic attempt was made to organize or explain the facts that had been gathered. Exponents of the institutional approach sought to provide detailed descriptions of political institutions, or detailed expositions of a particular political decision, and left the facts to speak for themselves (Isaak, 1981). "Hyperfactualism" was the term that David Easton would later coin to describe such an approach (Easton, 1953). To those who sought to explain political phenomena, the *naive empiricism* of institutionalism left a great deal to be desired. A small number of critics, including Arthur F. Bentley, Charles Merriam, and Harold Lasswell, charged that institutional and legalistic approaches to the study of politics both failed to capture "the rough-and-tumble public process in which individuals and groups struggle to achieve their ends in the cauldron of public life," and offered no conceptual framework in which to understand the facts that had been gathered (Susser, 1992). Arthur F. Bentley, in his *book Process of Government*, dismissed the ideas of his contemporaries as "verbiage" and accused them of ignoring "the activities which are politics" (Bentley, 1908). Charles Merriam, in an influential essay written in 1921, lamented the existing state of political inquiry and called for a more scientific approach to the study of politics (Merriam, 1921). In *New Aspects of Politics*, published four years later, Merriam enlarged upon his call for the political world to be studied scientifically (Merriam, 1925). A decade or so later, Harold Lasswell also urged colleagues to abandon the study of institutions as an end in itself and to concentrate instead upon the central question of politics: "Who gets what, when, how" (Lasswell, 1936).

Efforts to fashion a new approach to the study of politics flourished both at the University of Chicago where Charles Merriam was Chairman of the Department of Political Science, and in the work of individual scholars such as George Catlin and Stuart Rice, but were otherwise slow to develop (see Catlin, 1927; Rice, 1928). Not only was there uncertainty as to what would constitute a scientific approach to politics, but the political conditions did not exist for a new approach to flourish. The uncertainty about what a scientific approach to political inquiry would look like gradually dissipated in the 1930s and 1940s as the ideas of logical positivism with its stress on the need for "truths" to be empirically verifiable began to circulate in the United States, and new means of collecting and analyzing data became available. The development of survey methods, advances in statistics, and the gradual evolution of computer technology began to provide students of politics with the tools that would enable hypotheses to be tested. Funds to employ such expensive tools had to be solicited from government funding organizations and private foundations.

The necessary political conditions to support a new approach to the study of politics also began to develop during the 1930s and 1940s as bureaucratic growth and the advent of the atomic age produced a new governmental commitment to science. Not only did the bureaucratic state spawned by the New Deal depend upon science to legitimize decisionmaking, but the development of nuclear weapons established a clear link between scientific endeavor and national security. Science became an inherent part of the American state, in short, "in at least two dimensions" (Lowi, 1992). First, bureaucracy promoted a commitment to government by science. With bureaucratic decisions legitimized on the basis of what Karl Mannheim termed "measurement, formalization, and systematization," the language and methods of science began to permeate the discourse of the American state (Mannheim, 1936). Second, the recognition that science was essential to national security promoted a commitment by government to science (Smith, 1992). Government accepted the conclusions of the Vannevar Bush report of 1945 that science was a public good deserving of public support (Bush, 1945). Funding organizations to promote scientific research were established, and students of politics soon realized that they could gain access to government money if they could show that politics could be studied in a scientific manner. In the words of Somit and Tanenhaus: ". . . access to public funds was largely limited to the social sciences deemed worthy of the appellation 'behavioral sciences.' Widespread knowledge of this situation, it is safe to say, did not adversely affect conversions to the faith" (1967).

The new role of science in government created the conditions for a scientific approach to the study of politics to flourish. A final stimulus to the development of a new form of political inquiry, however, was provided by the advent of the Cold War in the late 1940s. The need to confront the scientific pretensions and collectivist impulse of Marxism created an environment in which a competing American science of politics containing an individualist impulse could thrive. In the words of David M. Ricci, an American science of politics was needed "to guarantee political confidence at home and, as the Cold War developed . . . to argue persuasively the American case abroad" (Ricci, 1984). What became known as behavioralism met such requirements perfectly.

The behavioral approach

Although a precise definition of behavioralism is probably impossible given the wide variety of studies that have appropriated the name over the last 40 years, two main imperatives may be identified as central to the behavioral revolution. First, behavioralists argued that the study of politics should be conducted with the same rigor as found in the natural sciences. "[In] its method of articulating its concepts and evaluating its evidence," the science of politics should be "continuous with the theories of the natural sciences" wrote Ernest Nagel in 1952 (Nagel, 1952). Just as the natural scientist had to prove hypotheses empirically, so it became incumbent upon the student of politics to test explanations of the political world against observable data. If political inquiry did not apply the rigorous methods of science, remarked Robert Dahl, it might as well take up permanent cohabitation with literary criticism (Dahl, 1960). Second, behavioralists argued that the study of politics should focus on the actual behavior of the individual in public life. Behavioralism, in the words of David Easton:

> indicates that the research worker wishes to look at participants in the political system as individuals who have the emotions, prejudices, and predispositions of human beings as we know them in our daily lives. . . . Behavioral research . . . has therefore sought to elevate the actual human being to the center of attention. Its premise is that the traditionalists have been

reifying institutions, virtually looking at them as entities apart from their component individuals (Easton, 1953).

The scope of political inquiry permitted by behavioralism, in short, was broader than that allowed under the legalist and institutional approaches to the study of politics. Behavioralism flourished in the 1950s, and soon became the dominant approach to the study of politics in the United States. Robert Dahl, writing in 1961, hailed the success of the behavioral revolution (Dahl, 1961). Behavioralism, Dahl argued:

. . . will gradually disappear. By this I mean only that it will slowly decay as a distinctive mood and outlook. For it will become, and in fact already is becoming, incorporated into the main body of the discipline. The behavioral mood will not disappear, then, because it has failed. It will disappear rather because it has succeeded.

A similar point was made by Evron M. Kirkpatrick in 1962: ". . . today, it is accurate to say that the behavioral approach has been incorporated into the mainstream of American political science" (Kirkpatrick, 1962). Although legalistic and institutional studies of political phenomena could still be found at the time that Dahl and Kirkpatrick were writing, and may still be found today, few could dispute the thrust of their observations. By the early 1960s the behavioral approach had gained wide acceptance in the United States as the proper way to conduct political inquiry.

The dominance of behavioralism was briefly challenged in the late 1960s when events such as the Vietnam War, student unrest, and urban riots "created a set of research and value priorities that were difficult to reconcile with the behavioralist world view" (Susser, 1992). Not only did behavioralism prohibit normative statements about such politically charged events, but the apparent failure of programs such as the War on Poverty seemed to cast doubt upon the very possibility of a science of politics. To a certain extent, the belief that government could engage in social engineering had been built upon the success of behavioralism. In the words of Samuel H. Beer, ". . . the social sciences . . . seemed to achieve in their 'behavioral revolution' the capacity for specific social control necessary to make them the foundation of government action"

(Beer, 1978). Doubts about the efficacy of government attempts at social engineering subsequently led to a reappraisal of some of the claims of behavioralism. "The somber fact of the matter was that, on most of the fundamental questions underlying disorder, the discipline of political science simply did not have anything to say one way or the other" noted Theodore J. Lowi (Lowi, 1972a). Uncertainty about the value of behavioralism when confronted with disorder led to an increased interest in approaches to the study of politics that did have something to say about events such as Vietnam. Marxism was rejuvenated and normative approaches to political inquiry that stressed the importance of finding the true ends of political life, such as that associated with Leo Strauss, became fashionable in certain quarters. Faced with such challenges, even prominent behavioralists conceded the need for more relevance. David Easton called for a post-behavioral approach to political inquiry whose "battle cries are *relevance* and *action*" (Easton, 1969). Beyond a stronger commitment to policy studies, however, post-behavioralism differed little in essentials from behavioralism. The imperatives of positivism and methodological individualism, for the most part, still remained *in situ*.

The rational choice approach

Behavioralism survived as the dominant approach to the study of politics because the disorder of the 1960s did not last long enough either to undermine the institutions that promoted political science or to change the values and needs of the prevailing regime. Although undoubtedly important, Straussian and Marxist approaches lacked the consonance with the values and needs of the regime to become dominant in the United States. A more serious threat to the dominance of behavioralism was posed by the growing popularity of rational choice as a means of political inquiry. The rational choice approach to the study of politics shared the twin imperatives of behavioralism: positivism and methodological individualism. Rational choice theorists and behavioralists agreed that the task of the student of politics is to generate hypotheses that can be tested empirically, and that the actions of individuals in political settings should be the starting point of political inquiry. Two important differences, however, distinguish the approaches.

The first difference is the way that behavioralists and rational choice theorists generated hypotheses about political phenomena. Behavioralists tend to employ inductive reasoning to generate hypotheses, whereas rational choice theorists proceeded deductively. Instead of basing their arguments on experience, rational choice theorists start with a set of *a priori* assumptions, which may or may not be true, and proceed to generate hypotheses through logical deduction. "Theoretical models should be tested by the accuracy of their predictions rather than by the reality of their assumptions," noted Anthony Downs (1957). The second difference in approach is in the way that behavioralists and rational choice theorists think about the individual. Behavioralists tend to focus upon the way in which the individual's behavior in a political setting is determined by socialization and adherence to roles, whereas rational choice theorists focus upon the way that the individual acts to achieve goals. In the words of Kenneth Shepsle: "A behavioral theory aggregates individual behaviors based on role, status and learned response. A rational theory aggregates individual choices based on preferences or privately held values" (Shepsle, 1989).

Rational choice theory originated in the classical microeconomics of Adam Smith, but its twentieth-century incarnation in the United States dates from the publication of *Theory of Games and Economic Behavior* by mathematician John von Neumann and economist Oskar Morgenstern (Neumann and Morgenstern, 1944). Over the next two decades scholars such as Kenneth Arrow, James Buchanan, Gordon Tullock, Anthony Downs, William Riker, and Mancur Olson used a rational actor approach to explore the provision of public goods, voting behavior, coalition-building, interest group formation, and other political phenomena. A different group of scholars, closely associated with the RAND Corporation, employed rational choice to examine some of the problems generated by the Cold War. Prisoner Dilemma Games and Chicken Games were used to analyze problems such as adherence to arms control agreements and whether to launch first strikes. The necessary conditions for rational choice to emerge as a dominant approach to the study of politics, however, only began to materialize in the late 1970s when economic and social malaise gave rise to a new conservative mood in the United States. Rational choice began to flourish in a political environment that saw a rebirth of classical, *laissez-faire* economics.

The rise of rational choice to challenge the dominance of behavioralism confirms the ascendancy of positivist approaches to the study of politics in the United States. Although normative, legalistic, and institutional means of political inquiry are still employed, most current studies of political phenomena fall either into the behavioral camp or the rational choice camp. As Nevil Johnson has noted: "Despite the survival and, indeed, the flowering of normative political argument in some American universities, it is a positivist science of politics which is dominant in the mainstream of political science education" (Johnson, 1989). Profound substantive consequences result from this dominance of positivism. Christian Bay, in an essay representative of many critiques of behavioralism and rational choice, has argued that the effort to produce a value-free political science means that important questions are not asked (Bay, 1965). The suppression of normative statements, such as conceptions of human welfare or the public good, leads to approaches to the study of politics that fail to discuss the *purpose* of political activity. In demanding that the political world be viewed in atomistic terms, the methodological individualism that underpins behavioralism and rational choice also prohibits explanations that make reference to "wholes." As Bernard Susser has noted: "Focusing on specific decisions in specific contexts closes off the option that the 'meaning' of the social process may lie in its integral wholeness, in its total structure" (Susser, 1992). The analysis of political phenomena that are not reducible to the level of the individual is made difficult by the behavioral and rational choice approaches to political inquiry. What can be studied, in short, is determined by the prescription of a particular method of studying.

Despite the rhetoric of their advocates, particular approaches to the study of politics do not become dominant because they are better at explaining political phenomena than competing approaches. No approach has a monopoly over truth and virtue. Each approach generates a peculiar vision of American politics that is no better or no worse than others. Approaches become dominant, rather, because they fit better with the political environment of the day. Behavioralism became dominant because the New Deal and Cold War generated an environment in which a particular approach to the study of politics could flourish. Bernard Crick even suggested that behavioralism was an example of American political thought of that time (Crick, 1959). Similarly, rational choice became dominant because the Reagan epoch generated an environment in which that approach could flourish.

Visions of American Politics

Each approach to the study of politics generates a different vision of American politics. The different starting points, concerns, and methods of legalism, institutionalism, behavioralism, rational choice, and the other means of political inquiry not only affect the way that political phenomena are studied, but also possess the potential to define what is to be studied. Legalism and institutionalism define politics in terms of government. The former approach examines constitutional codes, public law, and formal political structures, while the latter approach focusses on the nonlegal manifestations of government. Behavioralism and rational choice broaden the scope of political inquiry beyond government. The emphasis in both approaches is on activity rather than institutions. Politics is defined as ". . . a social process characterized by activity involving rivalry and cooperation in the exercise of power, and culminating in the making of decisions for a group" (Bluhm, 1965). Politics can be studied, according to this view, wherever conflict occurs over the distribution of resources. Legislatures, political parties, trade unions, social clubs, and the family are all arenas in which conflict is observable.

The problem with the expansive definition of politics allowed by the behavioral and rational choice approaches is that the term "political" loses some of its distinctiveness. Without a clear idea of what constitutes politics, the study of politics can become "a mountain of data surrounding a vacuum" (Schattschneider, 1969). To provide politics with some content and to delineate the boundaries of the subject, David Easton suggested that students of politics should be concerned with that activity which results in "the authoritative allocation of values for a society" (Easton, 1953). Neither too broad nor overly restrictive, Easton's definition of politics has been widely used (Isaak, 1981). The fact that government is viewed by most observers as the arena in which the authoritative allocation of values for society takes place in the United States has allowed behavioralists and rational choice theorists to focus upon the activity of government. Although acknowledging that forces outside what is commonly regarded as the government arena may have an influence on authoritative decisions, most behavioral and rational choice studies have examined either what goes on within the formal institutions of government, or the activity of overt political actors such as interest groups and political parties.

Mainstream acceptance of the definition of politics offered by David Easton has ensured some congruence between the subject matter of the legalistic, institutional, behavioral, and rational choice approaches to the study of politics. With their emphasis on activity rather than institutions, however, behavioralism and rational choice have tended to produce different visions of American government than those produced using the legalistic and institutional approaches. In contrast to the focus on government institutions that is found in the latter two approaches, some behavioralist and rational choice theorists have tended to play down the importance of institutions, albeit for different reasons. Behavioralism's focus on individual behavior has often resulted in a lack of interest in institutions. "To oversimplify, institutions were, in the thinking of many behavioralists, empty shells to be filled by individual roles, statuses and values. Once you had these individual-level properties, and summed them up properly . . . there was no need to study institutions; they were epiphenomenal" observed Kenneth A. Shepsle (1989). In a different vein, rational choice theorists have often suppressed institutional details in an effort to produce general theories. "Their view was that most empirical studies of institutions – of legislatures, courts, government bureaus, electoral systems – were so hopelessly time-and-location-bound, so hopelessly tied to specific details, that they had no place in a general theory" (Shepsle, 1989). At their most extreme, in short, behavioralism and rational choice have generated visions of politics lacking in institutional or organizational detail.

Concern that some behavioralists and rational choice theorists were not taking institutions seriously led to efforts to reassert their importance in the late 1970s and early 1980s. Although not a unified movement, advocates of "the new institutionalism," or neo-institutionalism, argue that politics cannot be reduced to social contexts or economic forces (March and Olson, 1984). Behavioralists must take into account not only the fact that the role, status, and values of the individual may be influenced by the institutional setting, but that institutions are also political actors in their own right. Rational choice theorists must take into account the fact that social outcomes are not only the product of agent preferences and optimizing behavior, but are also a consequence of institutional features. In the words of March and Olson: "Institutions seem to be neither neutral reflections of exogenous environmental forces nor neutral arenas for the performances of individuals driven by exogenous preferences and expectations" (1984).

One consequence of the new institutionalism has been an increased interest in the state. After decades of neglect by behavioralists who tended to regard concepts such as the state as meaningless, proponents of the new institutionalism have sought to place the state at the center of political inquiry. Theda Skocpol, in particular, has emphasized "the explanatory centrality of states as potent and autonomous organizational actors" (1985). None of this should be seen to imply a return to the "statism" of the legalistic and institutional approaches to political inquiry. What Skocpol and scholars such as Eric Nordlinger, Stephen Krasner, and Stephen Skowronek have sought to provide is a vision of the state that is informed by the theoretical and methodological rigor of behavioralism and rational choice.

The renewed interest in institutional or organizational detail engendered by the new institutionalism has reinforced the congruence between the subject matter of the legalistic and institutional approaches to the study of politics and the subject matter of the behavioral and rational choice approaches. Each approach, however, produces a different vision of American political phenomena. Legalism, institutionalism, behavioralism, and rational choice, in other words, produce different visions of political phenomena such as interest groups, voting, the presidency, Congress, the Supreme Court, bureaucracy, and the policy process. Some knowledge of these different visions is important if the content of American politics is to be evaluated.

Interest groups

The behavioral approach to political inquiry elevated the study of interest groups to a new level of importance. Whereas institutionalists had sought to detail the extent and influence of groups within the political system, the methodological individualism of behavioralism led scholars such as David Truman to examine the factors that caused individuals to join groups. In his classic book *The Governmental Process*, Truman advanced an explanation of group formation that was grounded in social psychology and anthropology (1951). Individuals join those groups that best meet their aspirations and values. An enormous range of interest groups, with different social bases and different objectives, is the result of this motivational diversity. Behavioralists since Truman have sought to explore more fully the motivational diversity that leads individuals to join groups, to chart the range of interest groups, and to explain why some groups are more successful at particular times than others.

Rational choice approaches to the study of interest groups have also tended to focus upon the problem of group formation. In his seminal book *The Logic of Collective Action*, Mancur Olson argued that it is often not rational for individuals to join public interest groups as the opportunity exists to "free-ride" on the efforts of others (1965). Contrary to the arguments of behavioralists like David Truman, Olson argued that individuals with common values would not necessarily form a group even if they had a reason to do so. Only if membership of a group brought benefits that are not available to nonmembers would it be rational to organize for collective action. Extraordinarily influential, *The Logic of Collective Action* has defined the research agenda for a generation of rational choice theorists.

The particular approach used to study interest groups has profound consequences. The motivational diversity suggested by behavioralists conjures up a vision of a society where individuals are free to join groups, where groups reflect the preferences of society, and where groups may compete against each other for influence over government. A pluralist vision of the United States, in short, is easily generated by using a behavioral approach to study interest groups. The vision generated by the rational choice approach, however, is much different. The "free-rider" problem means that private interest groups will find it easier to organize than public interest groups, and that as a consequence groups may not reflect the preferences of society. The rational choice approach tends to generate an elitist vision of American politics.

Voting

Institutional approaches to the study of voting attempt to explain electoral outcomes in terms of the larger context in which voting takes place. The focus of such studies is upon institutional features such as the social structure, party system, and electoral rules. In his book *The Political Consequences of Electoral Laws*, for example, Douglas W. Rae provides a detailed analysis of the ways in which electoral rules help determine electoral outcomes (1967). The importance of institutional features in explaining electoral outcomes is also explored by Frances Fox Piven and Richard A. Cloward in their book *Why Americans Don't Vote* (1988). Piven and Cloward argue that electoral rules determine the level of turnout in the United States.

Behavioral approaches to the study of voting reject the structural explanations of institutionalists in favor of individual-level explanations of voter turnout. A classic example of this type of behavioral analysis is *Who Votes?* by Raymond Wolfinger and Steven Rosenstone (1980). In this book, Wolfinger and Rosenstone attempt to show that turnout is related to demographic factors such as education, income, and occupation. Similar demographic factors are employed in another classic behavioral text, *The American Voter* by Angus Campbell, Philip E. Converse, Warren E. Miller, and Donald E. Stokes, as a means of explaining why individuals vote for particular parties (1960). In what has become known as the Michigan model of electoral behavior, Campbell *et al.* develop a social psychological model of the vote that emphasizes long-term psychological predispositions as a means of explaining voter choice.

Rational choice approaches to the study of voting also focus on individual-level explanations of voter turnout, but do so from a slightly different perspective. The concern of rational choice theorists, as articulated by Anthony Downs in his seminal book *An Economic Theory of Democracy*, is why people should vote when there is an opportunity to "free-ride" (1957). Given the fact that an individual's vote is unlikely to make a difference to the outcome of a presidential election, a rational voter, Downs suggests, should not incur the "cost" associated with voting, but rather should "free-ride" on the votes of others. In a further challenge to behavioral analyses of voting, Downs also suggests that voters calculate rationally when choosing whether to vote for a party or candidate. The idea of rational voter is developed by Morris Fiorina in his book *Retrospective Voting in American National Elections* (1981). Fiorina argues that voters make rational calculations about the "retrospective" performance of incumbent politicians and "prospective" judgments about the likely performance of their challengers.

The different visions that are generated by using different approaches to political inquiry are brought into stark relief in the study of elections. Employing an institutional approach leads to a focus on the general context in which voting takes place. Behavioral and rational choice approaches, on the other hand, focus on the individual. The latter approaches, however, view the individual in different ways. Behavioral analyses treat the individual as *homo sociological* and concentrate upon demographic characteristics, whereas rational choice analyses treat the individual as *homo economica* and concentrate upon calculations of interest.

The presidency

Legalistic and institutional approaches have dominated the study of the American president. *The President: Office and Powers* by Edward S. Corwin is the best example of the former approach (1957). Through a detailed analysis of constitutional codes and public law, Corwin provides an authoritative account of the legal basis of presidential power. A similar approach is taken by Louis Fisher, who also examines the conflict between president and Congress in terms of constitutional law (1985). Institutional approaches, on the other hand, seek to understand presidential power in much broader terms. Richard Neustadt, in his seminal book *Presidential Power*, examines both the legal and nonlegal bases of presidential power (1990). The sources and limits of presidential power are shown to be determined by a range of factors beyond legal prescriptions. Two other well-known studies – *The Imperial Presidency* by Arthur M. Schlesinger (1974), and *The Personal President* by Theodore Lowi (1985) – also employ an institutional approach to explain the development of the modern presidency.

The fact that only a small number of individuals have served as president has limited the scope for behavioral studies of the presidency. Obtaining sufficient data to test general hypotheses about the power or development of the presidency is extremely problematic given the small sample size. Perhaps the best attempt to overcome these difficulties is made by James David Barber in his book *The Presidential Character* (1972). Barber characterizes presidents into different psychological types in an attempt to produce a predictive theory about presidential behavior. On the whole, however, behavioral approaches have tended to focus on issues at the "periphery" of presidential studies where more data is available. Numerous behavioral studies exist on topics such as presidential approval ratings, presidential success rates in Congress, and presidential electoral success: topics where the behavior of actors other than the president are capable of being measured.

Rational choice is even more unsuited to the general study of the presidency than behavioralism. Characterized largely as an attempt to explain how collective decisions emerge out of the interplay of individual goals, the fact that there is only a single president makes a rational choice theory of the presidency next to impossible. Rational choice can only be employed in the study of the presidency where situations of collective choice pertain. Because of this fact, rational choice theorists have concentrated their attention upon "institutions" of the presidency such as the executive office of the presidency. It is an area that is beginning to provide fertile ground for rational choice theorists, and Terry Moe has confidently asserted that rational choice studies are on their way: "the positive theorists are coming anyway. They are going to invade presidential studies just as they invaded legislative and electoral studies" (Moe, 1993).

The US Congress

Institutional approaches dominated the early study of Congress. Books such as Woodrow Wilson's *Congressional Government*, first published in 1885, sought to examine "the real depositaries and the essential machinery of power" (1981). Wilson detailed the work of committees, the role of party leaders, and the interaction between president and Congress in a way that defined the scope of Congressional research for more than half a century. Even today, Wilson's aphorisms can still readily be found quoted in books on Congress. Perhaps the most famous is his remark that: ". . . Congress in session is Congress on public exhibition, whilst Congress in its committee rooms is Congress at work." Although no longer dominant, the institutional approach to the study of Congress that was pioneered by Wilson is still employed. Recent examples include *Bicameral Politics* by Lawrence D. Longley and Walter J. Oleszek (1989), and *Call to Order* by Steven S. Smith (1989). Both books provide detailed accounts of Congressional practices.

The fact that Congress contains clearly identifiable members whose behavior is susceptible to quantification has proved fertile ground for behavioralists. Early behavioral studies focussed on the socialization of members of Congress: their roles and the way that they learned norms of behavior. Classic examples of such studies are the essays by Ralph K. Huitt (1954, 1957, 1961a, 1961b), and the book *US Senators and Their World* by Donald R. Matthews (1960). Recent studies such as *The New American Politician* by Burdette Loomis have continued this tradition (1988). *Actors, Athletes, and Astronauts: Political Amateurs in the United States Congress* by David T. Canon develops the idea that the past experience of legislators determines their behavior in Congress (1990). Other behavioral studies of Congress have sought to relate phenomena such as voting to personal characteristics such as age, background, race, and gender.

The basic premise of rational choice studies of Congress is that members have a primary goal that they seek to maximize. Some of these studies generate complex spatial models of legislative organization and choice. *Information and Legislative Organization* by Keith Krehbiel presents what is perhaps the most developed example of such a model (1991). By far the most influential of the rational choice approach, however, is *Congress: The Electoral Connection* by David Mayhew (1974). In advancing the thesis that members act to maximize their chances of gaining reelection, Mayhew presented a vision of Congress that has become paradigmatic. Subsequent studies have sought to show how the reelection imperative can explain almost every aspect of the structure and activity of Congress: from the nature of the committee system to the role of party leaders to the production of legislation. In *Congress:*

Keystone of the Washington Establishment, Morris Fiorina shows how the desire to gain reelection underpins Congressional relations with the federal bureaucracy (1977). Richard Fenno, in his book *Home Style*, carefully details the different patterns of behavior that representatives exhibit in Washington, D.C., and their constituencies (1978). A more recent illustration of the way in which Mayhew's thesis has been developed by other scholars is *The Logic of Congressional Action* by R. Douglas Arnold (1990). Arnold seeks to show how members driven by the goal of maximizing their chances of gaining reelection can produce legislation that contains collective benefits.

Different visions of Congress have been produced by the different approaches to political inquiry. Institutional approaches focus on Congressional structures and processes. Congress is viewed in holistic terms. On those occasions when individual members are discussed, the focus is on the institutional position of the member: Speaker of the House of Representatives, party leader, or committee chairman. Behavioral and rational choice approaches, in contrast, focus primarily upon the individual member. The overwhelming vision of Congress that emerges from such approaches is that of an atomistic institution.

The Supreme Court

Legalistic approaches have tended to dominate the study of the Supreme Court. The emphasis in classic works such as *The Modern Supreme Court* by Robert G. McCloskey is on detailing the Court's decisions (1972). Typically legalistic studies proceed either chronologically or by issue area in an effort to elucidate the state of constitutional law. The volume *The Burger Court*, edited by Vincent Blasi, is an example of the latter approach (1983). Essays within the volume detail the Court's decisions on issues such as press freedom, the family, and race discrimination. Institutional approaches, in contrast, have focussed on the role of the Court in the political system. The legitimacy of "judicial review" has been a particular concern of many studies. Examples include books by John Brigham (1987) and William Lasser (1989).

Behavioral approaches to the study of the Supreme Court focus upon the attitudes, votes, and interaction of the individual Justices.

The emphasis is not so much upon the elucidation of constitutional law, but upon examining how the personal characteristics of the Justices influence judicial decisionmaking. An example of such a study is *Storm Center* by David O'Brien (1986). The book *Studies in US Supreme Court Behavior* by Saul Brenner and Harold Spaeth is an example of the "jurimetric" approach to the study of the Supreme Court (1990). Quantitative techniques are used in the book to analyze Court decisions.

Increased access both to current Justices and the private papers of past Justices has facilitated behavioral analyses of the Supreme Court. Conflict between the Justices is now observable where scholars previously had only the written opinions of the Court to examine. Unlike the study of most other areas of American government, however, behavioralism has not supplanted more traditional approaches as the dominant means of studying the Court. Rational choice has made even less of an impact, although some of the work of Gregory Caldeira has a "rational" component. In short, the way that the Court is studied stands outside the mainstream of American political science.

Bureaucracy

Institutional approaches to the study of bureaucracy have focussed upon concerns such as organizational structure, the recruitment of civil servants, and the relationship between the bureaucracy and other parts of government. An example of this type of approach is provided by Harold Seidman and Robert Gilmour in their book *Politics, Position, and Power* (1986). Seidman and Gilmour examine changes in bureaucratic structures, and explain how such changes have altered the balance of power between president, Congress, bureaucrats, the courts, and interest groups. The work of Theodore J. Lowi (1964–93), Hugh Heclo (1977; 1978), and James Q. Wilson (1989) also employs an institutional approach. What links the disparate work of these scholars is the conviction that institutions matter and the belief that a macro-level approach is the best way to study institutions.

The most important behavioral study of bureaucracy is *Administrative Behavior* by Herbert Simon (1945). Simon argued that an analysis of the way that individual bureaucrats make decisions is essential to an understanding of the way that bureaucracies function. Rational decisionmaking is impossible, according to Simon, because the individual bureaucrat possesses neither the capacity to process information, nor adequate computational ability, to predict all the consequences that would flow from making a decision. "Intended and bounded rationality" is the best that Simon believes is obtainable. "Satisficing" behavior rather than "maximizing" behavior among bureaucrats is the result.

Rational choice approaches to the study of bureaucracy assume that bureaucrats seek to maximize their goals. Anthony Downs, in his book *Inside Bureaucracy*, argued that bureaucrats are motivated by a number of possible goals: personal goals such as the desire for power, more money, greater prestige, an easy life, and job security; and broader goals such as organizational loyalty, mission-commitment, and even a desire to serve the public. Each bureaucrat acts in a way that maximizes his or her own particular goals. William Niskanen, in his book *Bureaucracy and Representative Government*, argues that the main goal of bureaucrats is to maximize their budgets (1971). The result of the efforts of bureaucrats to maximize this goal, Niskanen concludes, is the oversupply of government "goods."

The different visions generated by the different approaches to political inquiry can be seen clearly in the study of bureaucracy. Behavioral and rational choice approaches reduce the level of analysis to the individual bureaucrat rather than bureaucratic structures. Institutional approaches focus on the bureaucracy as the unit of analysis. Bureaucracies are seen in a much wider context than allowed using behavioral and rational choice approaches.

The policy process

The methodological individualism that underpins both behavioralism and rational choice creates certain problems when the subject to be studied would appear to require a holistic explanation. Means have to be found to fashion a holistic theory out of approaches to the study of politics that stress the importance of parts. Needed, in the words of Bernard Susser, is ". . . a theoretical construct that could translate the scattered bricks of data into a livable, unified edifice" (1992). Creating just such an edifice has plagued scholars of the policy process.

Almost all behavioral discussions of the policy process have employed, either explicitly or implicitly, the systems analysis developed by David Easton. In his book *A Systems Analysis of Political Life*, Easton argued that the policy process could be understood in terms of a series of interrelated parts (1965). Each part of the system coheres with other parts to form an integrated whole without losing its own individuality. Discussion of "wholes" is possible using Easton's model, therefore, without abandoning the methodological individualism of behavioralism.

The systems analysis of David Easton provides an intellectual framework to understand the policy process from demand articulation to policy formulation to policy implementation. Some scholars have concentrated on detailing the various stages of the policy process. Books by Charles O. Jones (1970), James Anderson (1975), and Guy Peters (1993) reduce the policy process to discrete stages. Other scholars have concentrated upon particular stages of the policy process. Examples include John Kingdon's innovative study of policy formulation (1984), and the classic study of implementation by Jeffrey Pressman and Aaron Wildavsky (1973). An effort to develop a causal model that explains how policy moves from stage to stage has been made by Richard Hofferbert (1974).

Rational choice studies of the policy process have started with the individual as the basic unit of analysis and then examined how institutional rules can affect decisionmaking. A good example of this approach is provided by the work of Elinor Ostrom. Ostrom views policy outcomes as a product of individual preferences and institutional rules (Kiser and Ostrom, 1982; Ostrom 1986, 1990). The suggestion is that the same individual may behave differently if the institutional rules change. Institutional rules, in effect, are the "rules of the game," which allow some individuals to express their preferences while limiting the impact of other individuals.

Indicative of the difficulties faced when attempting a behavioral or rational choice analysis of the policy process is the fact that the work that has probably had the greatest impact stands outside the two approaches. Theodore Lowi's argument that "policy determines politics" – that political behavior varies depending on the type of policy involved – employs neither the methodological individualism nor the positivism of behavioralism and rational choice (1964, 1972b). The basic unit of analysis is not the individual and the argument cannot be presented in the form of falsifiable hypotheses. Lowi's work, nevertheless, has been enormously influential.

The Study of Politics in the Post-Cold War Era

The symbiotic relationship that exists between the study of politics and the political world means that sustained changes in the nature of the political regime will eventually have an effect on both the content and the means of political inquiry. Changes in the content of politics will occur first as such changes are the most visible aspect of regime change. New subjects of study will replace subjects that have become obsolete. Changes in the means of political inquiry will follow at a later date as the values of the new regime feed into the mechanisms that promote the study of politics. The dominance of old approaches will fade as new approaches with biases that are more consonant with the needs and values of the regime emerge.

Changes in the content of American politics caused by the end of the Cold War are already observable. Students of politics are beginning to examine the consequences both of the transition from a bipolar to a multipolar world, and the transition from a world of strong nation-states to an interdependent world where nongovernmental institutions wield considerable power. William W. Boyer has summed up such changes as a move from the study of government to the study of governance (Boyer, 1990). Changes in the means of political inquiry have so far been less observable. Two changes are likely, however, if current trends continue. First, given the cultural pluralism of contemporary America it is unlikely that a single approach to the study of politics will dominate as in the past. Greater tolerance will be shown toward other approaches. Second, normative approaches will rise in importance as America seeks new certainties to replace the old certainties of the Cold War. The fundamentals of American democracy will have to be redefined to suit the new age. In the words of Alexis de Tocqueville: "A new political science is needed for a new world" (1956).

Guide to Further Reading

Chapter 2 The 1992 Presidential Elections: Voting Behavior and Legitimacy

For thematic accounts of the 1992 election, see Nelson (ed.) (1993) and Pomper (ed.) (1993).

For a more analytic approach to elections and voting behavior, see the two excellent collection of essays in Niemi and Weisberg (1993). For a reliable overview of Congress, see Jacobson (1992).

Chapter 3 Racial and Ethnic Politics

Browning, Marshall, and Tabb (1986) and Sonenshein (1990) are useful, as is Jackson (1991) Thernstrom (1987) offers a controversial view of voting issues.

Chapter 4 American Political Parties: Growth and Change

Epstein (1986) is a comprehensive overview, as is Wattenberg (1990) and Sorauf (1988), Herrnson (1988) gives particular attention to campaigning. Kessel (1992) focusses on the presidential campaign. The role of P.A.C.s is covered in Sabato (1981), Edsall (1993) draws attention to ideological divisions.

Chapter 5 Interest Groups and Policymaking

Schlozman and Tierney (1986) provide the best comprehensive introduction to the general topic of U. S. interest groups. Petracca (1992) brings together a rich collection of in-depth essays examining a number of current issues regarding interest groups. Lowi (1979) and McConnell (1966) are commentaries on the dangers of excessive power being wielded by organized groups. Truman (1951) and Olson (1965) relate dramatically contrasting views of the reason for, and resulting behavior, of interest groups. Finally, Schattschneider (1960) is both enlightening and enjoyable reading, providing astonishingly straightforward, penetrating insights into interest groups.

Chapter 6 The Presidency in the 1990s

The problems of presidential leadership in the post-Watergate era are addressed at length in Richard Rose (1991). For more on Clinton's election and mandate, see Pomper (1993). The best introduction to presidential–Congressional relations is still Nelson Polsby's classic, *Congress and the Presidency* (1986), but for a more recent study, see also Mark Peterson (1990). Presidential strategies with respect to the media are analyzed by Edwards (1983) and Kernell (1986). On the growth and power of the presidential branch, see Hart (1987). Waterman (1993) is a valuable collection of essays which addresses many of the themes raised in this chapter. The political science of the American presidency is assessed in Edwards, Kessel and Rockman (1993). Finally, no student of the presidency should be unaware of the superb four-volume *Encyclopedia of the American Presidency* edited by Levy and Fisher (1993).

Chapter 7 Congress in Crisis. . . . Once Again

A good introductory text is Davidson and Oleszek (1993). This text may be supplemented by the collections of essays edited by Dodd and Oppenheimer (1993) and Davidson (1992). The theme of Congressional capacity to act in the national interest is explored further in Arnold (1990) and Harris (1993). Highly readable accounts of Congressional lawmaking are Martin (1993) and Light (1992).

Chapter 8 The Supreme Court and the Constitution

Excellent recent interpretations of the Supreme Court are McKeever (1993), O'Brien (1993). For a journalist's view, see Savage (1992). The methodological problems of studying the Court can be gleaned from Segal and Spaeth (1993). Perry (1991) provides a highly illuminating account of the agenda setting process. Clayton (1992) and Salokar (1992) provide much needed analyses of the Attorney General and Solicitor General respectively. They may be supplemented with Caplan (1987) and Fried (1991). A recent general work on constitutional interpretation to be recommended is Wellington (1990). More specialized is Levy (1988) and Sunstein (1993), Abraham (1992) remains instructive and entertaining on the appointments process and Schwartz (1988) focusses on the Reagan administration's efforts to reshape the federal judiciary. Finally, the Kermit Hall's *1992 Oxford Companion to the Supreme Court* is a wonderful work of reference.

Chapter 9 Reinventing the Federal Government

It is too early for the National Performance Review and its impact to have received textbook coverage. However, the Review itself is well worth reading both as a statement of the entrepreneurial government perspective and as a valuable source of recent information on the federal government (Gore, 1993). Finally, Wilson's *Bureaucracy* is a stimulating and readable guide to the workings of the federal government.

Chapter 10 Governing the American States

For an overview of the problems of federal government, see Bowman and Kearney (1986). On intergovernmental relations, see especially Wright (1988), Conlon (1988), and Dilger (1989), Oates (1972) is still useful on fiscal federalism.

Zimmerman (1991) deals with the issue of federal preemption. For up-to-date discussion of trends in intergovernmental relations and federalism, reference should be made to the publications of the U.S. A.C.I.R. and to *Publius*.

Chapter 11 The Politics of Urban Policy

On urban politics, Judd (1983) and Jones (1983) provide good introductions. For individual cities, the following are valuable: Mollenkopf (1992) on New York City, Davis *et al.* (1990) and Sonenshein (1993) on Los Angeles, Grimshaw (1992) on Chicago, Stone (1989) on Atlanta, DeLeon (1992) on San Francisco, and Fuchs (1992) on New York City and Chicago. On urban machines, Banfield and Wilson (1963) and Erie (1988) are good introductions. The urban underclass and other social problems are thoroughly addressed in Katz (1993), Jencks and Peterson (1991), and Galster and Hill (1992). Black and minority politics are analyzed in Edsall and Edsall (1991), Persons (1991), Browning *et al.* (1990). The federal context and changes to it are discussed in Caraley (1992) and Gurr and King (1987)

Chapter 12 Economic Policy

Good collections of accessible articles on economic policymaking can be found in Hyde (1992) and Peretz (1994). The public choice approach is well represented in the articles in Alesina and Carliner (1991). The relation between the desires of the public and economic policy is explored in Hibbs (1987), Kiewiet (1983), and Peretz (1982). Two good books on the politics of monetary policy are Wooley (1984) and Kettl (1986). Histories of recent economic policy events can be found in Kettl (1992), and White and Wildavsky (1989).

Chapter 13 Social Policy

Useful background for American social policy can be found in Weir, Orloff, and Skocpol (1988). Browning (1986) provides a useful overview of policies and an excellent recent summary of the issues with a strong point of view can be found in Marmor, Mashaw, and Harvey (1990). An influential view from the political right can be found in Murray (1984). Hacker (1992) and Jencks (1992) emphasize the importance of race in understanding American social policy. Specialized concerns are covered by Levitan, Gallo, and Shapiro (1993), and Aaron, Bosworth, and Burtless (1989).

Chapter 14 Environmental Policy

Vig and Kraft (1990), Rosenbaum (1991), Portney (1992), and Smith (1992) are good general introductions to environmental politics in the United States. Bryner (1993) provides an excellent short introduction to efforts to control air pollution. Yeager (1991) provides an authoritative study of efforts to control water pollution. Mazmanian and Morell (1992) and Church and Nakamura (1993) are useful studies of the issues surrounding hazardous waste and toxic chemicals issues.

Chapter 15 Foreign Policy

A useful overiew of recent trends in American foreign policy is Deese (ed.) (1994). On the debate about American decline, see Kennedy (1987) and Nye (1990). Allison and Treverton (eds.) (1992) focus on American security issues. Rosenau (1990) and Manwaring (ed.) (1993) offer interpretations of the changing nature of international politics.

Chapter 16 Health Policy: The Analytics and Politics of Attempted Reform

For an overview of American health care politics see Paton (1990). The market approach to health service delivery is covered in Coddington and Moore (1987). Comparative approaches can be found in Fox (1986) and Jacobs (1993).

Chapter 17 Women in American Politics

Darcy, Welch, and Clark (1987) provide a useful, if now slightly dated overview of women and representation, as does Romney and Harrison (1987). Dodson (1991) is useful because it focusses on the role of women in office. Dodson and Carroll (1991) focusses on the role of women's elective politics at the state level.

Chapter 18 The Changing Media

For a general overview see Berger (1991) and Diamond (1991). Ranney (1983) remains useful. The relationship between politics and the media is explicitly covered in Dye (1992) and Graber, 4th edn (1993). Also relevant is Kern, (1989). Mann (1992) focusses on the role of media polls in politics. McCubbins (1992) and Nimmo (1990) provide thoughtful insights into the impact of the media on the presentation of political issues.

Chapter 19 Visions of American Politics

Ross (1991) provides the best account of the early development of American political science. Later developments are discussed in Barbrook (1975) and Susser (1992). Some of the controversy surrounding the historiography of the subject is evident in Crick (1959), Somit and Tanenhaus (1967), and Ricci (1984). A useful essay by Gunnell (1991) summarizes the historiography. Almond (1990) is a collection of important essays by one of the most prominent thinkers about political science.

Bibliography

Aaron, Henry J. (1991) *Serious and Unstable Condition: Financing America's Health Care*, Washington, D.C., Brookings Institution.

Aaron, Henry J., P. Bosworth and Gary Burtless (1989) *Can America Afford to Grow Old?*, Washington, D.C., Brookings Institution.

Aberbach, Joel D. (1990) *Keeping a Watchful Eye: The Politics of Congressional Oversight*, Washington, D.C., Brookings.

Aberbach, Joel D. (1991) "The President and the Executive Branch," in Colin Campbell and Bert A. Rockman, eds., *The Bush Presidency: First Appraisals*, Chatham, N.J., Chatham House.

Aberbach, Joel D., Robert A. Putnam, and Bert A. Rockman (1980) *Bureaucrats and Politicians in Western Democracies*, Cambridge, Harvard University Press.

Abraham, Henry (1992) *Justices and Presidents*, Oxford, Oxford University Press.

Acuna, Rudolfo (1981) *Occupied America: A History of Chicanos,* 2nd edn, New York, Harper and Row.

Agranoff, Robert (1972) "Introduction," in Robert Agranoff, ed., *The New Style in Election Campaigns*, Boston, Holbrook Press.

Alesina, Alberto and Geoffrey Carliner (1991) *Politics and Economics in the Eighties*, Chicago, University of Chicago Press.

Alexander, Herbert E. (1984) *Financing Politics: Money, Elections, and Political Reform*, Washington, D.C., Congressional Quarterly Press.

Allison, Graham and Gregory F. Treverton, eds. (1992) *Rethinking America's Security*, New York, Norton.

Almond, Gabriel A. (1990) *A Discipline Divided*, Newbury Park, Ca., Sage.

Anderson, James (1975) *Public Policy-Making*, New York, Praeger.

Arnold, R. Douglas (1979) *Congress and the Bureaucracy*, New Haven, Yale University Press.

Arnold, R. Douglas (1990) *The Logic of Congressional Action*, New Haven, Yale University Press.

Balz Dan and David Broder(1993) "Pessimism about Nation's Direction is Growing Again Among Voters" *The Washington Post*, 24 April.

Banfield, E.C. and James Q. Wilson (1963) *City Politics*, New York, Vintage.

Barber, James David (1972) *The Presidential Character,* Englewood Cliffs, N.J., Prentice-Hall.

Barbrook, Alec (1975) *Patterns of Political Behaviour*, London, Robertson.

Barr, Stephen (1993) "The President-Elect's Inheritance," *Washington Post*, January 8th.

Barringer, F. (1992) "Hire City Poor in the Suburbs, A Report Urges," *New York Times*, December 4th.

Barzelay, Michael and Babak J. Armajani (1992) *Breaking Through Bureaucracy: A New Vision for Managing Government*, Berkeley, University of California Press.

Bay, Christian (1965) "Politics and Pseudopolitics: A Critical Evaluation of Some Behavioral Literature," *American Political Science Review*, 59: 39–51.

Beck, Paul Allen (1984) "The Electoral Cycle and Patterns of American Politics," in Richard G. Niemi and Herbert F. Weisberg eds., *Controversies in American Voting Behavior*, Washington, D.C., Congressional Quarterly Press.

Beck, Paul Allen and Frank J. Sorauf (1992) *Party Politics in America*, 7th. edn., New York, HarperCollins.

Beer, Samuel H. (1978) "In Search of a New Public Philosophy," in Anthony King, ed., *The New American Political System*, Washington, D.C., American Enterprise Institute.

Behn, Robert D.(1991) *Leadership Counts*, Cambridge, Harvard University Press.

Behr, Roy L. and Edwards H. Lazarus (1984) *Third Parties in America*, Princeton, Princeton University Press.

Bell, Daniel (1965) *The End of Ideology: On the Exhaustion of Political Ideas in the Fifties*, New York, Free Press.

Bellah, R.N. (1985) *Habits of the Heart*, Berkeley, University of California Press.

Benedick, R.E. (1991) *Ozone Diplomacy*, Cambridge, Mass., Harvard University Press.

Bennett, W. Lance (1994) "The Media and the Foreign Policy Process," in David A. Deese, ed., *The New Politics of American Foreign Policy*, New York, St. Martin's Press.

Bentley, Arthur F. (1908) *Process of Government*, Chicago, University of Chicago Press.

Berger, A. (1991) *Media USA*, New York, Longman.

Berke, Richard (1993) "Perot Bloc Is Here to Stay, Clinton Pollster Finds," *New York Times*, July 8.

Berry, James (1989) "Fed Chief Supports Zero-Inflation Resolution," *Washington Post*, October 26.

Berry, Jeffrey M. (1977) *Lobbying for the People*, Princeton, Princeton University Press.

Bibby, John F. (1981) "Party Renewal in the National Republican Party" in Gerald M. Pomper, ed., *Party Renewal in America*, New York, Praeger.

Bibby, John F. ed., (1983) *Congress off the Record*, Washington, D.C., American Enterprise Institute.

Biskupic, Joan "Judge Ginsburg" *Washington Post*, 5 June 1993.

Black, Earle and Merle Black (1987) *Politics and Society in the South*, Cambridge, Mass., Harvard University Press.

Black, Earle and Merle Black (1992) *The Vital South: How Presidents Are Elected*, Cambridge, Mass., Harvard University Press.

Blasi, Vincent, ed. (1983) *The Burger Court*, New Haven, Yale University Press.

Bluestone, B. and B. Harrison (1982) *The Deindustrialization of America*, New York, Basic Books.

Bluhm, William (1965) *Theories of the Political System,* Englewood Cliffs, N.J., Prentice-Hall.

Blumenthal, Sidney (1992/1993) "All the President's Wars," *The New Yorker*, January 4.

Bond, Jon and Richard Fleisher (1990) *The President in the Legislative Arena*, Chicago, University of Chicago Press.

Booth, D.E. (1992) "Discussion Paper: The Economics and Ethics of Old Growth Forests," *Environmental Ethics*, 12.

Bowman, Ann O'M. and Richard C. Kearney (1986) *The Resurgence of the States*, Englewood Cliffs, N.J., Prentice-Hall.

Boyer, William W. (1990) "Political Science and the 21st Century: From Government to Governance," *PS*, 23: 50–4.

Brace, Paul and Barbara Hinckley (1992) *Follow the Leader*, New York, Basic Books.

Brady, David W. (1988) *Critical Elections and Congressional Policymaking*, Stanford, Stanford University Press.

Brenner, Saul and Harold Spaeth (1990) *Studies in US Supreme Court Behavior*, New York, Garland Press.

Brigham, John (1987) *The Cult of the Court*, Philadelphia, Temple University Press.

Brodsky, David (1988) *The South's New Politics: Realignment and Dealignment*, Columbia, University of South Carolina Press.

Brody, Richard A. (1991) *Assessing the President*, Stanford, Stanford University Press.

Browning, Rufus P., Dale Rogers Marshall and David H. Tabb (1986) *Protest is Not Enough*, Berkeley, University of California Press.

Browning, Rufus P., eds., (1990) *Racial Politics in American Cities*, New York, Longman.

Bryce, James (1888) *The American Commonwealth*, New York, Macmillan.

Bryce, James (1921) *Modern Democracies*, New York, Macmillan.

Bryner, Gary C. (1993) *Blue Skies, Green Politics*, Washington, D.C., Congressional Quarterly Press.

Burke, John P. (1992) *The Institutional Presidency*, Baltimore, Johns Hopkins University Press.

Burrell, Barbara (1992) "Women Candidates in Open-Seat Primaries for the US House: 1968–1990," *Legislative Studies Quarterly*, 17: 493–508.

Burrell, Barbara (forthcoming) *A Woman's Place is in the House: Campaigning for Congress in the Feminist Era*, Ann Arbor, University of Michigan Press.

Burnham, Walter Dean (1970) *Critical Elections and the Mainsprings of American Politics*, New York, W.W. Norton.

Bush, Vannevar (1945) *Science: The Endless Frontier: A Report to the President on a Program for Post-War Scientific Research*.

Button, J.W. (1989) *Blacks and Social Change*, Princeton, Princeton University Press.

Cain, Bruce E. and D. Roderick Kiewiet (1984) "Minorities in California," a Report for the Seaver Institute, California Institute of Technology.

Camia, Catalina *et al.* (1993) "1993 Budget-Reconciliation Act," *Congressional Quarterly Weekly Report*, September 18th, pp. 2482–97.

Campbell, Angus, Philip E. Converse, Warren E. Miller, and Donald E. Stokes (1960) *The American Voter*, New York, Wiley.

Campbell, Colin (1986) *Managing the Presidency: Carter, Reagan and the Search for Executive Harmony*, Pittsburgh, University of Pittsburgh Press.

Campbell, Colin and Bert A. Rockman, eds. (1991) *The Bush Presidency: First Appraisals*, Chatham, Chatham House.

Campion, Frank D. (1984) *The AMA and US Health Policy Since 1940*, Chicago, Chicago Review Press.

Canon, David T. (1990) *Actors, Athletes and Astronauts: Political Amateurs in the United States Congress*, Chicago, University of Chicago Press.

Caplan, L. (1987) *The Tenth Justice*, New York, Knopf.

Caraley, D. (1992) "Washington Abandons the Cities," *Political Science Quarterly*, 107: 1–30.

Catlin, George (1927) *The Science and Methods of Politics*, London, Kegan, Paul, Trench, Trubner and Co.

Chiras, D. (1990) *Beyond the Fray: Reshaping America's Environmental Response*, Boulder, Johnson Books.

Church, Thomas W. and Robert T. Nakamura (1993) *Cleaning Up the Mess*, Washington, D.C., Brookings Institution.

Clarke J.N. and D. McCool (1985) *Staking Out the Terrain: Power Differentials among Natural Resource Management Agencies*, Albany, State University of New York Press.

Clayton, Cornell W. (1992) *The Politics of Justice: The Attorney General and the Making of Legal Policy* New York, M.E. Sharp.

Cloud, David S. (1992) "House Passes Urban Aid Bill With Deal on Capitol Gains," *Congressional Quarterly Weekly Report*, July 4.

Cloud, David S. (1993) "Package of Tax Increases Reverses GOP Approach," *Congressional Quarterly Weekly Report*, February 20.

Clymer, Adam (1992) "Turnout at the Polls Best Since 68," *New York Times*, December 17th.

Clymer, Adam (1993) "Voices of New Women Resound at the Polls," *New York Times*. February 11th.

Coddington, Dean and K.D. Moore (1987) *Market-driven Strategies in Health Care*, San Francisco, Jossey-Bass.

Cohen, Richard E. (1993) "What Coattails?," *National Journal*, 29 May.

Committee on Political Parties, American Political Science Association (1950) "Toward a More Responsible Two-Party System," American Political Science Association: *supplement*.

Congressional Quarterly (1990) *Congressional Quarterly Almanac 1990*, Washington, D.C., Congressional Quarterly Press.

Conlon, Timothy (1988) *New Federalism: Intergovernmental Reform from Nixon to Reagan*, Washington, D.C., Brookings Institution.

Conlon, Timothy, Ann Martino, and Robert Dilger (1984) "State Parties in the 1980s: Adaption, Resurgence, and Continuing Constraints," *Intergovernmental Perspective*, 10: 1–23.

Conway, M. Margaret (1983) "Republican Political Party Nationalization, Campaign Activities, and their Implications for the Political System," *Publius*, 13, pp. 1–17.

Cook, F.L. and E.J. Barrett (1992) *Support for the American Welfare State*, New York, Columbia University Press.

Cook, Rhodes (1981) "Chorus of Democratic Voices Urges New Policies, Methods" *Congressional Quarterly Weekly Report*, January 17th, pp. 137–40.

Corwin, Edward S. (1957) *The President: Office and Powers*, 4th edn., New York, New York University Press.

Cotter, Cornelius P. and Bernard C. Hennessy (1964) *Politics Without Power: The National Party Committees*, New York, Atherton Press.

Cotter, Cornelius P. and John F. Bibby (1980) "Institutional Development and the Thesis of Party Decline," *Political Science Quarterly*, 95: 1–27.

Cotter, Cornelius P., James L. Gibson, John F. Bibby, and Robert J. Huckshorn (1984) *Party Organizations in American Politics*, New York, Praeger.

Council of Economic Advisors (1993) *Economic Report of the President 1993*, Washington, D.C., G.P.O.

Cox, Gary W. and S. Kernell (1991) *The Politics of Divided Government*, Boulder, Co. Westview.

Crick, Bernard (1959) *The American Science of Politics*, Berkeley, University of California Press.

Crotty, William (1983) *Party Reform*, New York, Longman.

Crotty, William (1984) *American Parties in Decline*, Boston, Little, Brown.

Crovitz, L. Gordon and Jeremy A. Rabkin, eds. (1989) *The Fettered Presidency: Legal Constraints on the Executive Branch*, Washington, D.C., American Enterprise Institute.

Culhane, P.J. (1981) *Public Lands Politics*, Washington, D.C., Resources for the Future.

Dahl, Robert (1960) "Political Theory: Truth and Consequence" *World Politics*, 12.

Dahl, Robert (1961) "The Behavioral Approach in Political Science: Epitaph for a Monument to a Successful Protest," *American Political Science Review*, 55: 763–72.

Danielson, M. (1976) *The Politics of Exclusion*, New York, Columbia University Press.

Darcy, R., Susan Welch, and Janet Clark (1987) *Women, Elections, and Representation*, New York, Longman.

Davidson, L. (1993) "Reforms Could Make Mining Towns Go Bust Forever, Mayors Warn DC," *The Deseret News*, October 19.

Davidson, Roger H., ed. (1992) *The Post-Reform Congress*, New York, St. Martin's Press.

Davidson, Roger H. and Walter J. Oleszek (1993) *Congress and Its Members*, 4th edn., Washington, D.C., Congressional Quarterly Press.

Davis, Charles E. and Lester, James B. (1989) "Federalism in Environmental Policy" in James B. Lester, ed., *Environmental Politics and Policy*, Durham, N.C., Duke University Press.

Davis, Karen *et al*, (1990) *Health Care Cost Containment*, Baltimore, Johns Hopkins University Press.

Davis, Mike (1993) "Who Killed LA? A Political Autopsy," *New Left Review*, 197.

Deering, Christopher J., ed. (1989) *Congressional Politics*, Pacific Grove, Ca., Brooks-Cole.

Deese, David A. (1994) "The Hazards of Interdependence: World Politics in the American Foreign Policy Process," in David A. Deese, ed., *The New Politics of American Foreign Policy*, New York, St. Martin's Press.

DeLeon, R.E. (1992) *Left Coast Politics: Progressive Politics in San Francisco 1975–1991*, Lawrence, K.S., University Press of Kansas.

De Parle, J. (1993) "Housing Secretary Carves Out Role As a Lonely Clarion Against Racism" *New York Times*, 8 July.

Destler, I.M. (1994) "A Government Divided: The Security Complex and the Economic Complex," in David A. Deese ed. *The New Politics of American Foreign Policy*, New York, St. Martin's Press.

Destler, I.M., Leslie H. Gelb and Anthony Lake (1984) *Our Own Worst Enemy: The Unmaking of American Foreign Policy*, New York, Simon and Schuster.

Diamond, Edwin (1991) *The Media Show*, Cambridge, Mass., M.I.T. Press.

Dilger, Robert Jay (1989) *National Intergovernmental Programs*, Englewood Cliffs, N.J., Prentice-Hall.

Dodd, Lawrence C. and Bruce I. Oppenheimer, eds. (1993) *Congress Reconsidered*, 5th edn., Washington, D.C., Congressional Quarterly Press.

Dodson, Debra, ed. (1991) *Gender and Policymaking: Studies of Women in Office*, Center for the American Woman and Politics, Eagleton Institute of Politics, Rutgers.

Dodson, Debra and Susan Carroll (1991) *Reshaping the Agenda: Women in State Legislatures*, Center for the American Woman and Politics, Eagleton Institute of Politics, Rutgers.

Doherty, Carrol J. (1993) "Foreign Policy: Is Congress Still Keeping Watch?" *Congressional Quarterly Weekly Report*, August 21st, pp. 2267–9.

Donahue, John D. (1989) *The Privatization Decision: Public Ends, Private Means*, New York, Basic Books.

Dowd, Maureen (1993) "Growing Sorority in Congress Edges Into the Ol' Boys' Club," *New York Times*, March 5.

Downs, Anthony (1957) *An Economic Theory of Democracy*, New York, Harper and Row.

Downs, Anthony (1967) *Inside Bureaucracy*, Boston, Little, Brown.

Drew, Elizabeth (1983) *Politics and Money*, New York, Macmillan.

Dugger, C.W.(1993) "Learning Homelessness First-Hand" *New York Times*, 10 July.

Duffy, Michael and Dan Goodgame (1992) *Marching in Place*, New York, Simon and Schuster.

Dwyer, Paul E. (1991) "Salaries and Allowances: The Congress," Washington, D.C., Congressional Research Service Report, 92–86.

Dye, T.R. (1992) *Politics in the Media Age*, Pacific Grove, Ca: Brooks/ Cole.

Easton, David (1953) *The Political System*, New York, Knopf.

Easton, David (1965) *A Systems Analysis of Political Life*, New York, Wiley.

Easton, David (1969) "The New Revolution in Political Science," *American Political Science Review*, 63: 1051–61.

Edsall, Thomas and Mary D. Edsall (1991) *Chain Reaction*, New York, W.W. Norton.

Edsall, Thomas and E.J. Dionne (1992) "Lower-Income, Younger Voters Spurn the G.O.P.," *Washington Post*, November 4th.

Edsall, Thomas (1993) "GOP's Volatile Mix: Mainstream Activists and the Evangelical Right," *Washington Post*, January 18th.

Edwards, George C. (1983) *The Public Presidency*, New York, St. Martin's Press.

Edwards, George C. (1989) *At the Margins*, New Haven, Yale University Press.

Edwards, George C., John Kessel, and Bert A. Rockman, eds. (1993) *Researching the Presidency*, Pittsburgh, University of Pittsburgh Press.

Egan, T. (1993) "Wingtip 'Cowboy' in Last Stand to Hold on to Low Grazing Fees," *New York Times*, October 29th.

Ehrenhalt, Alan (1991) *The United States of Ambition*, New York, Times Books.

Eisenhower Foundation (1993) *Investing in Children and Youth, Reconstructing Our Cities*, in Commemoration of the Twenty-Fifth Anniversary of the National Advisory Commission on Civil Disorders, Washington, D.C., Milton S. Eisenhower Foundation.

Elazar, Daniel (1990) "Opening the Third Century of American Federalism: Issues and Prospects," *Annals*, 509: 11–21.

Eldersveld, Samuel J. (1964) *Political Parties: A Behavioral Analysis*, Chicago, Rand McNally.

Enthoven, Alain (1988) *Theory and Practice of Managed Competition in Health Care Finance*, Amsterdam, North-Holland.

Epstein, L.D. (1985) *Conservatives in Court*, Knoxville, Tennessee University Press.

Epstein, L.D. (1986) *Political Parties in the American Mold*, 7th edn., Madison, University of Wisconsin Press.

Erie, Stephen P. (1988) *Rainbow's End*, Berkeley, University of California Press.

Fainstein, N. (1986/7) "The Underclass/Mismatch Hypothesis as an Explanation for Black Economic Deprivation," *Politics and Society*, 15: 403–51.

Feldman, D.L. (1991) "Tracking Global Climate Change Policy," *Policy Currents*, November, 1st.

Fenno, Richard F. (1973) *Congressmen in Committees*, Boston, Little, Brown.

Fenno, Richard F. (1978) *Home Style*, Boston, Little, Brown.
Finifter, Ada W., ed. (1993) *The State of the Discipline II*, Washington, D.C., American Political Science Association.
Fiorina, Morris (1989) *Congress: Keystone of the Washington Establishment*, 2nd edn., New Haven, Yale University Press.
Fiorina, Morris (1981) *Retrospective Voting in American National Elections*, New Haven, Yale University Press.
Fiorina, Morris (1991) "Elections and the Economy in the 1980s: Short and Long Term Effects," in Alberto Alesina and Geoffrey Carliner, eds. *Politics and Economics in the Eighties*, Chicago, University of Chicago Press.
Fiorina, Morris (1992) *Divided Government*, New York, Macmillan.
Firestone, B.J. (1982) *The Quest for Nuclear Stability*, London, Greenwood.
Fisher, Louis (1989) "Micromanagement by Congress: Reality and Mythology" in L. Gordon Crovitz and Jeremy A. Rabkin eds.
Fisher, Louis (1993) *Constitutional Conflicts Between Congress and the President*, 3rd edn., Princeton, Princeton University Press.
Foss, P.O., ed. (1987) *Federal Lands Policy*, New York, Greenwood.
Fox, Daniel (1986) *Health Policies, Health Politics: The British and American Experience 1911–1965*, Princeton, Princeton University Press.
Fox, Kenneth (1985) *Metropolitan America*, London, Macmillan.
Francis, John G. and R. Ganzel (1984) *Western Public Lands*, Totowa, N.J., Rowman and Allenheld.
Francis, John G. and C. Macmahon, "Comparative Interest Group Theory, Transboundary Politics and Acid Rain," Paper given at the biennial meeting of the Association for Canadian Studies, November 1991.
Frankovic, Kathleen A. (1993) "Public Opinion in the 1992 Campaign" in Gerald M. Pomper ed. *The Election of 1992*, Chatham, Chatham House.
Frantzich, Stephen E. (1989) *Political Parties in the Technological Age*, New York, Longman.
Fried, Charles (1991) *Order and Law: Arguing the Reagan Revolution – a firsthand account*, New York, Simon and Schuster.
Friedman, Jon (1993) "The Founding Mother," *New York Times Magazine* May 2nd.
Fuchs, E. (1992) *Mayors and Money*, Chicago, University of Chicago Press.
Fukuyama, *The End of History*.
Gais, Thomas, Mark Peterson, and Jack Walker (1984) "Interest Groups, Iron Triangles and Representative Institutions in American National Government," *British Journal of Political Science*, 14: 161–85.
Galbraith, John Kenneth (1992) *The Culture of Contentment*, London, Sinclair-Stevenson.
Galderisi, P.F., M.S. Lyons, R.T. Simmons, and J.G. Francis (1987) *The Politics of Realignment: Party Change in the Mountain West*, Boulder, Westview.
Galster, G.C. (1992) "A Cumulative Causation Model of the Underclass: Implications for Urban Economic Development Policy," in G.C. Galster

and E.W. Hill, eds., *The Metropolis in Black and White*, New Brunswick, N.J., Center for Urban Policy Research.

Galston, William A. and Elaine Ciulla Kamarck (1993) in Will Marshall and Martin Schram, eds. *Mandate for Change*, New York, Berkeley.

Garza, Rudolfo de la, Louis DeSipio, F. Chris Garcia, John Garcia and Angelo Falcon (1992) *Latino Voices: Mexican, Puerto Rican and Cuban Perspectives on American Politics*, Boulder, Westview.

Gibson, James L., Cornelius P. Cotter, John F. Bibby, and Robert J. Huckshorn (1985) "Whither the Local Parties? A Cross-Sectional and Longitudinal Analysis of the Strength of Party Organizations," *American Journal of Political Science,* 29: 139–59.

Godwin, R. Kenneth (1988) *One Billion Dollars Worth of Influence: The Direct Marketing of Politics*, Chatham, N.J., Chatham House.

Goldstein, Mark L. (1992) *America's Hollow Government: How Washington Has Failed the People*, Homewood, Ill., Business One Irwin.

Gore Al (1993) *National Performance Review: From Red Tape to Results*, Washington, D.C., GPO.

Gosnell, H. (1968) *Machine Politics: Chicago Model*, Chicago, University of Chicago Press.

Gottlieb, A.M. ed. (1989) *The Wise Use Agenda*, Bellevue, W.A., The Free Enterprise Press.

Graber, Doris (1993) *Mass Media and American Politics*, Washington, D.C., Congressional Quarterly Press.

Graham, G. (1993) "Still Asleep after the Wake-up Call," *Financial Times*, March 13.

Grantham, D.W. (1988) *The Life and Death of the Solid South,* Kentucky, University of Kentucky Press.

Greenhouse, Steven (1992) "Bush Calls on Fed for Another Drop in Interest Rates," *New York Times*, June 24th, pp. A1, D14.

Greenhouse, Steven (1993) "Judge in a Ruling that Could Delay Trade Pact," *New York Times*, July 1st.

Greenstein, Fred I. (1978) "Change and Continuity in the Modern Presidency" in Anthony King ed. *The New American Political System*, Washington, D.C., American Enterprise Institute.

Greve, M.S. and F.L. Smith, eds. (1992) *Environmental Politics*, New York, Praeger.

Grimshaw, W. (1992) *Bitter Fruit: Black Politics and the Chicago Machine*, Chicago, University of Chicago Press.

Grofman, Bernard, Lisa Handley and Richard Niemi (1992) *Minority Representation and the Quest for Voting Equality,* Cambridge, Cambridge University Press.

Gruberg, Martin (1968) *Women in Politics*, Oshkosh, W.I., Academia Press.

Gunnell, John G. (1991) "The Historiography of American Political Science," in David Easton, John G. Gunnell and Luigi Graziano, eds., *The Development of Political Science*, London, Routledge.

Gurin, Patricia, Shirley Hatchett, and James Jackson (1989) *Hope and Independence: Blacks' Response to Electoral and Party Politics*, New York, Russell Sage Foundation.

Gurr, T.R. and D.S. King (1987) *The State and the City,* Chicago, University of Chicago Press.

Guskind, Robert (1992) "Cable Connection," *National Journal,* September 19th.

Guterbock, T. (1980) *Machine Politics in Transition: Party and Community,* Chicago, University of Chicago Press.

Haber, S. (1964) *Efficiency and Uplift: Scientific Management in the Progressive Era 1890–1920,* Chicago, University of Chicago Press.

Hacker, A. (1992) *Two Nations: Black and White, Separate, Hostile, Unequal,* New York, Scribners.

Hage, David (1993) "Tonic for a Sick Economy," *US News and World Report,* August 20th, pp. 44–6.

Harris, Fred R. (1993) *Deadlock or Decision,* New York, Oxford University Press.

Harrison, B. and L. Gorham (1992) "What Happened to African-American Wages in the 1980s?," in G.C. Galster and E.W. Hill eds. *The Metropolis in Black and White,* New Brunswick, N.J., Center for Urban Policy Research.

Harrison, K. and G. Hoberg (1991) "Setting the Economic Agenda in Canada and the United States: The Cases of Dioxin and Radon," *Canadian Journal of Political Science,* 24: 2–28.

Hart, John (1987) *The Presidential Branch,* New York, Pergamon.

Hartz, Louis (1955) *The Liberal Tradition in America,* New York, Harcourt, Brace and World.

Hayes, Michael (1978) "The Semi-Sovereign Pressure Groups: A Critique of Current Theory and an Alternative Typology," *Journal of Politics,* 40: 1, pp. 134–61.

Hays, Samuel P. (1959) *Conservation and the Gospel of Efficiency,* Cambridge, Harvard University Press.

Hays, Samuel P. (1987) *Beauty, Health and Permanence: Environmental Politics in the United States 1955–1985,* Cambridge, Cambridge University Press.

Hays, Samuel P. (1992) "Environmental Political Culture and Environmental Political Development: An Analysis of Legislative Voting, 1971–1989," *Environmental History Review,* 16: 1–23.

Healey, Jon (1993) "Clinton Struggles with Hill But Still Gets His Way" *Congressional Quarterly Weekly Report,* 29 May.

Heclo, Hugh (1977) *A Government of Strangers: Executive Politics in the United States,* Washington, D.C., Brookings Institution.

Heclo, Hugh (1978) "Issue Networks and the Executive Establishment" in Anthony King, ed., *The New American Political System,* Washington, D.C., American Enterprise Institute.

Heclo, Hugh (1987) "The In-and-Outer System: A Critical Assessment," in G. Calvin Mackenzie, ed., *The In-and-Outers: Presidential Appointees and Transient Government in Washington DC,* Baltimore, Johns Hopkins Press.

Heclo, Hugh (1989) "The Emerging Regime," in Richard A. Harris and Sydney M. Milkis, eds., *Remaking American Politics,* Boulder, Westview.

Herrnson, Paul S. (1988) *Party Campaigning in the 1980s,* Cambridge, Mass., Harvard University Press.

Herrnson, Paul S. (1989) "National Party Decision Making, Strategies, and Resource Distribution in Congressional Elections," *Western Political Quarterly,* 42: 301–23.

Herrnson, Paul S. (1992) "Why the United States Does Not Have Responsible Parties," *Perspectives on Political Science,* 21: 91–9.

Herrnson, Paul S. (1994) *Campaigning for Congress: Candidates, Political Parties, and Political Action Committees,* Washington, D.C., Congressional Quarterly Press.

Hibbs, Douglas (1987) *The American Political Economy: Macroeconomics and Electoral Politics in the United States,* Cambridge, Harvard University Press.

Hicks, Richard C. (1992) "Environmental Legislation and the Costs of Compliance," *Government Finance Review,* 8: 7–10.

Hird, J.A. (1993) "Environmental Policy and Equity: The Case of Superfund," *Journal of Policy Analysis and Management,* 12.

Hofferbert, Richard (1974) *The Study of Public Policy,* Indianapolis, Bobbs-Merrill.

Horowitz, D. (1977) *The Courts and Social Policy,* Washington, D.C., Brookings Institution.

Howell, Susan E. and Shirley B. Laska (1992) "The Changing Face of the Environmental Coalition, A Research Note," *Environment and Behavior,* 24.

Hughes, M. and J. Steinberg (1993) *New Metropolitan Reality,* Washington, Urban Institute.

Huitt, Ralph K. (1954) "The Congressional Committee: A Case Study," *American Political Science Review,* 48: 340–65.

Huitt, Ralph K. (1957) "The Morse Committee Assignment Controversy," *American Political Science Review,* 51: 313–29.

Huitt, Ralph K. (1961a) "Democratic Party Leadership in the Senate," *American Political Science Review,* 55: 333–44.

Huitt, Ralph K. (1961b) "The Outsider in the Senate," *American Political Science Review,* 55: 566–75.

Huntington, Samuel (1973) "Transnational Organizations in World Politics," *World Politics,* 25: 3, pp. 333–68.

Hupp, D. (1992) "Lying About the Land: The 'Wise Use' Movement," *Western States Center Newsletter,* 7.

Hyde, Albert (1992) *Government Budgeting: Theory, Process, Politics,* Pacific Grove, Ca., Brooks/Cole.

Ifill, Gwen (1993) "Clinton in Prime Time, Spurned by Two Networks," *New York Times,* 18 June.

Ingraham, Patricia W. (1991) "Political Direction and Policy Change in Three Federal Departments" in James Pfiffner, ed., *The Managerial Presidency,* Belmont, Brooks/Cole.

Ingraham, Patricia W. and Donald W. Kettle, eds. (1992) *Agenda for Excellence: Public Service in America,* Chatham, N.J., Chatham House.

Ingram, H. and H.B. Milward and W. Laird (1990) "Scientists and Agenda Setting, Advocacy and Global Warming," unpublished paper.

Isaak, Alan C. (1981) *Scope and Methods of Political Science,* 3rd edn., Homeswood, Ill., The Dorsey Press.

Jackson, Bryan O. (1991) "Racial and Ethnic Cleavages in Los Angeles Politics," in Bryan O. Jackson and Michael B. Preston, eds., *Racial and Ethnic Politics in California,* Berkeley, I.G.S. Press.

Jacobs, Lawrence (1993) *The Health of Nations: Public Opinion and the Making of American and British Health Policy,* Ithaca, Cornell University Press.

Jacobson, Gary C. (1985–6) "Party Organization and the Distribution of Campaign Resources: Republicans and Democrats in 1982," *Political Science Quarterly,* 100: 603–25.

Jacobson, Gary C. (1990) *The Electoral Origins of Divided Government,* Boulder, Colo., Westview.

Jacobson, Gary C. (1992) *The Politics of Congressional Elections,* 3rd edn., Boston, HarperCollins.

Jargowsky, P.A. and M.J. Bane (1990) "Ghetto Poverty: Basic Questions" in L.E. Lynn and M.G. McGeary, eds., *Inner-City Poverty in the United States,* Washington, D.C., National Academy Press.

Jencks, C. (1992) *Rethinking Social Policy,* Cambridge, Mass., Harvard University Press.

Jencks, Christopher and Paul E. Peterson, eds. (1991) *The Urban Underclass,* Washington, D.C., Brookings Institution.

Johnson, D. (1990) "West that Is No More Turns Back Land-Use Fees," *New York Times,* April 4.

Johnson, Nevil (1989) *The Limits of Political Science,* Oxford, Oxford University Press.

Johnston, G.M. and P.M. Emerson, eds. (1984) *Public Lands and the US Economy: Balancing Conservation and Development,* Boulder, Westview.

Jones, B.D. (1983) *Governing Urban America,* Boston, Little, Brown.

Jones, Charles O. (1970) *An Introduction to the Study of Public Policy,* Belmont, Cal., Wadsworth.

Jones, Charles O. (1988) *The Trusteeship Presidency: Jimmy Carter and the United States Congress,* Baton Rouge, Louisiana State University Press.

Judd, D.R. (1983) *The Politics of American Cities: Private Power and Public Policy,* 2nd edn., Boston, Little, Brown.

Kaminer, Wendy (1992) "Crashing the Locker Room," *The Atlantic Monthly,* July, pp. 59–70.

Karnig, Albert K. and Susan Welch (1980) *Black Representation and Urban Politics,* Chicago, Chicago University Press.

Kasarda, J.D. (1985) "Urban Change and Minority Opportunities," in Paul Peterson, ed., *The New Urban Reality,* Washington, D.C., Brookings Institution.

Kasarda, J.D. (1989) "Urban Industrial Transition and the Underclass," *Annals,* 501: 26–47.

Kasten, Richard, Frank Sammartino, and Eric Toder (1992) "Trends in Federal Tax Progressivity: 1980–1993," unpublished paper.

Katz, M.B. (1993) *The Underclass Debate: Views from History,* Princeton, Princeton University Press.

Kaufman, Herbert (1981) *The Administrative Behavior of Federal Bureau Chiefs*, Washington, D.C., Brookings Institution.

Kearney, Richard C. and Reginald S. Sheehan (1992) "Supreme Court Decision Making: The Impact of Court Composition on State and Local Government Litigation," *Journal of Politics*, 54: 1008–25.

Keating, M. (1993) "The Politics of Economic Development," *Urban Affairs Quarterly*, 28.

Keller, L.F. (1992) "Leadership and Race in the Administrative City," in G.C. Galster and E.W. Hill, eds., *The Metropolis in Black and White*, New Brunswick, N.J., Center for Urban Policy Research.

Kennedy, Paul (1987) *The Rise and Fall of the Great Powers*, New York, Random House.

Kern, M. (1989) *Thirty-Second Politics*, New York, Praeger.

Kernell, Samuel (1986) *Going Public: New Strategies of Presidential Leadership*, Washington, D.C., Congressional Quarterly Press.

Kessel, John H. (1992) *Presidential Campaign Politics*, Homewood, Ill., Dorsey Press.

Kettl, Ronald E. (1986) *Leadership at the Fed*, New Haven, Yale University Press.

Kettl, Ronald E. (1992) *Deficit Politics: Public Budgeting in its Institutional and Scholarly Context*, New York, Macmillan.

Key, V.O. (1958) *Politics, Parties, and Pressure Groups*, New York, Thomas Y. Crowell.

Kiewiet, D.R. (1983) *Macroeconomics and Micropolitics*, Chicago, University of Chicago Press.

Kincaid, John (1985) "The American Governors in International Affairs," *Publius*, 14: 4, pp. 95–114.

Kincaid, John (1988) "State Court Protections of Individual Rights Under State Constitutions: The New Judicial Federalism," *Journal of State Government*, 61: 163–9.

Kincaid, John (1990) "State and Local Governments Go International," *Intergovernmental Perspective*, 16: 6–9.

Kincaid, John (1993) "Constitutional Federalism: Labor's Role in Displacing Places to Benefit Persons," *PS*, 26: 172–7.

Kincaid, John (1993a) "From Cooperation to Coercion in American Federalism: Housing, Fragmentation and Preemption, 1780–1992," *Journal of Law and Politics*, 9: 333–430.

King, Desmond S. (1990) "Economic Activity and the Challenge to Local Governments," in D.S. King and J. Pierre, eds., *Challenges to Local Government*, London, Sage.

King, Desmond S. (1992) "The Changing Federal Balance," in Gillian Peele, Christopher J. Bailey, Bruce Cain, eds., *Developments in American Politics*, London, Macmillan.

King, Desmond S. (1992a) "The Establishment of Work-welfare Programmes in Britain and the USA," in S. Steino *et al.*, eds., *Structuring Politics*, Cambridge, Cambridge University Press.

King, Desmond S. (1993) "The Longest Road to Equality: The Politics of Institutional Desegregation under Truman," *Journal of Historical Sociology*, 6: 119–64.

Kingdon, John (1984) *Agendas, Alternatives, and Public Policies*, Boston, Little, Brown.

Kirkpatrick, Evron M. (1962) "The Impact of the Behavioral Approach on Traditional Political Science," in Austin Ranney, ed., *Essays in the Behavioral Study of Politics*, Urbana, University of Illinois Press.

Kirkpatrick, Jeane (1976) *The New Presidential Elite*, New York, Russell Sage.

Kirschenman, J. and K.M. Neckerman (1991) " 'We'd Love to Hire Them, But.': The Meaning of Race for Employers," in Christopher Jencks and Paul Peterson, eds., *The Urban Underclass*, Washington, D.C., Brookings Institution.

Kiser, Larry and Elinor Ostrom (1982) "The Three Worlds of Action" in Elinor Ostrom, ed., *Strategies of Political Inquiry*, Beverly Hills, Sage.

Kitano, Harry (1981) "Asian-Americans: the Chinese, Japanese, Koreans, Filipinos and Southeast Asians," *Annals*, 454, pp. 125–38.

Kolbert, Elizabeth (1992) "Early Loss Cast Clinton as a Leader by Consensus," *New York Times*, September 28th.

Kosterlitz, Julie (1993) "Health Lobby Pushes Past the Beltway," *National Journal*, April 17th.

Kousser, J. Morgan (1984) "The Undermining of the First Reconstruction: Lessons for the Second," in Chandler Davidson, ed., *Minority Vote Dilution*, Washington, D.C., Howard University Press.

Kousser, J. Morgan (1992) "The Voting Rights Act and the Two Reconstructions," in Bernard Grofman and Chandler Davidson, eds., *Controversies in Minority Voting: A 25 Year Perspective on the Voting Rights Act of 1965*, Washington, D.C., Brookings Institution.

Kraft, Michael E. (1991) "Environmental Policy Studies and Political Science: New Directions in a Familiar Terrain," *Policy Currents*, November 1st.

Krauthammer, Charles (1991) "The Unipolar Moment," *Foreign Affairs*, 7: 8, pp. 23–34.

Krehbiel, Keith (1991) *Information and Legislative Organization*, Ann Arbor, University of Michigan Press.

Kurtz, Howard (1993) "Inaugurating a Talk Show Presidency," *Washington Post*, February 12th.

Lacey, Michael J. (1992) *Government and Environmental Politics*, Washington, D.C., The Woodrow Wilson Center Press.

Ladd, Everett Carl (1993) "The 1992 Vote for President: Another Brittle Mandate?," *Political Science Quarterly*, 108: 1–28.

Ladd, Everett Carl and Charles D. Hadley (1975) *Transformations of the American Party System: Political Coalitions from the New Deal to the 1970s*, New York, W.W. Norton.

Landis, J.D. (1987) "The Future of America's Central Cities," *Built Environment*, 13.

Lasser, William (1989) *The Limits of Judicial Power*, Chapel Hill, University of North Carolina Press.

Lasswell, Harold (1936) *Politics: Who Gets What, When, How*, New York, McGraw-Hill.

Lemann, N. (1991) *The Promised Land*, New York, Knopf.

Lengle, James I. (1987) "Democratic Party Reforms: The Past as Prologue to the 1988 Campaign," *Journal of Law and Politics*, 4.

Leopold, A. (1970) *A Sand County Almanac*, New York, Ballantine Books.

Leuchtenburg, William E. (1983) *In the Shadow of FDR*, Ithaca, Cornell University Press.

Levine, Charles H. (1992) "The Federal Government in the Year 2000," in Patricia W. Ingraham and Donald F. Kettle, eds., *Agenda for Legislative Change*, Chatham, N.J., Chatham House.

Levine, Charles H. and Rosslyn S. Kleeman (1992) "The Quiet Crisis in the American Public Service," in Patricia W. Ingraham and Donald F. Kettle, eds., *Agenda for Excellence*, Chatham, Chatham House.

Levy, Leonard (1988) *Original Intent and the Framer's Constitution*, London, Macmillan.

Levy, Leonard W. and Louis Fisher, eds. (1993) *The Encyclopedia of the American Presidency*, 4 vols, New York, Simon and Schuster.

Lewis, Gregory B. (1991) "Turnover and the Quiet Crisis in the Federal Civil Service," *Public Administration Review*, 51: 145–55.

Lewis-Beck, Michael (1988) *Economics and Elections*, Ann Arbor, University of Michigan Press.

Light, Paul C. (1992) *Forging Legislation*, New York, W.W. Norton.

Light, Paul C. (1993) *Monitoring Government*, Washington, D.C., Brookings Institution.

Logan, J.R. and H.L. Molotch (1987) *Urban Fortunes*, Berkeley, University of California Press.

Loomis, Burdette (1988) *The New American Politician*, New York, Basic Books.

Loomis, Burdette and Allan Cigler (1991) "Introduction: The Changing Nature of Interest Group Politics," in Allan Cigler and Burdette Loomis, eds., *Interest Group Politics*, 3rd edn., Washington, D.C., Congressional Quarterly Press.

Longley, Lawrence D. and Walter J. Oleszek (1989) *Bicameral Politics: Conference Committees in Congress*, New Haven, Yale University Press.

Lowi, Theodore (1964) "American Business, Public Policy, Case Studies, and Political Theory," *World Politics*, 16: 677–715.

Lowi, Theodore (1972a) "The Politics of Higher Education: Political Science as a Case Study," in George J. Graham and George W. Carey, eds., *The Post-Behavioral Era: Perspectives on Political Science*, New York, McKay.

Lowi, Theodore (1972b) "Four Systems of Policy, Politics, and Choice," *Public Administration Review*, 32: 298–310.

Lowi, Theodore (1979) *The End of Liberalism*, New York, W.W. Norton.

Lowi, Theodore (1985) *The Personal President*, Ithaca, Cornell University Press.

Lowi, Theodore (1992) "The State in Political Science: How We Became What We Study," *American Political Science Review*, 86: 1–7.

Lowi, Theodore (1993) "A Review of Herbert Simon's Review of My Review of the Discipline," *PS*, 26: 51–2.

Lupia, Arthur and Ken McCue (1990) "Why the 1980s Measures of Racially Polarized Voting are Inadequate for the 1990s," *Law and Policy*, 12: 353–87.

Lutz, Donald S. (1980) "From Covenant to Constitution in American Political Thought," *Publius*, 10: 101–33.

Maisal, L. Sandy, ed. (1994) *The Parties Respond: Changes in the American Party System*, 2nd edn., Boulder, Westview.

Maltzman, Forrest (1993) "A Spatial Understanding of Committee, Chamber and Party Preferences in the Postreform Congress," unpublished paper.

Mann, Dean E., ed. (1981) *Environmental Policy Formation*, Lexington, Lexington Books.

Mann, Dean E. (1986) "Democratic Politics and Environmental Politics" in S. Kamieniecki, R. O'Brien and M. Clarke, eds., *Controversies in Environmental Policy*, Albany, State University of New York Press.

Mann, Thomas E., ed. (1990) *A Question of Balance: The President, Congress and Foreign Policy*, Washington, D.C., Brookings Institution.

Mann, Thomas E. and Gary Orren, eds (1992) *Media Polls in American Politics*, Washington, D.C., Brookings Institution.

Mannheim, Karl (1936) *Ideology and Utopia*, New York, Harcourt, Brace Jovanovich.

Mannion, A.M. and S.R. Bowlby (1992) *Environmental Issues in the 1990s*, Chichester, John Wiley.

Manwaring, Max, ed. (1993) *Gray Area Phenomena: Confronting the New World Order*, Boulder, Westview.

March, James G. and Johan P. Olson (1984) "The New Institutionalism: Organizational Factors in Political Life," *American Political Science Review*, 74: 734–49.

Markey, J.P. (1988) "The Labor Market Problems of Today's High School Dropouts," *Monthly Labor Review*, June 3rd.

Marmor, T.R. (1973) *The Politics of Medicare*, Chicago, Aldine.

Marmor, T.R. and David Thomas (1972) "Doctors, Politics, and Pay Disputes," *British Journal of Political Science*, 2: 421–42.

Marmor, T.R., J.L. Mashaw, and P.L. Harvey (1990) *America's Misunderstood Welfare State*, New York, Basic Books.

Marshall, Will and Martin Schram, eds. (1993) *Mandate for Change*, New York, Berkeley.

Martin, Janet M. (1993) *Lessons from the Hill*, New York, St. Martin's Press.

Massey, D.S. and N.A. Denton (1993) *American Apartheid: Segregation and the Making of the Underclass*, Cambridge, Mass., Harvard University Press.

Matthews, Donald R. (1960) *US Senators and their World*, Chapel Hill, University of North Carolina Press.

Mayhew, David R. (1974) *Congress: The Electoral Connection*, New Haven, Yale University Press.

Mayhew, David R. (1991) *Divided We Govern*, New Haven, Yale University Press.

Mazmanian, Daniel and David Morell (1992) *Beyond Superfailure*, Boulder, Westview.

McAllister, Bill (1993) "Today's Raise May Be Last of its Kind," *Washington Post*, January 1st.

McAllister, Bill and Kenneth J. Cooper (1993) "Unions Applaud Personnel Plan," *Washington Post*, September 8th.

McCloskey, Robert G. (1972) *The Modern Supreme Court*, Harvard, Harvard University Press.

McConnell, Grant (1966) *Private Power and American Democracy*, New York, Vintage Books.

McCubbins, Matthew (1992) *Under the Watchful Eye*, Washington, D.C., Congressional Quarterly Press.

McKeegan, M. (1992) *Abortion Politics: Mutiny in the Ranks of the Right*, New York, The Free Press.

McKeever, Robert (1993) *Raw Judicial Power*, Manchester, Manchester University Press.

McWilliams, Wilson Carey (1981) "Parties as Civic Associations," in Gerald M. Pomper, ed., *Party Renewal in America*, New York, Praeger.

Merida, Kevin (1993) "Questions of Loyalty Among House Democrats," *Washington Post*, June 19th.

Merriam, Charles (1921) "The Present State of the Study of Politics" *American Political Science Review*, 15: 173–85.

Merriam, Charles (1925) *New Aspects of Politics*, Chicago, University of Chicago Press.

Merrifield, Bruce D. (1992) "Was This Recession Really Necessary?," *World Monitor*, September.

Meyer, Philip (1993) "The Media Reformation: Giving the Agenda Back to the People" in Michael Nelson, ed., *The Election of 1992*, Washington, D.C., Congressional Quarterly Press.

Milbrath, Lester W. (1989) *Envisioning a Sustainable Society: Learning Our Way Out*, Albany, State University of New York Press.

Miller, Warren E. and Kent M. Jennings (1986) *Parties in Transition*, New York, Russell Sage.

Mills, E.S. (1987) "Non-Urban Policies and Urban Policies," *Urban Studies*, 24.

Mladenka, K.R. (1989) "Blacks and Hispanics in Urban Politics," *American Political Science Review*, 83: 165–91.

Moe, Ronald C. (1990) "Traditional Organizational Principles and the Managerial Presidency: From Phoenix to Ashes," *Public Administration Review*, 50: 129–40.

Moe, Terry M. (1985) "The Politicized Presidency," in John E. Chubb and Paul E. Peterson, eds., *The New Direction in American Politics*, Washington, D.C., Brookings Institution.

Moe, Terry M. (1989) "The Politics of Bureaucratic Structure," in John E. Chubb and Paul E. Peterson, eds., *Can the Government Govern?* Washington, D.C., Brookings Institution.

Moe, Terry M. (1993) in George C. Edwards, John Kessel, and Bert A. Rockman, eds., *Researching the Presidency: Vital Questions, New Approaches*, Pittsburgh, University of Pittsburgh Press.

Mollenkopf, J.H. (1992) *A Phoenix in the Ashes*, Princeton, Princeton University Press.

Morgan, Dan (1992) "US Acknowledges Flaws in Contract Audit System" *Washington Post*, December 3rd.

Morin, Richard (1992) "Surviving the Ups and Downs of Election 92," *Washington Post Weekly Edition*, November 9–15.

Morin, Richard and Helen Dewar (1992) "Approval of Congress Hits All-Time Low, Poll Finds," *Washington Post*, March 20.

Mr X (1947) "The Sources of Soviet Conduct" *Foreign Affairs*, 4: 566–82.

Murray, C. (1984) *Losing Ground*, New York, Basic Books.

Musgrave, Richard A. (1959) *The Theory of Public Finance*, New York, McGraw-Hill.

Nagel, Ernest (1952) "Problems of Concept and Theory Formation in the Social Sciences," in *Science, Language and Human Rights*, Philadelphia, American Philosophical Association.

National Academy of Public Administration (1992) *Beyond Distrust: A Report by a Panel of the National Academy of Public Administration*, Washington, D.C., NAPA.

National League of Cities (1993) *Annual Survey*, Washington, DC, National League of Cities.

National Urban League (1991) *Playing to Win: A Marshall Plan for America*, Washington, D.C., National Urban League.

N.C.P.S. (National Commission on the Public Service) (1989) *Leadership for America: Rebuilding the Public Service*, Lexington, Lexington Books.

Nelson, Michael, ed., (1993) *The Elections of 1992*, Washington, D.C., Congressional Quarterly Press.

Neumann, John von and Oskar Morgenstern (1944) *Theory of Games and Economic Behavior*, Princeton, Princeton University Press.

Neus, Elizabeth (1993) "Health Care Reform Brings Ad Avalanche," *Garnet News Service*, May, 12.

Neustadt, Richard (1980) *Presidential Power*, 4th edn., New York, Wiley.

Neustadt, Richard (1990) *Presidential Power and the Modern Presidents: The Politics of Leadership from Roosevelt to Reagan*, New York, The Free Press.

Newland, Chester (1983) "A Mid-Term Appraisal – The Reagan Presidency: Limited Government and Political Administration," *Public Administration Review*, 43: 1–21.

New York Times (1993a) "Bill Clinton's Hundred Days," April 29th.

New York Times (1993b) "Was This Strike Necessary?," June 28th.

Nie, Norman H., Sidney Verba, and John R. Petrocik (1979) *The Changing American Voter*, Cambridge, Mass., Harvard University Press.

Niemi, R.G. and H. Weisberg (1993) *Controversies in Voting Behaviour*, 3rd edn, Washington, D.C., Congressional Quarterly Press.

Nimmo, Dan (1990) *Mediated Political Realities*, New York, Longman.

Niskanen, William (1971) *Bureaucracy and Representative Government*, Chicago, Aldine and Atherton.

Norris, Pippa (1993) "The 1992 US Election," *Government and Opposition*, 28: 51–68.

Nye, Joseph (1990) *Bound to Lead*, New York, Basic Books.

Oates, Wallace E. (1972) *Fiscal Federalism*, New York, Harcourt Brace Jovanovich.

O'Brien, David M. (1993) *Storm Center*, 3rd edn, New York, W.W. Norton.

O'Brien, David M. (1993) "The Rhenquist Court and Federal Preemption: In Search of a Theory," *Publius*, 23: 15–31.

Office of Inspector General, Environmental Protection Agency (1992) *EPA's Management of Computer Sciences Corporation Contract Activities*, Washington, D.C., EPA.

Olson, Mancur (1965) *The Logic of Collective Action*, Cambridge, Mass., Harvard University Press.

O.M.B. (Office of Management and Budget) (1993) *Budget Baselines, Historical Data, and Alternatives for the Future*, Washington, D.C., GPO.

Ophuls, W. and A.S. Boyan (1992) *Ecology and the Politics of Scarcity Revisited*, New York, W.H. Freeman.

Osborne, David (1993) "Reinventing Government: Creating an Entrepeneurial Federal Establishment," in Will Marshall and Martin Schram, eds.

Osborne, David and Ted Gaebler (1992) *Reinventing Government: How the Entrepreneurial Spirit is Transforming the Public Sector*, New York, Addison-Wesley.

Ostrom, Elinor (1986) "An Agenda for the Study of Institutions," *Public Choice*, 48: 3–25.

Ostrom, Elinor (1990) *Governing the Commons*, Cambridge, Cambridge University Press.

Pachon, Harry (1991) "US Citizenship and Latinos' Participation in California Politics," in Bryan O. Jackson and Michael B. Preston, eds., *Racial and Ethnic Politics in California*, Berkeley, I.G.S. Press.

Paehlke, R.C. (1989) *Environmentalism and the Future of Progressive Politics*, New Haven, Yale University Press.

Palmer, John and Isobel V. Sawhill, eds. (1982) *The Reagan Experiment*, Washington, D.C., The Urban Institute.

Parenti, Michael (1967) "Ethnic Politics and the Persistence of Ethnic Voting," *American Political Science Review*, 61, pp. 717–26.

Parker, Glenn R. (1980) "Sources of Change in Congressional District Attentiveness," *American Journal of Political Science*, 24: 115–24.

Parker, Glenn R. (1989) *Characteristics of Congress: Patterns in Congressional Behavior*, Englewood Cliffs, Prentice-Hall.

Paton, Calum (1990) *US Health Politics: Public Policy and Political Theory*, Aldershot and Brookfield, Vt. Avebury.

Peele, Gillian (1984) *Revival and Reaction*, Oxford, Oxford University Press.

Peele, Gillian (1992) "Civil Rights" in G. Peele, C.J. Bailey and Bruce Cain, *Developments in American Politics*, Basingstoke, Macmillan.

Peretz, Paul (1982) *The Political Economy of Inflation in the United States*, Chicago, University of Chicago Press.

Peretz, Paul, ed. (1994) *The Politics of American Economic Policy Making*, Armonk, N.J., Sharpe.

Perry, H.W. (1991) *Deciding to Decide: Agenda Setting in the Supreme Court*, Cambridge: Harvard University Press.

Persons, G.A. ed. (1991) *Dilemmas for Black Politics: Issues of Leadership and Strategy*, New York, HarperCollins.

Persons, G.A. (1992) "Racial Politics and Black Power in the Cities" in G.C. Galster and E.W. Hill, eds., *The Metropolis in Black and White*, New Brunswick, N.J., Center for Urban Policy Research.

Peters, B. Guy (1984) *The Politics of Bureaucracy*, 2nd edn., New York, Longman.

Peters, B. Guy (1993) *American Public Policy*, 3rd edn., Chatham, N.J., Chatham House.

Peterson, Mark A. (1990) *Legislating Together: The White House and Capitol Hill from Eisenhower to Reagan*, Cambridge, Harvard University Press.

Peterson, Peter C. with James K. Sebenius (1992) "The Primacy of the Domestic Agenda," in Graham Allison and Gregory F. Treverton, eds., *Rethinking America's Security*, New York, Norton.

Peterson, Paul E. (1991) "The Urban Underclass and the Poverty Paradox" in Christopher Jencks and Paul E. Peterson, eds., *The Urban Underclass*, Washington, D.C., Brookings Institution.

Petracca, Mark, ed. (1992) *The Politics of Interests*, Boulder, Co., Westview.

Petrocik, John (1987) "Realignment: New Party Coalitions and the Nationalization of the South," *Journal of Politics*, 49: 347–75.

Pfiffner, James P. (1988) *The Strategic Presidency: Hitting the Ground Running*, Chicago, Dorsey.

Pfiffner, James P., ed. (1991) *The Managerial Presidency*, Belmont, Brooks/Cole.

Phillips, Kevin (1970) *The Emerging Republican Majority*, New York, Anchor.

Pitkin, Hanna (1967) *The Concept of Representation*, Berkeley, University of California Press.

Piven, F.F. and R. Cloward (1988), *Why Americans Don't Vote*, New York, Pantheon.

Polsby, Nelson W. (1983) *Consequences of Party Reform*, New York, Oxford University Press.

Polsby, Nelson W. (1986) *Congress and the Presidency*, 4th edn., Englewood Cliffs, N.J., Prentice-Hall.

Polsby, Nelson W. and Aaron B. Wildavsky (1991) *Presidential Elections*, New York, Charles Scribners.

Pomper, Gerald M., ed. (1981) *Party Renewal in America*, New York, Praeger.

Pomper, Gerald M. (1992) *Passions and Interests: Political Party Concepts of American Democracy*, Lawrence, Ks., University Press of Kansas.

Pomper, Gerald M. ed. (1993) *The Election of 1992*, Chatham, N.J., Chatham House.

Portney, Kent E. (1992) *Controversial Issues in Environmental Policy*, Newbury Park, CA, Sage.

Pressman, Jeffrey and Aaron Wildavsky (1973) *Implementation,* Berkeley, University of California Press.

Radin, Beryl and Joseph N. Coffee (1993) "A Critique of TQM: Problems of Implementation in the Public Service," *Public Administration Quarterly,* vol. 17, 1 (Spring).

Rae, Douglas W. (1967) *The Political Consequences of Electoral Laws,* New Haven, Yale University Press.

Ranney, Austin (1975) *Curing the Mischiefs of Faction,* Berkeley, University of California Press.

Ranney, Austin (1983) *Channels of Power,* New York, Basic Books.

Rector, Robert and Michael Sanera, eds. (1987) *Steering the Elephant: How Washington Works,* New York, Universe.

Reich, Robert B. (1991) *The Work of Nations,* London, Simon and Schuster.

Rein, M. and L. Rainwater (1986) *Public/Private Interplay in Social Protection,* Armonk, N.Y., M.E. Sharpe.

Ricci, David (1984) *The Tragedy of Political Science,* New Haven, Yale University Press.

Rice, Stuart (1928) *Quantative Methods in Politics,* New York, Knopf.

Ricketts, E. (1992) "The Nature and Dimensions of the Underclass," in G.C. Galster and E.W. Hill, eds., *The Metropolis in Black and White,* New Brunswick, N.J., Center for Urban Policy Research.

Ricketts, E. and R. Mincy (1986) *Growth of the Underclass 1970–1980,* Washington, D.C., Urban Institute.

Ripley, Randall B. and Grace A. Franklin (1987) *Congress, the Bureaucracy, and Public Policy,* 4th edn., Homewood, Ill., Dorsey Press.

Romney, Ronna and Beppie Harrison (1987) *Momentum: Women in American Politics Now,* New York, Crown.

Rose, Richard (1991) *The Postmodern President,* 2nd edn., Chatham, N.J., Chatham House.

Rosenau, James (1990) *Turbulence in World Politics,* Princeton, Princeton University Press.

Rosenbaum, Walter A. (1991) *Environmental Politics and Policy,* Washington, D.C., Congressional Quarterly Press.

Ross, Dorothy (1991) *The Origins of American Social Science,* New York, Columbia University Press.

Rubin, Irene S. (1985) *Shrinking the Federal Government,* New York, Longman.

Ruggles, P. (1990) *Drawing the Line: Alternative Poverty Measures and their Implications for Public Policy,* Washington, D.C., Urban Institute.

Rule, Wilma and Pippa Norris (1992) "Anglo and Minority Women's Underrepresentation in the Congress: Is the Electoral System the Culprit?" in Joseph Zimmerman and Wilma Rule, eds., *The Impact of US Electoral Systems on Minorities and Women,* New Haven, Greenwood Press.

Sabato, Larry J. (1981) *The Rise of Political Consultants,* New York, Basic Books.

Sabato, Larry J. (1984) *PAC Power: Inside the World of Politcal Action Committees,* New York W.W. Norton.

Said, Lynda (1993) "Bush Leaves Office on a High Note," *The Gallup Poll Monthly*, January.

Salokar, Rebecca M. (1992) *The Solicitor General: The Politics of Law*, Philadelphia, Temple University Press.

Sammon, R. (1993) "Urban–Rural Rift Only Ripple at Cisneros' Senate Hearing," *Congressional Quarterly Weekly Report*, January 16.

Savage, David G. (1992) *Turning Right: The Making of the Rehnquist Supreme Court*, New York, John Wiley.

Savas, E.S. (1987) *Privatization: The Key to Better Government*, Chatham, Chatham House.

Savitch, H.V. and J.C. Thomas (1991) "Conclusion" in H.V. Savitch and J.C. Thomas, eds., *Big City Politics in Transition*, Newbury Park, Sage.

Schattschneider, E.E. (1960) *The Semi-Sovereign People*, New York, Holt, Rinehart, and Winston.

Schattschneider, E.E. (1969) *Two Hundred Million Americans in Search of a Government*, New York, Holt, Rinehart and Winston.

Schick, Allen ed. (1983) *Making Economic Policy in Congress*, Washington, D.C., American Enterprise Institute.

Schilling, Warner, Paul Hammond, and Glenn Snyder (1962) *Strategy Politics and Defense Budgets*, New York, Columbia University Press.

Schlesinger, Arthur M. (1974) *The Imperial Presidency*, New York, Popular Library.

Schlesinger, James (1993) "Quest for a Post-Cold War Foreign Policy," *Foreign Affairs*, 72: 17–28.

Schlesinger, Joseph A. (1985) "The New American Party" *American Political Science Review*, 79: 4, pp. 1151–69.

Schlozman, Kay and David Tierney (1986) *Organized Interests and American Government*, New York, Harper and Row.

Schneider, William (1992) "The Suburban Century Begins," *The Atlantic Monthly*, July.

Schroeder, Christopher (1991) "The Evolution of Federal Regulation of Toxic Substances" in Michael J. Lacey, ed., *Government and Environmental Politics*, Washington, D.C., Woodrow Wilson Center Press.

Schwab, Larry M. (1991) *The Illusion of a Conservative Reagan Revolution* New Brunswick, Transaction.

Schwartz, Herman (1988) *Packing the Courts: The Conservative Campaign to Rewrite the Constitution*, New York, Scribners.

Segal, J.A. and H.J. Spaeth (1993) *The Supreme Court and the Attitudinal Model*, Cambridge, Cambridge University Press.

Seidelman, Raymond (1985) *Disenchanted Realists: Political Science and the American Crisis 1884–1984*, Albany, State University of New York Press.

Seidman, Harold and Robert Gilmour (1986) *Politics, Position, and Power*, 4th edn., New York, Oxford University Press.

Shafer, Byron (1988) *Bifurcated Politics*, Cambridge, Mass., Harvard University Press.

Shafer, Byron, ed. (1991) *The End of Realignment? Interpreting American Electoral Eras*, Madison, University of Wisconsin Press.

Shapiro, I. (1991) *The States and the Poor*, Washington, D.C., Center for Budget Priorities.

Shepsle, Kenneth A. (1989) "Studying Institutions: Some Lessons from the Rational Choice Approach," *Journal of Theoretical Politics*, 1: 131–48.

Shoop, Tom (1992) "Sunshine on the Shadow Government," *Government Executive*, April, pp.16–19.

Sidey, Hugh (1993) "The White House Press Corps" in Leonard W. Levy and Louis Fisher, eds., *The Encyclopedia of the American Presidency*, New York, Simon and Schuster.

Sigal, Leon V. (1992–3) "The Last Cold War Election," *Foreign Affairs*, 72: 1–15.

Simon, Herbert (1945) *Administrative Behavior*, New York, Free Press.

Simson, G.J. (1993) "Thomas' Supreme Unfitness," *Cornell Law Review*, 78, 619–63.

Skocpol, Theda (1985) "Bringing the State Back In" in Peter B. Evans, Dietrich Rueschemeyer, and Theda Skocpol, eds., *Bringing the State Back In*, Cambridge, Cambridge University Press.

Smith, Bruce (1992) *The Advisors*, Washington, D.C., Brookings Institution.

Smith, Hedrick, (1988) *The Power Game*, London, Collins.

Smith, Steven S. (1989) *Call To Order: Floor Politics in the House and Senate*, Washington, D.C., Brookings Institution.

Smith, Steven S. and Christopher J. Deering (1990) *Committees in Congress*, 2nd edn., Washington, D.C., Congressional Quarterly Press.

Smith, Tom W. and Lance A. Selfa (1992) "When Do Women Vote for Women?" *The Public Perspective*, Storrs, C.N., The Roper Center for Public Opinion Research.

Smith, Tom W. (1993) "The Gender Gap at the State Level," *The Public Perspective*, Storrs, C.N., The Roper Center for Public Opinion Research.

Smith, Zachary, A. (1992) *The Environmental Policy Paradox*, Englewood Cliffs, N.J., Prentice-Hall.

Solomon, B. (1992) "Bush and Clinton's Urban Fervor," *National Journal*, May 16.

Somit, Albert and Joseph Tanenhaus (1967) *The Development of Political Science: From Burgess to Behavioralism*, Boston, Allyn and Bacon.

Sonenshein, Raphael (1990) "Biracial Coalition Politics in Los Angeles" in Rufus Browning, Dale Rogers Marshall and David H. Tabb, eds., *Racial Politics in American Cities*, New York, Longman.

Sonenshein, Raphael (1993) *Politics in Black and White*, Princeton, Princeton University Press.

Sorauf, Frank J. (1980) "Political Parties and Political Action Committees," *Arizona Law Review*, 22: 445–64.

Sorauf, Frank J. (1988) *Money in American Elections*, Glenview, Ill., Scott Foresman.

Stine, J.K. (1991) "Environmental Politics in the American South: The Fight over the Tennessee-Tombigee Waterway," *Environmental History Review*, 15.

Stokes, Donald and John DiIulio (1993) "The Setting: Valence Politics in Modern Elections," in Michael Nelson, ed. *The Election of 1992*, Washington, D.C., Congressional Quarterly Press.

Stone, Clarence (1989) *Regime Politics*, Lawrence, K.S., University Press of Kansas.

Sunstein, Cass (1993) *The Partial Constitution*, Cambridge, Cambridge University Press

Suro, R. (1992) "Clinton Selects Ex-Mayor for HUD," *New York Times*, December 8th.

Susser, Bernard (1992) *Approaches to the Study of Politics*, New York, Macmillan.

Swain, Carol M. (1993) *Black Faces, Black Interests*, Cambridge, Harvard University Press.

Tam, Wendy (1992) *Asian-Americans – A Monolithic Bloc?*, Berkeley, I.G.S.

Terry, S. (1993) "Troubled Water," *New York Times*, Sept 26th.

Thernstrom, Abigail (1987) *Whose Votes Count?*, Cambridge, Mass., Harvard University Press.

Thurber, James A., ed. (1991) *Divided Democracy*, Washington, D.C., Congressional Quarterly Press.

Tobin, G., ed. (1987) *Divided Neighbourhoods: Changing Patterns of Racial Segregation*, Newbury Park, Sage.

Tocqueville, Alexis de (1956) *Democracy in America*, New York, Mentor.

Tribe, L. (1990) *Abortion: The Clash of Absolutes*, New York, W.W. Norton.

Truman, David (1951) *The Governmental Process*, New York, Alfred Knopf.

Tyler, P.E. (1992) "Soviets' Secret Dumping Raises Fears for Arctic Waters," *New York Times*, May 4.

Uhlaner, Carole J. (1991) "Perceived Discrimination and Prejudice and the Coalition Propsects of Blacks, Latinos and Asian-Americans," in Bryan O. Jackson and Michael B. Preston, eds., *Racial and Ethnic Politics in California*, Berkeley, I.G.S.

Uhlaner, Carole J., D. Roderick Kiewiet, and Bruce Cain (1989) "Political Participation of Ethnic Minorities in the 1980s," *Political Behavior*, 11: 195–231.

U.S. Advisory Commission on Intergovernmental Relations (ACIR) (1992b) *Federal Statutory Preemption of State and Local Authority*, Washington, D.C., A.C.I.R.

U.S. Advisory Commission on Intergovernmental Relations (ACIR) (1993a and 1992a) *Changing Public Attitudes on Government and Taxes*, Washington, D.C., A.C.I.R.

U.S. Advisory Commission on Intergovernmental Relations (ACIR) (1993b) *Federal Regulation of State and Local Government*, Washington, D.C., A.C.I.R.

U.S. Advisory Commission on Intergovernmental Relations (ACIR) (1993c) *Significant Features of Fiscal Federalism: Revenues and Expenditures*, Washington, D.C., A.C.I.R.

U.S. Bureau of the Census (1992) *Statistical Abstract of the United States*, Washington, D.C., G.P.O.

U.S. Congress, Joint Committee on the Organization of Congress (1993) *Congressional Reorganization: Options for Change*, S. prt. 103–19, 103rd Congress, lst session.

U.S. Department of Housing and Urban Development (1982) *The President's National Urban Policy Report 1982*, Washington, D.C., G.P.O.

U.S. General Accounting Office (1992a) *Senior Executive Service: Opinions About the Federal Work Environment*, Washington, D.C., G.A.O.

U.S. General Accounting Office (1992b) *Political Appointees: Number of Noncareer SES and Schedule C Employees in Federal Agencies*, Washington, D.C., G.A.O.

U.S. General Accounting Office (1992c) *Quality Management: Survey of Federal Organizations*, Washington, D.C., G.A.O.

U.S. House of Representatives, Committee on Rules (1992) *To Establish a Joint Committee on the Organization of Congress*, 102nd. Congress, 2nd session.

Verhoek, S.H. (1992) "Power Struggle," *New York Times Magazine*, January 12th.

Verhoek, S.H. (1993) "Poor Would Tax the Rich in Texas Plan for Schools" *New York Times*, May 28th.

Vig, Norman J. and Michael E. Kraft eds. (1990) *Environmental Policy in the 1990s*, Washington, D.C., Congressional Quarterly Press.

Walker, Jack L. (1983) "The Origins and Maintenance of Interest Groups in America," *American Political Science Review*, 77: 390–406.

Waltz, Kenneth (1981) *The Spread of Nuclear Weapons: More May Be Better*, London, International Institute for Strategic Studies.

Washington Post (1993) "Emily's Lesson," April 12th, p. A18.

Waterman, Richard W. (1989) *Presidential Influence and the Administrative State*, Knoxville, University of Tennessee Press.

Waterman, Richard W., ed. (1993) *The Presidency Reconsidered*, Itasca, Ill., F.E. Peacock.

Wattenberg, Martin P. (1990) *The Decline of American Parties, 1952–1988*, Cambridge, Harvard University Press.

Wayne, Stephen J. (1978) *The Legislative Presidency*, New York, Harper and Row.

Weir, Margaret, Ann Shola Orloff, and Theda Skocpol, eds. (1988) *The Politics of Social Policy in the United States*, Princeton, Princeton University Press.

Weir, Margaret(1993) "Race and Urban Poverty," *The Brookings Review*, Summer.

Wekkin, Gary D. (1985) "Political Parties and Intergovernmental Relations in 1984: The Consequences of Party Renewal for Territorial Constituencies," *Publius*, 15: 1, pp. 19–37.

Welch, Susan (1990) "The Impact of At-Large Elections on the Representation of Blacks and Hispanics," *Journal of Politics,* 52: 1050–76.

Welch, Susan and Lorn Foster (1987) "Class and Conservatism in the Black Community," *American Politics Quarterly*, 15: 445–70.

Welch, Susan and Lorn Foster (1992) "The Impact of Economic Conditions on the Voting Behavior of Blacks" *Western Political Quarterly*, 45, pp. 221–36.

Welfeld, Irving (1992) *HUD Scandals: Howling Headlines and Silent Fiascoes*, New Brunswick, Transaction.

Wellington, Harry H. (1990) *Interpreting the Constitution*, (New Haven, Yale University Press.

West, C. (1992) "Learning to Talk of Race," *New York Times*, August 2nd.

White House (1993) *Health Security: Preliminary Plan*, Washington, D.C., The White House.

White, John Kenneth and Jerome M. Mileur, eds. (1992) *Challenges to Party Government*, Carbondale, Southern Illinois University Press.

White, Joseph and Aaron Wildavsky (1989) *The Deficit and the Public Interest*, Berkeley, University of California Press.

White, William S. (1957) *Citadel: The Story of the US Senate*, New York, Harper.

Wildavsky, Aaron (1991) *The Beleaguered Presidency*, New Brunswick, N.J., Transaction.

Wilson, C.A. (1992) "Restructuring and the Growth of Concentrated Poverty in Detroit," *Urban Affairs Quarterly*, 28: 187–205.

Wilson, James Q. (1962) *The Amateur Democrat*, Chicago, University of Chicago Press.

Wilson, James Q. (1989) *Bureaucracy*, New York, Basic Books.

Wilson, W.J. (1987) *The Truly Disadvantaged: The Inner City, the Underclass and Public Policy*, Chicago, University of Chicago Press.

Wilson, Woodrow (1981) *Congressional Government*, Baltimore, Johns Hopkins University Press.

Winant, H. (1993) "Difference and Inequality: Postmodern Racial Politics in the United States" in M. Cross and M. Keith, eds., *Racism, the City and the State*, London, Routledge.

Winks, R.W. (1993) "National Parks Aren't Disneylands," *New York Times*, April 19th.

Witcover, Julie (1993) *Mad as Hell, Revolt at the Ballot Box, 1992*, New York, Warner.

Wolfinger, Raymond E. (1965) "The Development and Persistence of Ethnic Voting," *American Political Science Review*, 59: 896–908.

Wolfinger, Raymond E. and Steven Rosenstone (1980) *Who Votes?*, New Haven, Yale University Press.

Wolfinger, Raymond E. and M.G. Hagen (1985) "Republican Prospects: Southern Comfort," *Public Opinion*, pp. 8–13.

Wolman, H. (1990) "The Reagan Urban Policy and Its Impacts" in D.S. King and J. Pierre, eds., *Challenges to Local Government*, London, Sage.

Woodward, Bob (1992a) "No Tax Vow Scuttled Anti-Deficit Mission," *The Washington Post*, October 5.

Woodward, Bob (1992b) "The Anatomy of a Decision: Six Words That Shaped – And May Sink – the Bush Presidency," *The Washington Post*, October 12th.

Wooley, John T. (1984) *Monetary Politics: The Federal Reserve and the Politics of Monetary Policy*, New York, Cambridge University Press.

Wright, Deil S. (1988) *Understanding Intergovernmental Relations*, Pacific Grove, C.A., Brooks/Cole.

Yeager, Peter C. (1991) *The Limits of Law*, Cambridge, Cambridge University Press.

Zimmerman, Joseph F. (1991) *Federal Preemption: The Silent Revolution*, Ames, Iowa State University Press.

Zuckman, J. (1992) "Enterprise Zone Alchemy: '90s-Style Urban Renewal," *Congressional Quarterly Weekly Report*, August 8th.

Index

Abortion 10, 27, 64, 326
  Supreme Court 153–4, 160,
    161–2, 169
Acheson, Dean 293
Administrative Procedures
    Act 178
African-Americans (see also
    race) 45, 47, 49–53, 54, 55,
    56, 59
  cities 221, 223, 225, 226–7, 231,
    234, 235
  elections 21, 27, 28
  health 312
  political parties 66, 72
  poverty 260–1
Aid to Families with Dependent
    Children 209, 254, 256, 259,
    260, 261–2, 267, 268
AIDS 27, 230, 234
Alabama 2, 24
Alaska 38, 262
American Medical
    Association 90, 91, 93, 94,
    96, 103, 107, 322
American Political Science
    Association 353, 354
Americans with Disabilities
    Act 208
Anderson, John 38
Arizona 26
Arkansas 2, 24
Arrow, Kenneth 359
Arsenio Hall Show 341–2
Asians 4, 8, 54, 55, 56, 57, 58, 59,
    60–6
  immigration 46, 48, 49–53
Atlanta 221, 227

Babbitt, Bruce 161, 281
Baird, Zoe 43, 157–8
Baker, Richard 80

Baltimore 227
Bell, Daniel 5
Bennet, William 5
Bentley, Arthur F. 354
Bentsen, Lloyd 12, 248
Biden, Joseph 339
Blackmun, Harry 155, 160, 166
Blendon, Robert 99
Blumenthal, Sidney 306
Bork, Robert 161, 162, 165
Bosnia 124, 293, 295, 304
Boston 51, 222–3, 227
Boxer, Barbara 81
Bradley, Tom 64–5, 227
Browner, Carol 281
Breyer, Stephen 161
Brown v. Board of Education 214
Bryce, Lord 134, 353–4
Buchanan, James 359
Buchanan, Patrick 72, 343
Budget deficit 6, 12, 32, 43, 115,
    121, 123, 125, 174, 306,
  economic policy 239, 242–4,
    246–9, 251–2, 269–70
Bureau of Land Management 282
Bureaucracy
  appointee 179–82, 189–91
  careerists 191–2
  Congress 182–5, 186–8, 195,
    198–9
  management 186–8
  president 179–82
  reform 172–5, 192–9
  role 175–6, 188–9
  structure 176–8
  theories 370–1
Burke, John 131
Bus Regulatory Act 212
Bush, George 1, 2, 3, 6, 11, 13
  bureaucracy 179, 181, 182, 183,
    192–3

Bush, George (*cont.*)
  cities 222, 229, 251, 235
  economy 33, 237, 240, 241–6,
    250–1, 252
  elections 18–21, 23, 24, 25, 26,
    28, 37, 38, 39, 41, 43, 72, 73,
    79, 119–20, 339, 341–2, 345
  environment 279–80
  evaluation 30–6, 117, 126, 306
  federalism 202, 206, 210, 213,
    217
  foreign policy 303, 306
  Gulf War 114, 134
  health policy 87–8, 320
  Supreme Court 158–9, 160,
    162–3
  welfare policy 267–8

Cabinet 179–80, 182
California 24, 25–6, 50, 51, 54, 56,
    57, 58, 59, 60, 200, 280
Cambodia 49
Canada 286–8
Cannon, Joseph 146
Carter, Jimmy 5, 74, 96, 149, 222
  economy 237, 238, 240
  elections 18, 20, 24, 28, 31, 41
  environment 280, 284
  foreign policy 292, 301
  presidency 115, 116
  Supreme Court 159, 161
Catlin, George 354
Census (1990) 3–4, 50–1, 52
Chicago 51, 59, 220, 221, 223,
    224, 225, 227, 233, 263
Children's Defense Fund 259
China 49, 291, 298
Cisneros, Henry 11, 232–3, 235–6
Cities (*see also individual cities*)
  crime 263–4
  machines 225–6, 230–1
  policy 229–33
  politics 224–9
  problems 11, 27, 220–4, 228–9
City of Richmond v. *Croson* 228
Civil Rights (*see also* African-
    Americans; race) 1, 45, 47,
    62, 158–9, 167–9

Civil Service Reform Act 180,
    191, 193
Clean Air Act 212–13, 280, 288
Cleaver, Eldridge 45
Cleveland 220, 223, 227
Clinton, Hillary 259, 320
Clinton, William J. 1–3, 4, 10, 11,
    16, 116, 124, 151
  abortion 27
  bureaucracy 172, 174, 175,
    179–80, 181, 182
  cities 232–3, 235–6
  divided government 115–17
  economy 12, 121, 123, 237,
    246–50, 257
  election 18, 19, 20, 23–4, 26,
    27, 28, 32, 33, 37, 38, 39, 41,
    73, 79, 118–20
  environment 271, 272, 280,
    284, 285, 287, 288
  federalism 175–6, 206, 210,
    212, 213, 216–17
  foreign policy 295–6, 302, 303,
    307, 309
  health policy 9, 15, 88, 103,
    104, 107, 121, 249, 315,
    320–2, 323
  inauguration 1, 7, 113, 120
  Justice Department 156–60
  media 335, 340–2, 343, 344–7
  policy 120–1, 130
  pragmatism 5–6, 122–3
  public opinion 43, 110–12,
    128–30, 134
  record 110–12, 123–30
  staff 130–1
  style 121–3, 125–30
  Supreme Court 153, 154, 155,
    160–3, 171
  welfare policy 13, 253,
    268–70
Coalitions for America 162
Cochran, Thad 149–50
Cold War 1, 2, 5, 14, 27, 33,
    117–18, 135, 289–93, 296, 298,
    300, 306, 308, 310, 350, 373
Collins, Barbara Rose 332
Colorado 26

Committee for Democratic
   Values 6
Conference of Mayors 231
Congress 7, 9–10, 11, 40, 45, 70,
   111, 113, 115, 116–17, 118,
   119, 120, 122, 123–4, 125–6
   assertiveness 113–14, 159
   bureaucracy 173, 175, 177, 178,
      182–5, 186–8, 195, 198–9
   committees 141–5, 148, 149,
      184, 187
   criticism 134–7
   economy 237, 238, 240, 241,
      242, 247–8, 251
   environment 271, 275–6, 287
   eras 147–50
   federalism 210–11, 212–13
   foreign policy 300, 305
   home style 138–9
   leadership 143, 145–7
   media 336
   parochialism 137–9
   reforms 136, 144
   scandals 135, 139
   staff 138–9, 148, 183–4, 191
   Supreme Court 153, 154–6,
      162–3
   theories 367–9
   turnover 141
   "two Congresses" 137, 150–1
   women 15, 327–8, 329, 330–4
Congressional Budget and
   Impoundment Control
   Act 114
Congressional Caucus for Women's
   Issues 332
Council of American
   Governors 11
Courts (*see also* Supreme
   Court) 10, 100, 155, 214–16,
   275–6
Cousins v. *Wigoda* 73
Cuba 49, 317
Cuomo, Mario 161
Cutler, Lloyd 159

Dahl, Robert 356, 357
Dallas 51, 227, 232

Darman, Richard 243
Daubert v. *Merrell Dow* 153
Days, Drew 158
Democratic Congressional
   Campaign Committee 77, 79
Democratic Leadership
   Council 5, 26
Democratic Party 2, 5, 13, 18,
   120, 121
   activists 72
   campaign strategy 21, 24, 27
   fundraising 76, 81
   national committee 68, 69, 71,
      73, 77, 78, 79
   nominations 115
   regional base 24–6
   renewal 74
   social base 7, 19, 20, 26–30,
      41–3, 57, 60, 63–5
Democratic Party of the U.S. v.
   LaFollette 73
Democratic Senatorial Campaign
   Committee 77, 79
Demographic changes 8, 28–30
Departments
   Agriculture 174, 177, 276
   Commerce 174, 276, 332
   Defense 175, 186, 196, 197
   Education 174, 188, 189
   Energy 188, 197, 276
   Health and Human
      Services 177, 269
   Housing and Urban
      Development 174, 185,
      197, 222, 232–3, 235
   Interior 177, 276, 281
   Justice 55–6, 124, 156–60, 168
   State 276
Detroit 220–1, 223, 224, 232, 345
Dewey, Thomas 353
Dirksen, Everett M. 148
Downs, Anthony 359, 365–6
Dukakis, Michael 2, 18, 24, 28,
   39, 72, 73, 339
Dworkin, Ronald 164

Easton, David 354, 356–7, 358,
   361, 362, 372

Economic policy   11–12, 14, 19
    Bush   33, 237, 240, 241–6,
        250–1, 252
    Clinton   237, 238, 240, 242,
        247–8, 251
    fiscal policy   240–4
    monetary policy   240–1, 244–6,
        249–50
    Reagan   237, 238–40, 242, 248
Education   27, 57, 258, 259,
    262–3
Eisenhower, Dwight   31, 148
Eisenhower Foundation   235
Elections (*see also* political parties;
    voting)
    1984   24
    1988   24, 25, 26, 27, 67, 72, 80,
        135
    1992   7, 18–20, 23, 26, 67, 72,
        80, 135
    candidate-centered   69, 74, 82,
        209
    congressional   15, 25, 73–4, 75,
        78, 80–2, 134–41
    electoral reform   62–4
    electoral system   53–4
    "Republican Lock"   18, 20–1,
        43
    state races   25, 82
    women   325–34
Ellwod, Paul   315
EMILY'S List   327, 328–9, 330–1
Endangered Species Act   279–80,
    284
Enthoven, Alain   315, 317, 320,
    321
Environment (*see also*
    pollution)   13, 57, 64
    agenda   272–4, 277
    Bush   279–80
    Clinton   271–7, 280, 281, 284,
        285, 287, 288
    Democrats   281
    federal land use   281–4
    international aspects   286–8
    litigation   276
    logging   284–5
    public opinion   271, 278

Reagan   279
Republicans   281
Environmental Protection
    Agency   178, 179, 182, 183,
        197–8, 276, 277, 281

Family and Medical Leave
    Act   332, 333
Family Support Act   13, 261
Federal Bureau of
    Investigation   163
Federal Election Campaign
    Act   74–5, 77
Federal Energy Management
    Act   212
Federal Pay Comparability
    Act   195
Federal Reserve Bank   237, 241,
    243, 245, 249–50, 252
Federalism (*see also* State
    Governments)   7, 11, 262,
    276–7
    contemporary   200–1, 208–16
    federal regulations   201–3,
        212–13, 275
    models   205–8
    origins   203–5
Federalist   15   204
Feinstein, Diane   332
Florida   2, 24, 51, 57
Flowers, Gennifer   343
Food and Drug
    Administration   176
Foodstamps   259, 268
Ford, Gerald   31, 126, 155
Foreign policy (*see also* Cold
    War)   3, 5, 13–14, 117, 118,
    307–10
    allies   293–4
    agenda   289–90
    Bush   303, 306
    Carter   292
    Clinton   295–6, 302, 303, 307,
        309
    détente   301
    domestic context   299–307
    issues   293–9, 303
    multilateralism   308–9

New World Order 292–3
nuclear profliferation 296–7
Reagan 301
uncertainty 290–2, 298–9
Fourteenth Amendment 66, 228, 263
Franz, Wanda 162
Fried, Charles 156
Friends of the Earth 287
Fuchs, Ester 228–9
Fund for a Feminist Majority 157, 328

Gans, Curtis 40
Garcia v. *San Antonio Metropolitan Transit Authority* 215
General Agreement on Tariffs and Trade 251
Georgia 24
Gergen, David 345–6
Ginsburg, Ruth Bader 161–2, 166
Gorbachev, Mikhail 292
Gore, Al 2, 24, 26, 27, 172, 195, 217, 249, 271, 281, 323, 344, 346
Gore Commission 10
Government Performance and Results Act 185
Gramm, Phil 232
Gramm–Rudman–Hollings Act 242
Great Society 5, 13, 148, 217, 222, 234
Greenspan, Alan 250
Greenwald, Glenda 327
Gregory v. *Ashcroft* 216
Growe v. *Emison* 167
Guinier, Lani 124, 159, 162
Gulf War 18, 31, 33, 114, 118, 134, 201, 274, 292, 293, 304, 306, 338

Hamilton, Alexander 137, 204
Hamilton, Lee 136
Hart, Gary 339
Hatch, Orrin 163
Hawaii 51
Hawkins, Paula 332

Health care (*see also* Medicaid; Medicare) 9, 12, 14–15, 19, 43, 57, 85–6, 254–5, 257, 265, 270, 306, 320
Bush 87–8
Carter 96
Clinton 88, 103, 104, 107, 121, 249, 315, 320–2, 323
diagnostic related groups 314
Health Maintenance Organizations 313, 314, 316, 318, 319, 321
interest groups 86–90, 95–6, 102–6
"Jackson Hole" Group 315–16, 317–18, 319–20
"Oregon" Plan 15, 322–3
political parties 87–8
problems 312–13
Reagan 314, 320
reform 312, 314–19, 321–2, 324
Hill, Anita 163
Hilsman, Roger 300
Hispanics (*see also* Latinos) 4, 27, 28, 57, 223, 260
Holoway, Clyde 80
Homeless 27, 232
Houston 51
Hughes, Mark 224
Human Rights Campaign Fund 162

Illinois 24, 26
Immigration 3–4, 45, 46, 47, 48, 49, 56, 224–5
Immigration and Naturalization Service 61
Inspectors General 185–6, 197–8
Interest groups 3, 8–9, 13, 85–6, 107–8, 203
bureaucracy 175, 177
Congress 145
environmental 272, 276, 278–9, 280, 285, 288
focus 86–90
involvement 90–1, 94
patterns of competition 94–6, 107

Interest groups (*cont.*)
representativeness 92–5
tactics 97–107
theories 364–5
typology 91–2
women 326–9
Iowa 50
Iran–Contra (Irangate) 130, 131,
174, 183
Irish-Americans 46, 47
Italian-Americans 27, 46, 47

Jackson, Andrew 205
Jackson, Jesse 5, 27, 72
Japan 14, 291, 293, 294, 304
Jews 21, 27, 28, 47, 64
Jipping, Thomas 162
Joint Committee on the
Organization of
Congress 135, 136
Johnson, Lyndon B. 4, 5, 26, 28,
31, 116, 131, 146, 148, 206,
217, 222, 259

Kansas 38
Kemp, Jack 5, 233, 238
Kennedy, Anthony 155, 165–6
Kennedy, Edward 5, 313
Kennedy, John F. 1, 28, 31, 155,
158, 325
Kerner Commission 221, 235
King, Gregory 162
King, Rodney 50, 66, 215
Kirk, Paul 71
Korea 49

LaFollette, Robert 38
Lamb's Chapel v. *Center Mariches
Union Free School
District* 170
Laos 49
Larry King Live 36, 341
Lasswell, Harold 354
*Late Night with David
Letterman* 346
Latino National Political
Survey 58

Latinos (*see also* Hispanics) 4, 8,
46, 48, 49–53, 54, 55, 56, 58,
59, 60–6, 225, 226, 231, 234
Lawyers Coalition for Civil
Rights 168
League of Women Voters 325
Limbaugh, Rush 342
Lincoln, Abraham 119
Lipinski, William 159
Locke, John 204
Louisiana 24–5
Los Angeles 25–6, 27, 59, 62,
63–4, 215, 224, 227, 231–2,
233
Lucas, William 159
Lugar, Richard 309
Lukumi Babalu Aye v. *Hialeah* 170

Madison, James 204
Maine 26, 38, 50
Malcolm, Ellen 327
Malcolm X 45
Marshall, John 205
Marxism 358
McGovern–Fraser
Commission 71
McGovern, George 72, 115
McNarry v. *Haitian Centers
Council* 165
Media 15, 19, 43, 114, 127–8
advertising 342
candidates 340–2
debates 344–5
elections 338–40, 342–4
foreign policy 304
new media 335–8
Medicaid 209, 213, 261, 313, 322,
323
Medicare 259, 266, 313, 322
Meek, Carrie 328, 332
Meese, Edwin 156, 165
Merriam, Charles 354
Metzenbaum, Howard 320
Mexico
immigration 49, 50
NAFTA 286–7
Meyer, Philip 127
Miami 51

Michigan 20
Mills, Wilbur 148
Minnesota v. *Dickerson* 166
Mississippi 2, 24, 262
Mondale, Walter 18, 24
Montana 26, 38
Morgan, John 229
MTV 127
Murray, Patty 332
Myers, Dee Dee 345

NASA 197, 198
National Academy of Public
  Administration 184–5
National Association of
  Counties 211
National Conference of State
  Legislatures 211
National Economic Council 303
National Environmental Policy
  Act 287
National Health Planning and
  Resources Development
  Act 313
National League of Cities 229
National Organization for
  Women 326, 327
National Performance
  Review 172, 174, 175, 193–6,
  199, 217
National Policy Council 303–4
National Right to Life
  Committee 162
National Security Council 303
National Urban League 234–5
National Women's Political
  Caucus 326
NATO 14
Negotiated Rulemaking Act 178
Nevada 26, 38
Newark 220
New Deal 68, 202, 207, 355
  Coalition 2, 19, 21, 24, 25, 27,
  41, 229, 300
New Hampshire 26, 50
  Primary 36, 343
New Jersey 24, 215
New Mexico 26

New Orleans 227
New York 24, 26, 50, 51, 220,
  221, 223, 225, 226, 227, 232,
  337
Nixon, Richard M. 31, 115, 131,
  155, 206
NLC v. *Usery* 215
North American Free Trade
  Agreement 151, 201, 251,
  274, 286–7, 346
North Carolina 2, 24, 55–6, 167–8
North Dakota 26, 50
Nunn, Sam 123
Nussbaum, Bernie 159

O'Connor, Sandra Day 155, 161,
  165, 167–8, 169, 216
Office of Economic
  Opportunity 259
Office of Management and
  Budget 181–2, 183, 197, 198,
  243, 348
Ohio 24, 26, 167
O'Neill, Thomas P. 137
Oregon 26, 322

Panama 33
Panetta, Leon 12, 248
Parker, Frank 168
Pauly, Mark 321
Pennsylvania 24, 26
Penry v. *Texas* 167
Perot, Ross 2, 7, 18, 19, 20, 33,
  36–41, 44, 79, 119, 120, 236,
  247, 248, 340, 341, 343
Perry, Michael 164
Peterson, Peter 306
Philadelphia 220, 223, 224, 227
Philippines 49
Phillips, Kevin 20
Pinkerton, James 5
Planned Parenthood v. *Casey* 169
Pluralism 93, 364
Polish-Americans 27
Political Action Committees
  60–70, 74, 77, 80, 81–2,
  99–100, 103, 140, 209, 330–1

Political parties (*see also*
    Democratic Party *and*
    Republican Party) 8, 67, 87
  decline 68–70
  elections 67, 68, 69, 70
  fundraising 76–7
  nominations 72, 79
  organization 67, 68–9, 70, 73,
    75–82, 83
  renewal 71–5, 78–9, 82–4
  state parties 78, 82
Political science 15–16, 350
  behavioralism 16, 352, 356–8,
    360, 361, 362–3
  bias 351
  Cold War 351, 356, 360
  institutionalism 16, 352, 353–6,
    357, 360, 361, 363
  legalism 352, 354, 357, 360,
    361, 363
  "New Institutionalism" 363
  normativism 351–2, 357, 358,
    360
  rational choice 16, 352, 358–61,
    362–3
Pollack, Ron 95
Pollution
  non-point 201
  problem 271, 273–4
  public opinion 271 .
  toxic substances 285–6
Populism 37
Poverty 12, 27
  cities 221, 226–7
  "New Poverty" 264–7
  problem 257–64
  welfare 253–7
  workfare 253
President (*see also individual
    presidents*)
  bureaucracy 179–82, 186–8
  Cold War 117–18
  Congress 113–14, 125–6
  institution 130–1
  leadership 111–12, 125,
    131–3
  media 114–15, 127–8
  modern 113

  power 112–18
  theories 366–7
Progressive Policy Institute 5
Public Citizen 287

Quayle, Dan 181, 342, 345

Race 3, 4, 8, 12, 19, 27, 53, 66
  cities 221, 223, 226–8, 234
  poverty 257, 260–1
Rangel, Charles 233
Rayburn, Sam 146, 148
Reagan, Ronald 1, 11, 13, 24, 31,
    72, 115
  bureaucracy 179, 181–2, 183,
    188–9, 192
  cities 222, 229, 231, 235
  economy 237, 238–40, 242, 243
  environment 279
  federalism 175, 176, 202,
    206–7, 208, 210–11, 213,
    217, 222
  foreign policy 301
  health policy 314, 320
  Reaganism 1, 6, 12, 149
  Supreme Court 153–5, 156
  welfare policy 267–8
Rehnquist, William 155, 166
Reich, Robert 269
Reinventing Government 10,
    172–3, 176, 188
Religion 3, 169–70
Reno, Janet 158
Republican Party 2, 5, 121
  fundraising 76–7, 81
  McGovern–Fraser 71
  National Committee 68, 69, 77,
    79
  renewal 73–4
  southern basis 24, 25
Reynolds, William Bradford 158
Rice, Stuart 354
Riker, William 359
Riley, Richard 161
Rockefeller, Jay 320
Roe v. *Wade* 153, 161, 169, 214,
    333
Roman Catholics . 27, 28

Roosevelt, Franklin D. 9, 21, 41,
    111–12, 113, 118, 129, 130,
    131, 132, 147, 205, 217
Roosevelt, Theodore 18, 206, 217
Rosenau, James 294–5
Russia 291–2, 297–8, 304
Russo, Marty 80

San Antonio 232
Scalia, Antonin 155, 161, 165–6,
    170
Schilling, Warner 299–300, 307
Schlesinger, James 300
Seattle 227
Shaw v. *Reno* 55–6, 167–8
Sierra Club 287
Sixteenth Amendment 207
Skocpol, Theda 363
Smeal, Eleanor 157, 328
Smith, William French 156
Social security 254, 258, 263
Somalia 293, 295
Souter, David 155, 161, 165
South Carolina 2, 24
South Dakota v. *Dole* 216
Soviet Union 2, 14, 117–18, 289,
    290, 293, 296–7, 300, 301
Stanford v. *Kentucky* 167
State Governments 6–7, 11, 13,
    200–1, 202, 280
Stephanopoulos, George 345
Stevens, John Paul 155, 161, 166
St. Louis 220, 221
St. Mary's Honor Center v.
    Hicks 168–9
Strauss, Leo 358
Supreme Court (*see also individual
    cases; courts*) 66, 118, 124,
    202, 204, 205, 212, 214–16,
    234, 281, 336,
  Burger Court 153, 166–7
  Clinton 153, 154–6, 160–3,
    171
  composition 160–3
  conservatism 165–9
  "Imperial" 153–4
  Rehnquist Court 155, 165,
    166

role 152–3, 163–5, 170–1
theories 369–70
Warren Court 153

Taylor, F. W. 353
Tenth Amendment 205, 215,
    216
Tennessee 2, 24
Texas 2, 24, 26, 50, 51, 55, 56, 58,
    263
Thomas, Clarence 155, 161,
    162–3, 165–6
Thornbaugh, Richard 156
Thurmond, Strom 18
Thurow, Lester 149
Tocqueville, Alexis de 13, 310,
    353, 373
Transnational Criminal
    Organizations 294–5, 298
Truman, Harry 147–8
Tsongas, Paul 343
Tullock, Gordon 359
Turner, Ted 338

United Nations 308
U.S. v. *Darby* 205
Utah 26, 38

Vermont 26
Vietnam 49
  war 1, 113, 114, 118, 301, 357
Virginia 2, 24
Voinovich v. *Quilter* 167
Voting
  dealignment 37, 39
  party identification 39–40
  realignment 25
  retrospective 18, 19–20, 30–6,
    43–4, 119
  theories 365–6
  turnout 19, 40
Voting Rights Act 55–6, 58, 61,
    63

Wallace, George 18, 38
War Powers Resolution 114

Washington   26, 51, 215, 322
  D.C.   224, 256, 337
Watergate   20, 31, 41, 73, 113,
  114, 130, 131, 183
Water Quality Act   201
Wesberry v. *Sanders*   209
White, Byron   155, 160, 166
Whitewater   2, 158
Wilson, Woodrow   119, 142, 217
Wisconsin   26, 73
WISH List   327

Women   15, 27, 28, 46, 65, 72
  elections   325–34
  poverty   226–7, 258, 282
Women's Campaign Fund   327
Woods, Kimba   158
Wright, Jim   146
Wyoming   26

Zobrest v. *Catalina Foothills School
  District*   170